Protests and Generations

Youth in a Globalizing World

Series Editors

Vincenzo Cicchelli (*Ceped, Université Paris Descartes/IRD*)
Sylvie Octobre (*GEMASS, Université Paris-Sorbonne/CNRS
and la DEPS au Ministère de la Culture, France*)

Editorial Board

Valentina Cuzzocrea (*University of Cagliari, Italy*)
Ratiba Hadj-Moussa (*York University, Canada*)
Claudia Jacinto (*PREJET-Instituto de Desarrollo Económico y Social, Argentina*)
Jeylan Mortimer (*University of Minnesota, United States of America*)
Andrea Pirni (*Unversità di Genova, Italy*)
Dan Woodman (*University of Melbourne, Australia*)
Chin-Chin Yi (*Academic Sinica, Taiwan*)

VOLUME 5

The titles published in this series are listed at *brill.com/ygw*

Protests and Generations

Legacies and Emergences in the Middle East, North Africa and the Mediterranean

Edited by

Mark Muhannad Ayyash
Ratiba Hadj-Moussa

BRILL

LEIDEN | BOSTON

Cover illustration: Original composition by Clara Motsch Hadj-Moussa. Drawing is inspired by an original photograph taken by Sunaina Maira of a Stencil in Ramallah, Palestine.

The Library of Congress Cataloging-in-Publication Data is available online at http://catalog.loc.gov
LC record available at http://lccn.loc.gov/2017008770

Typeface for the Latin, Greek, and Cyrillic scripts: "Brill". See and download: brill.com/brill-typeface.

ISSN 2212-9383
ISBN 978-90-04-44698-4 (paperback)
ISBN 978-90-04-33815-9 (hardback)
ISBN 978-90-04-34451-8 (e-book)

Copyright 2017 by Koninklijke Brill NV, Leiden, The Netherlands.
Koninklijke Brill NV incorporates the imprints Brill, Brill Hes & De Graaf, Brill Nijhoff, Brill Rodopi and Hotei Publishing.
All rights reserved. No part of this publication may be reproduced, translated, stored in a retrieval system, or transmitted in any form or by any means, electronic, mechanical, photocopying, recording or otherwise, without prior written permission from the publisher.
Authorization to photocopy items for internal or personal use is granted by Koninklijke Brill NV provided that the appropriate fees are paid directly to The Copyright Clearance Center, 222 Rosewood Drive, Suite 910, Danvers, MA 01923, USA. Fees are subject to change.

This book is printed on acid-free paper and produced in a sustainable manner.

Mark: to my parents Said and Samia Ayyash

Ratiba: to my sister Hafida Hadj-Moussa and Clara

Together, we dedicate this book to the countless protesters who continue the struggle for social justice, equality and freedom.

∵

Contents

Acknowledgments   IX
List of Illustrations   XI
Notes on Contributors   XII

Introduction: Conceptualizing Generations and Protests   1
Mark Muhannad Ayyash and Ratiba Hadj-Moussa

PART 1
Forms of Protest and the Production of Generations

1   Palestinian Youth in Israel: A New Generational Style of Activism?   27
Mohammad Massalha, Ilana Kaufman and Gal Levy

2   From Student to General Struggle: The Protests against the Neoliberal
Reforms in Higher Education in Contemporary Italy   55
Lorenzo Cini

3   Lawyers Mobilizing in the Tunisian Uprising: A Matter of
'generations'?   73
Éric Gobe

PART 2
Genealogies of Generational Formations

4   2003: A Turning Point in the Formation of Syrian Youth   99
Matthieu Rey

5   Together, but Divided: Trajectories of a Generation of Egyptian Political
Activists (From 2005 to the Revolution)   122
Chaymaa Hassabo

6   The Gezi Protests: The Making of the Next Left Generation in
Turkey   143
Gökbörü Sarp Tanyildiz

PART 3
Memory, History and the "New Generation"

7   'Freedom is a Daily Practice': The Palestinian Youth Movement and *Jil* Oslo   171
      Sunaina Maira

8   The Double Presence of Southern Algerians: Space, Generation and Unemployment   198
      Ratiba Hadj-Moussa

9   "We are not heiresses": Generational Memory, Heritage and Inheritance in Contemporary Italian Feminism   224
      Andrea Hajek

10   Echoes of Ricardo Mella: Reading Twenty-First Century Youth Protest Movements through the Lens of an Early Twentieth-Century Anarchist   245
      Stephen Luis Vilaseca

      Index   269

Acknowledgments

The protests that garnered the world's attention in the MENA and Mediterranean during the last two decades still beg numerous questions. In varied ways across the countries and regions, they have challenged social and cultural norms, the neoliberal economic order, gender and ethnic relations, political institutions, modes of governance, and the meaning of freedom and liberty. Some of the challenges and contributions of these protests are yet to be formulated, articulated and understood. Our book seeks to contribute to these discussions, and its uniqueness lies in its emphasis and focus on the question of generation in these protests. The terms "youth," "young generation" have been used extensively but rare are the scholars who have tried to reflect on them or to challenge the entrenched association between forms of protest that *seem* to appear from nowhere with the category of a "new" generation. Such an association often ignores an important question: is it the newness of a generation that produced the unexpected, or is the unexpected so difficult to understand that the notion of a "new" generation is then used to explain it? In exploring the relationship between protests and generations, we hope to invite scholars for a continuous re-thinking of these protest moments and events that have challenged not just powerful social, economic, political and cultural structures, but also some of the conventional models (e.g., "social movements") and categories (e.g., the definition of "activist") for understanding processes of social and political change.

This book could not have been possible without the support of many institutions and individuals. We would like to thank the Social Sciences and Humanities Research Council of Canada for their funding, and the Faculty of Arts and Professional Studies of York University for their generous support for the translation. Thank you to Vincenzo Cicchelli, who believed in our project from its inception and who encouraged us to pursue it. Our thanks also go to Kathryn Travis who pulled together the first draft of the manuscript, and to Peter Couto for the translation from French of some of the articles. We are heartedly grateful to Rana Sukarieh for her long-standing help at various stages of the manuscript preparation, her ability to work under great pressure while remaining cheerful and enthusiastic. We owe much to Jonathan Adjemian who not only translated some chapters from French but also worked on the indexing and provided much appreciated copy editing input at different times of the book preparation. His commitment in the final stage has been pivotal. Thank you Jonathan.

Among the friends who helped to refine our ideas, Karine Côté-Boucher was the barometer who provided us with much insights and our ideas benefited from her up-to-date theories and fieldwork. Last but not least, we would like to thank the contributors of this book for their dedication and willingness to review their papers more than twice, their positive responses to our inquiry and for their confidence in us and our collective project. Thank you all.

Ratiba is thankful to have had the opportunity to work with Mark, who she thought was one of the refined scholars she has known. Beyond that and beyond the great pleasure of working with him, she thanks him for seeing between what is essential and what is not. And this not a simple thing. Mark is thankful for Ratiba's guidance, mentorship, and for her original conception of the book's underlying thesis. Editing a book can often feel like a thankless job consisting of seemingly never-ending tasks that may or may not bear fruit at the end. It was Ratiba's continuous reminders that this was a project worth completing, which kept the seeds of doubt from growing. Now that we are at the end, I am fully convinced that it was worth it.

List of Illustrations

Tables

3.1   Father's profession by lawyer's bar admission date   78

3.2   Father's profession by lawyer's professional status   79

4.1   Population Growth   103

Graph

3.1   Number of lawyers registered in Tunisia from 1991 by professional status   77

Map

8.1   Map of Algeria   209

Notes on Contributors

Mark Muhannad Ayyash
is an Assistant Professor of Sociology and Director of The Peace Studies Initiative at Mount Royal University, Calgary. He specializes in social, political and postcolonial theory, the study of violence, social movements, decolonial conceptions of space and time, as well as culture and politics in the Middle East. His previous articles have dealt with the Iraq War, 'violent dialogue' between Hamas and the Israeli State, the exiling writing of Edward Said, the question of past violences in transnational Palestinian youth movements, and the paradox of political violence.

Lorenzo Cini
is a current research fellow at the Institute of Humanities and Social Sciences at the Scuola Normale Superiore of Pisa. He held a PhD degree in Social and Political Sciences at the European University Institute of Florence, conducting his research on the contentious politics of higher education in Italy and England. More notably, he investigated the array of university mobilizations arisen in England and Italy in opposition to the recent neoliberal reforms in higher education. On this topic, Lorenzo Cini published several articles and chapter contributions in edited volumes and journals. Over the past five years, he also carried out research in the field of political philosophy and theory by working on the concepts of democracy, justice and equality. On these topics, he recently published the book, Civil Society and Radical Democracy (2012), and, in collaboration with Professor Brunella Casalini, the volume of political philosophy on Justice, Equality, and Difference. A Guide to the Reading of Contemporary Political Philosophy (2012).

Éric Gobe
is Research Director at the Centre national de la recherche scientifique (Institut de recherche sur le Maghreb contemporain de Tunis). A political scientist and a sociologist, he was the chief editor of the journal L'Année du Maghreb (2004–2012). He authored Histoire de la Tunisie depuis l'indépendance (La Découverte, 2015, with Larbi Chouikha), Les avocats en Tunisie de la colonisation à la révolution (1883–2011): sociohistoire d'une profession politique (Karthala 2013), Les hommes d'affaires égyptiens (Karthala, 1999) and, with the collaboration of Saïd Ben Sedrine, Les ingénieurs tunisiens : dynamiques récentes d'un groupe professionnel (L'Harmattan, 2004). He has also edited L'ingénieur moderne au Maghreb (XIXe–XXe siècles) (IRMC-Maisonneuve & Larose, 2004).

NOTES ON CONTRIBUTORS

Ratiba Hadj-Moussa

is professor of cultural and political sociology in the Department of Sociology at York University, Toronto. She is a Board member of Cahiers de recherches sociologiques and a founder member of Sociétés arabes en mouvement within the Association Internationale de sociologues de langue française. Her research interests include the relations of the political and the margins, *laicité* in France and Quebec, art/visual expressive forms in North Africa and new forms of mobilisation. Her more recent publication is entitled, La télévision par satellite et ses publics: espaces critiques, espaces de résistance (Presses universitaires de Grenoble). She also the co-editor of several books and special journal issues.

Andrea Hajek

obtained her doctorate degree from the University of Warwick (UK), with a dissertation on the theme of memories of protest in 1970s Italy. She held a British Academy postdoctoral fellowship at the University of Glasgow, on the history and memory of Italian second-wave feminism. She is the Managing Editor for the journal Memory Studies and an Associate Editor of Modern Italy, and she is a founding member of the Warwick Oral History Network. Her research interests include cultural memory, protest movements, women's history, oral history, digital and visual memories, terrorism in history education, and collective trauma studies. She is the author of a monograph, entitled Negotiating Memories of Protest in Western Europe. The Case of Italy was (Palgrave Macmillan), and she has co-edited several special issues and a volume.

Chaymaa Hassabo

is a Fellow researcher at The Collège de France (Chair of contemporary history of the Arab world). She completed her PhD in Political Science in May 2012 at the University of Grenoble on the political transformation of Moubarak's regime during the period of 2002–2010, focusing on the factors that most threatened the stability of the then powerful Mubarak regime, especially on the eve of the challenges brought about by the newly created protest movements. Currently, her main research interest lies in the revolutionary process which has unfolded since January 25th, 2011, focusing particularly on the youth movements and networks, especially those on the side of a "revolutionary process." On a more general level, she is also working on a detailed chronological analysis of the individual events of the Egyptian revolution. She authored *Du rassemblement à l'effritement des jeunes pour le changement. Égyptiens: L'expérience de "générations qui ont vécu et vivent toujours sous la Loi d'urgence"* (Revue intern. de politique comparée. Vol. 16, 2009). As well, she co-authored

Socio-histoire d'un processus révolutionnaire: Analyse de la "configuration contestataire" égyptienne (2003–2011), in *Au cœur des révoltes arabes: Devenir révolutionnaires,* Paris, Armand Colin, 2013).

Ilana Kaufman

(Ph.D, UCLA) is the former Academic director of the M.A. program in Democracy Studies and a senior teaching faculty & researcher at the Open University, Israel. She does research in the area of comparative and ethnic politics, democratization, and specializes in the political history and political behavior of the Palestinian citizens of Israel. Her recent publications are I. Kaufman, G. Levy. The Public Sphere, 8, 2014. pp. 34–54 (in Hebrew); and "Communists and the 1948 War: PCP, Maki, and the National Liberation League" Journal of Israeli History, Vol. 33, No. 2 September, 2014, pp. 115–144. Her Current research project is the relationship between the state and the Islamic movement in Israel.

Gal Levy

(PhD, LSE) is a senior teaching faculty & researcher at the Open University, Israel. Gal has published on the intersection of education, ethnicity, religion and citizenship in both Jewish and Palestinian societies in Israel. His chapter on Contested Citizenship of the Arab Spring and Beyond has been published in The Routledge Handbook of Global Citizenship Studies (edited by E.F. Isin and P. Nyers, 2014). Current research projects include alternative education in the Arab-Palestinian society in Israel (with Dr. Massalha), education and conflict, and urban citizenship and political activism since 2011.

Sunaina Maira

is Professor of Asian American Studies at the University of California, Davis and is affiliated with the Middle East/South Asia Studies program as well as Cultural Studies graduate group. Her research and teaching focus on Asian and Arab American youth, citizenship, and popular culture. Her books include, Jil Oslo: Palestinian Hip Hop, Youth Culture, and the Youth Movement and Missing: Youth, Citizenship, and Empire After 9/11. She is the co-editor of Youthscapes: The Popular, the National, the Global and The Imperial University: Academic Repression and Scholarly Dissent. Her new book is The 9/11 Generation: Youth, Rights, and Solidarity in the War on Terror.

Mohammad Massalha

(PhD, Hebrew University, Jerusalem) is a teaching faculty & researcher at the Open University, Israel and Sakhnin Academic college for Teacher education. Mohammad has published on the intersection of Sociology of education, Youth and Adolescence and Generation Palestinian society. His chapter on

"The Intifada generation: Generation in the formation" has been published In: Rappaport, Tamar and Ahuvia Cahana (eds.) (2012) Between Order and Disorder: Informal Organizations as Platform to Social and Educational Thinking. Reslling.(Hebrew). Current research projects include alternative education in the Arab-Palestinian society in Israel (with Dr. Gal Levy), Home and Place making in the Arab society in Israel (with Dr. Zeev Shavit), Patterns of mobility in Arab society in Israel.

Matthieu Rey

is currently a Researcher at IREMAM in the CNRS (National Center for Scientific Research). As a Fellow doctorate in the French Institute of Near East in Damascus between 2009 and 2013, he has been a privileged witness of the Syrian events on the ground for two years. His research focuses on the political system in Iraq and Syria and aims at understanding policy-building and state-building during the fifties in the Middle-East. His work sheds light on political engineering of power and the centrality of parliaments in the decision-making processes.

Gökbörü Sarp Tanyildiz

is a PhD candidate in the department of Sociology at York University, Canada. He co-authored a book chapter on the public space, virtual space and protests, forthcoming in Urbanization in a Global Context with Oxford University Press. Also, he is currently co-editing a theme issue on planetary urbanization for Society and Space.

Stephen Luis Vilaseca

is Associate Professor of Spanish at Northern Illinois University and a co-Associate Editor of the Journal of Urban Cultural Studies. He is the author of Barcelonan Okupas: Squatter Power! (Fairleigh Dickinson University Press, 2013) as well as of articles in the Bulletin of Hispanic Studies (2006), Letras Hispanas: Revista de Literatura y Cultura (2009), the Arizona Journal of Hispanic Cultural Studies (2010), Transitions: Journal of Franco-Iberian Studies (2012), the Journal of Urban Cultural Studies (2014), and the Journal of Spanish Cultural Studies (2015). He is currently working on an English translation of and a critical introduction to Ideario [Idearium] (287 pages), a collection of Spanish anarchist Ricardo Mella's significant but underappreciated newspaper and journal articles written in the late nineteenth- and early twentieth-centuries.

INTRODUCTION

Conceptualizing Generations and Protests

Mark Muhannad Ayyash and Ratiba Hadj-Moussa

This book examines the relations between generations and protests in the Middle East, North Africa (MENA) and the Mediterranean. Most of the work on recent protests in these regions insists on the newness of their expressive forms but leave unexplored the various links that exist between them and the social, historical and political configurations that preceded them. The articulation between generations and protests, we argue, relies at once on historical ties and their rejection. It is, indeed, precisely this tension that the chapters of the book will address in documenting several case studies that highlight the processes by which generations and protests are connected.

The recent events in the MENA and the Mediterranean brought to the forefront the question of youth engagement and the development of new forms of protest. In public discourse, social media has been regarded as the principal means through which various groups with opposing interests have aggregated and represented a novel way to entice and maintain popular mobilizations. While the academic focus on information technology in 21st century protests has been discussed and sometimes criticized (Tilly and Wood 2009, 98; Kluber 2011; Ayari 2011), the demonstration of the interconnectedness between different protest 'moments' or constellations on a diachronic axis remains extremely thin if not absent. The aim of this book is to inquire and problematize the relations that exist between different periods of protest, the type of actors they mobilize and the processes of memory they generate in the MENA and the Mediterranean regions. Although there is no clear line between these periods, as will become evident in the following chapters, we contend that forms of legacies and relations are at play in the configuration of popular protests, each with its own temporal and spatial specificity. Whether it is the legacy of early twentieth century anarchist thought in Spain, the legacies of the Iraq War in Syria or the monumental history in Algeria, we argue that legacies and relations across complex temporal and spatial standpoints are not a given and that their actualization require a close analytical scrutiny. Indeed, whether accepted or adopted, legacies are sites of contention, formulation and reformulation.

The focus on the MENA and the Mediterranean is not incidental and requires much attention in so far as the countries of these regions have been described as dominated by neo-patrimonialism, tribalism as well as by totalitarian and authoritarian regimes that quashed contestation in its embryonic state, thus repressing and oppressing the populations for long periods of time. The extents to which this view predominates for each specific state and region discussed in this book will of course vary, but the general gist of this view nevertheless prevails, and always in relation to Western Europe and North America as the measure or standard against which these regions and states are judged. Such an interpretation partially faded with the events of the Arab Uprisings, but has arguably returned to its full force with more recent events, such as the discourse around the austerity measures in Italy, Spain and Greece, and the rise of Da'esh in the MENA. However, even when the Eurocentric and dominant interpretation of these regions did partially fade, it effectively called in reverse for the term 'generation' to explain this 'sudden awakening' of these regions.

Far from considering the term generation as a buzzword, there is a need to reassess it in light of the recent popular protests and conversely to analyze the latter through its lenses. What does the use of (new) generation bring to scholarly understanding of the protests and the ability to articulate them? The social sciences have been reluctant to limit the concept of generation to its integrative function and to factors such as age, location or historical conditions, nor have they totally accepted that the notion of 'contemporaneity' (Mannheim 1964 [1927]), which putatively federates specific groups of social actors, to be a strong analytical tool. However, without neglecting or refuting the contemporaneity that may (re)unite dispersed groups belonging to the same age cohorts or otherwise divided by their age but sharing the same 'spirit,' or the historical conditions that are constitutive in the production of a generation, considering the shared experience of various groups seems to provide a more complex understanding of the phenomenon. Indeed, not only does the shared experience refer to the contextual historical conditions but it also points to the reflexive capacity of actors who identify themselves (even marginally) as pertaining to the same generation (Eyerman and Turner 1998).

Based on both empirical and theoretical categories, the experience through which a generation is produced and maintained is thus located in opposition to intergenerational continuity and memory. This begs the question as to whether the closure that defines a generation configures the flux of social change or constitutes an analytical category in which recede unceasingly 'memories,' 'lessons from the past,' 'genealogies of remembrance,' 'ways of thinking,' and 'ways of doing.' If social change is inevitable, then how are histories of contestations and protests understood by the 'now' or 'new' generation? What roles do such histories play in the process of generational formation? Is the process of anamnesis, of selective forgetfulness of the past, a strategic recalling which serves to proclaim the birth of new ways of doing, feeling and belonging – or in short, to a different protest moment?

The relation between generations and protests is multi-faceted, and so we found it useful to organize the book into three interrelated parts. Each part constitutes a general dimension of the relationship between generations and protests. The first examines the ways in which the forms of protest and the production of generation shape and alter each other. The chapters in this section show that in some cases, the very form of the protests engenders either narrow or broad understandings of generation with important consequences to the protesters and their cause. In other cases, the very conception of generation as a 'new' generation that is in direct contrast to an 'old' generation, enables and inhibits certain forms of protest on the basis of this generational contrast.

The second part of the book explores entangled temporalities and the production of generations, particularly as this production revolves around the category of 'youth.' Chapters in this section examine questions such as, how are 'youth' produced as a generation. If it is not purely a biological category, then are 'youth' synonymous with the 'new'? That is, can we constitute as a 'new' generation, not a particular age group, but a new way of relating to the past, a production of memory in a manner that disrupts the normalcy of temporality? How do we make sense of the complex ways in which continuities and ruptures in memory constitute a generational consciousness? Furthermore, how might a generational consciousness neglect some historical continuities?

Finally, the third part of our collection challenges scholarly work that associates forms of protest that *seem* to appear from nowhere with the category of a 'new' generation. Such an association often ignores important questions that become visible with a generational analysis – for example, is it the newness of a generation that produced the unexpected appearance of protest? Or is the unexpected moment so difficult to understand that scholars then rely on the notion of a 'new' generation to explain what is, by definition, beyond the scope of conventional categories? How might we understand the production of the 'new' generation through memorialisation of past protests? In what ways does the (re)constitution of memory, the work of continuities and discontinuities across temporal layers of pasts-presents-futures, serve to enable the appearance of a 'new' generation? What is the role of scholars in analyzing these processes and how might scholars facilitate a different memorialisation of protests past?

We maintain that all of these questions do not, and perhaps cannot, have theoretical answers. That is, they all must be addressed and answered in the specificity of their contexts. And this is where we see the greatest contribution of this collection – in each of our chapters there is an attempt to deal with and answer one or more of these questions. Thus, we cannot go so far as to state that each chapter fits exclusively within one of the parts. Indeed, one of the strengths of our contributions is that they speak to all of the different parts in their own way, opening up a rich conversation in the process.

But before developing the three main themes of this book and tracing some of the ways in which the different chapters move through them, we begin with the concept of generation to provide the frame upon which the discussions are based.

Thinking Generation

The question of generation has been one of the central issues in social theory. In Ibn Khaldûn (2005 [1370]), the succession of generations within a dynasty was the key factor in explaining the rise and decline of social cohesion and 'group feeling' which, for him, was the real motor of history and animated great social change. Classical sociologists, such as Durkheim (1984, 2006) and Halbwachs (1995) in their efforts to explain and theorize social structures and agency through the concepts of collective consciousness, collective representation and social memory, have tangentially dealt with issues related to the concept of generation. However, it is Karl Mannheim's formulation of generations as a problem for sociological inquiry, which underscores the complexity of the contemporary questions on generations.

Mannheim states that the problem of generations has always been entangled with the question of human progress and the rhythm of history. He argues that two frameworks have dealt with the problem of generation, the positivist and the romantic, which reduced the problem into either a biological rhythm of birth and death, or have limited the problem to a specific historical mentality or spiritual rhythm while deconstructing the positivist linearity of progress. In contrast, Mannheim argues for a sociological examination of the very fabric of social processes through which the material of generations is formed (Mannheim 1964, 286). This material is made up of (a) 'generation location,' which refers to social and economic realities upon which a given generation positions itself; (b) 'generation as actuality,' which refers to its effective constitution as a generation; and (c) 'generation unit,' which refers to the shared experience and sense of belonging. These elements constitute recurring themes in the academic inquiry of generations, and it will become evident in the following case studies that they are always indeed at the heart of the analysis of generations and protests.

Mannheim argues that although 'class' and 'generation' share many similarities as 'social locations,' each is based on different grounds. Whereas class is based on historically specific economic and power structures, generation is, in addition, based on the biological rhythm of life and death (1964, 289–290), which calls for a re-elaboration of the constitutive elements of generational unities. The strengths and weaknesses of these unities can be illuminated through the ways their boundaries are formed and maintained. For example, one belongs to a generation in a temporally limited sense, and this temporal boundary determines who belongs to a generation and how they belong to it. However, 'contemporaneity,' to exist within the social whole at the same temporal moment, is not enough on its own to produce a generation; rather, contemporaneity gains significance when a concerted and collective unity is formed on its basis (Mannheim 1964, 298).

The tendency towards a continuous challenge to tradition is inherent to the generation location, but the actualization of this tendency is not automatically realized within the biological rhythm of life and death itself (Mannheim 1964, 302). To actualize this tendency into a unit of generation, which for Mannheim is the most concrete and binding attachment to a generation (Mannheim 1964, 304–307), is to actively "use the handicaps and privileges inherent in a generation location," and to commence a "*participation in the common destiny* of this historical and social unit." (Mannheim 1964, 303; original emphasis) This is distinct from an 'actual generation' which denotes loose ties between members of a given generation (e.g., the baby boomers, generation x), or which indicates the overall conflict between generation units within a larger actual generation. Regardless, these moments of generational formations constitute sociological relevance, the points at which generations are generated within the social, political and cultural landscape in specific ways and towards specific directions. Generation units are the most interesting for Mannheim. They are characterized by "partisan integrative attitudes" (Mannheim 1964, 307). Through their continuous and active participation, members become integrated into the generation unit in a close-knit concrete manner, and once created as such, these beliefs, values, goals and objectives of these generation units can then travel far beyond the immediate location of their creation.

In many ways, Mannheim offers a vitalist understanding of generation in which the new generation has to advance its claims against older generations. In privileging the romantic approach over the positivist one, Mannheim rightly problematizes the idea of progress and considers that the ruptures on which a generation builds its own demands and beliefs are key to establishing its boundaries and to emancipating itself from tradition (Scott 2014, 161–166).

But how is this inscribed and correlated to temporality? Abdelmalak Sayad's (1994) work on '*émigré* generation' is crucial in this regard since it tackles some of the important issues related to the temporal production of generation, which are not developed fully in Mannheim. Sayad's argument systematically puts into question the notion of generation indicating its shortcomings, such as the search for biological origins, but he also shows how generation could be useful in understanding the key issues at stake in society.

He argues that while indeed the notion of generation mobilizes two complementary axes, the 'diachronic' and the 'synchronic,' it needs to be complicated by the 'porosity' that characterizes contemporaneity. He uses Wilhelm Pinder's expression of the "non contemporaneity of contemporaneity" (also used by Mannheim) in order to distinguish between the "contemporaneity of the non contemporary" and the "non contemporaneity of the contemporary," and to denaturalize and disconnect the sense of belonging to the same time-frame and the meaning of simultaneity (Sayad 1994, 158). By contrast, groups who do not belong to the same period can be defined as contemporary because they share the "same engendering mode, the same generative social conditions...or what one calls the same social generation." (Sayad 1994, 158–159; our translation) Sayad short-circuits the time gap that separates two groups and puts them together, and brings to the fore the concept of habitus in exploring how under the same social conditions similar responses and 'behaviors' are produced. Hence, the title of his paper, "The Generation of Generation," refers both to the dynamic by which a generation is produced as well as to its products. As his main concern is to theorize the generative mode of the generation of émigré in France, he shows how different cohorts who emigrated at different periods of time but whose conditions of immigration were homologous produced the same categories ('class') of 'responses,' and therefore constitute what could be called the 'same generation,' which developed, despite the temporal distance, particular subjective dispositions.

One of Sayad's major contributions is his analysis of the reversed temporality that created 'generations' in the French migration context. He suggests that the reflection upon the 'internal' relations between generations is a trap, and instead he focuses on the articulation of generations with a third element, namely the society in which they are inscribed. He shows that the so-called 'first generation' was an absent reality before the émigrés were allowed to bring their family to France. Therefore, it is not the generation of the parents that produced the children's generation, but rather the reverse occurs. It is as if the parents came to existence by the very presence of their children, which leads to the question as to whether the strong but implicit inversion of temporality between the two doesn't reveal the incapacity to think this population.

Thus, the temporal reversibility of generation is based less on the linearity of successive age groups than on the exteriority of immigration that is imposed on this immigrant population, namely, the notion that this population is an alien, an external problem to the (French) Nation-State. Thus, it could be that the temporal modes of generation are defined – delimited in their reciprocal relations – by the *spatial location*, and that the temporal deployment of generation is also indebted to external factors. While insisting on the practices or the discursive construction of generation, the latter remark departs from most of the works on generations that either ignore or brush aside this dynamic. While Sayad is critical towards the notion of generation, it helps him to think its 'externality' upon social actors and the shared experience of various generations belonging to different periods of time. But the imposition that is unleashed by the temporality of experience is counterbalanced by the consideration of space (before immigration) that reinstates social actors' subjectivity.

Taken together, Mannheim and Sayad show that a generational analysis can shed light on the spatial and temporal processes through which social and political landscapes become transformable through the production and formation of generations, whether the process is based on ambiguous linkages with past social experiences and conditions or expresses ruptures and continuities or both. Those linkages to, and expressions of, spatiality and temporality in the formation/transformation of generations can be triggered in a unique way by protests. Because of that, the analysis of the relationship between generations and protests becomes central to our book.

In explaining the relationship between generations and protests, researchers often considered 'the event' of protest as the anchoring locus for the actions and the practices defining 'generations units.' Two kinds of interpretations prevail which basically favor on the one hand, macro structures that lead to the events, and on the other, rely on meso-structures and micro-structures. The first relies on the events often seized as the result of a long process that affects the entire social structure, as demonstrated by the functionalist perspective, in particular by Shmuel Eisenstadt (2009). In his analysis of the intergenerational configuration, the author analyzes how social change that has affected the family, the occupational world and the growing demand to the participation in the socio-cultural order (2009, XXXVI–VII), and how that change that characterized the transition to industrial society has produced unprecedented youth organizing and 'youth rebellion.' Eisenstadt (2009) also brings to our attention the supra-national feature of these youth rebellions. In more critical philosophical approaches, such as Alain Badiou's (2012) *The Rebirth of History*, there is similarly an emphasis on the event – for Badiou, on a 'massive popular event' where the rare conjunction of an event and an Idea takes shape.

Badiou (2012) situates the Arab Uprisings and others around the world within the framework of a Historical Idea (Communism) – an opening of History that does not perpetuate the dominant system of politics but reinvents politics.

While we find much theoretical value in this macro approach, *Protests and Generations* situates each case within its own historical specificity and then within its comparative cross-regional connections. Our book does not seek to find a universal dimension to recent protests nor does it simply enumerate differences between varied contexts. Rather, it points to the historical, social, cultural and political (dis)continuities within and across specific localities on the meso and micro levels, and to understanding the comprehensiveness that the actors give to the events they have experienced, thereby reinstating agency and the accomplishment it performs on its epoch, to paraphrase Achille Mbembe (2001). Our collection, therefore, considers that the event can be produced and oriented by a combination of factors, both internal and external to the nation-state. Increasingly, the boundaries of these events move and exceed the national territories and require more complex temporal and spatial interpretations.

1   *Forms of Protest and the Production of Generations*

Much has been written on the 'young' component among the protesters of the Arab Uprisings. Challenging this observation or discussing the participation of other segments of society is important, but just as important is examining if and how the protesters' practices are novel – forms of occupation of public space, providing training in non-violence to protestors, the emphasis on new thematizations of social justice, the use of social media, forms of organization and so on – and how such practices are inscribed within a chain of protest events whose intensities, implications and effects are various and uneven. Thus, for example, protest events in remote areas are often known only by their inhabitants and remain within the confines of the region where they have occurred, while other events are bigger and have longer-term echoes and effects. In addition, we heed Charles Tilly's warning to avoid a conceptualization of protests as consisting of a continuous and coherent life-history (forming, flourishing, evolving and finally dying). While such historical coherence is often central for activists and protestors themselves in terms of how they frame their grievances, objectives, ideas, etc., such frames and narratives are precisely what need to be explained and analyzed (Tilly 1993–1994, 3).

Much like Tilly's notion of 'clusters of political performances,' we favor a conception of protest moments and events as intermittent interactions between challengers, power-holders, audiences, allies, enemies, rivals, reporters and so on. Unlike Tilly, however, we are less concerned with defining these protests as 'social movements,' since the latter term is unnecessarily restrictive and excludes 'civil wars,' 'insurrections' or 'riots' on the basis of a distinction between indirect action (social movements) and direct action (insurrections, civil wars, riots) (Tilly 1993–1994, 7). Protests in the regions of interest to this book have challenged the rigid distinction between direct and indirect actions, and rendered misleading the conception of social movements as, more or less, an invention of Western European and North American democracies that was then transported to the rest of the world. We maintain that scholars cannot understand these complex protest practices as somehow constituting endogenous developments within specific regions of the world (Western Europe and North America) and not others (the 'Rest' as termed by Stuart Hall (1992)), under particular contexts (democracy) and not others (authoritarian regimes) (see Schock 2005 for an analysis that challenges the rigidity of such distinctions). For example, Gökbörü Tanyildiz in Chapter 6, challenges the idea that the Gezi protests were developed elsewhere and then were simply exported to Turkey. Instead, Tanyildiz examines the complex ways in which Gezi protestors in a sense amalgamated a varied array of ideas, strategies, tactics and forms of protest in their own unique ways, producing a new and different kind of politics in Turkey.

In explaining this different kind of politics, scholarly attention has turned to the horizontalism that characterizes large-scale contemporary protests in the MENA region and beyond. Hamid Dabashi (2012), for example, argues that the people of the region were creating a new public, both conceptually and spatially, reshaping all political and social relations in the process. Race, class, and gender relations, for instance, cannot escape the effects of this new public sphere, this new language that treats these differences, not as fixed and separate positions speaking to one another across an abyss, but rather as relational points that are discovering the intricate complexities of their connectivity (Dabashi 2012, 171–202; a point that Tanyildiz makes in the Turkish context as well). While we do not downplay this unique element of the Arab Uprisings, it is important to keep in mind that these forms of protest in MENA and the Mediterranean are similar to the struggles of neighborhood groups and workers in Argentina, described by Marina Sitrin (2012) and Denis Merklen (2009), even as they differ from them because of the sheer magnitude of the Arab Uprisings for example. Certainly, Asaf Bayat (2008) shows how what he calls 'the non-movement movement,' i.e., the workers, the poor, the disenfranchised and the unemployed in large cities have developed 'street politics' and shook the structure of the 'commandment,' to borrow a term from Mbmebe (2001), but he does not think the struggles of these social actors within the perspective of horizontalism, which is a genuine contribution of the politics-from-below, as he does not reflect on them within the perspective privileging subjectivity formations.

However, approaches to horizontalism and 'non-movement movements' both agree on the centrality of the class component present in the struggles during recent decades around the world. While class struggles seem to be subsumed by the claims for democracy in the many accounts on the Arab Spring there has been little work on how these class struggles are at work in the protests and how they are supported by generations who have not had direct experience of colonialism, with the notable exception of Palestine. For example, in his insightful *The People's Spring*, Samir Amin (2012), while remaining within the paradigm of the unequal exchange and considering the new functions of the comprador bourgeoisie in the deployment of neoliberalism, fails to envision the role played by new fractions of classes and the intersections between generations and social classes, as he is unable to foresee the challenges of reality to theoretical categories. The macro-analysis of these types of processes that hinge upon claims of large scale historical changes of a new kind of politics has serious limitations, which include the non-consideration of popular protests that have no centralized leadership such as riots, the difficulty to think of other types of governance which refuse to take the State as their sole interlocutor, or to oversee the political change that non-organized movements can produce.

While our collection does not fall within an overarching framework of a 'new politics of horizontalism' it does not overlook the interconnections between the different protest moments either. The flight of ideas, tactics, strategies, frames and narratives across borders has been an important aspect and feature of all the different forms of protest across history, and therefore we prefer the notion of 'a chain of protest events' in order to better locate the generation of generations in this complex process. We contend that this generation of generations is a crucial feature of these protests in terms of how they frame the novelty of their protest practices as illustrated by Mohammad Massalha, Ilana Kaufman and Gal Levy in Chapter 1, and in terms of how they frame their struggle as shown by Lorenzo Cini in Chapter 2.

Against the backdrop of an Israeli Jewish state that treats them as second class citizens, a political party system that does not represent their needs and demands, and a colonial context that separates and fragments Palestinian Arab communities, Massalha, Kaufman and Levy identify a growing number of Palestinian Arab Israeli youth groups and activists that have developed a unique political style. By refusing, for example, to adhere to mainstream political party orientations, they have initiated a series of actions that spans along a large spectrum of individual acts of resistance, to artistic actions to more organized action. While intergenerational conflicts do not seem to explicitly figure into their worldview, these young activists in a sense create their novelty through their mobilization tactics and techniques and in the process propel themselves forward as a 'new' generation. That is, the generation of the generation is largely shaped by the mobilization techniques and tactics of these protesters.

In Italy, a slightly different dynamic can be observed. Lorenzo Cini outlines the strategic maneuver the Italian student movement has undertaken in the lapse of a few decades (1968 to 2012) when it changed its identity from a generation defined by its student occupation to a generation unit immersed within a broader social movement. In this case, generation became less significant than the strategic and tactical goals of the protests. It was the protests that oriented the visibility or the merging of a given generation. This is an important insight, as Cini shows how activists' construction of the protest frame is key to building collective identities, scope of actions, and political goals, Cini illustrates how structural factors (neoliberal economic policy in this case) impact on not only the decision making of a group of protesters (forms of protests, frames of protest, etc.) but also the identity formation of a group – that is, how they identify their sense of generational belonging. Both of these chapters are important in that they illustrate the fluidity of generational formations in these protest moments – generation units shape, as much as they are shaped by, protest practices, tactics, techniques and strategies.

Even though class occupies an important analytical space in the first two chapters, it figures more prominently in the third chapter. In emphasizing class and class struggles in the formation of protests in Tunisia, Éric Gobe challenges attempts at downplaying the element of class in understanding the Arab Uprisings. Gobe shows how the lower bar, mainly invested by the children of Tunisian lower middle class, has played a significant role during the revolution and has been at the crossroads of two generational modes of habitus, combining its own practices with that of the cohort that preceded it. Here again, the return on some individual trajectories within the senior judiciary body shows how the links were forged between the different protagonists and the actions of the lower bar members who not only defied the regime by physically protecting the protesters against the police – the lawyers dressed in black robes formed a cordon during one of the demonstrations in Tunis – but also managed to make significant political gains. In this respect, the case analyzed by Gobe is as well a great example of the "non-contemporaneity of contemporary" developed by Pinder (cited in Mannheim 1964, 283; Sayad, 1994, 158) and shows the convergent political vision at a turning point between two groups that had little to share during the Ben Ali régime.

11 *Genealogies of Generational Formations*

The second and third dimensions of the relationship between generations and protests concern the question of entangled temporalities/spatialities, with each focusing on a different aspect of this question (Section 11 in the book focuses on the youth, while Section 111 on memory). In order to set the stage for both sections, we add to Sayad's notion of reversibility Mbembe's (2001) notions of fluctuation and interlocking of temporalities. Mbembe's work (2001, 24–65) suggests that the postcolonial condition contains multiple configurations of temporality that must be analyzed. As opposed to acting as a stable framework or horizon of analysis, temporality itself, for Mbembe, becomes the object of analysis. In his attempt at a different writing of Africa and the African subject, Mbembe suggests a move away from an evolutionist/linear model of time as well as models of rupture, and towards a view of every 'age' as "a combination of several temporalities" (Mbembe 2001, 15). To understand how several temporalities are conferred by a set of material practices and signs, Mbembe posits a 'time of entanglement' for which he asserts three postulates of time as (a) an interlocking of various past-present-future configurations that contain both temporal and spatial depths (as opposed to a fixed set of a mono past-present-future),[1] (b) a fluctuating movement of sudden occurrences that cannot be understood as a momentary event or chaos that disturbs an otherwise normal smooth rhythm of time but as intelligible features of time, as disruptions that are constitutive of the rhythm of time, and (c) reversible in its movement in the sense that the past-present-future are not articulated in their near linear unfolding, but are rather intermingled within a fluid and complex process (2001, 16).

When these three postulates – interlocking, fluctuation, reversibility – are viewed in relation to the generation of generations, crucial questions become visible. First, and back to Sayad, the notion of reversibility introduces an analytical dimension otherwise missed if we conceive of temporality as moving only in a forward linear direction. Generations can and are formed through both forward and reverse movements. Second, generations are always constituted within multiple levels of temporal depth. Every configuration of past-present-future inevitably interlocks with other configurations of past-present-future, which opens the door for an analysis of how it is that a 'new' generation, despite its efforts to situate itself within a stable and new past-present-future configuration, interlocks with previous generations' configurations of past-present-future, which shapes and formulates the very

---

1 Similarly, David Scott argues that a generation's ways of living pasts-presents-futures are organized by "intersecting planes of temporality." (Scott 2014, 166).

framing of a generation in a given protest moment. Andrea Hajek's work on the feminist movement in Italy in Chapter 9, for example, shows how young feminists, despite their attempts to temporalize their movement as belonging horizontally with previous movements, nonetheless interlock with the vertical depths of older generations' temporalities. Such interlocking produces some very complex and important questions for the young feminists particularly surrounding the transmission of memory.

Third, fluctuation brings to view the instability and flux of generations without positing such instances as anomalies or temporary events. A fluctuating time suggests that the generation of generations can and does indeed operate in a state of flux that does not lend itself to a final resting place where the 'new' generation has 'arrived.' Sunaina Maira's ethnographic work with young Palestinian activists in Chapter 7 offers a window into the workings of this fluctuating dynamic. In her analysis, it becomes evident that young Palestinian activists have abandoned the notion that Palestine, as a dream and goal of the national liberation struggle exemplified in the Palestine Liberation Organization (PLO), could arrive through the political process initiated by the Oslo Accords of 1993. As a 'new' generation, these activists seek to create themselves as subjects in constant self-formation who turn to cultural forms (graffiti and hip hop) in order to maintain the dream and goal of a Palestine decolonized.

Put together, these three postulates of time indicate that the 'newness' of the new generation is perhaps an important element in the generation of generations but does not, on that account, constitute an analytically essential feature of generations. Succinctly put, the 'newness' of a generation is part of what is to be analyzed in the generation of generations. Both Sayad (1994; 1999) and Mbembe (2001) also bring to the fore the critical importance of understanding the location of this process of generation. They emphasize the significant social, political, economic and cultural factors that inscribe temporality in specific ways on the lived and living daily experience. This inscription can be observed on a multitude of levels (the body, the family, identity, the nation and so on), and in a variety of forms (cartoons, graffiti, music, labor practices, political parties, sexuality and so on), all of which are important. The focus of the second section of the book is on the manner in which the generation of generations, in and through the category of 'youth,' simultaneously operates within and itself creates entangled temporalities.

Unlike works on the causes of the Syrian civil war that emphasize the 'Damascus Spring' events (2001) as the endogenous and original moment that has profoundly shaken the Syrian political system, Matthieu Rey in Chapter 4 shows that the young people he met during the civil war have kept only a scarce memory of that spring, if not almost nothing. The latter's existence was dispersed and was mainly relayed by family transmission. In face of the memory eclipse of this significant internal event, the bold traces of the war in Iraq in 2003, in particular the 'fall of Baghdad,' have instead remained alive for them. For Rey, the 'empty memory' and the absence of a historical relay left a vacuum that was filled up by the war in Iraq, which served as a substitute. In what Rey calls the 'empty memory,' an active memory of the war in Iraq and the capture of Saddam Hussein were at play; it flashed to Syrian youths that their own president was not as invincible as his propaganda machine had made him seem. Rey hints indirectly to the idea of a utopian space, a 'possible' future, to which the capture of Saddam alluded to, that may have transformed the parameters of the generation he names 'Generation 2003.' The broadcasting of what became the death of an 'ordinary man' in the hands of the Americans and the flows of satellite television images break in some ways the national borders and render them pervious to other ideas and influences. This type of experience corresponds to the plea made by Ulrich Beck and Elizabeth Beck-Gersheim (2009). In their defense of "cosmopolitan youth movement," these authors and others (Bracke 2012, 640) have criticized "methodological nationalism" which, according to them hinders the globalizing capabilities of youth movements. Likewise, although more attentive to the significance of local experiences and interpretations, Rey demonstrates how the 'exit' through the border is as important as the real encounters with Iraqi refugees which helped the '2003 Syrian generation' to forge its identity and its consciousness. The endogenous characteristics, in space (Damascus) and time (2001), still sketches then this generation's contours without blocking the aperture to other territories and temporalities.

While Rey starts from the 'event' and reflects on its impact on the experiential dimension of Syrian youth generation formation, Chaymaa Hassabo in Chapter 5 begins with the concept of 'youth' and deconstructs it while looking at its formations in the Egyptian Revolution. She underscores the coming together of several generations that were, according to her, at play in the process. These generations are both the result of other events and the fabricants of the revolution-as-an-event. Reflecting within a short time framework, while anchoring her analysis on the most important protest event in decades within Egypt, Hassabo problematizes the putative homogeneity of the youth movement and emphasizes its diversity. For her, it is more appropriate to refer to 'generation units' adopting various methods of protest rather than using the term 'youth' as a generic rendering of this category of actors within the revolution. In doing so, she sheds some light on the crisscrossing influences, notably on those more traditional features such as the Muslim Brotherhood and other conventional political parties. Similarly, but in a more accentuated ways than the approach developed by Rey, Hassabo develops a typology of generational units through personal trajectories of individuals who position themselves in relation to the conjunctures and not to specific political parties' directions. However, both authors discuss social and political contexts pertaining to authoritarian regimes.

Tanyildiz's chapter on Turkey lies at the nexus of the intersection between the youth and subjective formation. Tanyildiz attempts to describe how the protesters in the Gezi Park in Istanbul are bound up with the 'accumulation by dispossession' deployed by the machinery of the new Turkish bourgeoisie class and its neo-liberal dispositions. Tanyildiz proposes to rethink the words and the practices that accompany the fights for Gezi Park to remain to its people, to allow from the emergence of the not yet seen and the not yet known subjectivities that saw the birth at the protest event and are intrinsically part of it. He theorizes the event itself to be more or less the place of the "subject formation of Turkey's next left generation." Not that the concept of class and the reality that it represents no longer exist or do not count, but rather that the revolutionary subjects of the old left, epitomized by the working class or the middle class understood as immanent realities, should be replaced by the revolutionary subjectivity, based on the actors' 'fragility,' to use Miguel Benasayag's term (2004), the recognition of the other and the ethic of solidarity that unites them.

III   *Memory, History and the 'New Generation'*

The third dimension of the relationship between generation and protest concerns questions of memory. Most pertinent for our book are the following two questions: how do memories and histories of protests produce generational consciousness and lead to the formation of a new generation? How do continuities and ruptures in memory re-dispose protest practices that inflect the formation of a generation?

In his reflection on the relationship between generations and the past, Mannheim (1964) distinguishes between the generations that have been formed as a result of a major or a significant event they have experienced firsthand, and those that have crystallized through their relations to a specific event they inherited. Within this distinction, he gives precedence to what he calls 'acquired memories' that emerge from the very experience of the event, in contrast to the 'appropriated memories' which he considers to be diffused and leading to milder forms of generational affiliations. In and through the formation of acquired memories, the traumatic event enables the aggregation of group members and further substantiates and clarifies its generational features. In light of new social developments, social scientists have challenged some of these ideas. Perhaps most significantly, June Edmunds and Bryan Turner (2002) consider that events, traumatic events in particular, are the ones that *prompt* 'generation consciousness' which is framed as an ideological factor that distinguishes one generation from another, consciousness being the defining point of the very concept of generation as it stands in contrast with other types of aggregation such as group, cohort or membership.[2]

However, the interest in the event, as a temporal matrix in the formation of generation, highlights the focus on social change as a converging point for many disciplinary approaches including history. For example, historians aim to show "how the event is transformed into a mentality" (Ihl 2002, 118; our translation). In other words, in this process, the event is transmuted into an element of the structure and becomes more strictly based on what Pickering and Keightley (2012) call the 'in time' of the communal experience at the expense of its various reception modes 'though time'; modes potentially leading to other types of linkages with the triggering event.

Two slightly different analytical perspectives both dealing with the relationship of memory and generations are of interest here. Given the complexity of the issues raised by them, we will focus our arguments only on the aspects that are relevant to the relations between memory and generation. The first perspective is best illuminated in the work of the historian Pierre Nora (1997), who sees generation as the quintessential producer of 'lieux de mémoire'; the second perspective more akin with Cultural Studies and trauma studies, is developed among others by Michael Pickering and Emily Keightley (2012) who emphasize the fluidity and diversity of generational memory production. Both perspectives aim to understand how memory is constitutive of generation production and conversely how generation owes its very existence to memory processes.

Nora answers more directly to the question on the types of relatedness between generation and event. He identifies the event of the French Revolution as the founding moment of the idea of generation. In particular, the Revolution has resulted in producing for the first time a 'youth' category as a generation, which becomes an important actor in the social and political fabric. In this sense, youth is far from being "only a word" (Nora 1997, 2986), as stated by Pierre Bourdieu (1984, also quoted in Nora, op. cit.). The very birth of

---

2   Edmunds and Turner replaced the expression 'generation actuality,' originally contrasted in Mannheim with generation as potentiality, by 'active generation' and 'passive generation,' but without questioning their predecessor's distinction between 'acquired' and 'appropriated' memories. This view, according to Michael Pickering and Emily Keightley (2012, 118), hardens the "separation between commonality of time and the relations that exist over time," and abandons the idea that "inherited experience is involved in the development of shared generational consciousness."

a youth generation serves to 'immemorialize' history (i.e. the Revolution) and produces what Nora (1997) calls 'historical memory.' For Nora, this production of historical memory alludes to something more important than itself, that is to "better memorialize the present," through essentially "Lieux de mémoires" (Nora 1997, 3005), as belonging to a generation of youth.

In other words, the 'acquired memories' (Mannheim 1964), that is the memories, that are formed through the experience of the event, are not necessarily the key moment in the formation of a 'generation.' Indeed, although the Revolution revealed that the 'youth' was the real engine of change, the generation of the Revolution does not coincide with those who have initiated it but is incarnated by those who have carried it out a decade later, the 'youth.' Hence, there is no necessary coincidence between generation and past event. Nora's remark on the importance of the present in the formulation of generation does not mean the rejection of the past (Nora 1997), because the constitution of youth is shaped by the 'Lieux de mémoire,' which remains the main mode of its manifestation.

In a slightly different way than Nora, Maira's article shows that the distinction between an 'appropriated' and an 'acquired' memory can be superseded by a moment that could be called 'creative' memory. Her analysis focuses on the ways in which protest practices and continuities and ruptures in memory reciprocally interact to inflect the formation of a generation. The Palestinian activists she worked with reveal how they formed a generational consciousness in three important ways: first, by virtue of their firsthand experiences, their acquired memory, of the Oslo Accords and its aftermath, which is the major political event of their time; second, through their formulation of a relation to the past, of an appropriated memory of the Palestinian *Nakba* that was for them betrayed and its struggle abandoned by the Oslo Accords; and third, through cultural forms of protest that are reshaping the meaning of politics for this *Jil Oslo*. The third element is particularly interesting as Maira illustrates how the cultural idioms of the youth, such as graffiti and hip-hop, in their very form, draw on and revive past political discourses in order to create and recreate political vocabularies in the present moment. One of the key features of this new vocabulary is its dissociation between political progress as it was understood in the Oslo Accords and a decolonial world that is created in the cultural realm for Palestinian youth to inhabit. Maira's article reveals the analytical importance of examining the varied ways in which memory infuses the reciprocal formation of generations and protests.

While Maira insists on the encounters between memory and artistic production as performance protest on their own and on the novel understanding of realities such as nation, territory, struggles as well as the ways they have been redefined through sometimes ephemeral modes of expression, Ratiba Hadj-Moussa's work in Chapter 8 discusses how monumental history, forcibly visible through the 'November generation,' the very generation who started the Algerian liberation war, is appropriated and redesigned through the claims for social justice in Southern Algeria. Hadj-Moussa's analysis articulates basic claims for jobs – through the unemployed movement – and a unique voice that has emerged from its Southern membership, which recomposes monumentality by adding to it silenced memory events and by making visible the inscription of their space and territory. The conjunctive gesture of space and memory re-elaborates the spatial characteristics (here Southern Algeria) as the central point to the definition of generational claims for justice in contemporary Algeria. Neither monumental history nor spatiality can unilaterally be abstracted from this juncture while notions such as region, periphery give voice to marginalized generation.

While in these examples the performativity of generation is inscribed within the present and somehow instrumentalized producing temporal reversibility, the second perspective on memory and generation develops a resolutely 'through time' generational memory, where the founding event is conceived of as an important moment albeit without the weight it has in Edmunds' and Turner's work. This perspective can be resumed under the auspices of family lineage or family generation (Attias-Donfut and Arber 2000, Mauger 2009). Using Rothberg's (2009) and Hirsch's work (2008), Pickering and Keightley strongly advocate for a view that takes into account the relatedness of vertical and horizontal modes of mnemonic transmission and appropriation and insist that we should be attentive to "how stories can be heard, not just expressed" (2012, 119). To assert this view comprises many fold analytical tasks comprising first, the disentanglement of any putative correspondence between identity and memory, and between the past and generational memories, second, the assertion that patterns of cross-generational identification are mutable and contingent (Pickering and Keightley 2012, 120) and, finally, the restoration of the second hand experience as a significant builder of criss-crossing and multi-layered generational connections. Along with the now accepted view – already stated by Mannheim – according to which generation memories are not handed down without selection and re-elaboration, the authors stress their creative impulse and imaginative recombination of ideas and practices and the potentiality of their projection in future experiences. What these analytical attempts bring to the discussion could be summarized in two points: the first concerns the dispersed production of memory and its possible fading into something that relate to generation as 'a concrete groups' (Mannheim 1964). The second refers to the transformation brought by new media to the pair generation and memory. The latter point is exemplified by 'second' and other generations and the transformative outcome brought by individuals who, like the children of Holocaust survivors, re-sketch their individual family experiences and enunciate critically and imaginatively their own relation to the past. Imagination is then an additional dimension that marks the liminal position of those who record bits and pieces of past experiences and articulate them to the collective present: "moving memory beyond a solely private, vertical mode of transmission is crucial if we are to avoid mnemonic inheritances from one another" (Pickering and Keightley 2012, 128).

But if Pickering and Keightley base their analysis on generation memory on more 'traditional' texts, several other authors mentions the role played by new media in the elaboration of memory and generation. This additional piece to generation consciousness is best illustrated by Alison Landberg's concept of 'prosthetic memory' (2004), which problematizes the role and use of media in the stitching of past events and narratives with individuals who have never experienced them directly. Prosthetic memory's virtue is to unbound 'traditional' identifications to nation and territory, and move them into the transnational terrain where they are commodified and individually appropriated. For example, in their work on Sikh and Indo-Caribbean diasporic second generation, Michael Nijhawan and Andrea Shultz (2014), inspired by Landberg's concept, show how this generation while being immersed in an act of mass consumption – using photographs of their indentured ancestors in what could be seen as a virtual nostalgia scene – tell the stories of their families and the exploitative journey they went through and putting forward recognition claims (Hadj-Moussa and Nijhawan 2014). Although they are personally deeply immersed their engagement with these narratives should in any way solely to be seen as an individual search and inquiry but also as a collective memory 'through time,' pertaining to one of the "communities of memories" (Pickering and Keightley 2012, 129) that strive to imagine its relations to the past.

Andrea Hajek, in her study of the feminist movement in Italy, speaks to the complex ways in which the transmission of memory takes place. We often think of the transmission of memory as a straightforward process of handing down, of bequeathing tradition, beliefs, values and practices. Hajek's analysis, however, reveals how the rejection of such a process of entrustment in itself transmits memory nonetheless and produces a generational consciousness in the process. The young feminists, most prominent of which is *Femministe Nove*, in Hajek's paper, do not necessarily reject the beliefs, traditions, and values of earlier feminist struggles, of earlier feminist generations (or waves), but rather reject the very idea of a linear progression of feminist generations or waves, whereby they are viewed as the heiresses of the work and struggles of older generations. However, in their attempt to resituate their generational positionality on a more horizontal plane with historical feminists, these young feminists nonetheless interlock with the temporalities of these older generations, where memory is transmitted through carriers, media, contents, practices and forms. Even though not always explicitly stated by young feminists, Hajek's analysis demonstrates the interlocking between the generations that takes place despite the intentions and claims of the activist groups concerned.

Observing a similar dynamic in Spain where young activists do not necessarily or explicitly observe their connections to the past, Vilaseca's work in Chapter 10 examines the ways in which contemporary Spanish youth movements would benefit from a more direct encounter with the writings of the turn of the twentieth century anarchist intellectual, Ricardo Mella. Vilaseca takes on the task of enabling this encounter. His work is simultaneously an analysis of the generational consciousness of present-day activism in Spain and an intervention in this activism.[3] Vilaseca's analysis strives to facilitate an encounter with the past in order to reenergize and reinvigorate anarchist praxis. In showing activists their connectedness to past practices and ideas, Vilaseca points out some of the potential limits of present-day practices and as well some of the potential solutions to those limits. Perhaps most significant here for studies of generations more generally is the idea that the workings of memory in the formation of generational consciousness, while sometimes hidden as it is in the case of anarchist politics in Spain, must be unearthed by scholarly analysis in order to not just analyze forms of protests but to help clarify their historicity for them. This is the kind of work that activists do not often have the resources and time to carry out, and it is precisely where academic analysis can explicitly become part of what it analyzes.

***

On a final note, we acknowledge that the relationship between religion and politics remains largely unexplored in our book. Only Hassabo's chapter on the Egyptian Uprisings deals with this question, albeit tangentially. This is not to suggest that we do not think it is an important area of academic analysis. In our efforts to counter Western European/North American dominant discourse

---

3 This is similar to a longstanding trend in feminist literature on social movements where the analysis strives to directly contribute to a social movement, often by helping activists better frame their issues and objectives (e.g., see Nixon & Humphreys 2010 on domestic violence; Moravec 2012 on feminist/women's art; Frazer & Hutchings 2014 on pacifism and non-violence).

that has more or less forgotten about the protests of the early 2010s, and has obsessively focused on the rise and spread of political Islam, we have neglected the question altogether. But we maintain that a generational analysis of the varied movements that self-identify under the banner of political Islam remains an urgent and necessary task. Here again, we believe that a generational analysis would not yield to a framing of such protests as 'religious movements,' but would rather introduce them as complex forms of protest that incorporate religious doctrine in their formations of generation, as shown for example in the case of Saudi Arabia in Pascal Menoret's (2011) work.

Finally, our underlying assumption in this collection is that the articulation and production of a generation is a key dynamic in these protests, both for the protesters and for the academic representation of their actions. Our collection reveals a rich area of study that goes unexplored when the concept of generation is taken for granted. Generation can act as a frame of reference that enables a tactic/strategy of protest, a sense of unity and solidarity, and as constituting the novelty of protest practices. Understanding how generation works in those three different ways is a crucial aspect of further understanding the challenges that these protests raise and, just as importantly, the obstacles that they themselves might face.

References

Amin, Samir. *The People's Spring. The Future of the Arab Revolution*. Cap Town, Dakar, Nairobi: Pambazuka Press, 2012.

Attias-Donfut, Claudine and Sara Arber. "Equity and Solidarity Across the Generations," in *The Myth of Generational Conflict: The Family and State in Ageing Societies*. edited by Claudine Attias-Donfut and Sara Arber, 1–21. London: Routledge, 2000.

Ayari, Michaël Béchir. "Non, les Révolutions Tunisienne et Egyptienne ne sont pas des 'Révolutions 2.0'," *Mouvements* 2, 66 (2011): 56–61.

Badiou, Alain. *The Rebirth of History: Times of Riots and Uprisings*. Translated by Gregory Elliott. New York: Verso, 2012.

Bayat, Asef. "Workless Revolutionnaries. The Umemployed Movement in Revolutionary Iran," in *Subalterns and Social Protest. History. From Below in the Middle-East and North Africa*, edited by Stephanie Cronin, 91–115. London and New York: Routledge, 2008.

Beck, Ulrich and Beck-Gersheim, Elizabeth. "Global Generations and the Trap of Methodological Nationalism For a Cosmopolitan Turn in the Sociology of Youth and Generation," *European Sociological Review*, 25, 1 (2009): 25–36.

Bourdieu, Pierre. "La Jeunesse n'est qu'un Mot," in *Questions de Sociologie*, 143–154. Paris: Les Éditions de Minuit, 1984.

Bracke, Maud Anne. "One-dimensional Conflict? Recent Scholarship on 1968 and the Limitations of the Generation Concept." *Journal of Contemporary History* 47, 3 (2012): 638–646.

Dabashi, Hamid. *The Arab Spring: The End of Postcolonialism*. New York: Zed Books, 2012.

Durkheim, Émile. The *Division of Labor in Society*. New York: Free Press, 1984.

Durkheim, Émile. *On Suicide*. New York: Penguin, 2006.

Edmunds, June and Bryan S. Tumer. *Generations, Culture and Society*. Buckingham: Open University Press, 2002.

Eisenstadt, Shmuel. N. *From Generation to Generation. Age Groups and Social Structure*. New Brunswick: Transaction, 2009.

Eyerman, Ron and Bryan Turner. "Outline of a Theory of Generations." *European Journal of Social Theory* 1, 1 (1998): 91–106.

Frazer, Elizabeth and Kimberly Hutchings. Revisiting Ruddick: Feminism, Pacifism and Non-Violence. *Journal of International Political Theory* 10, 1 (2014): 109–124.

Hadj-Moussa, Ratiba and Michael Nijhawan, (eds). Suffering, Art, and Aesthetics. New York: Palgrave Macmillan, 2014.

Halbwachs, Maurice. *Les Cadres Sociaux de la Mémoire*. Paris: Albin Michel, 1995.

Hall, Stuart. "The West and the Rest: Discourse and Power." In *Formations of Modernity*, edited by Stuart Hall and Bram Gieben, 275–320. The Open University: Polity Press, 1992.

Hirsch, Marianne. "The Generation of Postmemory." *Poetics Today* 29, 1 (2008): 103–128.

Ibn, Khaldûn. *The Muqaddimah: An Introduction to History*. Translated by Franz Rosenthal (1958). Princeton: Princeton University Press, 2005 [1370].

Ihl, Olivier. "Socialisation et Evénements Politiques." *Revue Française de Sciences Politiques* 2–3 (2002): 125–144.

Kluber, Johanne. "Les Révolutions Arabes et le Web. 2.0. Tunisie et Égypte." Revue Averroes, August 7, 2011. https://revueaverroestest.wordpress.com/category/numero-4-5 -082011/special-printemps-arabe/. Retrieved September 2011.

Keightley, Emily and Michael Pickering. *The Mnemonic Imagination: Remembering as Creative Practice*. New York: Palgrave Macmillan, 2012.

Landsberg, Alison. Prosthetic Memory: The Transformation of American Remembrance in the Age of Mass Culture. New York: Columbia University Press, 2004.

Mannheim, Karl. "The Problem of Generations," in *Essays on the Sociology of Knowledge*, edited by Karl Paul Kecskemeti, 276–322. London: Routledge & Kegan, 1964 [1927].

Mauger, Gérard. "Générations et rapports de générations." *Daimon Revista Internacional de Filosofía* 46 (2009): 109–126.

Mbembe, Achille. *On the Postcolony*. Translated by A.M. Berrett, Janet Roitman, Murray Last and Steven Rendall. Berkeley and Los Angeles: University of California Press, 2001.

Menoret, Pascal. "Leaving Islamic Activism. Ambiguous Disengagement in Saudi Arabia," in *Social Movements, Mobilization and Contestation in the Middle East and North Africa*, edited by Joel Beinin and Frédéric Vairel, 43–69. Stanford: Stanford University Press, 2011.

Merklen, Denis. *Quartiers Populaires, Quartiers Politiques*. Paris : La Dispute, 2009.

Moravec, Michelle. "Toward a History of Feminism, Art, and Social Movements in the United States." *Frontiers: A Journal of Women Studies* 33, 2 (2012): 22–54.

Nijhawan, Michael and Anna C. Schultz. "The Diasporic *Rasa* of Suffering: Notes on the Aesthetics of Image and Sound in the Indo-Caribbean and Sikh Popular Art," in *Suffering, Art and Aesthetics*, edited by Ratiba Hadj-Moussa and Michael Nijhawan, 177–205. New York: Palgrave, 2014.

Nixon, Jennifer and Cathy Humphreys. "Marshalling the Evidence: Using Intersectionality in the Domestic Violence Frame." *Social Politics: International Studies in Gender, State and Society* 17, 2 (2010): 137–158.

Nora, Pierre. "La Génération," in *Les Lieux de Mémoire*, edited by Pierre Nora, 2975–3015. Paris: Gallimard, 1997.

Rothberg, Michael. *Multidirectional Memory. Remembering the Holocaust in the Age of Decolonization*. Stanford: Stanford University Press, 2009.

Sayad, Abdelmalek. *La Double Absence. Des Illusions de l'Emigré aux Souffrances de l'Immigré*. Paris: Le Seuil, 1999.

Sayad, Abdelmalek. "Le Mode de Génération des Générations Immigrées." *L'Homme et la Société* 111–112 (1994): 155–174.

Schock, Kurt. *Unarmed Insurrections: People Power Movements in Non Democracies*. Minneapolis: University of Minnesota Press, 2005.

Scott, David. "The Temporality of Generations: Dialogue, Tradition, Criticism." *New Literary History* 45, 2 (2014): 157–181.

Sitrin, Marina. *Everyday Revolution: Horizontalism and Autonomy in Argentina*. London and New York: Zed Books, 2012.

Tilly, Charles and Leslie Wood. *Social Movements, 1768–2008*. Second Revised Edition. London: Paradigm Publishers, 2009.

Tilly, Charles. "Social Movements as Historically Specific Clusters of Political Performances." *Berkeley Journal of Sociology* 38 (1993–1994): 1–30.

PART 1

Forms of Protest and the Production of Generations

∵

CHAPTER 1

Palestinian Youth in Israel: A New Generational Style of Activism?[1]

Mohammad Massalha, Ilana Kaufman and Gal Levy

Introduction

In the last decade, there has been substantial growth in the numbers of groups of adolescent and youth activists within Arab-Palestinian society in Israel. These groups are active in a wide range of issues: politics, social issues, ideology, culture and religion, on both local and societal levels. Activism is not a new phenomenon among Arab-Palestinian youth, but hitherto, they were predominantly active in bodies affiliated with political parties or extra-parliamentary movements. Thus, what makes the new activist groups unique is that their activism is mostly channeled through independent, primarily local, initiatives of their own. This chapter seeks to account for the emergence of this new type of activism, and particularly for the motives for political action by youth. These motivations, as distinguished from the political identity of young Arab Palestinians in Israel, have hardly attracted academic interest, probably due to the dominance of party politics in setting the political agenda (Ghanim 2009).

The immediate historical political context of this activism is the deterioration over a decade in the relationship of Palestinian citizens with the state. After a short period of political liberalization, and a temporary thaw in the conflict with the PLO upon the signing of the Oslo Accords in 1993, a severe crisis of trust erupted at the turn of the millennium. The faltering of the Oslo process in 1996 brought about the outbreak of the second Intifada in the Palestinian territories in 2000. This was followed by the October Events, during unprecedented days of rage, protest and civil disobedience: 13 young Palestinian citizens – protestors – were shot and killed by the Israeli police (Rabinowitz,

---

1 We would like first and foremost to thank our interviewees for their time and willingness to share with us their experience and views. We also wish to thank our assistants during this study Samaher Hafi and Michal Milerman. The Open University Research Authority is also acknowledged for its financial support of this project. Finally, we are thankful to the editors of this volume for their interest in our work and for the reviewers for their helpful comments.

© KONINKLIJKE BRILL NV, LEIDEN, 2017 | DOI 10.1163/9789004344518_003

Ghanim and Yiftachel 2000). The October Events became a formative experience for young Palestinians who were born in the 1980s.

While it is widely acknowledged and agreed that October 2000 marked a watershed event in the relationship between the Palestinian citizens and the state, few scholarly writings relate specifically to its impact on the young generation of Palestinians. Based on discussions conducted hard on the heels of the events, in 2000–2001 with students from a class of high school seniors and student leaders, Rabinowitz and Abu Baker (2002) concluded that the consciousness of the generation involved in the events was now more strongly linked to the historical narrative of the anti-colonial Palestinian struggle and the collective memory of the 1948 *Nakba* (catastrophe). Furthermore, they suggested that this protest included a critical view of the political strategies of their parents' generation (Rabinowitz and Abu Baker 2002, 20–70). A similar conclusion was drawn by Ghanim in a study of three generations of Palestinian intellectuals (Ghanim 2009). She concluded, on the basis of interviews conducted between 2001–2002 with the youngest intellectuals, that the attempt by previous generations to reform the state and reach a solution for the national conflict through electoral politics and civil society organizations has seemingly reached a deadlock (Ghanim 2009, 150). These events, nonetheless, as several researchers observed, formed the grounds for a new definition of Palestinian patriotism based on the growth of Palestinian civil society in the 1990s (Haklai 2004; Jamal 2011, 188–225). Using these NGOs as their platform, intellectuals as well as activists put forward new identity based agendas emphasizing authenticity, autonomy and collective rights as an indigenous population (Kaufman 2010; Jamal 2011, 36–39).

This study focuses on a specific group of young Palestinian activists who were mostly born between the mid-1980s and late 1990s. The interviewees were almost equally male and female and were either during or after their BA education. They were of diverse geographical background and different types of localities (mixed cities, exclusive Arab settlements in the north, center and south), many were politically active, but all were of middle class background (though this term in the Arab-Palestinian society must be taken cautiously). While most were too young to actually take part in the October Events, they were impacted by them so they share the political consciousness of those born a decade earlier. This chapter addresses the following question: are we witnessing early signs of a generational phenomenon involving the consolidation of a new generational unit of youth bearing a new style of activism and patriotism, meant to intervene in history and change its course? Specifically, by focusing on these activists and their particular type of activism we ask whether we are seeing more than simply the rise of a new cohort of politicized Palestinian youth who are seeking to resist and to act against their structural marginality in the Jewish state of Israel and the Israeli society. We are equally interested in their style of collective action and its new content matter, distinguished from that which characterizes the established political parties, and which attests to a shift from ideology to practice in contemporary political activism across the globe.

This question will be discussed in the context of three analytical frameworks: Manheim's theoretical framework on generations and generational units; the impact of neoliberalism on the rise of individualism, and the decline of political parties as a vehicle for political activism under the impact of new media on the style of collective action. As part of an ongoing research on political activism in the Palestinian society, this chapter is based on data collected from focus groups and in-depth interviews with leading activists, some of them acting *ad hoc*, others are active in more structured groups of youth activists, including 'The Movement of Jaffa's Youth' (*Harakat A-Shabiba al-Yaffaweeya*), 'Youth on the Move' (*Hirak al-Shababii*), 'Our Country' (*Baladna*), and 'Stepping Forward' (*Khutwe*). The interviews were conducted between 2013 and 2014 in Jaffa, Beer Sheba, Ramle, Haifa and Qufur Qara. The data were systematically analyzed for traces of generational events, including historical events, collective memory and personal/familial/generational experiences that shape generational consciousness.

Generations and the Course of History – A Conceptual Introduction

Karl Mannheim's classical essay, "The Problem of Generations," remains, to date, the point of origin for any study of generations in sociology as well as in other disciplines. For Manheim, a generation is an explanatory factor in social change and one of the cornerstones in rendering intellectual and social movements explicable (Mannheim 1952 [1923], 286–287). Accordingly, social position and shared fate of youth of the same cohort, as well as shared activism in social movements and intellectual circles shape and determine the historical trajectory (Corsten 1999; Braungart 1984). The social cohesiveness of the generational phenomenon manifests itself on three levels.

The generational location is first. This refers to the structure of opportunity in which individuals are located. In turn, this defines the potential range of social opportunities and experience for them. A shared location in the case of a generation is derived from biological rhythm, and hence, an objective fact, analogical to class position. Thus, by shifting our understanding of the generational phenomenon from biological to societal sites, the notion of location is imbued with a sociological significance that turns it into a multifaceted, dynamic concept.

The subjective level is second. The impact of social location has a bearing on the individuals' psychological and emotional state beyond the affiliation with a specific group or social category. It impacts the individuals' way of thinking, the meaning they ascribe to their experiences, and their social engagements. Furthermore, relations of location determine the accessibility of cultural heritage to them. Different generations may experience varied levels of accessibility and a different attitude towards the society's cultural heritage (Mannheim 1952; Lambert 1972; Braungart 1984).

However, social location alone will not explain the generational phenomenon and its crucial role in the historical development of human society. A generation as actuality also requires a will to act. The question is, therefore, under what social conditions people of a shared social location crystallize into a conscious generation willing to act upon their shared consciousness.

By way of an answer, Mannheim suggested that mutual experience of the same historical events and sharing the meaning of those events is what turns this aggregate of people into an actual generation (Mannheim 1952, 304; Corsten 1999, 254). Hence, the importance of the early impressions which shape one's basic worldview and become influential in rendering later experiences meaningful (Corsten 1999, 298). Shared experience is similarly central to the understanding of the generational phenomenon in the eyes of many other scholars (e.g. Esler 1984; Rintala 1974; Braungart 1984).

Social cohesiveness of a generation is formed when generational units consolidate. It is at this point that the objective and subjective shared locations become distinctive in the individual's response to generational problems. The characteristics of each generational unit are shaped by the *zeitgeist*, or 'the spirit of the epoch.' Youth absorb their knowledge of society which is integrated into their worldview and becomes part of their identity (Mannheim 1952, 305). However, one generational cohort may breed several units (Mannheim 1952, 304). In other words, in one actual generation several generational units may coexist, sometimes antagonistic to each other, each deriving its uniqueness from different ideological or social sources. Thus, the choice a generational unit makes in its ideological inclinations and cultural ideas is the source of social dynamics and a new social order (Braungart 1984, 19).

The importance of youth in the process of social change stems from the tension between the need of human societies to transmit their heritage from one generation to the next, and the youth's fresh contact with their heritage. This generates the potential on the part of the youth to challenge acceptance of their heritage as is (ibid, 293–294). The potential for social change is therefore embedded in the young generation as it shapes and articulates its worldview, under the impact of its own unique experiences.

Mannheim's theorization of the role of youth in instigating social change, particularly through an outburst of protest against existing institutions survived the transition to late modernity with its primacy on post-material values and self-actualizing individualization (Beck 1997). For example, the concept of generational units has been found useful in explaining intergenerational differences in activism and attitudes towards civil liberties and partisanship in the United States from the mid-1960s to the late 1990s (Jennings 2002). More recently, the 2011 Arab Spring protests initiated by the young against long established, rigid authoritarian regimes has been heralded as a transformative event (Sika 2012). After it unleashed a wave of similar protests of youth in cities around the globe (Castells 2012), it has been predicted that the year 2011, "will be remembered in history" since it is "a year, where dreams of a different world were put into political practice" (Fuchs 2012, 797). While the political contexts of the mass protest activity of the young in 2011 in Madrid, Santiago, and Tel Aviv were unique and different from that in Tunis and Cairo, all the protestors had in common the experience of living in a global, neoliberal, depoliticized digital age. Their activism shared the characteristics of a grassroots, rhizomatic, leaderless ad hoc activities that went beyond the spectrum of electoral politics, political parties, and civil society associations (Castells 2012; Levy 2014). It is in this theoretical context that we set out to examine the consciousness of Palestinian youth activist groups in Israel. We hypothesize that they are part of the solidification of a generational unit. In the interviews, we therefore searched for the social sites where their collective generational identity has been forged. We assume that experiences of the interviewees have a phenomenological effect upon the structural formation of common generational experiences. Similarly we assume that their experiences create feelings of a common destiny in the form of generational identity (Gasset 1974).

Findings – Sites of Concretization of Generational Identity

(a) *The Universities*

All our interviewees were either students or graduates of a university. Their experience as students comes out clearly in the interviews as a transformative process which dramatically shaped their consciousness, their points of view and their incentives for action.

I think that all the work, my preoccupation, as well as that of all the Arab activists, begins mainly at the university. For those who grow up, in the Palestinian society, the student movement is the place for politics. It's also historically the place. But in the universities we were still [identified with] *Hadash* [a political party] *Balad* [a political party] and the Islamic movement. This was the [nature of] activism.

As we can see, the student describes the university as a major site of political socialization, as well as a site for political mobilization and action. This mode is typical of other universities in the Middle East and Africa in which militant activism of students against colonialism, occupation and social injustice brew (Aya 1979; Cross 1993; Comarof 1985; Foran 1997; Vilas 1986). According to Cross (1993) and Comarof (1985), the schools and universities in South Africa provided students with opportunities for informal meetings which served to help them translate their experiences to political consciousness and to taking action against the Apartheid regime. In Israel too, the meeting with other young Palestinians at these sites has served to raise consciousness. One activist credits the *Balad* party cell in the student body with politicizing him:

> ...from the activities *Balad* initiated, from the meetings we held, I learned a lot, and this is very important. Their activities here are very important, and it is very good that they help raise a generation of activists...

Furthermore, the meeting at the university with other students empowers them *vis a` vis* their personal sense of discrimination and the collective experiences of suppression. As one activist described her experience at the university:

> Life at the university was really interesting...Here along with a number of other students, we established *Jamaatna* [literally in Arabic: Our Group] as the Arab Students' Forum at Ben-Gurion University in order to fight for cultural rights at the university for the Arab students. We had a big quarrel with the dean...He was a number one racist, and he said he will not allow an official cell of an Arab students' organization as long as he is in office. We recorded him and reported it in a message to the president of the university. [When] we wanted to organize a Students Day' for the Arab students parallel to the [general] Students Day and they refused to let us organize on campus, we wrote to the president and we also published it in the media, so it appears in *Ha'aretz* [a daily national newspaper] and on Facebook. [The president] got very nervous and contacted us and asked for a meeting. We met and she promised that from now on they

PALESTINIAN YOUTH IN ISRAEL

will appoint Arab members to the student union. I am not sure if it did happen, since I graduated. However, there are two Arab coordinators for cultural issues in the student union.

(b)   *Political Parties*

The Arab political parties and movements (*Hadash, Balad*, Islamic Movement) are another venue where political consciousness is cultivated and materialized. As mentioned above, these bodies have an active presence of party cells on the campuses. A significant number of our interviewees told us that they were recruited to political activism by these cells. Consequently, their initial political activities were carried out under the auspices of the political parties on campus.

However, the picture depicted by our interviewees is that these party activities among students are not always well organized, and often tend to mirror the electoral politics outside the student bodies. This is how one of our interviewees, from the Jaffa group of activists, described the effort of one of the political parties, and of the students affiliated with it, to launch more continuous and organized activities on campus:

> ...They [the party student activists] decided to set up a party cell on campus. But, having had experience of at least three years as party activists they came to the task with the goal of building something which was lacking, not only to organize for elections [for the student council] and to *go to sleep* for four years after that...Things started to move from this [elections] because we used to meet at election times. So, from here the need for a new thing was created. In my opinion, if I recall well, all of them were *Balad* party members. Yes, from the activities that *Balad* used to organize, from the meetings we had, I learned a lot, and this is important, here it's important...If you check most of the Palestinian activists in Israel, you will find that most of them have been members of a party, grew up in a party.

Being members of political parties did not prevent our interviewees from harboring reservations regarding the parties and their conduct on campuses. Some of the interviewees even discontinued their party memberships on account of the cumbersomeness of the parties, being bogged down with internal political squabbles, and too constricting with regard to political action. Following is the description of one interviewee from Jaffa:

> ...you don't have power when things are not moving, because of political issues, [and you start asking yourself] to be in the party or not to be in

the party. And this is because if you are active in the party, you cannot be independent...

Another interviewee criticizes the political party of which he was a member for its opportunism, especially at times of elections to the Knesset or to the Arab student councils at the various campuses:

> Let us say that the only activity, and this is one of my arguments against *Balad* that connected us geographically with other campuses was at times of elections and this is very wrong. At election time, members of the party's cell at Haifa University that was an older and more experienced cell, used to arrive on our campus. A.B.'s sister [senior activist] used to show up, would not leave us, and instruct us what to do...

Disappointment with the mainstream activism of the party eventually led to his resigning from the party altogether:

> ...With all due respect, what *Balad* is doing is serving the interest of the Zionist regime by sitting in the Parliament. I do think they are a little over militant (in rhetoric) but have lost their focus in the last ten to twenty years...They don't know what they want...Each one of them talks about different things...They are afraid to act. So, they don't push others to act. This is sheer cowardice.

(c) *Informal and Civil Society Organizations and the New Media*

As mentioned above, since the mid-1980s, there has been remarkable growth of civil society organizations in Palestinian society in Israel (Jamal 2011). The NGOs have been active in political and socio-political, religious-political fields.

Although there is no agreement among researchers with respect to the extent to which they have been effective overall, there seems to be a consensus that in some areas their activities made a contribution to social change and to socio-political, gender, and religious consciousness (Jamal 2011; Zeidan and Ghanim 2000). One of the main audiences targeted by these NGOs are youth. Hence, informal organizations and NGOs also operate as important sites for solidifying generational consciousness in Arab society in Israel. Furthermore, the NGOs connect members of this generation and transform them into activists' groups. As we discovered, the boundaries between young party activists, young NGO employees, and youth activists are consequently, sometimes, blurred. We learned from one of our interviewees in Haifa who works for *Baladna*, an association for Arab youth, on the logistical and financial assistance that this organization provides for activities to promote political youth agendas. These include direct mass protests in the struggle against the government's Prawer Plan of displacing and resettling the Arabs in the south.

> Each NGO acts by itself and each organization has its mechanisms, but in the final analysis, the role of the NGOs…[e.g.] *Baladna* because it is an organization for youth, and because the main leaders and its workers are young, [and I am part of them], we were among the ten organizers [of the Prawer protest]. So there is a feeling that *Baladna* is involved…but on the other hand, I think that the main role of the *Baladna* was to support [the protest], but they are not its main organizers [which were *Hiraq*]. But I still say that those who are active in the NGOs and in the parties are the same people. So, formally whether *Baladna* is attending or *Hiraq* is attending [a specific organizational meeting] it is the respective organization that is being represented.

The young activists mostly emerge from the universities seeking a way to channel their rage and urge to change the socio-political status quo. An activist from Ramla-Lydda thus told us about his experience:

> I completed my studies in Jerusalem where I was active in the *Balad* cell on campus, and I came back here to live with my parents in the town of Lydda. My friends who were also active in cells of different parties or volunteer social activists [such as assisting sick children with cancer, or hospitalized, sick, non-citizen Palestinian children], we just did not know what to do with ourselves, and this was really a catastrophic situation. We had so much rage, such a lot of energy that we desperately wanted to go out and do something and we did not know how to do it. So we decided to establish a non-partisan movement, [because] we got fed up with Arab political parties. We became convinced that their struggle is not conducted correctly and we established our activist movement *Khutwe* [A Step], during the 2009 Israeli war on Gaza. Our first act was to bring to town Palestinian hip hop artists for a concert in aid of the children in Gaza…

Given the age cohort of the activists, it is similarly not surprising that the new media plays an important role in the activists' organizations. Most of the young activists in this study came of age in the later stages of the digital revolution in the late 1990s and early 21st century. Their lifestyles are therefore embedded in what Castells has termed as the network society, characterized by the mass use of interactive horizontal networks of Internet and wireless communication (Castells 2000). A 2012 survey by the Central Bureau of Statistics has shown that almost half (47.6%) of the Palestinians in Israel use the Internet for communication and information (The Social Survey, CBS 2014, 482). Research has further shown that the Palestinians in Israel have demarcated their own web space as a national community (Ben David 2014). The network has been used by members of the community as a primary tool for both political communication, as well as for consumption of local news and commerce (Kabha 2007; Mesch and Talmud 2011; Jamal 2009). Palestinian civil society organizations show a strong presence of websites, through which they spread their information and organize their activities (Ben David 2014, 142).

As in other parts of the world, members of this generation, particularly the more educated, are the most proficient section of the population in digital technology, and hence have also been associated with the high level of mobilization by means of social networks (Salvatore 2013, 221–222; Valenzuela et al. 2012; Bennett and Segerberg 2012; Sika 2012). They feel at home in the net and share its language. As an activist of *Baladna* from Haifa explained with regard to the central role Facebook plays in the activity of all groups:

> Facebook is not only a platform for recruiting people. I think that the language and discourse used there is very much suited to the young generation, it appeals to them. If you put a two-page lecture on Facebook, it will not have an impact. So it is not only the platform, it is also the manner in which you fit it to the language used by the young generation which mobilizes them...The bottom line is that it is a very significant tool.

Similar to their cohorts in other societies, being relatively more privileged in their community, the youth activists have been socialized and act within the context of the network society. Their manner of political engagement fits in with their social lifestyle in which individual expression, participation, and sharing in social networks plays a major role as a medium for connecting with other individuals. Political activism for a collective cause, with or without the use of digital technology, also becomes an act of personal expression. Grassroots activism based on individual initiatives is preferred over being active in more institutionalized bodies, such as political parties and NGOs. An activist from the Jaffa group explained his motivation for joining the group:

> I don't come from a family that is involved politically; on the contrary, from a family that is reserved and tries the whole time to keep a big

distance [from politics]. I always felt I needed a place where I could share *my* own thoughts and also decide to put into practice *my* own ideas. I always used to participate independently, and through this group I am able to carry out projects…

For this generation, worldwide, researchers argue, "participation becomes self-motivating as personally expressive content is shared with and recognized by others, who, in turn repeat these networked sharing activities" (Bennett and Segerberg 2012, 752). An old school activist, of the pre-digital era, who acts as a mentor for the Jaffa youth activists observed with unconcealed admiration how the Jaffa youth group initiates events:

They have outstanding creative ideas. This new [digital] language gives them tools that were not available previously…On Nakba Commemoration Day, they decided to have a whole day sit-down demonstration in the central roundabout square in Jaffa. They came with Palestine flags and banners with crazy stuff written on them. Now, you enter the roundabout and you see 'Welcome to Palestine,' and they are sitting there. They take pictures, post it on Facebook, and then start getting 'likes' from friends and some groups…One of them gets all excited because his picture received 100 'likes.' It means a whole lot to him, it strengthens him. Through Facebook, if you do it right, you can reach tens of thousands of your target audience.

The *Harakat al-Yaffaweeya*, and the *Hiraq* youth are well aware of the digital rules of the game in the network society and designed their successful campaigns accordingly. Instead of organizing (as the Jaffa mentor suggested) a mass demonstration to release a Palestinian detainee in Israel who went on a hunger strike, they held a daily sit-in at the Jaffa square for two months. After two weeks of publication on Facebook, buses from Jerusalem and from Haifa, arrived to join the sit-in. They were interviewed and covered by Israeli, and Palestinian media and by *al Jazeera*…The *Hiraq* activist described the network of support they built abroad for their struggle against the government land settlement plan:

We have a team for so-called international marketing of the struggle. We have a Facebook page in English, Hebrew and Arabic. We rely on the usual networking of global civil society organizations. So we put out a call for action to organize protests and rallies (of solidarity) in their localities, and people responded.

Activism on the net is considered by one activist as even preferable to sporadic and conventional forms of protest demonstrations. The activist from Ramla-Lydda, whose group dispersed after some four years of intensive action, and who is also a blogger on a radical website explained:

> Our group, *Khutwe*, is no longer very active. We are active in other things. I for instance, am focused on my own individual life, on my own self-fulfillment, in writing. A sort of substitute for activism. For me, if an article or written piece that I write changes the opinion of two or three Israelis [Jews], it is better than ten demonstrations that I used to go to.

At the same time, the shortcomings of digital age activism have not escaped the eyes of some activists. They noticed the implications of the digital divide: that the less privileged, whose lifestyle does not include the use of the net are excluded from participating in the youth's grassroots contentious politics. Sami, the Jaffa Youth's mentor remarked that:

> Today you are present everywhere in the world online. A good video that you make reaches directly. That wasn't so in the past. But now you are not asked the big political questions: who is your audience? Your audience are those who are on Facebook. For whom are you protesting? For people on Facebook.

The *Baladna* activist from Haifa was even more critical:

> Facebook is two-faced. We think that the world will be revolutionized through Facebook. But it will not. That is why we are reaching only 3000 people. After all, a young women who stays in the village, has no Facebook account. She is not included in the target audience. We are counting on Facebook for recruitment but it delimits us to the same sector. You are not in real contact with people, [those who are workers and do not study] and therefore you do not recruit more people. You are drawn constantly to the same group. As much as it is big, in the final account it is a defined percentage of the population.

(e)   *Neoliberalism*

It is almost trivial to relate the popular mass protest of this era to the growing inequalities and the deepening depoliticization of the public sphere since neoliberalism took hold in the 1970s (Brown 2011; Calhoun 2013; Levy 2014, 2015). As mentioned, among its many economic, social, and cultural effects, the shift to neoliberalism manifested itself in the distancing of mainly young voters from parliamentary politics and in the dwindling of mass social movements as conveyers of the political plight of the younger generation (e.g. Furlong and Cartmel 2007, 124; Harris, et al. 2010). The salience of the alter-globalization movement, which rendered territoriality of lesser importance in political struggles (Hardt and Negri 2012; Levy 2014), had its own effect on the political consciousness of millennial generation voters (Cammaerts et al. 2014). Since the turn of the millennium, it has become common wisdom that young voters are politically apathetic, and, given the processes of individualization, their identities are less fixed, or more liquid (Bauman 2001).

The shift to neoliberalism in Israel dates back to the 1985 Emergency Economic Stabilization Plan that was designed to curb the skyrocketing inflation and to restore economic stability. This was an opportunity for the state, under the leadership of a National Unity government, to inaugurate a considerable structural change, and thus "to regain [state] autonomy by strengthening market discipline" (Shalev 1999, 126). In the following years, this shift was reflected in various indicators that showed broadening income inequalities, growing employment insecurity, increasing cost of living (Shalev 2012; Swirski and Konor-Atias 2013). Consequently, the welfare state underwent retrenchment that cut across many programs (Shalev, Gal and Azary-Viesel 2011, 413). Similarly, the level of unionization declined by about half with a parallel decline in the rate of workers covered by collective agreements (Cohen et al. 2004). Furthermore, the notion of privatization and the idea of individual choice have become common sense-like and hegemonic in almost any field (Ram 2008). These trends further deepened the new spirit of individualization and the inclination amongst youth to distancing themselves from anything collective, more saliently in Jewish society compared to Palestinian-Arab society (Sagy et al. 2001).

Contemporary activists came of age around the millennial turn, which, as mentioned above, was marked in Israel/Palestine by the rekindling of the Palestinian Intifada (September 2000). Thus, the political atmosphere in which young Palestinians grew up was shaped by the deepening distrust between Palestinian society and the state, and the ensuing political and social polarization between Jewish and Palestinian societies as manifested by the Arab boycott of the 2001 premiership elections (Bishara 2001; Peled and Navot 2005; Waxman 2012). These developments were accompanied by a deep structural economic transformation, when PM Sharon co-opted his rival to the leadership of the Likud party, Benjamin Netanyahu, by appointing him Minister of Finance and giving him a free hand to privatize and shrink the welfare state (Ram 2008). Consequently, young Palestinians were affected not only by the deepening mistrust between the Palestinians and the state, but also because their prospects for enjoying a rising standard of living, which have always been lower when compared to their Jewish counterparts, actually dropped (Shalev 2012, 195).

Whereas Israelis from marginalized groups were protesting against the neoliberal shift all along (Lavie 2014; Levy 2015), it was, nonetheless, the young Jewish middle class cohort that initiated the anti-neoliberal protests in Israel. Inspired by the young men and women of the Arab Spring, as well as by the mass protest against neoliberal authoritarianism in Spain (May 2011), they took to the streets calling for 'social justice for the people.' As has been noted, the popular, unarmed revolts in Egypt and Tunisia which led to the unseating of well entrenched authoritarian regimes revealed a new subjectivity in Arab societies, particularly of youth (*al shabab*) and gave inspiration to similar protests around the globe (Challand 2011).

The Palestinians in Israel also initially greeted the events with considerable approval. In a poll taken close to the events on March 2011, 74% of the Palestinians in Israel followed them with a high degree of interest, and 65% viewed them as positive for the people in the area. However, for the most part this approval was expressed as a view of observers from afar, not as a potential model for civic action for Palestinians in the Israeli context. Almost 80% of the Palestinian respondents to the poll estimated that the chances of such an uprising of the Palestinians within Israel were low (Peace Index, March 2011).

Indeed, when the Jewish middle class youth in the summer of 2011 mimed the Tahrir social protest against the outcomes of neoliberal policies in Israel, joining the protest or refraining from it was a matter of contention within the Palestinian public (Kaufman and Levy 2014). Our interviews and surveys among participants in the 2011 Tents Protest reveal that some of those who decided to join in cited the Arab revolt as having had an impact on their decision to do so, but it was not the prevalent factor. Only a handful of Palestinian and Jewish activists framed their actions in the summer of 2011 in terms of regional solidarity against colonial and capitalist oppression. In a public statement during the protest, they hailed "the major role that the men and women of our generation are playing so courageously in the demonstrations for freedom and change across the Arab World" (Monterescu and Shaindlinger 2013, 231). Furthermore, as the Arab popular revolt turned into a bloody civil war in Libya and in Syria with the outside involvement of global powers, the mood in regard to the Arab revolt within the Palestinian public turned sour (Rinawie-Zoabi 2013).

Our findings support the same mixed trends. Amongst our interviewees, only one (from *Hiraq al-Shababi*) cited the Arab popular revolt as an initial inspiration for organizing the group. In Jaffa, the spontaneous sentiment of joy and the distribution of Egyptian and Tunisian flags by the activists after the fall of Hosni Mubarak was met with apathy on the street. Among the activists, after an initial sense of pride, disappointment with the Arab popular revolt set in, in view of its deterioration into a bloodbath, orchestrated, so it seemed, by the Western powers and their allies in the region.

New Generational Style: New Forms of Socio-political Activism and Protest

Political protests in the post-2011 era are characteristically different in form and structure (e.g. Milkman et al. 2013). Thus, the mass mobilization of New Social Movements, characteristic of the 1960s and 1970s, was gradually diminishing when non-governmental organizations shifted the political battles from the streets to the courts in the 1980s and 1990s. While the state was losing its primacy in favor of the force of globalization, so did the nomadic alter-globalization which hopped from one summit of the G-20 or G-8 to another become the main cites of protest and politicization (Hardt and Negri 2012; Levy 2014, 2015). In the aftermath of the major sit-ins and occupy style protests, the protesters were adopting and shaping new forms of political mobilization. Its main characteristics were their flat network rhizome and ad hoc structure, being leaderless and non-hierarchical, with a greater salience of women activists, and their reliance on social media as its main vehicle of mobilization and communication. The activists that we met were no different in these respects, and at times, they were the entrepreneurs of these new structures.

(a)   *Rhizomatic Forms of Organization*
The Palestinian activists are organized in several, basically locale-based activists' groups, each comprised of a nucleus of committed activists. One interviewee from the *Naqeb* Bedouin activist group – *Hiraq al-Shababi* – described it as a spread of small circles, each independent of the other and yet ready to be called upon to support and back up each other's activities.

> Circles, and around it more circles, and it spreads as far north as possible…The inner circle is the people who thought [about this] in the beginning and connected at the university.

This group seems to be the most structurally organized, having several coordinators who work vis-à-vis the Israeli and international press, the Israeli

[Jewish] street, and other groups. The Haifa group seems, however, to be rather more unstructured, or fluid in the words of one of its activists:

> It is said that it's a group, but it's really fluid. It's not that there are 50 people who were the original founders. People change, it's informal, very fluid, so people come and go. If we're talking about the first Prawer Protest [against the implementation of the Prawer Plan for resettling the Bedouins in the *Naqeb*] last July, so the people who organized it are not necessarily those who organized the protest in Arara, and not necessarily those who organized the third protest in Haifa. It's not that there's a block of people, highly organized and with a division of labor. This is the meaning of *Hiraq*, that there aren't the same people.

Internally, the structure is flat and non-hierarchical, as the same activist explains:

> It is very, very important that there is no hierarchy in the group, because we don't want to replicate the reasons for us [choosing a new form of political struggle]. So it was really important that it be horizontal, that there's no hierarchy...there's a division of labor, there were a few committees. There's a press committee, a committee that mobilizes people for demonstrations, and a financial committee, etc. There is a division of labor, but we try to bring in as many people as possible and not to feel that there's someone who dictates and someone [else] who executes. For it would have been fatal had we done this.

This pattern repeats itself in the various groups, each comprised of a nucleus of more active agents. Yet each one is capable of recruiting several more activists for particular actions and also coordinating among the various groups when the need arises. Thus, spontaneity and immediacy also became characteristics of the action. It took the will of only a couple of activists for a new action to be initiated.

> There are [actions] that began outside the movement, like the vigil in support of Samer Al-Isawi [who was held in administrative custody and was on months long hunger strike]. It began in a café, where some four people talked and decided on this. We're not alone here in Jaffa, there are activists outside the movement, independent, or from other groups ...There was no specific decision in the movement to go for it. At the end, the only person who was active backed off...and we remained three

activists from the Jaffa Youth who led [the daily vigil], and in the first days, the rest of the activists joined and led it through the end. So sometimes it starts off outside the movement and the movement joins in and adopts it. (*Harakat A-Shabiba al-Yaffaweeya*).

Once the vigil assumed its shape and structure, held in Jaffa in the early afternoon hours on a main street that traverses the city, activists from other groups and different places joined in. Thus, the horizontal rhizome shape was not only a characteristic of the internal structure of each group, but also of the relationship between the groups. Not at all times did this work well. One activist attested to the difficulties in coordinating between the groups.

Another activist in Jaffa told us a similar story of how, when the revolution in Egypt began, he was with two friends drinking. They reportedly were saying to each other that they will soon be holding a demonstration in support of the rebels in front of the [Egyptian] embassy. After that, there were two more demonstrations in front of the embassy... However, in other cases, the organization of the protests or actions took more planning.

(b) *New and Old Forms of Protest*
While demonstrations and vigils are still the most common way of protesting and mobilizing citizens for political action, these were not the only methods of action for these young activists. In one case, a few activists performed a mock wedding to protest the amendment to the Israeli citizenship law which prevents Palestinians from the West Bank or Gaza Strip who married Israeli-citizen Palestinians from moving into Green Line Israel (Barak-Erez 2007). On another occasion, the *Khutwe* activists in Ramla-Lydda organized a live concert with a local hip hop band to raise money for children in Gaza, as well as to cultivate the consciousness of the citizens of these cities. They also organized a camp for children from the unrecognized village of Dahamsh in the city of Lydda which faced demolition orders. Subsequently, they mobilized the children to a big demonstration, It was the first time in the history of Ramla that there was an Arab demonstration in the main street of Ramla, that the street was actually closed. The demonstration ended in the village of Dahamsh with a big concert. According to the interviewee, this was a big success since it shifted the court's ruling to their side.

Perhaps the most impressive demonstration was the Day of Rage that was held on November 30, 2013. This was the first time that the *Hiraq* activists actually initiated and implemented a large scale demonstration that did not only mobilize protesters on a national scale, but also extended beyond the boundaries of the state. This was a protest against the implementation of the government led Prawer Plan to resettle the Bedouins in the unrecognized villages, thus allowing the state to expand Jewish settlement in the *Naqeb*. The plan was the culmination of the work of several committees and involved high ranking politicians, and it was met by opposition from most Bedouin citizens and the Palestinian activists, who were barely involved in its articulation, and saw it as a way of further confiscating most of the lands on which the Bedouins resided. Thus, after proving their political commitment already in the 2013 Land Day and the following Nakba Day, *Hiraq* was ready to pull together its own protest.

The Day of Rage proved the organizational capacities of the youth. They mobilized their own activists and their sister groups around Israel, but also many Jewish political activists, the Arab political parties, and activists in the Palestinian Territories. More significantly, they mobilized support from activists around the globe. In the words of the activist from *Hiraq al Shababi*:

> We too initiated it [The Day of Rage], but there's also the international team, the marketing of the struggle team. We have three Facebook pages, in Hebrew, in Arabic, and in English, and there are many supporters of the English page. The civil society organizations did a lot of lobbying work around the world, they met with people in [international] conferences, so there is a basis for cooperation between us and people who can organize [support abroad]. Then people started, we issued a call to people to organize rallies and demonstrations in their own place. We called it a call for action, and people responded. We used the platform of the BDS, they have their own network.

An activist from Haifa also attested to the uniqueness of this action:

> I think that [the Prawer protest] is not just an example, because there's something unique, and it's not that we've not had similar things before, and therefore it was innovative. [It was] innovative not only in the outcomes and in form. It is also innovative that the youth find their own space and that they are the organizers, they make the decisions. They do everything despite being [active] in the political parties. And I emphasize that we're in the parties, but not acting on their behalf. The political parties were not directly involved.

Thus, what has made the demonstrations of the Palestinian youth different was that it was their own to initiate and shape. In principle, they refused to apply for permits from the police, which emphasized for them their autonomy

PALESTINIAN YOUTH IN ISRAEL

and they insisted that their struggle would be non-violent and peaceful. In fact, one of the activists published a post just before the 2013 general elections in Israel where he called upon the Arab citizens to boycott the elections and demanded from the Palestinian political parties to abandon the parliamentary route in favor of non-violent civil struggle.

(c)   *New Contents*

The new forms of political actions are different not only in structure, but in content. In the past, ideologies and big 'isms' were underlying the action and political mobilization of social groups, and the political map itself was characteristically ideological. In the neoliberal era, politics has rendered this ideological debate obsolete (e.g., Dean 2009). This does not imply that political activists and groups do not have ideas and do not hold on to certain goals and visions. However, these ideological structures are also fluid and rarely do we see a group that identifies itself by a known ideology (Bennett and Segerberg 2012, 748). Of course, the activists share a common background and adhere to certain main goals. In the case of the Palestinian citizens in Israel, these include the two pillars of the Israeli political debate on the national issue – the struggle for the national liberation of the Palestinian people and the quest for civic equality for the Arab citizens of the Israeli state (Peled 1992; Levy 2005; Jamal 2007). While these goals underlie the politics of the Palestinian youth, we did detect a new post-nationalist consciousness among some of the activists which devalues nationalism as an ultimate goal, assigning it a temporary, instrumental role in the struggle for liberation. The de facto goal, or vision, is therefore to look beyond the two state solution to a single, *civic* state in the whole of the territory of Palestine. An activist from Haifa explained:

> Nationalism, I think, is a necessity right now. We need to organize ourselves...Nationalism in this context, at this period, is a need because the Zionist project is actually against your own nationality, so this is the front, the danger zone, the context for the struggle...but once there is a state, nationalism takes on a different form. It becomes common history, common culture, and common language.

The grounds for this position are not merely academic and sterile, but derived from an analysis of the upheaval in Syria since 2011:

> ...with all due respect, I do not want nationalism in Syria, if it means massacring the nation. I do not want nationalism which is based on bloodshed. If there is no nationalism with human values, I have no need for

it...are we fighting Zionism with the same instruments? Are we Zionism under a different name?

An activist from Jaffa rejects her Israeli citizenship as being completely hollow, by declaring "I am not Israeli, this is not my state." The Palestinians as a whole are the indigenous and rightful owners of the territory on which a state for all national groups is envisioned. Nevertheless, she declares:

> There is no such thing as a Palestinian nation. I am against nationalism. There is a Palestinian nation because there is an Israeli [Jewish] nation. I am a nationalist because I am in a struggle for identity and existence, and in the current political vocabulary, a nationality means existence...[but] nationality in the final analysis is a matter of symbols...Let the [future] state be called Isratin where people of all nationalities have rights.

But in the 'here and now,' the same activist acknowledges that her Israeli citizenship has a confusing effect on her own consciousness, particularly when facing Palestinians under occupation:

> I am a Palestinian but I am not like the Palestinian who lives in the West bank, or the Palestinian in exile, nor am I like the Israeli (Jew). When I sit with Palestinians [in the occupied territories], the power that I have by being an Israeli is very strong and has a strong impact, because "those who come from there, know what is happening there"...what is my nationality or identity then? I haven't a clue, I really don't know...I am a Palestinian here [In Israel] much more than an Israeli. But I am also Israeli...

This consciousness of multiple positioning of the activists most probably contributes to the fact that the current political struggles of the activists are primarily issue-oriented. Indeed we found that their political action has been characteristically issue-oriented, sporadic, and chiefly as a response to contingent political issues.

Thus, each activity was focused on a single issue, big or small. Notably the most salient one was the struggle against the implementation of the Prawer Plan. The Prawer-Begin Plan is the common name of the outline for resettling the Bedouins in the *Naqeb*/Negev which was approved by the cabinet in January 2013. It was the culmination of a long, deliberative process which began in 2007 and was passed in its first reading as a government bill in the Knesset in June 2013. The bill purported to settle the land dispute with some 100,000 Bedouins who live in unrecognized, makeshift villages. However, provisions of the plan drew fierce opposition in the Knesset from both the ranks of the ruling party (Likud) and its right wing coalition partners, as well as from the Arab parties in opposition. The provisions included granting title to the land of some of the Bedouins and permits to settle on it, but also called for the resettlement of most others (Rinat 2013). Unsurprisingly, this was the main issue on the political agenda of *Hiraq al-shababi* that was based in the Bedouin community in the Naqeb. After successfully organizing protests on two Palestinian memorial days in 2013, Land Day on March 30, and Nakba Day (Israeli Independence Day) on May 15, in the summer of 2013 *the Hiraq* activists turned their efforts to fighting against the implementation of the Prawer Plan. On November 30, 2013, they were the main driving force behind one thousand protesters in the *Naqeb* and some 3000 more up north (Shani, Mandel and Altman 2013), in what has been termed as a Day of Rage:

> We began organizing...towards the Land Day, because we didn't want these speeches, [from] the traditional leadership with whom we don't really agree. In parallel, we saw that the struggle against the Prawer Plan legislation proposal is not conducted at the level that we thought it should be. Then we said, if the youth don't come, don't participate and boycott everything, then, *yalla*, it's the end of the Negev and of the future for us and our children. Then we decided to get organized.

The protest was a success in three senses: first, it drew huge crowds, and as a consequence of the violent response of the police, it also became a media event. It therefore managed to draw the attention of the Jewish public to the high level of grassroots opposition to the plan. Second, it contributed to the decision by Prime Minster Netanyahu in December 2013 to halt the legislative process of the Prawer-Begin Plan (Azoulai and Blumenthal, 2013). Third, it mobilized the Palestinians of the north to become active in the cause of the Arab-Bedouins of the south. According to one of our interviewees, this cause has not been high on the agenda of the rest of the northern Palestinians. The November Day of Rage, claims the activist from Haifa [in the north], changed this mood:

> It was meaningful that [Arabs] in Northern Israel started to say Prawer. I remember before [the demonstration] when we wanted to organize a bus [of protesters] to something in the Negev, people [asked] what is Prawer? Why is it of interest to me? It's the Negev. They don't feel as if it's a part of the Palestinian people, it's Egypt...For me it is a success that it penetrated the consciousness of people in the north who didn't see this as relevant,

as meaningful...It's not another march in *Arrabbe* [a Palestinian village in the north] where people walk down the road and go back home, happy.

The condition of Palestinian prisoners from the West Bank and Gaza in the Israeli prisons who went on a hunger strike was another issue that concerned Arab youth. As noted above, the initiative to protest in support of Samer Al-Isawi who has been held in custody since August 2012 after allegedly violating his parole raised the more general issue of administrative custody, a common practice that almost exclusively sends Palestinians to serve an undetermined time in prison. The vigil initiated by the activists was the unique manner in which they as Palestinian citizens showed their solidarity with the Palestinian national struggle. But it also demonstrated the pattern of the youth action noted above: focusing on a single issue and extending the struggle from the virtual space to the streets. This struggle, at least in the eyes of its participants, was successful in facilitating the eventual agreement between Al-Isawi's lawyers to the security forces that brought about his release in April 2013 (Khoury 2013). It also asserted their will to strengthen the sense of "one same struggle for one same people and one same space." The *Shabab al-Yaffoia* celebrated his release on the streets of Jaffa where they protested for 54 days, and called for the continuation of the struggle on behalf of another prisoner.[2]

There were other issues on the agenda of the youth activist groups. The Haifa group became involved in the struggle against the drafting of Christian Palestinian citizens to the military, claiming this move by the government is designed to drive a wedge between them and the Muslim majority. The *Khutwe* group, (which is no longer active) focused on the condition of Palestinian residents in the city of Lydda who were subject to evacuation orders, and to house demolition. Another group of activists, as mentioned above, chose to demonstrate against Israeli restriction on marriage between citizens and non-citizen Palestinians from the Occupied Territories by arranging the performance of a mock wedding on the Green Line, with the embarrassed Israeli soldiers looking on.

Finally, these activists seem to shun or have a critical opinion of the set ways and *politics as usual* of the Arab political parties, movements and NGOs. Even those who remained party members insisted on drawing a line between the two forms of activity. On the eve of the 2013 general elections, one activist even called for a boycott of the elections, publicly denouncing the political parties for failing to represent the Palestinian citizens (Younes 2013). After visiting

---

2 See https://www.facebook.com/events/261307564000421/permalink/312224252242085/.

Bab-al-shams, an encampment of Palestinians on the West Bank set up to protest against Israeli settlements, he wrote:

> While *Al Jazeera* and the Israeli news channels open their magazines with reports from *Bab al shams*, the Arab parties are engaged in petty quarrels and in failed attempts to garner one more mandate. I couldn't but feel the vast detachment, and how deeply did the Zionist establishment blind us, making us incapable of understanding what is a true, non-violent struggle for justice. [*Bab al shams*] has proven that there're other ways [than participating in elections]. The establishment is shaking in front of popular non-violent struggles, because they are just (Younes 2013).

Conclusion

An extensive range of political action is being carried out within the Palestinian-Arab society in Israel. This paper delineates the new developments, which we argue have come out of the consolidation of a new generational unit, acting in its unique political style. The novelty is reflected mainly in its direct mode of political action, in the scope of its actions and mode of organization. This generational unit and its generational style take their form in interaction with different though related, contexts. For some activists, their action is a product of their conception of the context being colonial. Hence, their political action requires cross-boundary joint action with Palestinian youth in the Occupied Territories in the West Bank and Gaza. Although the saliency of the youth in the Arab spring protests did not seem to have a direct influence on the Palestinian activists, we did find a similar use of the new media for organizing the struggle and mobilizing support through networking locally and globally. Similarly, we found that the social media facilitated a fluid, horizontal type of organization, but also short-lived issue-oriented activities. Along with this mode of operation, we found a strong tendency to move away from political parties.

We suggested that this generation's style was shaped by their social positioning, or, generational location, as well as by the neoliberal era of individualism. We therefore suggest that as a group their consciousness is composed of different and partly conflicting realms.

The source of the contradictions and conflicts are rooted in their civic status as Palestinian Arabs in the Jewish state, as well as, and directly related to, their place in the economic market and their limited structural ability to move within it freely, and as they see fit, in accord with their skills and capabilities.

The conflicting and contradictory components of this consciousness are also expressed in their attitudes towards structures and forces in their own society who oppose, and even obstruct change. The activists share a view of themselves as fighting on multiple fronts. In the general political arena, they are struggling against occupation and against the Jewish structure of the state. In their own political arena of Palestinian society, they are challenging the rigid party frameworks' *modus operandi* and hierarchies, and regard part of the leadership, as lacking in revolutionary zeal. In the socio-cultural realm, they are agents of change, particularly with regard to gender: among the activists, women have a strong presence in the public arena at the forefront of the struggle.

And yet, intergenerational conflicts were merely alluded to, but were not brought up explicitly by the activists. However, we found that despite their strong commitment to collective political goals, at least some of the activists in this group subscribe to an individualistic liberal world view, which places their own individual socio-political mobility and success at the center. A tentative conclusion, for which more research is required, is that neoliberalism and the regional political deadlock is shaping a new style of patriotic activist. Together with his or her new patriotism, the activists are also seeking socio-economic upward mobility within the Israeli market economy and society.

References

Aya, Rod. "Theories of Revolution Reconsidered: Constructing Models of Collective Violence." *Theory and Society* 8 (1979): 39–99.

Azoulai, Moran and Itay Blumenthal. "Netanyahu shelves the Prawer Plan." *Ynet*, December 1, 2013. Accessed May 29, 2015. http://www.ynet.co.il/articles/0,7340, L-4464682,00.html.

Barak-Erez, Daphne. "Terrorism and Profiling: Shifting the Focus from Criteria to Effects." *Cardozo Law Review* 1, 29 (2007): 1–10.

Bauman, Zygmunt. *Community: Seeking Safety in an Insecure World.* USA: John Wiley and Sons, 2001.

Beck, Ulirch. *The Reinvention of Politics: Rethinking Modernity in the Global Social Order.* Cambridge: Polity Press, 1997.

Ben David, Anat. "Mapping Minority Web-spaces: The Case of the Arabic Web-space in Israel." In *Ethnic Minorities and Media in the Holy Land*, edited by Dan Caspi and Elias Nelly, 137–157. Vallentine-Mitchell Academic, 2014.

Bennett, Lance and Alexandra Segerberg. "The Logic of Connective Action." *Information, Communication & Society* 15, 5 (2012): 739–768.

Bishara, Azmi. "Reflections on October 2000: A Landmark in Jewish-Arab Relations in Israel." *Journal of Palestine Studies* 30, 3 (2001): 54–67.

Braungart, Richard. "Historical and Generational Patterns of Youth Movements: A Global Perspective." *Comparative Social Research* 7, 1 (1984): 3–62.

Brown, Wendy. "Occupy Wall Street: Return of a Repressed Res-Publica." *Theory and Event* 14, 4 (2011).

Calhoun, Craig. "Occupy Wall Street in Perspective." *The British Journal of Sociology* 64 (2013): 26–38.

Cammaerts, Bart, Michael Bruter, Shakuntala Banaji, Sarah Harrison and Nick Anstead. "The Myth of Youth Apathy: Young Europeans' Critical Attitudes Toward Democratic Life." *American Behavioral Scientist* 58, 5 (2014): 645–664.

Castells, Manuel. *The Rise of the Network Society (2nd edition)*. Oxford and Malden, Massachusetts: Blackwell Publishers, 2000.

Castells, Manuel. *Networks of Outrage and Hope: Social Movements in the Internet Age*. Cambridge, UK: Polity Press, 2012.

CBS, The Social Survey, 2014 (Chart 5). Accessed October 18, 2015. http://www.cbs.gov .il/publications16/seker_hevrati14_1648/pdf/t05.pdf. (In Hebrew).

Challand, Benoit. "The Counter-Power of Civil Society and the Emergence of a New Political Imaginary in the Arab World." *Constellations* 18, 3 (2011): 271–283.

Cohen, Yinon, Yitchak Haberfeld, Guy Mundlak, and Ishak Saporta. "Union Density and Coverage: Past, Present, and Future." *Labor, Society and Law* 10 (2004): 15–49. (In Hebrew).

Comaroff, Jean. *Body of Power, Spirit of Resistance: The Culture and History of a South African People*. Chicago: University of Chicago Press, 1985.

Corsten, Michael. "The Time of Generations." *Time and Society* 8, 2–3 (1999): 249–272.

Cross, Michael. "Youth, Culture and Politics in South African Education: The past, Present and Future." *Youth and Society* 24, 4 (1993): 377–389.

Dean, Jodi. *Democracy and Other Neoliberal Fantasies: Communicative Capitalism and Left Politics*. Durham, North Carolina: Duke University Press, 2009.

Esler, Antony. "The Trust Community: Social Generations as Collective Mentalities." *Journal of Politics and Military Sociology* 12 (1984): 99–112.

Foran, John. "Discourses and Social Forces: The Role of Culture and Cultural Studies in Understanding Revolutions: Why Few Succeed, Why Most Fail," in *Theorizing Revolutions*, edited by John Foran, 203–266. London and New-York: Routledge, 1997.

Fuchs, Christian. "Some Reflections on Manuel Castells' book, Networks of Outrage and Hope. Social Movements in the Internet Age." *tripleC* 10, 2 (2012): 775–797.

Furlong, Andy and Fred Cartmel. *Young People and Social Change, New Perspectives (2nd edition)*. Berkshire: Open University Press, 2007.

Gasset, Ortega. "The Importance of Generationhood," in *The Youth Revolution: The Conflict of Generations in Modern History*, edited by Antony Esler, 3–6. Lexington, MA, Toronto, London: D.C. Health and Company, 1974.

Ghanim, Honaida. *Reinventing the Nation: Palestinian Intellectuals in Israel*. Jerusalem: Magness, 2009. [Hebrew].

Haklai, Oded. "Palestinian NGOs in Israel: A Campaign for Civic Equality or 'Ethnic Civil Society'?" *Israel Studies* 9, 3 (2004): 157–168.

Hardt, Michael and Antonio Negri. *Declaration*. New York: Argo Navis, 2012.

Harris, Anita, Johanna Wyn, and Salem Younes. "Beyond Apathetic or Activist Youth 'Ordinary' Young People and Contemporary Forms of Participation." *Young* 18, 1 (2010): 9–32.

Jamal, Amal. "Nationalizing States and the Constitution of 'Hollow Citizenship': Israel and its Palestinian Citizens." *Ethnopolitics* 6, 4 (2007): 471–493.

Jamal, Amal. "Media Culture as Counter-Hegemonic Strategy." *Media, Culture, and Society* 31, 4 (2009): 559–577.

Jamal, Amal. *Arab Minority Nationalism in Israel*. Oxon: Routledge, 2011.

Jennings, M. Kent. "Generation Units and the Student Protest Movement in the United States: an Intra- and Inter-generational Analysis." *Political Psychology* 23 (2002): 303–324.

Kabha, Mustafa. "A Net without Borders," in *Online Newspapers in Israel*, edited by Altshuler Shwartz, 17–197. Jerusalem and Beer Sheba, Israel: Israel Democracy Institute and Ben-Gurion University of the Negev, Burda Center for Innovative Communications, 2007.

Kaufman, Ilana. "Escalating Minority Claims: The Arab 'Vision Documents' of 2006–2007 in Israel," in *Nationalism and Democracy*, edited by Andre Lecours and Luis Moreno, 184–207. Oxon: Routledge, 2010.

Kaufman, Ilana. And Gal Levy. "The Palestinians in Israel in the 2011 Protests." *Hamerchav Hatziburi*, Winter 8 (2014): 34–54 (In Hebrew).

Khoury, Jackie. "A Deal Was Reached for the Release of Samir Al-Isawi Who is on Hunger Strike for 8 Months." *Haaretz*, April 23, 2013. Accessed 29 May 2015. http://www.ha-aretz.co.il/news/politics/1.2001196.

Lambert, Allen. "Generation and Change, Toward a Theory of Generations as Force in Historical Process." *Youth and Society* 4 (1972): 21–45.

Lavie, Smadar. *Wrapped in the Flag of Israel: Mizrahi Single Mothers and Bureaucratic Torture*. New York: Berghahn Books, 2014.

Levy, Gal. "From Subjects to Citizens: On Educational Reforms and the Demarcation of the Israeli-Arabs." *Citizenship Studies* 9, 3 (2005): 271–291.

Levy, Gal. "Contested Citizenship of the Arab Spring and Beyond," in *The Routledge Handbook of Global Citizenship Studies*, edited by Engin Isin and Peter Nyers, 23–37. New York: Routledge, 2014.

Levy, Gal. "From Rights to Representation: Challenging Citizenship from the Margins Post 2011." *Mathal: A Journal of Islamic and Middle Eastern Multidisciplinary Studies* 4, 1 (2015): 1–26.

Mannheim, Karl. "The Problem of Generation," in *Essays on the Sociology of Knowledge*, edited by Karl Mannheim. London: RHP, 1952 (first published 1923).

Mesch, Gustavo and Ilan Talmud. "Ethnic Differences in Internet Access." *Information, Communication & Society* 14, 4 (2011): 445–471.

Milkman, Ruth, Stephanie Luce, and Penny Lewis. *Changing the Subject: A Bottom-Up Account of Occupy Wall Street in New York City.* New York: The Murphy Institute, City University of New York, 2013.

Monterescu, Daniel, and Noa Shaindlinger. "Situational Radicalism: The Israeli 'Arab Spring' and the (un)making of the Rebel City." *Constellations* 20, 2 (2013): 229–253.

Peace Index, March 2011. Accessed May 27, 2015. http://bit.ly/1XMSJzB.

Peled, Yoav. "Ethnic Democracy and the Legal Construction of Citizenship: Arab Citizens of the Jewish State." *The American Political Science Review* 86, 2 (1992): 432–443.

Peled, Yoav and Doron Navot. "Ethnic Democracy Revisited: On the State of Democracy in the Jewish State." *Israel Studies Forum Berghahn Journals* (2005): 3–27.

Rabinowitz, Dan, and Khawala Abu Baker. *The Stand Tall Generation: The Palestinian Citizens of Israel Today.* Jerusalem: Keter, 2002.

Rabinowitz, Dan, As'ad Ghanim and Oren Yiftachel. *After the Rift: New Directions for Government Policy Towards the Arab Population in Israel.* An Emergency Report by an Inter-University Research Team Submitted to the Prime Minister of Israel, 2000. (English, Hebrew and Arabic).

Ram, Uri. "Why Secularism Fails? Secular Nationalism and Religious Revivalism in Israel." *International Journal of Politics, Culture, and Society* 21, 1–4 (2008): 57–73.

Rinat, Tzafrir. "What is the Prawer Plan." *Haaretz* June 25, 2013. Accessed May 29, 2015. http://www.haaretz.co.il/news/whatis/.premium-1.2013154.

Rinawie-Zoabi, Ghaida. "The Arab Spring and the Palestinians of Israel," in *Israel and the Arab Spring: Opportunities in Change*, edited by Nimrod Goren and Jenia Yudkevich, 26–30. Israel: Mitvim, 2013.

Rintala, Marvin. "Generation in Politics," in *The Youth Revolution: The Conflict of Generations in Modern History*, edited by Anthony Esler, 15–20. Lexington, MA, Toronto, London: D.C. Heath and Company, 1974.

Sagy, Shifra, Emda, Orr, Dan Bar-On and Elia Awwad. "Individualism and Collectivism in Two Conflicted Societies Comparing Israeli-Jewish and Palestinian-Arab High School Students." *Youth and Society* 33, 1 (2001): 3–30.

Salvatore, Armando. "New Media, the 'Arab Spring,' and the Metamorphosis of the Public Sphere: Beyond Western Assumptions on Collective Agency and Democratic Politics." *Constellations* 20, 2 (2013): 219–228.

Shalev, Michael. "Have Globalization and Liberalization 'Normalized' Israel's Political Economy?" *Israel Affairs* 5, 2–3 (1999): 121–155.

Shalev, Michael. "The Economic Background of the Social Protest of Summer 2011," in *State of the Nation Report: Society, Economy and Policy in Israel 2011–2012*, edited by Dan Ben-David, 161–220. Jerusalem: Taub Center for Social Policy Studies in Israel, 2012.

Shalev, Michael, John Gal, and Sagit Azary-Viesel. "The Cost of Social Welfare: Israel in Comparative Perspective," in *State of the Nation Report: Society, Economy and Policy in Israel 2011–2012*, edited by Dan Ben-David, 367–426. Jerusalem: Taub Center for Social Policy Studies in Israel, 2011.

Shani, Rami, Kobi Mandel and Yair Altman. "Thousands of Protesters against the Prawer Plan: 11 Police Officers were Lightly Injured." *Walla News*, December 1, 2013. Accessed May 29, 2015. http://news.walla.co.il/item/2699195.

Sika, Nadine. "Youth Political Engagement in Egypt: From Abstention to Uprising." *British Journal of Middle Eastern Studies* 39, 2 (2012): 181–199.

Swirski, Shlomo and Etty Konor-Atias. *Israel: A Social Report 2012*. Tel Aviv: Adva Center, 2013. http://tinyurl.com/adva-soc-rep-2012.

Valenzuela, Sebasti'an, Arturo Arriagada and Andr'es Scherman. "The Social Media Basis of Youth Protest Behavior: The Case of Chile." *Journal of Communication* 62 (2012): 1–16.

Vilas, Carlos. *The Sandinista Revolution: National Liberation and Social Transformation in Central America*, translated by Judy Butler. New York: Monthly Review Press 1986.

Waxman, Dov. "A Dangerous Divide: The Deterioration of Jewish-Palestinian Relations in Israel." *The Middle East Journal* 66, 1 (2012): 11–29.

Younes, Rami. "What is seen from bab alshams". *Haokets*. January 16, 2013. Accessed May 7, 2015. http://tinyurl.com/younes2013.

Zeidan, Elias and Asad Ghanim. *Contribution and Voluntarism in the Arab-Palestinian Society in Israel*. Beer Sheba: Ben Gurion University, Israeli Center for Third Sector Research, 2000.

CHAPTER 2

From Student to General Struggle: The Protests against the Neoliberal Reforms in Higher Education in Contemporary Italy

Lorenzo Cini

Introduction

The present chapter tackles the issue of the strategic decision over the political identity that the Italian student movement has faced in the recent cycle of struggles against two neoliberal reforms in the field of higher education in 2008 and 2010. Although this protest cycle lasted several years (from 2008 to 2012), it had two protest peaks (or, more specifically, two distinct protest campaigns) concurrently with the implementation of Law 133 in 2008 (cuts in public higher education) and Law 240 in 2010 (managerial restructuring of university governance). In opposing these reforms, Italian students have faced the dilemma concerning the adoption of the collective identity and of the related protest frame.

Whilst in 2008 the protesters had stressed the student and generational aspect of their struggle by framing their mobilization as the protest of a 'lost generation' of students under the neoliberal assault, in 2010 mostly the same actors targeted the political system as a whole by framing their struggle as an instance of the general opposition of all the social forces against the neoliberal policies of the Italian government. If the focus of the mobilization of 2008 was principally on student issues and related to the field of higher education, the mobilization of 2010 aimed at addressing the ensemble of neoliberal policies as a whole. In this sense, the mobilization of 2008 can be thought of as fostering a student identity against the neoliberal reforms of higher education, where that of 2010 was a more social and general identity against all the neoliberal policies implemented by the government.

Although the year 2010 witnessed both a widespread worsening of the life conditions of Italians due to the economic recession and the implementation of austerity measures by the government, the student activists attempted to broaden their movement 'constituency' and make alliances with other social actors (such as precarious workers, researchers, public and private employees) to build a broader and more effective opposition against the Italian government

© KONINKLIJKE BRILL NV, LEIDEN, 2017 | DOI 10.1163/9789004344518_004

and its neoliberal policies. Despite the significant change of some contextual factors, such as the worsening of the economic crisis and the adoption of austerity policies, the shift in the protest framing between 2008 and 2010, from a student to a general scope, was a deliberate decision taken by the student leadership and organizations in the effort to make their struggle more effective in terms of political impact.

Why did the same generation of student activists change its protest frames and goals, and, therefore, its political identity in the period of only three years? More broadly, what is the specificity of the student condition that makes such a change possible? The youngsters, and especially the students, are the most politically and socially active segment of the population. Since the advent of modern society they have been the core of the political and social movements of all sort (Sukarieh and Tannock 2015). By drawing on social movement theory (della Porta and Diani 2006) and literature on generation (Mannheim 1952), I argue that one of the reasons of this specificity is related to the ambivalent socio-existential condition that students live: their social identity is never fixed and defined. The ambivalent character of this condition is even more evident when students mobilize and join political and social movements. Collective mobilizations make the process of identity formation even more fluid and open-ended (Johnston and Noakes 2005): during mobilizations, students are more able and freer to decide upon and select their own (political) identity. This has been clearly the case of the recent student protests in Italy, where the same cohort of student activists and leaders has attempted to modify the political identity of the movement between 2008 and 2010. By and large, this chapter aims at showing the centrality of the concept of generation in explaining how and to what extent the strategies of mobilization are deeply connected with the identity that the student activists provide of themselves.

Student Protests: Generational, Social Uprising, or Both?

The decision regarding the collective identity is very crucial for student movements, as their political goals and protest frames have been historically ambivalent (Cockburn and Blackburn 1969). More generally, the analysis of the causes, goals, and targets of student mobilizations has been problematic, especially with reference to the political year of the global student protest par excellence, namely 'the 1968' movement (Gill and De Fronzo 2009). Was such a protest social and general or only student-centred? Radical and revolutionary or moderate and reformist? Vanguard or mass mobilization? The political ambivalence of student protests is essentially due to the socially ambiguous and ill-defined location in which students find themselves, a peculiar socio-existential condition of a specific age cohort which is neither part of the adolescence anymore nor adulthood yet (Ortoleva 1988).

This indecipherable life condition necessarily affects the personal and political experiences of such a cohort; especially when this age group, massively increased in number in the highly differentiated society of twentieth century, is about to initiate a process of mobilization. In this sense, student movements, more than any other movement, are an open-ended process of social formation of collective identity, claims, goals, and action repertoire. It is precisely the open-ended nature of these movements that provides their leaders and activists with an array of strategic options over several issues in the course of mobilization. In other words, these leaders and activists deal with several 'strategic dilemmas,' meaning, situations where there are "two or more options, each with a long list of risks, costs, and potential benefits" (Jasper 2006, 1). The dilemmas that they must, time by time, face and solve in their engagement are various and different, such as the type of collective identity, protest frames, of movement goals, and of action tactics (Gamson 2004).

Student uprisings have often been considered as a manifestation of generational conflict: students in mobilization have been seen as instances of contentious generations demanding for social and political change (Edmunds and Turner 2005; Braungart 2013). This has been, at least, the dominant sociological interpretation concerning the student protests of the 1968 (Rootes 2013). However, more recent studies exploring the causes of student mobilizations have shown that the picture of student protest is much more complicated and cannot be so narrowly reduced to the idea of intergenerational conflict (della Porta 2010; della Porta 2015).

Student protests have constantly been part of broader cycles of struggle, such as those associated with nationalist movements, with labour movements, and more recently with the so-called 'new social movements' (i.e. environmental, urban, feminist, peace movements) (Touraine 1987; Melucci 1996; Fasano and Renosio 2002). In other words, student mobilizations do not arise in a social vacuum, but are always embedded within the dynamics of contention that the society in which they show up constantly generates and develops (della Porta 1996). In this sense, too much attention devoted to the generational dimension of student movements has limited the analysis of the broader nature and causes of student demands and mobilizations (Andretta et al. 2006; della Porta 2010).

It is only for analytical ease that some student mobilizations can be read and explained more narrowly as instances of a generational conflict experienced by an age group in a given historical moment (such as the anti-authoritarian movement of 1968), whilst some others are explained more broadly as instances of social antagonism, expression of the discontent that a society exhibits in a specific moment (such as the urban youth movements, squatting and housing movements). Yet this analytical distinction is not so sharp in practice. Although one can easily retrace the nature, cause, and origin of their discontent, student uprisings can be hardly defined as a simple manifestation of generational conflict or as part of a broader episode of social contention. As exhibited in the empirical part of this chapter, the two dimensions are always strongly interwoven in any situation of student mobilization: students can bring forward some generational concern on their socio-existential condition and, at the same time, convey broader feelings of social discontent. In short, student movements can address both university conditions and more general and social issues. In other words, such movements always carry on the problems experienced by the generation of their activists and, at the same time, are often part of broader protest cycles in society. As mentioned above, it is precisely due to the structural ambivalence of the student condition that several strategic dilemmas can arise in the course of mobilizations among their activists.

Why and how, then, the mobilization strategies of students are deeply connected with the formation processes of their collective identity? This is where the concept of (political) generation (Mannheim 1952) combined with some concepts from social movement theory (della Porta and Diani 2006) can be of help. Without explicitly referring to student uprisings, Karl Mannheim had already dealt with and realized how and to what extent the rising and potential mobilization of segments of a specific age-group can be associated with a social movement like phenomenon in his seminal work on the concept of political generation (2000 [1936]). Some features of his elaboration on this concept can be adopted to highlight the linkages between the rising of a political generation and what in social movement studies are identified as the processes of collective mobilization and protest. More notably, Mannheim's notion of 'generation unit' turns out to be very useful in grasping why a process of collective identity formation may emerge, how a collective identity can 'travel' from a generation to another, and even to what extent a movement can be seen as the intersection of several generational units.

For Mannheim, generational units can be understood as different fractions of an age group sharing the same concrete socio-historical experience, but working up the material of this experience "in different specific ways" (Mannheim 2000 [1936], 304). A generational unit can be understood as an active group of people, which is aware of being part of a common thing, experience, or condition and, therefore, of sharing determined values and

FROM STUDENT TO GENERAL STRUGGLE

behaviors.[1] A generation unit represents, thus, the segment of an age group that actively shares specific political values and material interests and, for this reason, is often eager to collectively mobilize in society (Bettin Lattes 1999, 34).

It is precisely in this latter sense that the concept of social movement and that of generational unit seem to overlap in certain aspects. Social movements can be seen as a collective enterprise initiated by a generation of activists united by some common values, behaviors and/or interests, who aim at triggering or resisting some type of social change (see Melucci 1996; della Porta and Diani 2006). The mobilization of a segment of a specific age-group can thus intersect with the mobilization campaign of a social movement. This is certainly the case in student protests, in as much as students in mobilization are seen as an active segment of a specific age-group building and sharing a distinctive cultural and/or political identity. In this case, one can easily identify Mannheim's concept of generational unit with that of a generation of activists, which is adopted in social movement literature. The activists composing a student movement are seen as the active expression of a specific generation.

What is more, given their student condition, these activists are more active and freer than other social segments and cohorts of the population to renew their action repertoires, to change their political goals and claims, to invent their protest frames, and to decide upon and select their own collective identity (della Porta 2010). In short, the ambivalent socio-condition of the student activists provides them with more collective freedom and strategic options, when they start and/or keep going in mobilizing (Snow 2004).

On the Student Protests of 2008 and 2010: 'getting your way'

The neoliberal agenda on matter of higher education brought forward by the third Berlusconi government (2008–10) included: cuts to public spending for

---

1 One can better understand the distinction between generation unit and actual generation, if one takes into account historical examples, as recently Beck and Beck-Gernsheim (2008) have carried out in their work on the concept of global generation. The authors' interpretation of the concept of global generation echoes the Mannheim notion of actual generation, insofar as they define it as a specific segment of the global population sharing common "cosmopolitan experiences and events," but divided "into different fractions [connected] in a conflictual relationship with each other" (*idem,* 34). The contemporary global generation is grasped by the concept of actual generation. Beck and Beck-Gernsheim (ibid.) also provide an example of two distinct and opposing generational units that belong to the current global generation (actual generation): the "migration generation" which protests "against the international order of inequality and its guardians" and the "European insecure generation" which protests "against short-term contracts and falling incomes."

higher education; the support for the entry of private providers; the centralization of the university leadership; the managerialization of decisional bodies; the support for the entry of firms and companies in such decisional bodies; and the reduction of power of the collegial organs (Palermo 2011; Regini 2014).

Facing this neoliberal attack undermining the right to public higher education, masses of students started mobilizing by occupying squares and universities as a form of opposition against such a plan in the fall of 2008. More notably, Italian students undertook two distinct protest campaigns in concomitance with the processes of enactment of two national laws, Law 133/2008 introducing significant cuts to the public system of funding, and Law 240/2010 providing for the restructuring of the university governance towards a managerial pattern. The first student campaign lasted three months (between October and December 2008), the second one two months (between October and December 2010). More notably, the two campaigns had two distinct protest targets and pursued diverse goals. While in 2008 Italian students had pointed at opposing the dismantling of the national system of public funding (Law 133), in 2010 their mobilization also aimed at arresting the process of managerialization of the university governance (Law 240). Both student campaigns contested two national reforms and, therefore, had the government as the main target of their protests. However, this is not the whole story. If in 2008 the Italian students had framed their protests and the scope of their action as student-centred (*studentista*) by focusing on their student condition (Cini 2013b), in 2010 both frames and scope of their protest were much broader by pointing out how and to what extent the legislative measures on higher education that the then government was bringing forward were part of a neoliberal project aimed at restructuring the Italian society as a whole (Cini 2013c).

"*Noi non paghiamo la vostra crisi!*" (We do not pay your crisis) This was the slogan chanted in the student protests that took place in many Italian cities and universities since October 2008. More precisely, this slogan indicated the refusal by the generation of students that was attending Italian universities in 2008 to undergo the effects of the economic crisis, epitomized by the cuts affecting the sector of higher education provided for by the law 133 (1,5 billions of euro in 5 years). The main measures regarding the Italian university system provided for by the law 133/2008, and contested by the university students, were three: cuts to the fund for ordinary financing ("*Fondo per il Finanziamento Ordinario*" – FFO), the turn-over and recruitment of new professors, and the transformation of universities into private foundations. By chanting "we do not pay your crisis," Italian students tried to make manifest their willingness not to undergo a generalized process of social downgrading affecting the condition of their generation (Raparelli 2009; Roggero 2011).

By contrast, in 2010 the scope of the student protests was much wider. Students were not the only university actors who were protesting against a national law on higher education. Law 240/2010 did not only provide for the managerial restructuring of the university governance, but it also established the extinction of the role of researchers (until their depletion), and simultaneously the introduction of a new figure of fixed-term researcher (TD – *"Tempo Determinato"*). In the plan of the government, the fixed-term researcher should have gradually replaced the researcher with position, more expensive and unmovable. Facing this blackmail, the researchers rejected what was regarded as 'a race at the bottom' and started organizing and mobilizing from the early months of 2010. Additionally, the sharpening of the economic crisis combined with the implementation of austerity measures brought about a generalized worsening of the conditions of living experienced by the vast majority of Italians. In 2010, the social discontent was not only limited to the students and their 'professional' conditions within the university system.

While in 2008 the situation of discontent had been mainly felt by the students, in 2010 this situation was generalized throughout Italian society. Besides students and other university actors (researchers, cleaners, and so on), other social sectors of Italian society, such as public and private employees, pensioners, underwent a generalized process of impoverishment. The transformation of these conditions between the years 2008 and 2010 led the core groups of the student activists to modify their protest frames and claims in the effort to broaden the movement 'constituency' and, thus, to get more people mobilized against the neoliberal measures of the government.

The issue of which identity and interpretive frames protesters are allowed to choose in the effort to successfully pursue their goals is of paramount importance (Gamson 1990 [1975]). The capacity of a generation of activists to broaden their base, to build up a larger coalition of actors in mobilization, and forge clear goals and demands depends, indeed, upon this strategic decision. Decisions like these may concern symbolic as well as material domains of strategic choice, ranging from cultural matters such as the creation of collective identities and cognitive framings to the material ones such as the pursuit of economic profit and the take-over of political power (Snow and Benford 1992). In the case of the Italian student movement, the strategic decision concerned the shift in the political identity between the campaign of 2008 and that of 2010. Why did the same student activists manage to change the political identity of the movement between the two protest campaigns?

Methodology

In order to respond to this research question, I have adopted the following qualitative methods: semi-structured interviews and frame analysis. I have carried out semi-structured interviews with student activists and leaders to collect information concerning the collective identity formation process of the Italian student movement with particular reference to the political goals promoted and pursued by various groups of the movement. More specifically, I have conducted around thirty interviews with student activists belonging to the movements of Turin, Rome, and Naples. In the selection of the people to be interviewed, I have tried to follow the criteria suggested by Herbert Rubin and Irene Rubin in *Qualitative Interviewing: The Art of Hearing Data* (1995). Rubin and Rubin argue that sampling for qualitative interviews must follow two principles.

On the one hand, researchers should strive for the value of completeness, meaning seeking for respondents who are knowledgeable about the topic under investigation. On the other hand, researchers should follow the principle of similarity and dissimilarity, that is – seeking for respondents who may provide the interviewer with similar interpretations on different situations and different interpretations on similar situations (Blee and Taylor 2002). In my fieldwork in Turin, Naples and Rome, I have sought for students belonging to the same national organization and/or political area in the three cities. In doing so, I have been able to interview people with similar interpretations (affiliation to the same political organization) in different contexts (Turin, Naples and Rome). Secondly, in each of the two cities I have interviewed students belonging to diverse and, to a certain extent, competing organizations.

In addition, I have conducted a frame analysis of the documents produced by the student movement to assess the changes in the protest frames and goals between the campaigns of 2008 and 2010. In this respect, I have looked at the main documents produced by the student organizations in the period of mobilization (2008–2010). In particular, I have analysed the official documents presented and discussed during key national student meetings and/or produced by national student organizations.

From Student to General Struggle

To begin with, the analysis I have conducted to explore the protest frames of the mobilizations of 2008 and 2010 confirms the shift in terms of collective identity I mentioned above. Whereas in 2008 the vast majority of the student organizations and activists stressed the negative effects that Law 133 would have produced on the field of higher education, in 2010 their concern was much more focused on the general and social effects that the neoliberal reforms would have brought about on Italian society as a whole.

In 2008, the main goal of the student movement was to radically reform the university system in order to oppose the 'neoliberal assault' (Bailey and Freedman 2011) that the Italian sector of higher education had been undergoing. To this end, the Italian students promoted a national assembly at the University of Rome in November 2008 to discuss what they called the 'self-reform from below,' that is an attempt to elaborate a program of alternative proposals for higher education to oppose the neoliberal hegemony. For two days (15 and 16 November), more than 4000 students representing all the Italian universities debated and confronted each other on this issue. The stressful conditions under which students lived was evident in the claims and frames of the protest, epitomized by the name that the student activists gave to their movement, that is '*Onda Anomala*' (anomalous wave) (Aruzza et al. 2008).

In the view of the activists, this name alluded to the fact that, for the first time after years, a generation of university students had finally decided to recognize itself as a political group facing the same problems (i.e. social and professional precarity) and, thus, was willing to mobilize to demand better life conditions (Raparelli 2009; Caruso et al. 2010). The rise of the student movement of 2008 represented – adopting the terminology formulated by Edmunds and Turner (2005, 562) – the shift from being a passive cohort ("generation in itself") into a politically active and self-conscious cohort ("generation for itself"). In other words, facing neoliberal policies on the matter of higher education in a context of high rates of youth unemployment, the students involved in this protest epitomized the most active part of the Italian young generation of the time, who felt losing the hope in the idea of higher education as a vector of social mobility (Sukarieh and Tannock 2015). Like the student protests in other European countries of the time, this protest represented a response to growing structural contradictions in the relationship that post-secondary education had with the Italian society and economy at large. Post-secondary education had been promoted by the Italian governments as the most important vehicle for individual social mobility, promising access to good jobs and high standards of living. Yet, due also to the structural rigidity of the Italian labor market, when the economic crisis sparkled, those students realized that it was impossible to obtain the high quality and high wage employment that they believed had been promised to them through the vehicle of higher education. From this angle, the student protest of 2008 can be seen as inherently generational, in the sense that it conveyed the feelings of disillusion and of hatred of a generation with no longer expectations of social mobility. In short, this protest represented the first contentious public episode of a generation without future.

By contrast, the political claims and the movement identity emerged from the 2010 protests were less 'student-oriented' and politically more 'universal.' As mentioned above, two politico-economic conditions were at the basis of this change: the worsening of the economic crisis and the implementation of the austerity package by the Italian government. When the negative effects of the first and biggest crisis of the new phase of capitalism that several sociologists had enthusiastically baptized as 'knowledge society' or 'cognitive capitalism' (Cini 2012) started to spread across Italian society, also other social segments began to feel betrayed in their hope of social upgrading. In addition, the adoption of austerity policies, that the government had brought forward as the best (neoliberal) way to exit the economic crisis, generalized the social discontent lived by large strata of the Italian population.

More notably, a widespread 'process of relative deprivation' (Cini and Drapalova 2014), affecting the social and economic conditions of the vast majority of the Italians took place from the early 2010. These structural factors were, thus, at the basis of the 'generalization' of claims and identity that the Italian student movement put forward in 2010. While the end of neoliberal policies was the key demand of this movement, its peculiar and shared trait was to be 'anti-austerity.' In this sense, the 'collective identity' of the movement of 2010 was clearly broader than that of the movement of 2008. As in the cases of Spain and Greece, the Italian protests of 2010 included, thus, the mobilization of students and young unemployed, workers from the public as well as from the private sector, along with pensioners and housekeepers (della Porta 2015).

Bearing in mind the transformation of these conditions in the Italian society between the two protest campaigns of 2008 and 2010, it is now possible to answer the main research questions of this chapter: why did the student activists change the collective identity of the movement (from 'student' to 'general') in the course of the two campaigns? Was this transformation of the movement identity a real strategic dilemma?

All the student activists and leaders participating in both campaigns I have interviewed confirm this interpretation. Not all of them were aware of facing what social scientists call a 'strategic dilemma,' but they seemed to reflect upon the previous experiences of struggle and the present political options as if they were aware of it. The departing point of all the activists' reflections was that in 2008 the Italian student movement underwent a big political defeat because, despite the huge and massive student protests of the autumn, the Italian parliament eventually approved the Law 133 in December 2008. The experience and memory of this failure undergone in 2008 seemed to be internalized and overcome in 2010 as the student activists (many of them now leaders of the various national student organizations) started a second and more 'general' protest campaign against the Italian government.

Regardless of their heterogeneous political orientations (ranging from the most radical and autonomist to the most moderate and institutional), all these activists agreed on the idea that the only way to try to politically achieve something in 2010 were to 'universalize' the struggle and make social alliances with other oppressed segments of Italian society. In 2008, the protests did not reach their goals to halt the cuts in higher education, and to secure more rights and roles for students in building more democratic university (Cini 2013a). In 2010, a significant part of this generation of students still involved in politics shared the idea that a better strategy was needed in order to achieve those goals. They agreed to broaden the social opposition against the government by joining forces with other actors and sectors of Italian society (Cini 2013c).

In the mobilization of 2010 and similarly to past cycles of protest, this generation of student activists flowed into a more general protest, made up also of other social components suffering the economic recession and the package of austerity measures. These measures encompassed significant cuts and a neoliberal restructuring not only of the higher education sector, but of all the public services and sectors within the Italian welfare system, ranging from public education to healthcare, pensions, unemployment benefits, and social housing. Besides the students, the implementation of this wide gamut of measures triggered the mobilization of various social actors and organizations, such as the researchers, the militants of the housing movement and social centers, rank-and-file unions representing public employees, and pensioners (della Porta 2015). In a nutshell, the mobilization of 2010 was less narrowly focused on student issues and more on social and general issues.

Just as the generations of students mobilized in 1968 joined the social movements of the 1970s, a significant part of the generation of students socialized into protest politics in 2008 favored the rise and kept mobilizing in the more general protests against austerity in 2010. All the student activists I interviewed reflecting upon the two campaigns agreed on this interpretation. As Gianluca, student activist at the University of Turin in 2008 and 2010 and member of the social center belonging to the movement of the Italian autonomia (Askatasuna), told me:

> The student movement of 2008 lost a big battle. The Gelmini [the then Minister of Education] won. The university has changed and the reform passed. However, if we look at the protests of 2008 and 2010, one can

see that there has been an increase in the politicization of the students. Campaign by campaign the movements become less '*studentista*' (student-centred) and more explicitly connected with the rest of society. This is precisely what happened from 2008 to 2010. There is always a gap between what the militants see in the movement and the mobilization that they try to trigger and the ordinary people willing to join the movement. I provide you with an example. Our main political merit [as militants] in 2010 was precisely to provide the students with a more universal political identity. We were not only mobilizing as students for a better higher education, but as people for a better society.

Andrea, from a more moderate student collective of the University of Turin, seems to confirm this interpretation by highlighting that the main difference between the protest of 2008 ('student focused') and that of 2010 ('general') was the active presence of other social actors taking part in the mobilization of 2010. The broadening of the social opposition against the Italian government was fully supported and, to a certain extent, even planned by the student activists in their effort to build up a stronger movement between 2009 and early 2010. As Alice, part of the same student organization with Andrea, well explained to me that, "the 2010 has been created, almost politically organized by us [the student militants]. Throughout 2009 there has been a big information campaign from and among us to trigger the mobilization of 2010."

Similar political learning experiences between the protest campaign of 2008 and that of 2010 are done by the student activists and leaders of the several and politically heterogeneous collectives of the University of Rome (Sapienza). All the students I interviewed seem to confirm the interpretation of the existence of this strategic dilemma (student vs. general) of which also the activists from Turin seemed to be aware. In this respect, Giorgio, one of the national leaders of the Trotskyist student organization '*Atenei in Rivolta*,' well explains the generational significance of the student struggles of 2008 in this passage of our interview:

> [in 2008] the students were the first to realize that the university does not ensure any future. Once completed a university degree, we are unemployed and if we find a job, it's precarious and poorly paid. For this reason, the myth of knowledge society has fallen apart and the students have begun to rebel. A generation which has no future, and a precarious present, eventually rose up. In 2008, a young generation of unemployed and precarious workers (not only in Italy) broke into the political scene.

On the other hand, the novelty of the mobilization of 2010 was precisely its more universally recognized 'general character' and the 'inclusion of other various social actors and segments' in such protests. As already highlighted by the activists of the movement of Turin, also for the vast majority of the Roman activists I interviewed, this shift in terms of political claims and collective identity was also due to a political strategy adopted by the students to generalize the struggle. This view well reflects Fabio's thought, a student activist at the University of Rome in both the campaigns and, in 2009, one of the founders of the national student union LINK:

> The 2010 was not only made up of students (like in 2008). Segments of the housing movement, rank and file unions, social centers, and so on. More generally, this was a much more political movement that had built social alliances compared to 2008. The movement of 2010 had a broader political view, had more radical slogans, produced political analyses that looked at Europe and the rest of the world. Social alliances! One says that students alone do not count. We understood this. With the water movement, the squatters, the precarious workers, the unions, our movement in 2010 was much stronger and broader: from the CGIL to the social centers and the people from the water movement.

Similar processes of generalization of the struggles, of the issues at stake and of the political claims have, finally, also taken place in the mobilizations brought forward by the Neapolitan movement in the period of the two campaigns. All the six student activists, coming from student organizations with different political orientations, that I have interviewed agree both on the main aspects of difference between the protests of 2008 and of 2010 and on the reasons which brought to such a difference. As in the cases of the mobilizations of Turin and Rome, all the Neapolitan activists agree on the fact that the main difference between the movement of 2008 and 2010 was the level of 'social generalization' of the latter. Giancarlo from a Marxist-Leninist collective, Roberta from a moderate student union, Giovanni and Luca from an autonomist political group all shared the idea that the "movement of 2010 was more general and social than the movement of 2008."

For Giovanni, the movement of 2010 was "the first movement against the crisis. Less generational, more radical movement against the economic crisis; more political and general." In this respect, there was a widespread awareness that the movement had to 'block everything,' to stop the austerity measures and the neoliberal policies. According to Giancarlo, the peculiarity of the movement of 2010 was its 'class dimension': "that movement represented the needs of the new urban proletariat." In the same vein, Luca adds that in 2010 "in Naples, there were not only students; rather, the real aim was to block the government. Put it in crisis. There was the clear perception that we were all poorer. The crisis had started to bite. The movement of 2010 constituted the first strong and general reaction to the economic crisis." This idea of the movement of 2010 as the manifestation of a 'general movement' was shared also by the most moderate faction of the student activists. Roberta, at the time leader of the student union LINK at the University of Naples (Federico II), referring to the mobilizations of 2010, told me that: "[in that movement] there was everything, including the movement against biocide. In this sense, the movement of 2010 was more general and social."

However, the most interesting remarks that all of them provided concerned the reasons of this transformation of the political identity between the movement of 2008 and 2010. If, on the one hand, they seemed to confirm the idea offered by their comrades from Turin and Rome on the fact that the movement of 2008 was 'student' whereas that of 2010 'general,' on the other, the Neapolitan students added up a more explicit element to the interpretation that the transformation of the movement identity between 2008 and 2010 was principally carried out by the student activists and their organizations. In explaining such an identity shift (from 'student' to 'general'), all the six student activists interviewed have emphasized the function played by the student organizations and, within them, the role played by the most experienced and skillful militants. In other words, the 'universalization' of the political identity of the movement of 2010 was perceived as a deliberate strategic act brought forward by the most organized and expert militants of the movement to avoid the political errors of the mobilization of 2008 and in order to build up a much more credible and effective social opposition to the Italian government. According to Giancarlo, this transformation "was a political merit of the movement organizations, which in 2010 were much more active and powerful than in 2008." In this respect, Luca was even more explicit than Giancarlo in highlighting the active role played by the most politicized militants (and their learning capacity) in this process of identity transformation. As Luca put it:

> The movement of 2010 was the result of the political growth of the comrades accumulated in the two preceding years of political experience. There was a widespread awareness that the movement of 2008 had failed because of its inability to produce social force and a general impact. In 2010, we understood this and, as militants and organized political groups, we tried to solve such problem. Our effort to generalize the struggle was precisely our way to deal with it.

Concluding Remarks

This chapter has shown how and why the strategic decision over the type and nature of the collective identity is one of the most important political tasks that student activists face during a mobilization. The youngsters, and especially the students, live an ambivalent socio-existential condition which allows them to choose different identities according to the type of circumstances and of opportunities: their identity is never fixed and defined. The ambivalent character of their condition is even more evident when students mobilize and join political and social movements. As illustrated in this chapter, students engaging in protest politics tend often to face several strategic dilemmas concerning their political objectives, identity, and position in the broader sector of social movements. This represented the case of the Italian generations of students involved in the protests of 1968, as it was for the student generation mobilized between 2008 and 2010.

The students involved in these protests have, indeed, faced a strategic dilemma concerning the collective identity of their movement. If in 2008 these activists had brought forward a strategy centred upon the idea that their struggle had to be fought within the field of higher education and, thus, only involve the other university students, in 2010 they realized that the most effective way to successfully oppose the neoliberal plan of the government was to broaden their struggle to all the other groups and actors of Italian society that were, in that phase, undergoing a similar neoliberal assault. In terms of collective identity, these activists decided, thus, to undertake a process of generalization of their struggle between the campaign of 2008 and that of 2010, namely from a 'student' to a 'general' identity. By and large, this chapter has stressed the importance to combine social movement theory with generation literature in order to see and explain how and why specific generations of student activists adopt and build different political identities in their strategies of mobilization.

References

Andretta, Massimiliano, Donatella della Porta, Lorenzo Moscaand and Herbert Reiter. *Globalization from below. Transnational Activists and Protest Networks*. Minneapolis and London: Minnesota Press, 2006.

Aruzza Cinzia, Gioliu Calella, Salvatore Cannavo, Daniele D'Ambra, Antonio Montefusco, Giorgio Sestili, Massimiliano Tomba and Giovanna G. Vertova. *L'Onda Anomala. Alla Ricerca dell'Autopolitica*. Rome: Edizioni Alegre, 2008.

Bailey, Michael and Des Freedman. *The Assault on Universities. A Manifesto for Resistance*. London: Pluto Press, 2011.

Bettin Lattes, Gianfraco. "Sul Concetto di Generazione Politica." *Rivista italiana di scienza politica* XXIX, 1 (1999): 23–54.

Blee, Kathleen, and Verta Taylor. "Semi-Structured Interviewing in Social Movement Research," in *Methods of Social Movement Research*, edited by Bert Klandermans and Susanne Staggenberg, 92–117. University of Minnesota Press: Minneapolis, 2002.

Braungart, Richard. "Political Generation," in *Encyclopedia of Social & Political Movements*, edited by David Snow, Donatella della Porta, Bert Klandermans and Doug McAdam, 949–951. Malden: The Wiley-Blackwell, 2013.

Caruso, Loris, Alberto, Giorgi, Alice, Mattoni and Gianni Piazza. *Alla ricerca dell'Onda. I nuovi conflitti nell'istruzione superiore*. Milano: FrancoAngeli, 2010.

Cini, Lorenzo. "Lavoro e Differenza. Il Paradigma del Capitalismo Cognitivo," in *Giustizia, Uguaglianza e Differenza. Una Guida alla,* edited by Brunella Casalini and Lorenzo Cini Firenze University Press: Firenze, 2012.

Cini, Lorenzo. 2013a. *The Impact of the "Onda Anomala" Movement on the Italian Universities: The Student Perspective*. Paper Delivered at the 7th ECPR General Conference, Discussion Panel: "The Consequences of the New Wave of Mobilization," Bordeaux, 4–7 September.

Cini, Lorenzo. "Imagining an Alternative Higher Education. Conceptions of the University in the 'Onda Anomala' Movement." Paper presented at ESA 11th General Conference, "Crisis, Critique, and Change," Turin, Italy, 2013b.

Cini, Lorenzo. "Radical is Beautiful. The Radicalization of the Italian Student Movement Onda Anomala between 2008 and 2010." Paper delivered at the XXVII Conference, Società Italiana di Scienza Politica (SISP), Discussion Panel: "Repertoire of Contention and the Intersection of Agency and Structure," Firenze, Italy, 2013c.

Cini, Lorenzo and Eliska Drapalova. "Protests Out of the Economic Crisis. The Movimento 5 Stelle in Italy and 15M in Spain: Two Instances of a New Politics?" Paper delivered at the Conference "Alternative Futures and Popular Protests," Manchester, UK, 2014.

Cockburn, Alexander and Robin Blackburn. *Student Power*. London: Penguin, 1969.

della Porta, Donatella. *Movimenti Collettivi e Sistema Politico in Italia. 1960–1995*. Roma-Bari: Laterza, 1996.

della Porta, Donatella. "Prefazione. Movimenti degli Studenti: Riflessioni Comparate," in *Alla ricerca dell'Onda. I nuovi conflitti nell'istruzione superiore*, edited by Loris Caruso, Alberta Giorgi, Alice Mattoni and Gianni Piazza, 9–15. Milano: FrancoAngeli, 2010.

della Porta, Donatella. *Social Movements in Times of Austerity: Bringing Capitalism Back Into Protest Analysis*. London: Polity Press, 2015.

della Porta, Donatella, and Mario Diani. *Social Movements. An Introduction*. Malden: Blackwell Publisher, 2006.

Edmunds, June, and Bryan Turner. "Global Generations: Social Change in the Twentieth Century." *The British Journal of Sociology* 56, 4 (2005): 559–77.

Fasano, Nicoletta, and Mario Renosio. *I Giovani e la Politica: Il Lungo '68* Torino: Edizioni Gruppo Abele, 2002.

Gamson, William. "Bystanders, Public Opinion, and the Media," in *The Blackwell Companion to Social Movements*, edited by David Snow, Sarah Soule and Hanspeter Kriesi, 242–261. Oxford: Blackwell Publishing, 2004.

Gamson, William. *The Strategy of Social Protest*. Homewood: The Dorsey Press, 1990 (1975).

Gill, Jungyun, and James De Fronzo. "A Comparative Framework for the Analysis of International Student Movements." *Social Movement Studies: Journal of Social, Cultural, and Political Protest* 8, 3 (2009): 203–224.

Jasper, James. *Getting your Way. Strategic Dilemmas in the Real World*. Chicago and London: The University of Chicago Press, 2006.

Johnston, Hank, and John Noakes. *Frames of Protest. Social Movements and the Framing Perspective*. Oxford: Rowman & Littlefield Publishers, 2005.

Mannheim, Karl. "The Problem of Generations," in *Essays on the Sociology of Knowledge*, edited by Karl Paul Kecskemeti, 276–320. London: Routledge & Kegan Paul, 1952.

Melucci, Alberto. *Challenging Code: Collective Action in the Information Age*. New York and Cambridge: Cambridge University Press, 1996.

Ortoleva, Peppino. *Saggio sui Movimenti del 1968 in Europa e America*. Roma: Editori Riuniti, 1988.

Palermo, Giulio. *L'Università dei Baroni. Centocinquant'anni di Storia tra Cooptazione, Contestazione e Mercificazione*. Milano: Edizioni Punto Rosso, 2011.

Raparelli, Francesco. *La Lunghezza dell'Onda. Fine della Sinistra e Nuovi Movimenti*. Roma: Ponte alle Grazie, 2009.

Regini, Marino. *La Riforma Universitaria nel Quadro dei Sistemi di Governance Europei*. Firenze: Firenze University Press, 2014.

Roggero, Gigi. *The Production of Living Knowledge. The Crisis of the University and the Transformation of Labor in Europe and North America*. Philadelphia: Temple University Press, 2011.

Rootes, Christopher. "Student Movements," in *Encyclopedia of Social & Political Movements*, edited by David Snow, Donatella della Porta and David McAdam, 4864–4869. Malden: The Wiley-Blackwell, 2013.

Rubin, H., and I. Rubin. *Qualitative Interviewing: The Art of Hearing Data*, Thousand Oaks: California, 1995.

Snow, David. "Framing Processes, Ideology, and Discursive Fields," in *The Blackwell Companion to Social Movements*, edited by David Snow, Sarah Soule and Hanspeter Kriesi, 380–412. Oxford: Blackwell Publishing, 2004.

Snow, David, and Robert Benford. "Master Frames and Cycles of Protest," in *Frontiers in Social Movement Theory,* edited by Aldon Morris and Carol McClurg Mueller, 133–155. New Haven and London: Yale University Press, 1992.

Sukarieh, Mayssoun and Stuart Tannock. *Youth Rising? The Politics of Youth in the Global Economy,* Routledge: New York and London, 2015.

Touraine, Alain. *The Workers' Movement.* Cambridge and New York: Cambridge University Press, 1987.

CHAPTER 3

Lawyers Mobilizing in the Tunisian Uprising: A Matter of 'generations'?

Éric Gobe

On January 14, 2011, the day President Ben Ali fled from Tunisia, images of young Tunisian lawyers protesting in their black robes in front of the Ministry of the Interior were broadcast around the world on television and on the web. These images made people think these young lawyers had played a fundamental role in the protest movements that led to the fall of the authoritarian regime which had ruled the country since Independence. Although one should avoid establishing a causal link, the fact is that during the popular uprising many lawyers came out of courthouses to join the protests against the Ben Ali regime. The 'profession' had already shown a higher ability to resist and protest against the strongman than other social groups. For a while after the 'despot' fled, lawyers appeared to be the professional group that would be able to symbolically and materially profit from the transition phase. However, they lost their 'revolutionary euphoria' after the election of the National Constituent Assembly (NCA) on October 23, 2011. This brief summary of the visible role of Tunisian lawyers during the 2011 revolutionary events leads one to question the possible generational,[1] social and political logic that underlies the collective efforts by a professional group that contested Ben Ali's authoritarian regime and contributed to its fall.

The research we present here, however, is not the result of an analysis in generational terms. It flows from research work that was carried out mainly between 2006 and 2011 on collective efforts by lawyers from the beginnings of the profession in Tunisia to the overthrow of the Ben Ali regime. Without going into the details of the approach developed by us, the goal of our socio-historical investigation is to propose a critical reading of the exclusive approach assumed by the current research on the sociology of collective action by lawyers. We link it to a neo-Weberian approach within which the issues of professional market control and obtaining a higher social status is at the core of understanding political action by the legal profession in Tunisia.

---

1 Here, I position myself within a perspective that considers generations in terms of belonging to a cohort and its position in the life cycle.

© KONINKLIJKE BRILL NV, LEIDEN, 2017 | DOI 10.1163/9789004344518_005

The main stream of research on 'political lawyering' highlights the legal profession's underlying 'liberal' biases, starting in the 18th Century. Represented mainly by Terence Halliday and Lucien Karpik (1997), research work within this approach posits that starting in the 18th Century, lawyers as 'collective actors'[2] got involved in one way or another in defence of fundamental freedoms, the assertion of an 'independent civil society' and a 'moderate state.' As adherents to a 'narrow political liberalism,'[3] lawyers seem to have put in place, unwillingly or willingly, a dual mobilization strategy: within the courthouses, where the legal space can become a political arena during a trial or while on strike; and without, by becoming public spokespersons due to their professional ethos and the autonomy enjoyed by their representative bodies.

The central hypothesis of Lucien Karpik and Terence C. Halliday is that there is an elective affinity between the legal profession and liberalism. This seems to overly 'substantialize' the legal profession by seeing it as a homogeneous whole and by focusing on professional organizations' actions. Without denying the existence of a liberal ethos in the profession, we have tried to show that there are no contradictions between its 'civic professionalism,'[4] formalized by American sociologist Terence C. Halliday (1987), and lawyers' promotion of their economic interests, aimed at increasing their professional autonomy thereby legitimizing and imposing a monopoly on a large part of the legal services market. To develop our discussion of the ability of Tunisian lawyers to establish themselves as collective actors, we have also analyzed social segmentations and hierarchies established within the profession, as well as their efforts to define the issues at the core of the profession and the manner in which some members of the legal profession came to rethink their professional activity in terms of political objectives.

To be able to find answers to our questions, we undertook two types of field work between 2005 and 2010, a quantitative and a qualitative survey. The first study surveyed a sample of 626 lawyers (about 10% of the legal profession in

---

2 Lucien Karpik means by this concept "any entity that has the means to establish contact among its members and to design and implement outside common action. Specifically, we posit that the collective actor exists around arrangement, it establishes regulations and intervenes by specific actions." [Our translation] Karpik (1995, 22–23).

3 Lucien Karpik and Terence Halliday consider that lawyers defend a particular form of political liberalism that is limited to "civil and political individual rights," promoting also "fundamental freedoms" protecting citizens from arbitrary measures by the State, such as freedom of conscience, freedom of speech, freedom of movement, due process of law, etc.

4 Lawyers are thus the defenders, beyond "an advantageous market situation" (hence the book's title) of a "collective interest in an efficient and effective legal system, in the legitimacy of law as an institution, and in the intrinsic merits of procedural justice and legalism" (Halliday 1987, 369).

2008, trainees included), representative of large cities in Tunisia where more than 90% of the country's lawyers are concentrated. The second study, carried out between 2005 and 2009, was a qualitative survey of 85 lawyers in which we asked these members of the legal profession to talk about their family, their training, their professional practice, their perceptions of the profession's situation, and their view on how the justice system worked in Tunisia. The qualitative survey sample included lawyers from different age brackets, various political affiliations, and diverse socio-economic status.

Our analysis regarding the 2010–2011 protest movements, and related to post-Ben Ali Tunisia is based on ongoing research.[5] The interviews carried out so far have been with lawyers in Tunis, including some who were in contact with colleagues in the cities where the uprising against the Ben Ali regime started.

Although we have not used in our research a generational approach, we have been drawn to analyze to what extent age is an explanatory variable for lawyers' attitudes and representations. From this point of view, our approach is similar to that taken by Karen Foster (2013), who used in her work the concept of generation based on its use in the actual discourse by the actors themselves. In other words, according to the Canadian sociologist the important thing is not to ponder beforehand what a generation is or what the characteristics of such and such generation are, but rather to start from what those responding say regarding the concept and how to can we construct a generational identity from their answers.

However, from the qualitative interviews that we did with 'young lawyers' there emerged a 'generational conscience,'[6] at least in the collective discourse of the legal profession, undergirded by a devalued image of lawyers being harassed by an authoritarian regime accused of wanting to starve (*tajwi'*) the legal profession. If these lawyers did not explicitly use in their interviews the term 'generations,' they saw themselves under Ben Ali as young lawyers having in common a much lower status than their socio-professional expectations. We postulate here that this representation, together with other variables, constituted the strong seed for the 'lower-level legal profession' (*bas barreau*)[7] mobilizing during the people's uprising in December 2010/January 2011 (1st part).

---

5   The results presented here are thus partial and further investigation will be carried out specifically in the regions where the protest movement started.

6   This notion refers originally "to the hypothesis of a collective mentality shaped by a founding event" [Our translation] (Tournier 2002, 230). If it is not possible here to mention a 'founding event,' the interference by the Ben Ali regime in matters of the legal profession, combined with the effects of the large increase in the number of legal professionals, contributed to shaping a common devalued image of the profession among young lawyers.

7   Meaning the majority of the profession and its youngest group (born in the 1980s) dominated both economically and politically. See below.

The collective action by these 'lower-level' lawyers was encouraged and supported mainly by politically active opposition lawyers – those most oppositional having been politically socialized as far-left under Bourguiba. Most of the political action took place outside of, even against, professional organizations whose leading instances (Bar Association's President and Governing Council) took a hesitating, wait-and-see approach during most of the uprising (2nd part).

Social Structures and Age in the Legal Profession under Ben Ali

The key phenomenon that marked the legal profession over the last 20 years was its large increase. From 1991 to 2011, the number of lawyers in Tunisia grew to almost six times its previous size, going from 1,400 members to 7,759 (ONAT 2011), whereas during the same period the total active population grew only 1.6 times. This growth accelerated in the late 2000s, leading to unprecedented rejuvenation of the profession. Thus between June 2008 and June 2011, 1,500 new lawyers became bar members, such that in 2010 almost 75% of lawyers were younger than 40. Trainees were in 2011 almost 40% of the legal profession and 95% of them were younger than 30 (Gobe 2013a). These young lawyers, trainees or registered with the Court of Appeal, comprised 80% of what I have called the Tunisian 'lower-level legal profession.'[8] This large increase in numbers in the legal profession was favoured by the regime, as it masked some of the joblessness among recent graduates (See Graph 3.1).[9]

The large increase in the number of lawyers also contributed to amplify, throughout the 2000s, the classic refrain of the profession's overcrowding and the pressure that young lawyers were putting on the legal services market. The recruitment 'democratization' in the legal profession, or at least its large increase in number, is accompanied by a relative reduction of lawyers having inherited wealth, and thus reduced the ability of young lawyers to make a living from their legal fees. If this 'career congestion' is in large part a 'social

---

8 Generally, the 2000s were a decade during which graduate unemployment grew, as did the difficulties in entering the job market. See the last report by the World Bank on the issue of youth employment in Tunisia. It shows that unemployment affects increasingly more university graduates (Their number has almost doubled in 10 years, as unemployed university graduate numbers rose to 336,000 in 2006–2007 from 121,800 in 1996–1997). Furthermore, it is in the tertiary sector (management, finances, law) that the rate of unemployment is the highest, reaching 68% for Master of Law graduates, 18 months after graduation (République Tunisienne 2008).

9 Statistically, someone who is registered with the Bar Association is no longer unemployed, even if he/she is not working.

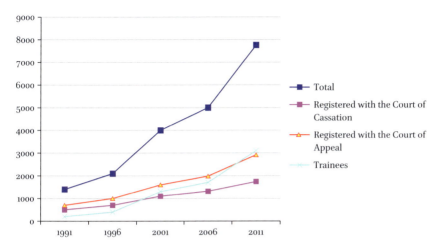

GRAPH 3.1   *Number of lawyers registered in Tunisia from 1991 by professional status.*
SOURCE: REPORTS AND TABLES FROM THE TUNISIAN NATIONAL BAR ASSOCIATION, 1991, 1997, 2002, 2007, 2011.

fantasy' commonplace in the profession's history across many countries, the fact remains that this 'impression of oversupply' in the profession (*image du trop-plein*) as noted by historian Christophe Charles (1994, 22) "extrapolates uncontested morphological and social changes in the legal profession." In fact, Table 3.1 denotes a cross-generational increase in the number of lawyers whose father belongs to low- and middle-salary strata.

Table 3.2 shows professional differences between fathers of lawyers registered at the Court of Cassation, those registered with the Court of Appeal and unpaid trainees[10] – which mirror a distinction between those longest in the profession and new entrants – but it also brings out the social disparities between different age brackets of lawyers.

The clients of the 'lower-level legal profession' were almost exclusively drawn from the working class, often from the same neighbourhoods in which the lawyers themselves grew up in. These legal professionals intervened in the areas of family law (divorces, alimony), real estate law (writing of sales agreement with small amounts involved), petty crimes (mainly misdemeanors) and neighbourhood disputes. Within the profession, they collected the lowest legal fees from a clientele of modest means (Gobe 2013a, 236–241).

Directly confronted with competition from adjoining professions, such as paralegals, in matters in which being a member of the bar is not a requirement,[11]

---

10 Almost 85% of the total number of articling lawyers. Source: Éric Gobe, study 2008–2009.
11 In matters where the persons in proceedings are not obliged to use the services of a barrister.

TABLE 3.1   *Father's profession by lawyer's bar admission date (n=610).*

	1945–1979	1980–1989	1990–1999	2000–2009	Total
Small farm operator, hired farm worker, employee and labourer	8	20	18	25	19
Middle and large farm operator	16	12	4	3	6
Skilled tradesman, small business owner, business manager	20	20	18	15	17
Professional, senior executive	31	23	26	25	27
Middle manager, senior technician, elementary school teacher	25	25	34	32	30
Total	100	100	100	100	100

SOURCE: ÉRIC GOBE, STUDY 2008–2009.

these lawyers often experienced financial difficulties, especially in the first ten years of their professional practice.

In the late 1990s, talk started among lawyers as to the legal profession being a safe haven for the unemployed looking for a job. This phenomenon was particularly difficult for young lawyers, who saw it as something that devalued the legal profession and felt as if there was a social downgrading of their professional practice. The overcrowding in the legal profession exacerbated competition and led to illegal practices, such as widespread soliciting of clients.

This economic situation is particularly difficult for trainee lawyers that cannot always be helped by their families. Thus, the distribution of court appointed lawyers has become an important economic issue at the end of the Ben Ali era. Some trainees are required to spend days in courtrooms in the hope of being appointed by a judge. A young lawyer who had just finished his internship views a political will in this practice that is geared towards new entrants to the profession:

> The trainee who spends his day in court may have two to three cases a day. He makes over 300 DT per day. But he will never become a lawyer. He has no pressure from clients which helps to form lawyers. He feels

LAWYERS MOBILIZING IN THE TUNISIAN UPRISING   79

TABLE 3.2   *Father's profession by lawyer's professional status (n = 610).*

	Lawyer at the Court of Cassation (>45 years)	Lawyer at the Court of Appeal (31 to 45 years)	Unpaid Trainess Lawyer (25 to 30 years)	Paid Trainees Lawyer (25 to 30 years)	Total
Small farm operator, hired farm worker, employee and labourer	15	16	30	8	19
Middle and large farm operator	13	4	3	4	6
Skilled tradesman, small business owner, business manager	22	20	13	14	17
Professional, senior executive	26	28	25	55	27
Middle manager, senior technician, elementary school teacher	24	32	29	19	30
Total	100	100	100	100	100

SOURCE: ÉRIC GOBE, STUDY 2008–2009.

submissive in court. He is not even able to request an adjournment. He cannot defend his clients. He only says two words. The lawyer, who enters into this new world without training, feels adrift. All of these drawbacks were wanted by the authorities, it did not happen by chance. At a certain moment, the lawyers have become the first opposition party. They need to look after their livelihood, they do not earn much. Increasing the number of lawyers is purposeful. The lawyer has no credibility within society.[12]

During the 2000s, in professional organization elections, these lawyers voted in large numbers for Bar Association leaders close to the opposition, such as

---

12   Interview with Amenallah Mourou, son of Abdelfattah Mourou, former n° 2 of Ennahda Islamiste Movement, 26 octobre 2008.

BéchirEssid, an Arab nationalist who had been imprisoned under Ben Ali, Abdessatar Ben Moussa (a left-winger, close to the Ettajdid movement, a party in the legal political scene under Ben Ali and a successor to the Tunisian Communist Party) or still AbderrazakKilani, an Arab nationalist close to political Islam (Gobe 2010).

Their main work-related demand (take new professional areas from competing professions[13]) became in fact the leitmotif of speeches by the Bar Association's President and Governing Council. Faced with an influx of newcomers, leaders in the Tunisian National Bar Association led a two-pronged policy. On the one hand, they tried to stop some categories of law graduates from becoming bar members, while on the other hand they demanded the Ministry of Justice implement a reform giving them the means to monitor and force standards onto new entrants in the profession. On both counts, the Bar Association saw its wishes quashed by the Ben Ali regime, which blocked their actions (Gobe 2013a, 258–264).

The professional difficulties experienced by the lower-level legal profession created strong resentment among these lawyers, as legal professionals who were active members of the party in power (RCD – *Rassemblement constitutionnel démocratique*, the Democratic Constitutional Rally) benefited from many privileges. Given patronage by the Ben Ali regime, these politically connected lawyers (around 500, about 7% of the profession) benefited from a virtual monopoly in terms of litigation work from public administration and state-owned companies. In exchange for these financial advantages, the governing elites expected them to watch and counter the collective action by their colleagues (Gobe 2013b, 49–53).

Even so, belonging to the RCD did not necessarily mean one had public institutions as clients, as more than 40% of lawyers who were members of the ruling party had only private individuals and companies in their client portfolio.[14] Some young lawyers, members of the RCD, hoped to eventually have public institutions as clients, but complained that even among party members some had a monopoly on representing the administration and state-owned companies.[15]

---

13   "Potential clients involved in cases where recourse to a lawyer is not compulsory may decide to act on their own behalf or call upon the services of members of other paralegal professions (notaries, bailiffs, clerks of the court) or professions whose members have some legal expertise (accountants, legal advisors, financial advisors, public writers). Non-specialist lawyers have been particularly sensitive to competition from other professions accused of poaching on their professional territory." See Éric Gobe (2013b, 56).

14   The percentage is even higher if articling lawyers are included (almost 60%).

15   Interview with BAR, a young lawyer, member of the RCD, and registered with the Court of Appeal, Tunis October 3, 2009.

The committee in charge of examining the files of lawyers dealing with administrative and public institutions, made up of RCD party bosses, regularly drew up lists of lawyers eligible to represent public institutions. At the same time, this committee listed the so-called 'harmful' lawyers that public sector managers were supposed to dismiss. The party hierarchy was thus able to select the lawyers that could benefit from public-funded work. They established categories of lawyers according to their zeal in serving the Ben Ali regime, and differentiated lawyers, RCD members, on the list of strong supporters (*mutahammisin*) from those considered as 'ordinary lawyers' (Secrétariat général 2000).

To aspire to this privilege, a lawyer member of the RCD had to have a sufficiently good track record of service. First of all, he had to be an active member, in other words participate in party association activities to prove his allegiance, so as to see a public institution use his services. In fact, RCD members joined non-professional associations in higher proportions than did lawyers who were members of opposition parties or had no political affiliation. The associations were for the most part RCD satellite organizations. There was ferocious competition among young RCD members who sought to get privileged clients. Those that could be taken under the wing of a senior party figure, or better yet the President of the Republic or his family circle, would see their public client roll grow.

Although lawyers who were active in the RCD conducted counter-mobilization operations during the protest movement in December 2010–January 2011, the younger ones, who had joined the party in the hopes of getting litigation work from public institutions, did not try to thwart their colleagues movement, namely during the profession's general strike on January 6, 2011. This apathy among RCD's young lawyers can be explained mainly by the loss of patronage resources by the party in power (Ayari 2013, 245). Having been unable to give its protégés enough work, those in power were not able to mobilize the young lawyers who were members of the RCD and who had the same sociological profile as their fellow members of the lower-level Tunisian legal profession.[16]

Another segment of the profession did not get mobilized, specifically the specialized lawyers at the top of income hierarchy (less than 10% of lawyers), too busy making money or too worried that the political troubles would affect their income negatively (Gobe 2013a, 225–236).

Between the lower-level legal profession and the business lawyers, there was a generalist lawyer segment that possessed social capital letting them have a

---

16   Interview with BAR, a young lawyer, member of the RCD, and registered with the Court of Appeal, Tunis April 21, 2013.

mixed clientele, including small businesses, individuals belonging to the higher middle class and the top tier of society. They mainly mobilized against the Ben Ali regime a week before its fall.[17]

Generally speaking, the young general practitioners at the bottom of the income ladder and professional experience whom we met during our survey, were particularly sensitive to the disconnect between their difficult financial situation and their hopes for professional success. Their socioeconomic conditions, regarded as an injustice, made them receptive to the activities carried out by the activist lawyers, political opponents to the regime well before the uprising in Sidi Bouzid (Gobe 2010).

In fact, there is a distinction to be made between two groups of political activist lawyers, according to their age and activist socialization. First, the opponent lawyers born in the 1950s,[18] who carried out highly transgressive activist activity following a political path marked by socialization and activist mobilization previous to Bourguiba's era. These lawyers, concentrated in the capital Tunis, also extended their opposition activities on the far left (Marxist-Leninists and Maoists, sometimes tinted by Arab nationalism) and to a lesser extent their affiliation to political Islam, to their legal practise.

Most of them had experienced varying lengths of prison stays and all of them were arrested and beaten up by police at least once in their life. These prison stays became biographical breaking points, fertile periods that redefined their activist identity and their professional vocation. The activists that experienced a long prison stay (one to various years) mentioned it as a fundamental phase in their life that shaped both their political militancy and their vision of practising law.[19] Their involvement as opposition lawyers was the continuation of their past political involvement. Defending Human Rights and defendants' rights gave a 'moral dimension' (Agrikoliansky 2010)[20] to their previous political activism, as well as to their later professional work.

---

17   Interview with Mohamed Ali Gherib, a lawyer registered with the Court of Appeal, Tunis April 19, 2011.

18   Very few, about fifteen people, they started their militancy career under Bourguiba and thus were for the most part over 50 years old in 2011 (Gobe 2013a, 242–247).

19   This incarceration period corresponds to one of the turning points mentioned by Everett C. Hughes (1996). It was a pivotal moment, a trying period which following the discourse of Human Rights became the evident thing to do.

20   The reference to human rights enabled previous political involvement different from the present (for lawyers having been far left movements) and gave more soul to political activity in step with society but considered by adversaries as a contradiction with the values held up by the universality of Human Rights (for Islamist lawyers).

LAWYERS MOBILIZING IN THE TUNISIAN UPRISING 83

They constitute a 'political generation' to the extent that age is here correlated to "a collective political behaviour" (Braungart and Braungart 1989, 9). Their profession has allowed them to benefit from symbolic resources that contributed to sustain their political involvement within the profession, either through activist groups or directly before the courts or within professional organizations once they were elected into positions therein. Harassed by the state's repressive machinery (beatings, car tampering, telephone wiretapping, tax inspections, etc.), these lawyers were, like their younger fellow members of the lower-level legal profession, in a difficult financial situation (Gobe 2013a, 242–247).

As for the opposition lawyers from the second group (about sixty people), they were younger professionals, born in the 1970s, involved in less transgressive political activities than their elders, as they were faced with the repressive apparatus that had overcome the Ennahdha Islamist party in the early 1990s. Most often Arab nationalist, members of radical left fringe groups, Islamists or even defenders of Human Rights, they continued their political involvement as lawyers in trials for labour and/or political activists. Furthermore, they mobilized against the lawyers members of the RCD in the Bar Association elections and also in the Tunisian Association of Young Lawyers (*Association Tunisienne des Jeunes Avocats* – ATJA).

These activist professionals in the second group, who according to their socioeconomic status belong to the lower-level legal profession, became the spokespersons of the young lawyers' financial demands, while at the same time supporting the values held up by the profession (invoking Human Rights and fundamental freedoms, protecting the right of defence, etc.). By their ethos and their vision, these lawyers demanded both 'civic professionalism' and professional independence while supporting the economic agenda of widening the scope of work carried out by lawyers, as expressed by the lower-level legal profession.

The commitment to minorities by the political activist lawyers of both the first and second groups was a "revealing element of the groups' principles and functioning logic" (Champy and Israël 2009, 14).

All these opponent lawyers acted in concert in the mobilizations that took place throughout the 2000s. They pushed their professional organizations to condemn the repressive policies of the Ben Ali regime and to organize hearing strikes. They also pushed for, set-up and supported the sit-ins organized to protest against the arrest, imprisonment, and conviction in 2005 of their colleague Mohamed Abbou (Gobe 2013a, 290–293).[21]

---

21 A political activist lawyer, member of the Congress for the Republic (*Congrès pour la République* – CPR), a party not recognized under Ben Ali. He was arrested and jailed in 2005

84 GOBE

It became easier to mobilize the low-level lawyers as the gap in the image of lawyers' professional activity and the reality of their practise deepened during the 1990s–2000s, leading to relative frustration among vulnerable young lawyers faced with financial difficulties at the start of their careers.

Lawyers were one of the few groups that participated in the political challenges to the regime in the 2000s. But until the start of the protest movement that eventually led to President Ben Ali fleeing, their collective action took place within their sector of activity. The popular uprising in 2010–2011 in fact changed the scale of the lawyers' mobilization that became part of widespread protests against the Ben Ali regime.

Lawyers' Mobilizations within the Protest Movement: 'lower-level legal profession' versus Organizations?

The entry of the lower-level legal profession in the collective action is not indicative of generational tensions or conflicts between senior lawyers and young members of the profession. Political activist lawyers of all ages got involved to support the large number of lower-level legal professionals who, from the day after the death of Mohamed TarakBouazizi, came out onto the streets to denounce the crackdown. The tensions between the camps against and in favour of participating in the uprising became polarized; there was a divide between representatives of the profession reluctant in calling for mobilizing, and the lower-level lawyers with its spokespersons (political activist lawyers) who were pushing for the profession to get involved as an institution.

The collective action of lawyers between December 2010 and January 2011 had its start in the courthouses. Activist lawyers spoke out at these to encourage their young colleagues in the lower-level legal profession to get out of the courthouses and to express their solidarity toward the protesters by participating in demonstration marches, protest meetings and other sit-ins.[22] Defense lawyers joined some public protests by using the local network that first

---

for having published an Internet article comparing President Ben Ali to Israeli Prime Minister Ariel Sharon, while the World Summit on the Information Society (WSIS) was being held in Tunis, and to which Israel had been invited. He was named Minister in charge of Administrative Reform in the first troika government.

22 Interview with Koutheïr Bouallègue, a lawyer and an activist in the second group, April 23, 2013. He considers himself an independent professional, without any specific affiliation. He was in phone contact with activist colleagues in SidiBouzid, Regueb and Kasserine during the uprising.

instance courts are. They were able to appear in political protests as a collective body, visible in the public sphere (by wearing lawyers' black robes). The various provincial courthouses, as the one in the capital, symbolic places at the core of urban life (and of protest movements), topographical embodiments of justice (and of the injustice of the Ben Ali regime), became thus the sites where the lawyers mobilization crystallized.

However, the mobilization in December 2010 was not a result of the profession having organizational representation and deciding to act. Inactive for a part of the protest movement, the professional organizations were in fact a brake on mobilization rather than a player in the uprising.

Seen under this angle, action or rather inaction by the profession's spokespersons confirms the thesis developed by law sociologists Kieran McEvoy and Rachel Rebouché (2007, 275), for whom professional organizations representing lawyers tend to take conservative positions in favour of the status quo in the name of the profession's neutrality and independence. Rarely do they use their resources to defend Human Rights and the rule of law or to challenge a political regime.

Although Bar Association President Abderrazak Kilanihad a history of political involvement that would naturally make him an opponent to Ben Ali's power,[23] after his election to the position in June 2010 he tried to find a *modus vivendi* with the authorities. He wanted to find a compromise that would satisfy at least some of the professional demands by the low-level legal profession in exchange for control of professional requests perceived by the powers that be as essentially political (defending Human Rights, respecting the rule of law, protecting public and private freedoms). In this regard, as soon as he was elected to the position on June 30, 2010, Abderrazak Kilani convened a 'scientific council' for the purpose of drafting new legislation regarding the profession. Comprised of three former Bar Association Presidents and of 43 fellow members including its Governing Council members, this council's membership was designed to reflect all political and ideological currents across the profession.

---

23   The authorities were critical of him, among other things, for having signed in 1993 a petition in favour of RadhiaNasraoui (an activist lawyer socialized under Bourguiba, wife of the leader of the Tunisian Workers' Communist Party (PCOT) – Hamma Hammami), having published a communiqué denouncing the conditions imposed on his detained clients (1994), having made 'murky' relationships with certain Ennahda activists (1995), having signed a petition that mentioned the authorities taking away the passport from some political opponents (2000), having called on lawyers to heed the call for strike on April 28, 2000, etc. See Secrétariat général (2000).

Later, over the fall, a select committee was given the task of drafting a final bill.[24]

How the protest momentum played out within the profession revealed this hiatus between the mobilization at the grassroots level and the wait-and-see attitude by the Bar Association leadership. In order to facilitate negotiations, the association President and some members of the Governing Council tried to steer the action by grassroots lawyers. Within the Council, lawyers close to the RCD did not want the leading instances to be associated with the protests, whereas other members were hesitant.[25] Even those who were aligned with a more oppositional line (the majority of Governing Council members were political Islam and Arab nationalism supporters, along with other individuals without a declared political affiliation) attempted to play for time and did not take any public position denouncing the wait-and-see approach by the professional organization's higher instances.[26]

In some aspects, lawyer mobilization during the phase of popular uprising can be classified as belonging to 'cause lawyering' (Sarat and Scheingold 1998). Indeed, it was a specific category of lawyers focused on "a marked political cause" (Israël 2003, 600) already engaged in protest activities and having an activist know-how that mobilized its colleagues. Responding to the protest circumstances, it was the Human Rights defenders and political activists that were instrumental in waking up the profession's 'collective conscience' and in pushing for the leading instances to call for mobilizing against the Ben Ali regime's repressive action (McEvoy and Rebouché 2007, 277).

Although the lawyers elected for the organization's higher instances were experienced men (between 45 and 60 years old) that did not fully represent the profession's age profile, a reading in terms of generations does not seem to help in understanding the reticence by the Bar Association leadership to officially engage the legal profession in the protest movement. Institutional logic makes it possible to understand the timidity by the Bar Association President and its Governing Council. The uncertainty regarding the uprising outcome, as the association leaders prepared to negotiate new legislation with the Ben Ali regime, in large part explains the prudence shown by the association President and Governing Council members, some of whom moreover were close to the powers that be.

---

24   Interview with a Court of Cassation lawyer, Mongi Ghribi, Tunis, April 19, 2013. A journalist by training, this lawyer monitored the lawyer protest movement in Tunis.

25   Ibid.

26   Ibid.

LAWYERS MOBILIZING IN THE TUNISIAN UPRISING

In some respects, the Bar Association position vindicates the defenders of organizations' cast-iron laws, according to whom leaders ought to "focus the strength of numbers into the confined space of meeting rooms," and thus would be "inclined to find a compromise with the elites at the time to sustain its position" (Pierru 2010, 23).

The first lawyer mobilization took place in SidiBouzid on December 18, 2010, the day after the self-immolation suicide of Tarek Mohammed Bouazizi. A first event, a solidarity sit-in, was organized in front of the city's lower court. On December 19, some lawyers acting on their own behalf, joined militants from the UGTT (*Union générale tunisienne du travail*–Tunisian General Labour Union, then the country's sole central union) calling for the release of protesters arrested the previous day (Hmed 2012, 38). On December 24, as the social uprising spread throughout the governorate and a first protestor was fatally shot by police in MenzelBouzaïane, a group of about thirty lawyers in SidiBouzid left the courthouse and started protesting on the city streets.[27]

On the same day, in Kasserine, about forty lawyers including the leaders of the second group of activist lawyers, linked to the radical left fringe groups (Watad, PCOT) and the PDP,[28] after having harangued their young colleagues within the lower court to go protest, left the courthouse and called on a reticent UGTT local union to protest and show their solidarity with the residents of SidiBouzid. On December 27, 28 and 29, the repression of the rioting affecting the cities surrounding SidiBouzid, led to sit-ins by lawyers in front of the courthouses in Médenine, SidiBouzid and Kasserine.[29] These sit-ins became wider protests joined by other segments of the population, and came on top of nightly clashes organized in neighbourhoods by local residents. In Kasserine, protesting lawyers marched to the working-class neighbourhood of al-Zouhour where they were joined by some young people making the march bigger, whence it returned to the city centre where is located the first instance courthouse. The slogans chanted in the lawyers' march took from the outset a

---

27   Information given by Chawki Tabib in a June 7, 2011 email. Most of this lawyer's political/ professional career took place in lawyers' professional bodies: he was President of the ATJA in late 1990s, member of the Bar Association's Governing Council in the 2000s, then its interim President from January 2012 to July 2013.

28   Interview with Koutheïr Bouallègue, The PDP (*Partidémocrateprogressiste* – Progressive Democratic Party) was, during the 23 years in power by Ben Ali, the only legal political party to refuse swearing total allegiance to the authoritarian regime. The Watad (Democratic Patriots' Movement) was under Ben Ali a political groupuscule mixing Marxism and pan-Arabism. The PCOT is a Marxist-Leninist party stemming from the academic far left.

29   Information given by Chawki Tabib, There were about 60 lawyers in the sit-in and political march in Médenine out of the 280 that the city had.

political connotation, and were not very different from the ones used by the working-class young rioters: they denounced the political regime and the predatory behaviour by the in-laws of President Ben Ali (Hmed 2012, 31).

There was a similar phenomenon in Tunis. On December 22, spurred on by opposition lawyers, far-left activist and Arab nationalist lawyers from the first and second category, a first sit-in, by around one hundred lawyers, was organized on the fly in front of the Courthouse and the 'Maison de l'avocat' in the city centre. Moreover, supported by dozens of colleagues, activist lawyers carried out a daily siege of the association President's office to demand he officially stake a position and denounce the repression against residents in SidiBouzid and in other urban centres in the west central region. The fact that Abderrazak Kilani organized "coordination and consultation meetings" in the association's offices with lawyers known to be linked to the RCD raised disapproval among these lawyers, who brought their protest as far as his office door.[30]

It was precisely these same activist lawyers that organized a sit-in the morning of December 28, 2010 in front of the Courthouse: speeches, cheers and applause followed each other for almost two hours, under the watchful eyes of law enforcement forces. This opportunity was seized by Abdenasser Laouini, a 'progressive' activist and Arab nationalist lawyer, who spoke to "send a message to the regime, to the President, to his mafia and his family." He repeated the slogans chanted by protestors in SidiBouzid, calling for the right to have a 'dignified life' (*hayât karîma*) and against the 'gang of thieves' (*'isâbat al-surrâq*) that governs and pillages the country.[31]

A few hours later, two opponent lawyers socialized under Bourguiba, Abderraouf Ayadi (a former far-left activist, member of the CPR) and Choukri Belaïd (a pan-Arabist radical left supporter) were arrested not far from their homes. The pressure by activist lawyers prompted the Bar Association President to convene a 'public information meeting' for December 29. Abderraouf

---

30   "There were young colleagues with us. They were furious with the inaction by the Bar Association President." Interview with Koutheir Bouallègue.

31   Interview with Mokhtar Jallali, lawyer accredited at the Court of Cassation, April 24, 2013. Of Arab nationalist allegiance, Mokhtar Jallali was in late 1990s member of the Chamber of Deputies for a co-opted opposition party, the Unionist Democratic Union (UDU – *Union démocratiqueunioniste*). Married to the intellectual activist in the CPR (under Ben Ali), NazihaRjiba also known as Om Ziyed, he became increasingly radical in the 2000s, to the point he was jailed for a few weeks in 2008. Originally from SidiBouzid, he went shortly after the beginning of the uprising to his birth city, before returning to Tunis on December 27 and witnessing the information public meeting organized by the Bar Association President.

Ayadi and Choukri Belaïd, released during the night, went to the offices of the 'Maison de l'avocat' across the Tunis Courthouse, where the 'public information meeting' was taking place. Abderraouf Ayadi showed those present at the meeting his clothes ripped to shreds by his kidnapers and denounced the physical abuse he suffered.[32] However, in this first 'information meeting,' the Bar Association President remained pusillanimous. Although denouncing the physical mistreatment suffered by the two activist lawyers, he stated that "the Bar Association is not a political party" and that he had to take care of "5,000 lawyers who are starving" (Bouallègue 2011). Despite different proposals being formulated by the lawyers present at the meeting on how to behave in relation to the regime's coercive policy, they ultimately put the Governing Council in charge of deciding what position to adopt.[33]

The professional organization leading instances, which had not yet officially reacted to the protest movement repression, decided then to issue an official statement expressing their solidarity with the residents in SidiBouzid who, according to them, were only demanding to exercise their right to work and to have a decent life. At the same time, the communiqué from the Governing Council denounced "the kidnapping and arrest of colleagues Abderraouf Ayadi and Choukri Belaïd by security officers in clear violation of the law." To protest against how the security forces had dealt with the protests, the Governing Council called for a day of solidarity by lawyers with the residents of SidiBouzid: the black-robed men would wear a red ribbon in all lower courts in Tunisia on December 31, 2010 (ONAT 2010a).

However, the Bar Association President asked that lawyers remain within the courthouses and not protest on the street.[34] On their part, the authorities reacted to this statement by putting in place repressive measures outside and inside the courthouses. The former to forcibly stop lawyers from coming out of courthouses, while the latter, which consisted of deploying security officers inside the court precincts, sought to ban lawyers from wearing the red ribbons and express their solidarity towards the residents of SidiBouzid. In Tunis, law enforcement officers closed the Courthouse gates thus preventing lawyers to come out onto the street.[35] Lawyers that refused to abide by the law enforcement directives were man-handled, injured, and had their black robes ripped apart.[36]

---

32   Interview with Mokhtar Jallali.

33   Information given by Mongi Ghribi in an email on May 12, 2013.

34   Information given by Mongi Ghribi.

35   Information given by Mokhtar Jallali and Mongi Ghribi in emails on May 12, 2013.

36   Interview with Hichem Belhadj Hamida, a Court of Cassation lawyer who is close to Bar Association President Abderrazak Kilani, Tunis, April 20, 2011.

This violent action by the security services, within the court precinct itself, led the Governing Council to make a stand in favor of the manhandled colleagues. By denouncing the 'savage aggression' (ONAT 2010b) by the security forces on lawyers, the GoverningCouncil called for a general strike on January 6, 2011. But this stand, decided by Bar Association leading instances, is once more indicative of the prudent position taken by its President.

Furthermore, the wording of the call to strike did not make any reference to the riots nor their repression in the west central region of the country, but to the "violence and aggressions against lawyers by security forces within courthouses, offices, the 'Maison de l'avocat,' and in front of the Courthouse" (ONAT 2010b).

The strike had massive participation, despite lawyers from the RCD attending court hearings and denouncing other lawyers as using the courts as a 'political tool.' As for the Bar Association President, he insisted on how responsibly the Association carried out its action. Furthermore, Abderrazak Kilani invited his colleagues to "turn the page, now that the profession expressed its view that bashing lawyers is not allowed" (AFP 2011).

Much more than the success of the strike, it was in fact the momentum of political mobilizations that radicalized the Association's leading instances in the wake of the UGTT leadership that, although largely subservient to the regime before, realized that Ben Ali's power was faltering. The crushing of rioting in Thala, and especially in Kasserine, on January 8 and 9, led to a geographical and social widening of the protest movement. The political insurrection spread to all the country's urban centres, including the capital, and from that point on, the 'middle class' alongside the lawyers, fed the protests which had originally mostly consisted of young people from the working-class neighbourhoods.

Even so, Abderrazak Kilani had not come to the end of his hesitation. On January 11, the meeting by the lawyers 'select committee,' which had the task to finalize drafting new legislation concerning the profession (see above), could not run its normal course due to the high human cost of the rioting in the country's central region. One of its members, Mongi Ghribi, proposed to adjourn the discussions concerning that legislation, so as to focus on the events in Kasserine, Thala and SidiBouzid. Supported by lawyer Moncef Djerbi, his proposal was endorsed by the other members of the committee present who asked the Bar Association President to report on the profession's situation in the regions affected by the popular uprising.[37] Abderrazak Kilani mentioned the phone contact he had had the day before with lawyers in Kasserine, who had informed him that security forces had opened fire on people and that they

---

37   Interview with Mongi Ghribi.

themselves had tried using their bodies as shields to protect the protestors. They had asked him to intervene with Ben Ali on their behalf. The association President then specified that he had spoken with the President of the Republic by phone, and reminded those present that the Minister of Health, Mondher Zeneidi, had contacted him to ask him to bring lawyers in Kasserine to calm and order. In exchange for doing so, Abderrazak Kilani stated having demanded the release of arrested rioters and that the police forces not intervene in the funeral processions of deceased protestors. At the end of the meeting, the members present decided to create two committees, one to follow up issues and the other a defence committee for lawyers so as to track closely how events where unfolding.[38]

In fact, that same day the UGTT national leaders, by deciding under pressure from its rank and file to allow regional unions to organize general strikes across the Tunisian territory starting on January 12, opened an avenue for a clearer engagement by the Bar Association President and its Governing Council alongside the uprising players. This decision by the union federation finally pushed the association's higher instances to follow the protest movement momentum more strongly. Following a special session which met in the association President's office on January 12, its Governing Council called for "a lawyers' general strike across all courts on Friday January 14 in solidarity with the victims, and in support of the demonstrators' demands." It also planned to send a delegation to Kasserine on January 13 to monitor the "safety of colleagues" in the martyr city (ONAT 2011).

Whereas in Tunis the general strike was planned by the UGT regional union for January 14, the strike took place on January 12 in Sfax, the country's second city, and had massive participation. In Médenine, Kasserine and SidiBouzid, lawyers wearing their black robes left the courthouses to take position at the head of demonstration marches side by side with union members. Faced with multiplying riots that now affected the capital and "cracks at high levels of the State" (Baduel 2013, 53–56), President Ben Ali was starting to be in a precarious position. In the morning of January 14, Prime Minister Mohamed Ghannouchi invited the Bar Association President and a delegation from its Governing Council to meet him to inform him of lawyers' grievances. The association President, accompanied by the Tunis section head (Néjib Ben Youssef, Islamist) and the Governing Council's secretary-general (Mohamed Rached Fray, RCD) accepted to attend the meeting with some of the lawyers present in front of the Courthouse. He refused to lead the march that, stopped in front of the 'Maison de l'avocat,' was about to go down to Bourguiba Avenue to join

---

38   Information given by Mongi Ghribi.

up with other protestors.[39] Hundreds of lawyers, including some members of the Bar Association Governing Council (namely Chawki Tabib and Boubaker Bethabet), marched and stopped first in front of the Ministry of Justice to demand independence for the judicial institution. They then went down towards Habib Bourguiba Avenue and the Ministry of the Interior to join the protest. As for the lawyers accompanying the delegation led by the association President, as they did not see it leave the Prime Minister's office, they decided to join the other lawyers on Habib Bourguiba Avenue.[40] Around the Ministry of the Interior, agroup of activist lawyers formed a cordon while the crowd, all social classes together, gathered in front and shouted "Ben Ali Get Out."[41]

Conclusion

If the young lawyers from the lower-level legal profession joined in massive numbers the marches, protests, and sit-ins that fed the protest movement, it was the professionals with experience in political activism that were the organizers of the lower-level lawyers mobilization. From this point of view, political engagement by the lawyers appears as 'transgenerational.' But their participation in the protest movement was mainly due to its young segment, which followed the large increase in numbers in the legal profession. The feeling of sharing a common socio-economic status and perceiving the Ben Ali authoritarian regime as fundamentally hostile to them, contributed to the creation among most lawyers of a generational conscience and a rejection of the authoritarian status quo. Ultimately, the uprising in December 2010–January 2011 contributed to crystallizing this conscience, or in a more general way, "the interaction between historical resources, the contingency of circumstances, and a social formation" is susceptible to render pertinent a generation as a sociological category (Edmunds and Turner 2002, 7). But in the case of lawyers, the generational reading of the uprising in 2010–2011 must be balanced with the lower-level legal profession identity crisis, itself a consequence of the policies directed by the authoritarian regime towards the profession.

With the fall of the authoritarian regime led by Ben Ali, 'young lawyers' exacted their revenge following years of humiliation during his regime. At the

---

39   Information given by Chawki Tabib. On the subject, Koutheïr Bouallègue (2011) specified that during the phase preceding the fall of President Ben Ali, the Bar Association President did not participate in any march or protest, including on January 14, 2011.

40   Interview with Mohamed Ali Gherib, lawyer at the Court of Appeal, Tunis, April 19, 2011.

41   In French "Ben Ali dégage." Ibid.

same time, the professional organization, although reticent at first to get involved in collective action, was able to capture and profit from the dividends of mobilization by its grassroots and political activist lawyers.

Afterwards, the latter, especially the most senior, leaned heavily on their revolutionary legitimacy to get politically involved: two-thirds of the lawyers from the first category, as well as the most politicized lawyers in the second inserted themselves in the official political scene and became professional political figures. These opposition lawyers, whose politico-professional engagement is anchored in the continuation of a political trajectory marked by their socialization and their previous activist mobilizations in the 1970s and early 1980s, had developed under Ben Ali a professional practice in support of union and political activists repressed by the authoritarian regime. In so doing, these lawyers had continued their oppositional practice within the framework of their professional activity. Two fundamental areas in their life, their career and their political engagement, had thus mingled "thanks to their profession" (Willemez 2003, 145). At present, thanks to their protesting political action within the popular uprising of 2010–2011, they have been able to convert the activist and oppositional political resources accumulated since their university days into official political positions and status in post-Ben Ali's Tunisia.[42]

References

AFP (*Agence France Presse*), January 6, 2011.

Agrikoliansky, Éric. "Les usages protestataires du droit," in *Penser les mouvements sociaux*, edited by Olivier Fillieule, Éric Agrikoliansky and Isabelle Sommier, 225–243. Paris: La Découverte, 2010.

Ayari, Michael Bechir. "La 'révolution tunisienne,' une émeute politique qui a réussi?" in *Au cœur des révoltes arabes. Devenir révolutionnaires*, edited by Amin Allal and Thomas Pierret, 241–260. Paris: Armand Colin, 2013.

Baduel, Pierre-Robert. "Le temps insurrectionnel comme moment politique. Tunisie 2011." *Revue internationale de politique comparée* 20, 2 (2013): 33–61.

Bouallègue, Kautheïr. "Shay' min al-haqīqah 'an al-muḥāmah wa istiḥqāqhihā." *al-Sabah*, February 13, 2011. (In Arabic).

Braungart and Braungart. "Les générations politiques," in *Générations et politique*, edited by Jean Crête and Pierre Favre, 7–51. Paris and Laval: Economica and PUL, 1989.

---

42   With 33 members, lawyers were the second profession in numbers (behind teachers, 77 members) in the National Constituent Assembly elected on October 23, 2011.

Champy, Florent and Israël, Liora. "Professions et engagement public." *Sociétés Contemporaines* 73 (2009): 7–19.

Charles, Christophe. "Le recrutement des avocats parisiens 1880–1914," in *Avocats et barreaux en France 1910–1930*, edited by Gilles Le Béguec, 21–34. Nancy: PUN, 1994.

Edmunds, June and Bryan S. Tumer. *Generations, Culture and Society*. Buckingham: Open University Press, 2002.

Foster, Karen. "Generations and Discourse in Working Life Stories." *The British Journal of Sociology* 64, 2 (2013): 195–215.

Gobe, Éric. "The Tunisian Bar to The Test of Authoritarianism: Professional and Political Movements in Ben Ali's Tunisia (1990–2007)." *Journal of North African Studies* 15, 3 (2010): 333–347.

Gobe, Éric. *Les Avocats en Tunisie de la Colonisation à la Révolution (1883–2011): Sociohistoire d'une Profession Politique*. Paris: Karthala, 2013a.

Gobe, Éric. "Of Lawyers and *Samsars*: the Legal Services Market and the Authoritarian State in Ben 'Ali's Tunisia (1987–2011)." *The Middle East Journal* 67, 1 (2013b): 44–62.

Halliday, Terence C. *Beyond Monopoly. Lawyers, State Crises, and Professional Empowerment*. Chicago: The University of Chicago Press, 1987.

Halliday, Terence C., and Lucien Karpik. *Lawyers and the Rise of Western Political Liberalism: Europe and North America from the Eighteenth to Twentieth Centuries*. New York: Clarendon Press and Oxford University Press, 1997.

Hmed, Choukri. "Abeyance Networks, Contingency and Structures." *Revue Française de Science Politique (English)* 62, 5 (2012): 31–53.

Hughes, Everett C. *Le regard sociologique. Essais choisis*. Textes rassemblés et présentés par Jean-Michel Chapoulie. Paris: Édition de l'EHESS, 1996.

Israël, Liora. "Dossier – La justice comme espace politique. Trois études de cas: Israel, Inde, Argentine." *Droit et Société* 55 (2003): 599–603.

Karpik, Lucien. *Les Avocats Entre l'État, le Public et le Marché XIIIe–XXe siècle*. Paris: Gallimard, 1995.

McEvoy, Kieran, and Rachel Rebouché. "Mobilizing the Professions: Lawyers, Politics, and the Collective Legal Conscience," in *Judges, Transition, and Human Rights*, edited by John Morison, Kieran McEvoy and Gordon Anthony, 275–314. New York: Oxford University Press, 2007.

ONAT (Ordre national des avocats de Tunisie). Communiqué (*balagh*) December 29, 2010 (2010a). Tunis: Tunisian Bar Association.

ONAT (Ordre national des avocats de Tunisie). La'ihat al-waqfah al-ihtijājiyyah li-yawm December 31, 2010 (2010b) [Motion de protestation du 31 Decembre 31, 2010]. Tunis: Tunisian Bar Association.

ONAT (Ordre national des avocats de Tunisie). Communiqué (*balagh*) January 6, 2011. Tunis.

Pierru, Emmanuel. "Organisations et ressources," in *Penser les Mouvements Sociaux*, edited by Olivier Fillieule, Éric Agrikoliansky and Isabelle Sommier, 19–38. Paris : La Découverte, 2010.

République Tunisienne. *Dynamique de l'emploi et adéquation de la formation parmi les diplômés universitaires.* Volume 1: *rapport sur l'insertion des diplômés de l'année 2004.* Ministère de l'emploi et de l'insertion professionnelle des jeunes, Banque mondiale, 2008. http://siteresources.worldbank.org/INTTUNISIAINFRENCH/Resources/Dynamique.de.lemploi.pdf.

Sarat, Austin, and Stuart A. Scheingold. "Cause lawyering and the Reproduction of Professional Authority," in *Cause Lawyering: Political Commitments and Professional Responsibilities*, edited by Austin Sarat and Stuart A. Scheingold, 3–28. New York: Oxford University Press, 1998.

Secrétariat général, présidence de la République [al-Kitaba al-'âmma, ri'assat al-jumhuriyya]. *Mémorandum adressé par le secrétaire général de la présidence à la haute attention de son Excellence le président de la République, Objet : la liste des avocats traitant avec les établissements publics* [*Mudhakkirailasami 'inâyatsiyâdatra'îs al-Jumhuriyya, al-mawdu' : qa'imat al-muhamin al-muta'aqidinma'aalmunsha'at al-'umumiyya*], 2000.

Tournier, Vincent. "Générations politiques," in *Le Nouveau Désordre électoral*, edited by Bruno Cautres and Nonna Mayer, 229–252. Paris: Presse de science po, 2002.

Willemez, Laurent. "Engagement Professionnel et Fidélités Militantes: les Avocats Travaillistes dans la Défense Judiciaire des Salariés." *Politix* 16, 62 (2003): 145–164.

PART 2

Genealogies of Generational Formations

∵

CHAPTER 4

2003: A Turning Point in the Formation of Syrian Youth

Matthieu Rey

When the United States invaded Iraq in April 2003, it attempted to change an internal political situation by toppling Saddam Hussein's regime, which was supposed to establish democracy. Then, following the plan for a new Middle East promoted by the neo-conservatives (Yetiv 2007; Little 2008), other countries might be reshuffled and, in a few years, the clash of civilizations as described by Samuel Huntington (1996) would be over. This perspective collapsed soon after, as Iraq entered a deep and long internal crisis. Violence, sectarianism, massive waves of refugees and, in return, a deep moral crisis in the United States could be seen between 2003 and 2011. Rather than focusing once again on the Iraqi crisis, a topic which has occasioned some very insightful studies and has scholars' interest back to this country (Allawi 2007; DeFronzo 2010; Haddad 2011; Keegan 2004; Tejel et al. 2013), I will argue in the present chapter that the 'Iraqi-American war' of 2003 impacted the whole region, and that its effects on the populations in neighbouring countries need to be studied as elements of the crisis. While researchers have considered refugees and refugee settlements (Doraï 2009), the indirect outcomes of the crisis have been overshadowed by the direct and highly mediatized violence that spread across Iraq. However, this crisis cannot be isolated from the regional stage, nor can its importance be underestimated; indeed, an 'Iraq War generation' emerged from these events. I will attempt to show how the televised destruction of Baghdad and the increase in sectarian violence (as the war made things worse), the image of Saddam as an ordinary man in the face of death, the influx of refugees fleeing Iraq and the everyday interactions with these refugees – the impact of the Iraq War on the neighbouring countries – converged with other important social trends to shape a new age group.

The Syrian situation highlights the crisis' regional echoes. A generation there developed a new way of looking at the world around it, a view that was shaped by the events it had suffered. Certainly, it is not possible to reduce the social transformation of Syria in the last decade to the social and cultural effects of foreign events. I will argue that a whole set of phenomena led to the emergence of a new group in Syria, which might be called the Iraq War

© KONINKLIJKE BRILL NV, LEIDEN, 2017 | DOI 10.1163/9789004344518_006

generation. It is this phenomenon that created the underpinnings of the current protest movements in Syria. It has been argued that the so-called Arab spring was produced by youth, leading some Middle Eastern specialists such as Thierry Boissiere (2012) to speak about a 'new generation' that emerged from current events. Others have emphasized a 'lost' generation (Hosseini 2014). These analyses are relevant to the change introduced by the conflict, but they overlook the pre-existing patterns of Syrian society that made the uprising possible. It is necessary to define the term 'generation' in order to clarify its use. The word 'generation' refers to a certain mass of population sharing the same age group. But, as Karl Mannheim (1972) argues, the criterion of age is not sufficient[1] as such a group is unified by experiencing a common event which frames its perception of the world. Within this general perspective, wars have been highlighted as a useful criterion for understanding generational processes. Jean-François Sirinelli (2008) refined this notion by underlining the limits of Mannheim's conception. Mannheim emphasizes an event as crucial to sparking generational emergence while, to the contrary, Sirinelli (2008) foregrounds the diversity of trajectories of different groups in the same generation. He does not refuse to identify some age groups as generations, but uses them as a key factor to clarify the social changes that occur during a certain period.

Academic studies have linked generations and youth. Focusing on the latter allows many researchers to target the former. It seems obvious that, for some analyses, inquiring about a generation implies tackling the trajectory taken by youth. This approach proves relevant – and I will adopt it – but it is important to clarify its underlying hypothesis. First, it is clear that a generation might designate age groups other than youth. For example, in Syria, generations emerged from the series of wars between Israel and Arab countries. In his memoirs, Bashīr al-ʿAzmih called his generation the 'generation of the defeat,' to remind the public how the dissolution of the United Arab Republic constituted a clear breaking point in the trajectories of the country and its population (al-ʿAzmih 1991). However, in considering the new order in Syria from 2000 onwards, the youth seem to be the main group that conducted the uprising in Syria. Second, while some studies have been undertaken on Arab youth, they have focused on countries other than Syria.[2] If Syrian studies have seen a renewal since 2000,[3]

---

1 More generally on the notion of generation and its use in social sciences, see Attias-Donfut (1988, 38–43).
2 Herrera and Bayat 2010. The two out of thirty-eight chapters in Bonnefoy and Catusse (2013) that concern Syria remain exceptional. On Syrian studies and its shortcomings, see Chiffoleau 2006.
3 See for example Pierret 2013 and Dupret et al. 2007.

mainly due to better access to fieldwork, mainstream research addresses culture, social life, the religious apparatus, and foreign policy. This research has not paid attention to the youth in Syria as an issue for scholarship. Youth can be defined as a group because it encompasses a certain amount of population, and because actors refer to it in their own narratives (Murphy 2012). However, youth cannot be simplistically defined as a homogeneous group; rather, its diversity reflects the social and economic differences that prevail in a given country (Bourdieu 1984; Gauthier 1999). But if heterogeneity is important in understanding the 'youth,' the category of *shabab* still constitutes an interesting reference point, where objective and subjective elements intertwine. *Shabab* appears as a relevant demographic group, and is determined by a social representation according to which people who do not have children belong to this group. The objective criteria are based on the fact that *shabab* are not the head of a family, and therefore have free time. From this point of view, they are equivalent to teenagers in that term's earlier meaning.[4] This representation of youth enlarges the scope of what is meant by a generation. Consequently, I will suggest some insights that help understand how and why a specific generation emerged in Syria and underpinned the ongoing uprising.

In the present chapter, three main events determine the formation of a particular political generation. First, 1982 can be considered as a landmark in Syrian history. Over one month, the Assad regime violently crushed the opposition, killing several thousand of its members in Hama. In the aftermath, the public sphere was violently repressed. My hypothesis is that young Syrians in 2011, who cannot remember these events, as they were 5 or younger (if born) in 1982, constitute a new group.[5] They show the importance of these events without having been part of them. Then, the events of 2003 – the consequences of the Iraqi invasion – shaped their political identities and social awareness. Finally, in 2011, the uprising paved the way for their individual involvement in politics. Consequently, speaking about 'the generation of 2003' means that a group formed by the end of the demographic transition in Syria was gathered together by a common heritage – the outcomes of the 2003 war – which underpinned their political action a decade later.

---

4   The notion of teenagers emerged in the beginning of the contemporary period, and designated young people who were able to leave the home after childhood. It was directly correlated to the invention of the childhood (Becchi and Julia 1998).

5   I selected the interviewees by range of age (born in 1977 and 1992) who agreed to meet with me. Interviews were conducted in Damascus mostly, in June 2012. Security conditions limited greatly the selection.

The methodological underpinnings of the present chapter are mainly qualitative, while second-hand quantitative resources highlight the importance of the group under study. This has been made possible by the growing number of surveys conducted by United Nations agencies, which have brought a new picture of the country, cataloguing new trends and drawing a clear panorama of Syrian society.[6] These analyses provide the background of this study. I also use qualitative approaches my study, knowing they do not exhaust reality but rather hint to certain points that I think remain either unknown or hastily described. As Everett H. Hughes reminds us (1996), some situations demand other methodological stances. Quantitative approaches presuppose access to statistical tools and categories. In the case of Syria, these tools simply do not exist and the researcher is left with few options. Moreover, some cases require observations and interviews to access actors' significations as personal narratives shed light on the meaning an individual ascribes to events. These are not restricted to facts, but take part in a broader picture. They also provide some insights on aspects which cannot be quantified. I conducted a dozen semi-open interviews with people who were between 20 and 35. They all shared a common experience: they had not witnessed the events in Hama,[7] and they could be qualified as Bashar al-Assad's generation, as they were teenagers when he came to power in 2000. But rather than defining them by this event, I will prove that their generation emerged from the seismic shock of 2003. My study works through the socio-political history of Syria and attempts to provide elements for a Middle Eastern sociology.

Demographic Importance

How and why can we speak about a generation of people born between 1977 and 1992, people who were 20 to 35 in 2011? Is it possible to define a demographic group, as Emma Murphy discusses for other Arab countries? It is necessary to question the importance of this generation (1977–1992) in relation to other generations.

The number of children born between 1977 and 1992 was roughly equivalent each year, ranging from 360,000 and 440,000 individuals (See Table 4.1).

---

6 UNFPA 2008. The first report was issued in 2000 but the enterprise was then blocked, probably for political and security reasons.

7 After an uprising of political forces, the Syrian regime led by Hafez al-Assad violently crushed the protests by sending in troops and helicopters. Between 10,000 and 35,000 people died in the repression. Afterwards, the Syrian public sphere was shut down.

TABLE 4.1   *Population growth*[8]

Year	Natural growth rate in Syria	Natural growth rate in Tunisia	Age group population in Syria[1]	Percentage of this age group in the global population in Syria[2]	Life expectancy in Syria
1977	3.33	2.53	366,972	4.55	
1978	3.38	2.68			
1979	3.45	2.71			
1980	3.52	2.67	394,961	4.43	65
1981	3.56	2.65			
1982	3.55	2.62	412,069	4.31	
1983	3.48	2.58			64
1984	3.38	1.97			
1985	3.26	2.05	431,631	4.08	
1986	3.16	2.15			
1987	3.08	2.53	438,284	3.88	65.4
1988	3.03	2.22			
1989	2.99	1.28			66.3
1990	2.97	2.43	441,129	3.57	66.1
1992	2.94	1.99	442,066	3.58	
1993	2.87	2.04			
1994	2.76				
1995	2.62		444,251	3.54	

1: This number is provided each time that official data is available defining the Syrian population.
2: Official data is not available for every year.
SOURCE: UNFPA (2008) *MASHRU' DA'M AL ISTRATIJIYA ALWATANIYA LILSHABÂB FI SURIA.*
Data for Tunisia is calculated from World Bank data available online.

Regarding the total population, each group represented between 3.8% and 4.4%. Taken together, they represent 6.7 million inhabitants or 34% of the Syrian population. Therefore, this group constitutes a significant segment of the population: the 'youth' of Syria can be considered a *generation*. Certainly, its

---

8   I chose Tunisia as a comparison because it exemplifies how Arab countries entered a demographic transition in the late 1970s. In addition to Tunisia being the launching point of the Arab Uprisings, the comparison to Tunisia underlines a key element – the chronological difference between Tunisia and Syria. In Tunisia, the turning point in the demographic growth was in the 1990s while in Syria it was the 2000s.

members are not the same. Some live in cities, others in the countryside; some received a degree, others are illiterate. As Pierre Bourdieu points out, 'youth is just a word' (Bourdieu 1984). However, it makes up a significant section of the population. Studying it allows us to understand continuities and change within the population more broadly.

Comparing the Tunisian and the Syrian natural growth rates, several points need to be underlined. First, both countries witnessed a decline in death rates, which became non-significant. Life expectancy is equivalent in both countries, around 65 years. As well, in the Syrian case, the high birth rate mostly explains the number of children born in the same year. Syria remained at the second stage of demographic transition, where high growth is noticed. However, this process seems to end beginning in the mid-nineties. Consequently, Syrian youth is somehow exceptional both in comparison to other national situations and in comparison to other Syrian generations. It is numerically larger than previous and the future generations, and it can be considered as a demographic peak in Syria.

Understanding this specific demographic history requires looking at political decision-making. As Onn Winckler clarifies (Winckler 1999), most Arab countries long favoured high birth rates in their legislation. This was the case in Syria. After independence, the general project was to increase the population (which was 2.9 million in 1946), in order to become more important in the region. This was directly associated with the national defence project against Israeli forces. Moreover, growth was considered as a proof of development – which it was. During the four first decades of Syrian history, governments improved education and sanitary conditions. This led to a general growth of the population during the next decade due to a sharp decrease in mortality rates. This did not impact demographic behaviour, as most families, who lived mainly in rural areas, continued to have more than five children.

Contrary to other Arab countries, policies in favour of a high birth rate were not changed before 1986. Comparing Tunisia and Syria clearly indicates the discrepancy between the two nations' birth trends. As Youssef Courbage pointed out (1994), while most Arab countries started to undermine the birth rate in the late 1970s, the Syrian authorities kept promoting it in order to generate a general population growth. Three main factors explain this policy: (1) Syria was still at war with Israel and needed to mobilize new soldiers; (2) Baathist ideology promoted the renaissance of the Arab nation, which supposed a general growth of the population; and (3) it seemed difficult for the authorities to promote certain pieces of legislation which attempt to curb the birth rate while they were facing a major uprising by the Muslim brotherhood. In 1986, several reforms were initiated in order to restore global levels of economic stability

(Kienle 1994). Demographic approaches shifted towards limiting the number of births, now considered a burden rather than an opportunity. This policy impacted behaviour at the beginning of the 1990s, and the birth rate started to decrease. Consequently, the generation under study here belongs to the peak of demographic growth in Syria.[9]

This generation shared a common background, which led it to become aware of the political situation in a particular manner. First of all, this generation followed other highly symbolic ones. The first generation who built the country took power in the late 1930s, fighting the French mandate. Shukrī al-Quwwātlī, the first president, was born in 1891 and represented the generation of notables. As Philip Khoury and Patrick Seale highlight (Khoury 1987; Seale 2010), this generation slowly moved away from the Ottoman pattern to behave as a single Syrian entity. They implemented constitutionalist ideas in order to build a new political order in Syria. They remained in power from the 1930s to the 1960s. During the 1960s, they were progressively ousted from power as new generations emerged and claimed their right to take part in the political decision-making process. A high level of instability characterised Syria during the 1950s and 1960s, which led to a shift in the generations governing Syria. Hafez al-Assad and the inner circle who came to power at the end of this process won the support of the old classes at the beginning of 1970s, and managed to establish their government in the country for almost forty years (Batatu 1999). If Hafez al-Asad symbolised the new Baathist regime after 1971, he did not rule alone but through collegiums of trusted people. All shared the same characteristics of age, economic and social background, and level of education. This second generation came together by confronting the previous one and consequently defined itself in competition with the previous one which, in its vocabulary, had become corrupted. Its reign ended at the beginning of 2000, when Hafez al-Assad died and his son was nominated, and then elected, president. The old guard was progressively moved aside. Consequently, the generation which emerged in 2011 may be seen as the third one in Syrian national history.

The general political background of the generation under survey was established during the 1980s. When the oldest of the group (born in 1977) were 10, Syria moved towards a highly personalised system of power guided by Hafez al-Assad. Previous attempts to remove him from power failed. After a long and growing movement of protests between 1976 and 1982 the opposition shifted towards Islamic and jihadist approaches. The disorganization of the protests

---

9 This is not to presume the outcomes of current events, nor a possible adjustment after the civil war, but simply to state that those who were between 20 and 35 in 2011 belong to the most numerous generation in Syria.

and their radicalisation led to the crackdown during the Hama episode. This event exemplified the long-term process of establishing a harsh regime. This was stabilised in the mid-1980s after the 'succession' crisis. When Hafez al-Assad had a heart attack, his brother Rifa`at al-Assad, head of security, led a failed coup attempt in Damascus. He was forced to leave the country (ibid.). A new political order emerged, which remained unchallenged until the late 1990s. As Lisa Wedeen (1999, 27–30) argues, this system was not totalitarian but rather an authoritarian regime in which the population had to behave 'as if' it believed in the ruler and his message, while preventing themselves from taking part in political activities. The youth were educated in this context, which many described as one of stagnation and repression. They were well aware of the cult of personality, as they had to take an oath every day in school. During the 1990s, the youth grew up in a very tense context, in which it inherited from the previous generation the internalisation of the 'normality' of the regime. As I will mention later, intergenerational memory failed, and the long fight of the late 1970s was forgotten. This was mainly due to the educational and coercive systems established in the country.

It is not my purpose here to describe the general framework of the Syrian regime. Several polices competed one against another to control the public sphere, while the inner circle around Hafez al-Assad was balancing the influence of each services. Therefore, no forms of expression were permitted apart from governmentally tolerated ones. This 'informal system' (Zisser 2000; Kienle 1992) was effective at curbing all independent voices. During the 1980s, the generation under study grew up in Soviet-inspired educational institutions. Two main characteristics of these can be emphasized. First, they remained heavily organised and controlled by the Baath party and its agencies. One interviewee said, looking back on the shift away from this mode:

> It was a great change. We did not have to wear the uniform anymore. Previously, we were, as school kids, members of the *futuwa*. Have you heard about this institution? Like the army... (Interviewee A)

Uniforms, anthems, and oaths were used as tools to reinforce the regime and to create a new and homogenised generation. History was a highly sensitive subject in school, as its mission was to raise awareness among the new generation about the corruption of the past and its consequences, as well as colonial encroachment (Freitag 1999). Programs and books were severely controlled to avoid any kind of undesirable presentation of the past. Most of contemporary history was silenced, and when it was spoken about the curriculum focused solely on the Arab struggle rather than on overall Syrian history. Then, during the 1980s, educational institutions were affected by a deep crisis produced by economic shortages:

> Between 1991 and 1994, we left for Libya. My father found a position in Tripoli. The financial situation in Syria was very harsh. As a university professor, he was earning no more than 500 LS... (Interviewee B)

These shortages damaged the educational system which, for many Syrians, became synonymous with a useless and corrupt regime (Huitfeldt and Kabbani 2007). They undermined the transmission of knowledge, and created the potential for a counter-discourse as these youth were becoming teenagers. The destruction of educational institutions created a vacuum in the official version of contemporary history, which was filled by alternative narratives when they became available. Were the changes introduced later by Bashar al-Assad relevant for the group studied? His reforms were formulated at the beginning of 2000 and implemented in 2005–2008, while the generation was exiting educational institutions. They could not have impacted the curriculum used by children born between 1977 and 1995.

Transmission of knowledge and experimentation took place in arenas other than public ones. The family and the neighbourhood seem more relevant to understand their processes of socialization. As Asef Bayat notes (Herrera and Bayat 2010, 7–9), cities – from which most of the interviewees came – allow some room for liberty without control by families. This generation, the most urbanised in Syrian history (more than 55%), represented in this matter a shift compared to previous ones in terms of the decrease of social control on their activities. Since the public sphere was controlled, free education and discussions were sheltered in the family:

> My father explained to me a lot of things about his studies during the sixties. In his school, there were Muslim Brethren, the left, Nasserists, and rich people or rightist guys...at the university, Muslim Brethren and socialists were the most active of them...During this period, it was not possible to be neutral in the political conflict. (Interviewee B)
> During the 50s, it was the golden age. There were Bakdash, Azm, Khuri... It was the only time of freedom in this country, as my father explains to me. (Interviewee C)
> My brother had some difficulties getting access to Lebanese newspapers in the 90s. Therefore, he had the news only ten days later. It was by this process that we heard about the events in 1991...Do you understand? It was very different from 2003. (Interviewee D)

Each answer pointed out the importance of family connections. The father – in both cases these figures belonged to the opposition to the Baathist regime – or the brother played a key role in the promotion of political awareness. But these private talks did not aim to mobilise the youth into political activities and parties. They were rather a private transmission. As studies of European countries have pointed out, political awareness does not emerge from the same mechanisms in the 2000s as it did in the 1960s. Family context seems very important in framing the world's perception of youth, and here the Syrian case is no different. Retreat from the public sphere – highly scrutinized – led the family to become the new arena in which youth had access to other voices. At the same time, this does not imply that the family as a social institution was not criticized. A global shift had affected social institutions such as the family (Hasso 2011).[10]

On the one hand, some interviewees highlighted their problem with the familial environment:

> Family, it's a failed institution (*mu'assassa fashila*). In the whole world, it is important but problems come with it...and 'forever,' what does that mean? (Interviewee E)
> I don't like the family much. It's a support, but as an institution, it is problematic...It gives much too power to somebody, like a king over his subjects. There is something of an arbitrary system (*istibdad*). (Interview EEJ)

Most of the interviewees pointed out how social dynamics reinforce the parents' social power. They articulated clear criticism against the standard or model that prevails in the Arab world, in which they – as kids, teenagers and young adults – had to obey without any reciprocal obligation. But at the same time, they pinpointed how family remains their first support:

> Family, it is eternal relations, it is my priority. My family was always an example of solidarity and harmony. (Interviewee F)
> In everyday life, I can't imagine to live without my family. Relations are very strong. If someone is sad, we're all...If I can do anything for them, I will do it. (Interviewee G)

A shift took place in this generation. While young Syrians keep in mind their familial genealogy and some social aspects of its importance, they emphasize

---

10   This is of course not exclusive to Syria.

privacy above the public role of the family. The inner circle – parents and brothers and sisters – seems more important than other family connections, even if they have some connection to different branches of their families. The family has become a private institution which provides support and understanding, while at the same time its social mechanisms need to be criticised. These different aspects clarify the youth's background and primary socialisation. Does the family's inner circle constitute a homogenous place of political education? This is not easy to answer: it seems that the political involvements of their parents – who had often been imprisoned – meant the second generation was raised in a context of political awareness. On many occasions, however, it is hard to conclude that a lack of concern or a precise political position can be explained by the parents' attitude towards politics.

Institutions of 'secondary socialisation' (Dubar 1998, Gauthier 1999) also played a role in framing the world for this generation. It seems clear that for all the interviewees, schools and universities did not meet their demands in terms of training in knowledge and skills. 'Absence of dialogue,' 'nullity,' 'waste of time' or 'corrupted institution' were common responses. These institutions' functional significance was clearly criticised. However, personal trajectories – which reflect a general trend in Syria – prove that most of the interviewees obtained degrees in university. The global scholarly level had improved and universities and schools had become an important arena of socialisation.

> I refused to continue in Pharmacy. I preferred French literature. There, I met a lot of young guys who shared the same point of view on current issues. We were discussing a lot, particularly our artistic projects. In my opinion, art and freedom come together. I can decide so I am free. (Interview D)
>
> We were following the news with some friends at the university. When Baghdad fell, we went to demonstrate on the campus. We were angry and shocked...We gathered with friends and students...Of course it was not allowed but they let us do it. (Interviewee H)

The university was where groups of closely connected people first met. Shared activities and discussion were the two main means of forming informal groups. Kastrinou Theodoropoulou (2012) highlights as well how financial issues affected this process: paying for rent or basic commodities led some of students to organise 'tontine' – informal financial groups of brokers and credit – to face the difficulties of day-to-day student life. The role of these informal groups in Syria should not be underestimated. They have constituted an important arena for introducing people to one another, and one of the nuclei of the civil movement in 2011. As was the case with the family, youth hijacked the social meaning of an institution that they viewed as an inefficient tool. A second institution which sociologists have investigated is work, which continues to be a life goal for this generation. Job scarcity deeply affects the youth's trajectory, and if the global situation during the 2000s was definitively better than the economic context that prevailed in the 1980s and 90s, the job market was unable to match the new generation's growing demand. It has been estimated that a third of this generation was unemployed.[11] This caused disturbances, as marriage is often linked to young adults' ability to buy an apartment. The age of marriage has increased for men, after a decrease during the 1990s (Balanche 2006). When young people have the opportunity to work, they ascribe it a high value:

> It is a priority. It gives us our achievement in life. (Interviewee G)
> It is important. Contrary to university where we don't learn anything, we can create in work, invent new things. (Interviewee H)

The job environment is conceived of as a space for freedom and change. It provides financial support and independence from the family's control. Moving away from the home gives young people some time away from family obligations. It permits young people to have leisure and funds for non-essential matters. Institutions of secondary socialisation allow the young generation to frame its speech and to extend its abilities in private life. They create the conditions for a new space and time between childhood and adulthood, and therefore permit the emergence of youth as a category. If these new processes are not so different from other contexts – they constitute the Syrian path towards the emergence of youth – their implications seem quite distinct. This became obvious in 2011 when this generation rose against the regime. As mentioned above, the political change was part of a broader dynamic that undermined social control and the social order. Nevertheless, pointing out the social conditions of change does not amount to providing insightful analysis on the conditions of political awareness. It is necessary to focus on this generation's political trajectory in order to understand which events were most important.

Several strata can be studied as key components of historical consciousness. Is the past idealized as a golden age? Was there a particular event that impacted the youth? Did this generation experience particular circumstances such as

---

11   It is very hard to properly estimate unemployment in Syria, as surveys remain highly controlled by the authorities, who refused to recognize the full extent of the crisis (see Lahcen 2011).

wars, upheavals or natural disasters? If so, did members of this group constitute core actors in those movements? I will argue that for this generation, a peripheral event deeply changed their view of the world and current affairs. First of all, how did this generation look at Syrian history? Did they see any glorious periods? It had been quite common to see teenagers reciting classical poems and songs. They have adopted a long-term history as part of their patrimony. But they do not refer to it while acting in daily life, nor when they framed their involvement in social life or political activities. And they gave little attention to contemporary history:

> In 1946...Was it independence? You should know better than me? (Interviewee G)
> In 1946 there was something with Palestine I guess, maybe a war between Israel and Palestine... (Interviewee D)
> In 1946, it was the moment when Sultan Atrash[12] made an alliance with Jordan. He was not yet in favour of Syria and that created some problems. (Interviewee F)

The first two answers clearly indicate the disconnection between an event – the independence of Syria in 1946, which is celebrated every 17th April – and social memory (Halbwachs 1994). Young people did not particularly note this date, but they think about it as one of the elements of the official narrative. In many aspects, the official narrative seems like a strange history without links with their own life. They disregard part of the official discourse as vain propaganda.[13]

The third answer points out another element. The interviewee comes from Suweida, the hometown of Sultan Atrash and capital of the Druze region. He mentioned a local event rather than a national one, and focused on local history. A clear tension between unity and division animates Syrian history and society. Town and village neighbourhoods remain very important, as most events are reframed through local understanding. While questions focus on the first event that comes to the interviewee's mind, most answers point out locality as one of the main aspects of their memories:

---

12 Born in 1879, near Suwayda, Sultan Atrash headed the Druze uprising against the French which turned into a Syrian upheaval in 1925. He had to flow in exile on Jordan. He went back after World War II and pursued some political activities. He is recognised today as a great leader of the Syrian independence movement.

13 This was confirmed by answers about 1963 and 1971. Moreover, the first decade of the Baath party's regime is not well known.

> The most important event I remember...When we came back in Syria. I remember when we were back to our neighborhood. We were living with my family in two different buildings. I had always known these places. It was like a dream to be back. (Interviewee B)
> Can you tell me something about your family?
> In my town, we can see many different people. It was a crossroad between Bedouin and urban people. (Interviewee J)

The interviewees ascribed a high emotional value to their place of birth and life. It may be assumed that the neighbourhood is one of the key units in defining and framing individual understandings. From this point of view, if sectarian division exists in Syria, sectarian oppositions and divisions seem less relevant than geographic ones. This process has roots in the long-term history of Syria. As `Alī al-Wardī (2005) clarifies for the Iraqi case, the neighbourhood was a very important unit of urban life and it is possible to argue, following Michel Seurat's analyses (1985), that a strong sentiment of belonging to a group can emerge from local life in a neighbourhood. It may also carry sectarian characteristics, as in Damascus or Homs where Alawite, Christian and Sunni neighbourhoods stand side by side, but the formal unit remains the neighbourhood rather than sectarian belonging. Local identities filter the news and lead to a specific framing of the world. This largely explains why the election of Bashar al-Assad in 2000 has not been remembered as a key event.

Many analyses identify the so-called Damascus spring between 2000 and 2005 as one of the main causes behind the currently ongoing events (for example, see Lesch 2012). Some argue that the protests had already started during that period. In that case, one would expect it to be well-remembered by the young population. Two questions focused on this event, and their answers are relevant:

> Damascus spring... I don't see what you are talking about... do you mean the Syrian spring? (Interviewee G)
> In 2001, there was a new president. He was the son so everything was normal...I was not aware of the beginning of the Damascus spring in 2011. I became involved and interested during the summer. (Interviewee I)[14]
> I remember 2000. Was it the moment when Basel [al-Assad] died? No sorry, that should be earlier...In all cases, the Damascus spring was for me

---

14   This interviewee confused the Damascus spring in 2001 – a series of conferences, meeting and debates which called for the removal of the emergency law – and the Syrian spring in 2011 – a peaceful uprising.

an aborted experience. There was maybe something but nothing clear. People from another time put forward some requests but we [the youth] were not concerned. (Interviewee D)

Damascus spring? No idea, I was living in Homs. (Interviewee C)

I became aware of the political processes during the Damascus spring. They arrested X; previously, we met him every day and talked to him. One day, they came and caught him. There were at least a hundred *mukhabarat* [intelligence services] men. (Interviewee B)

Two kinds of answers were collected. Most interviewees did not ascribe any importance to these events for two main reasons. First, from their point of view, they concerned another generation and dealt with issues without any practical and immediate meaning. Second, for others, it was a process that occurred in the capital and to which the other inhabitants of Syria were not bound. Third, for many different reasons, mainly the longevity of Hafez al-Assad's rule and its normalization for the youth, as mentioned above, the transition between the two presidents did not raise hopes as it did for older Syrians. The generation under survey was too young to realize what this process meant and how processes could follow different paths. Somehow, the arrival of the new president and the protests which resulted from it did not impact the youth.

The last answer is different from the others. It shows that some of the interviewees witnessed the events as unusual in ordinary life. As the sociology of mobilisation argues (Traïni 2009), it created a moral shock for the protagonists, who suddenly faced the arbitrary violence of the regime. This was not new at the beginning of the 2000s, since most activists from the Muslim Brotherhood and opposition groups were remembered in memoirs and testimonies (Benkorich 2012, Khalifé 2007) as people who had entered the opposition after witnessing violent events and seeing people arrested. However, this raising of awareness did not lead the whole population to rise against the system; therefore, the concept of moral shock is sufficient to explain some mobilisation but remains one cause among others. Several other aspects can be underlined. Rather than pretending that one reason explains the process, it is necessary to put forward a multi-causal model. From this point of view, the Damascus Spring involved the interplay of three dynamics. First, the events took place in privacy, and could be interpreted as an intrusion, the invasion of a personal environment. Second, violence broke down the normal way of doing politics. Third, most witnesses belonged to families committed to politics, and in some cases these families had members in jail. The events consequently took place in a chain of events, and added to older stories. But it is not possible to see the Damascus Spring as the only event which triggered political awareness.

When the Iraqi war broke out in 2003, the youth had been impacted by long-term changes such as the decrease of social control or the economic changes in the country. Certainly, the reforms introduced by the new president Bashar al-Assad exemplified some changes, like the appearance of the Internet in the country (Zisser 2000), although it remained marginal. In this context, the war created a deep crisis. Studies point out how it shook the regime, while the neo-conservative administration justified the possibility of overthrowing a regime in order to promote their vision of a new Middle East. Their attempts on Syria finally failed and at the end of the 2000s relations improved. However, this political stance overshadowed some important outcomes of the crisis. Formal relations between Iraq and Syria have been well-documented and studied. But informal links and ordinary relations have also occasioned some clear and insightful analyses. Since 1991 and the embargo on Iraq, smuggling networks passed through Syria:

> We were aware of Iraqi affairs. Trucks went from Homs to Iraq almost every week. There was some business to do. And in 2002, when the two countries became closer, it became even easier than before. (Interviewee I)

This testimony sheds light on the different connections between localities across the two countries' borders. When the war started, followed by an insurgency against the American occupation, these networks increased Syrians' sensibility towards the Iraqi population. Some mechanisms fuelled the departure of sections of Syrian fighters to Iraq, to fight against the 'colonial' power. Although many of these people turned out to be jihadists or Islamists, most reports clarified that their primary motives remained more nationalistic than religious. On the ground they became radicalized and came closer to al-Qaeda affiliated groups. A great bulk of these newcomers on the Iraqi stage came from the regions of the Hawran and Euphrates rivers.[15] When they tried to return after the mid-2000s, they were arrested by the political police, and labelled as terrorists by their former recruiters. This does not mean that they had not taken part in such operations, but it shows a process which turned ordinary Syrians into jihadist prisoners. This was the first and the most well-known consequence on the Syrian population of the events in Iraq.

Further outcomes can be noticed and analysed. Two events received great concern from the young Syrians interviewed: the fall of Baghdad in 2003, and the execution of Saddam Hussein. These two events are not always separated in the narrative:

---

15   Interviews with Wladimir Glasman, Paris, April 2012.

The War in Iraq, it was the first time I became aware of world issues. This came through my collaboration with Palestinian refugees and the Taneq camp issue. I had many conversations. It was the moment when words such as freedom and dangers received a concrete meaning...Through discussions with Iraqi refugees, these words received a new meaning. It was not anymore a 'bomb' or an 'explosion.' I could understand through their stories what happened, how it was. I discovered the reality of the event. We [Syrians] saw people from inside. It was not just a show on television... I remember when Baghdad fell. At the beginning, it was a surprise: how quickly it all happened. It took only an hour to conquer the city...When they caught Saddam...It was a shock. There was a gap between 'the Great guy' and 'the prisoner he was'...Moreover, his execution took place during the festivities ['aid al-kabir]...he was just an ordinary man. He might have been any ordinary guy. At the end, he was just a guy. (Interviewee D)
The Fall of Baghdad, it was terrible. I got the impression that the world crumbled, that the Americans would be here [Syria] the next day and that everything would be upside down.
What is the first event that you remember?
Nothing before the revolution [in March 2011]
What can you tell me about the Damascus spring?
Nothing, as I told you, before the uprising [*intifada*] nothing was important.
And about the war in Iraq?
Yes! I clearly remember it! I keep a clear memory of this war. If something could happen there, it might occur everywhere. If they did it in Iraq, they would do it everywhere. Iraq was the first Arab country...I don't speak about its system, it's different. Iraq had a high standard of living, high level of education...In the 90s, we talked a lot about Iraq. We developed strong ties with Iraq during the embargo. From the human point of view (*min al-nahia al-insaniyya*) we felt the oppression (*zulm*). (Interview I)

These different answers highlight three points about Iraq. First, these events can be qualified as a social trauma which greatly affected significant segments of the populations without any direct ties between them. The different images they presented refer to the end of the world, the collapse of ordinary life, or destruction and chaos. They showed violent death as something ordinary rather than exceptional. Violent confrontation has to receive further investigation, as it can generate new perceptions on the world: it breaks the sense of the future as an already known path. What would have been unthinkable – brutal death – suddenly emerged as a potentiality. A second set of feelings emerges from the two events. Globally, this underscores a shift toward Arab affairs. These were not understood though the Arab nationalist lens, as had been the case in the previous decades. Interviewees rather looked at the events through the spectrum of a humanitarian crisis. This confirms Caroline Donati's (2009) insightful remarks about the Palestinian situation: Arab people were no longer a single political unit, but they were perceived as belonging to particular one (Iraqi, Palestinian, etc.); as people, their suffering sparked strong feelings of solidarity and attempts to help. Third, the political signification of the events raises two contradictory outcomes. On the one hand, the Iraqi system was denounced as oppressive and brutal; although the American invasion and its consequences seemed to have created a more violent situation. The regime's collapse was seen as an offence and a surprise. On the other hand, the quick overthrow proved how weak Saddam Hussein's rule had become. Moreover, his execution showed him as an ordinary man: it was possible to bring one of the most powerful and brutal dictators to a common death. Processes of desecration and disenchantment overthrew the old-fashioned idols. None of the regimes and their rulers were eternal or invincible. This change deeply affected a generation that had been raised on the idea that the chief of the nation would normally be ruling the country forever.

Why did these events impact the youth to this extent? First of all, this was a result of the revolutionary change brought by satellite channels. For the very first time, news was streamed continuously, and events could be followed on a day to day basis without the filter of official propaganda. Unlike the war of 1991, which was not really covered by the Syrian press – the events were silenced, as Syria took part in the international coalition, and the case was presented as a struggle against a traitor to the Arab cause – the war of 2003 was highly scrutinized by Syrians and the authorities allowed information to spread throughout the country. From their point of view, it gave proof of imperialist aggression against the Arab nation; but they underestimated the outcomes. Awareness arose at first from the news and its images, but this was not the only factor in the sensitivity that the events created. Progressively, between 2003 and 2008, Syria welcomed hundreds of thousands of refugees fleeing sectarian violence in Iraq. The exact number remains controversial, but the phenomenon represented a clear social event, as thousands of inhabitants came to live in the suburbs. A dual process took place in the city. As prices increased heavily in the 2000s, mostly in real estate, a large bulk of the middle class moved to new suburbs in the large cities. Jaramana, next to Damascus, exemplified this. These locations were also the places where Iraqis had found shelter (Chatelard and Doraï 2011). Daily exchanges and shared experiences took place. Moreover, the Iraqi refugee issue led to some change in Syrian charity networks, which started to collaborate with new foreign NGOs to support this population. This clearly indicates that the arrival of Iraqis shed new light on the crisis, and that each Syrian community could identify some common points with the discourse on Iraq. This was particularly true for Christian communities, which were traumatized by their arrival, seeing it as the revelation of the extermination of the Christians in the Middle East. The same events were refracted into different interpretations among the different groups. For Christians it resonated as a disaster, for Sunnis as a massive humanitarian crisis, etc. The twin processes – satellite television and the flow of refugees – deeply undermined Syrians' shared views, especially among the youth. To some extent, we might wonder how this process could be compared to the Nakba in 1948.[16] In both cases, the displaced people revealed a crisis which led soon afterwards to turmoil. But this assertion would need to be explored in more detail. The main result was the emergence of a new generation marked by the massive flow of refugees.

Echoing Jean-François Sirinelli's argument (2008), it would be simplistic to sum up this generation's trajectory by pointing to the upheaval in 2011. Several factors came into play, and they led to several different paths. However, it is true this generation made up the bulk of the actors in 2011 and thereafter. On both sides, which can be qualified generally as 'regime' and 'opposition,' groups of young people gathered in protests and then later on in armed groups.[17] Their awareness could be traced directly to the Iraqi crisis. The events there proved that some changes can occur even if a regime seems irremovable and brutal. They also led this generation to confront general destruction and massive death. They certainly created a dual reaction. On the one hand they increased fear of sectarianism and division, which fuelled inaction for some Syrians and discourses of national harmony for others (such as the revolutionary slogan, 'Syria, onc, the Syrian people are one'). On the other hand, they broke down the imaginary boundaries – what the French historian Lucien Febvre (1942) qualifies as 'outillage mental' or mental tools – which prevented the youth from

---

16   In 1948, more than 80,000 Arabs from Palestine reached Syria, mainly to Damascus where they gathered in a new area – the Yarmuk camp. Their arrival was highly commented in the press and shocked Syrians, as it materialised Arab defeat and failure.

17   While this article was being written (October 2014), fighters in Syria were mostly Syrian. On the opposition side, the number of foreign fighters has slowly increased since the end of 2012, to reach 10 to 30,000 (depending on sources). The number of Syrian in the opposition forces has been estimated as between 90,000 to 120,000 at the end of summer 2014. On the regime side, the size of the Syrian troops is hard to estimate, but probably 150.000 to 200.000, while foreign fighters (from Lebanon, Iraq, Yemen etc.) are estimated at between 30,000 to 60,000 at the beginning of the summer 2014.

thinking about the exceptionality of the regime. They undermined its 'normality' and created a space of opportunity. I will not conclude that the Iraq war alone triggered the uprising in 2011. Nevertheless, it contributed to the political awareness of a new generation. This generation had already been affected by several social processes which changed its social position. The convergence of the political crisis and social dynamics sparked the upheaval in 2011.

The ongoing events in Syria shed light on this country and its society, which previously had not been subject to much clear insight. Political phenomena and foreign policy were the two main topics of mainstream research, even if a new generation of scholars pointed out new subjects. These questions were linked to the social changes which affected the different classes and communities of Syria. The present chapter attempts to shed light on one of these constituencies, the youth, and more precisely on how young people in Syria became a generation during the 2000s. This group is particularly important as it has been the mass force in the present conflict, but also because it represents a third of the population. This generation – defined as a demographic group – was the most numerous population in Syrian history and it remained so for a decade. It was affected by certain very important social dynamics. Out of these trends, including among others urbanisation, population growth, and a rise in the level of education, a process of individualization resulted. Social controls were undermined and new social spaces and time were available for these youth to build their environment. Certainly, new technologies contributed to extending and strengthening these new worlds by creating connection where there had been discontinuities. But, the decrease of social control lifted the fear somewhat and created the social opportunity for the emergence of a youth. Turmoil in the region, mainly the Iraq war, impacted this generation's path. They became aware of the humanitarian crisis and its outcomes; they faced the possibility of changing a political regime well known for its sustainability and its brutality. The turmoil shook the mental and social boundaries of the core of the Syrian population. In several aspects, it opened the road to the uprising. Certainly, the events since 2011 have reframed this generation's way of thinking and its practices. They have exacerbated its divisions, its social and confessional profiles, and its different opportunities in life. However, the Iraqi war provided the decisive step in the generation's emergence and formation.

References

Al-`Azmih, Bashīr. *Jīl al-hazīma bayn al-wahda wa al-infiṣāl: mudhakkarāt*. London: Riyad al-Rayyes, 1991.

Allawi, Ali. *The Occupation of Iraq: Winning the War, Losing the Peace.* New Haven: Yale University Press, 2007.

Al-Wardî, `Alî. *"Lamhât ijtimâ`iyya mîn târîkh al-`irâq al-hadîth"* (Social elements of the history of the Modern Iraq). Bagdad: Dâr wa Maktaba al-mutanayya 1, 2005.

Attias-Donfut, Claudine. *Sociologie des Générations, l'Empreinte du Temps.* Paris: Presses Universitaires de France, 1988.

Balanche, Fabrice. *La Région Alaouite et le Pouvoir Syrien.* Paris: Karthala, L'Harmattan, 2006.

Batatu, Hana. *Syria's Peasantry, the Descendants of Its Lesser Rural Notables and Their Politics.* Princeton: Princeton University Press, 1999.

Becchi, Eglia and Dominique Julia. *Histoire de l'enfance.* Tome I : *De l'Antiquité au xviie siècle. Tome II : Du xviiie siècle à nos jours.* Paris : Seuil, 1998.

Benkorich, Nora. "La Tentation de la Lutte Armée Contre le Pouvoir Baasiste en Syrie. Passé (1976–1982) et Présent (2011)." *Le débat* 168, 1 (2012): 155–167.

Boissière, Thierry. "Les Limites d'une Approche Confessionnelle de la Crise Syrienne." *Libération*, June 12, 2012.

Bonnefoy, Laurent and Myriam Catusse. *Jeunesses Arabes.* Paris: La Découverte, 2013.

Bourdieu, Pierre. "La Jeunesse n'est qu'un Mot," in *Questions de Sociologie 1978*, 520–553. Paris: éd. Minuit, 1984.

Chatelard, Géraldine and Mohamed Kamel Doraï. "Les Irakiens en Syrie et en Jordanie: Régimes d'Entrée et de Séjour et Effets sur les Configurations Migratoires." CERISCOPE *Frontières*, 2011. http://ceriscope.sciences-po.fr/content/part2/les-irakiens-en-syrie-et-en-jordanie.

Chiffoleau, Sylvia. "La Syrie au Quotidien. Cultures et Pratiques du Changement Présentation." *Revue des Mondes Musulmans et de la Méditerranée* 2006: 115–116. http://remmm.revues.org/3008#text.

Courbage, Youssef. "Evolution Démographique et Attitudes Politiques en Syrie," *Populations* 49, 3 (1994): 725–749.

DeFronzo, James. *The Iraq War: Origins and Consequences.* Boulder, Colombia: Westview Press, 2010.

Donati, Caroline. *L'Exception Syrienne: Entre Modernisation et Résistance.* Paris: La Découverte, 2009.

Doraï, Kamel. "Le Rôle de la Syrie dans l'Accueil des Réfugiés Irakiens Depuis 2003: Espace de Transit, Espace d'Installation." *Méditerranée* 113 (2009): 139–146.

Dubar, Claude. *La Socialisation, Construction Sociale et Professionnelle des Identités.* Paris: Armand Colin, 1998.

Dupret, Baudoin, et al. *La Syrie au Présent. Reflets d'une Société.* Paris: Sindbad, Actes Sud, Ifpo, 2007.

Febvre, Lucien. *La Religion de Rabelais, le Problème de l'Incroyance au xvie Siècle.* Paris: Albin Michel, 1942.

Freitag, Ulrike. "In Search of Historical Correctness: the Ba'th Party in Syria." *Middle Eastern Studies*, 35 (1999): 1–16.

Gauthier, Madeleine. "La Jeunesse, un Mot. Combien de Définitions?" in *Définir la Jeunesse?: D'un Bout à l'Autre du Monde*, edited by Madelaine Gauthier and Jean-François Guillaume, 6–15. Sainte Foy: Ed. IQRC, 1999.

Haddad, Fanar. *Sectarianism in Iraq: Antagonistic Visions of Unity*. London: C. Hurst and Co, 2011.

Halbwachs, Maurice. *Les Cadres Sociaux de la Mémoire*. Paris: Albin Michel, 1994.

Hasso, France Susan. *Consuming Desires: Family Crisis and the State in the Middle East*. Stanford: Stanford University Press, 2011.

Herrera, Linda and Asef Bayat. *Being Young and Muslim, New Cultural Politics in the Global South and North*. Oxford: Oxford University Press, 2010.

Hosseini, Khaled. "The Lost generation." The New York Times. April 11, 2014. https://www.nytimes.com/2014/04/13/opinion/sunday/syrias-lost-generation.html?_r=0

Hughes, Everett H. *Le Regard Sociologique: Essais Choisis*. Paris: ed. EHESS, 1996.

Huitfeldt, Henrik and Nader Kabbani. *Returns to Education and the Transition from School to Work in Syria*. Beirut: American University of Beirut, 2007.

Huntington, Samuel. *The Clash of Civilizations and the Remaking of World Order*. New York: Simon and Schuster, 1996.

Keegan, John. *The Iraq War*. New York: A.A. Knopf, 2004.

Khalifé, Moustapha. *La Coquille: Prisonnier Politique en Syrie*. Paris: Actes Sud, 2007.

Khoury, Philip. *Syria and the French Mandate*. London: I.B. Tauris, 1987.

Kienle, Eberhard. *Entre Jama`a et Classe: le Pouvoir Politique en Syrie*. Berlin: Das Arabische Buch, 1992.

Kienle, Eberhard (ed.). *Contemporary Syria. Liberalization between Cold War and Cold Peace*. London: British Academic Press, 1994.

Lahcen Achy. "Syrie: les Difficultés économiques Alimentent les Tensions Sociales," Carnegie Middle East Center. March 31, 2011. http://carnegie-mec.org/2011/03/31/syrie-les-difficult%C3%A9s-%C3%A9conomiques-alimentent-les-tensions-sociales/b785.

Lesch, David. *Syria: The Fall of the House of Assad*. New Haven: Yale University Press, 2012.

Little, Douglas. *American Orientalism: The United States and the Middle East since 1945*. North Hill: University of North Carolina Press, 2008.

Mannheim, Karl. "The Problem of Generations," in *Essays on the Sociology of Knowledge*, edited by Karl Paul Kecskemeti, 276–320. London: Routledge, 1972.

Murphy, Emma. "Problematizing Arab Youth: Generational Narratives of Systemic Failure." *Mediterranean Politics* 17 (2012): 1–5.

Pierret, Thomas. *Religion and State in Syria. The Sunni Ulama from Coup to Revolution*. Cambridge: Cambridge University Press, 2013.

Seale, Patrick. *Riad al-Solh and the Makers of the Modern Middle East.* Cambridge: Cambridge University Press, 2010.

Seurat, Michel. "Le Quartier de Bab Tebbane à Tripoli (Liban): étude d'une 'Assabiyya Urbaine," in *Mouvements Communautaires et Espaces Urbains au Machreq.* Beirut: ed. CERMOC, 1985.

Sirinelli, Jean François. "Génération, Générations." *Vingtième Siècle, Revue d'Histoire* 98, 2 (2008): 113–124.

Tejel, Jodi, et al. (eds.). *Writing the Modern History of Iraq: Historiographical and Political Challenges.* Singapore: World Scientific Company, 2013.

Theodoropoulou, Kastrinou. "A Different Struggle for Syria: Becoming Young in the Middle East." *Mediterranean Politics* 17 (2012): 1–5.

Traïni, Christophe. "Choc Moral,"in *Dictionnaire des Mouvements Sociaux,* edited by Olivier Fillieule, Lilian Mathieu and Cécile Péchu, 101–107. Paris: Presses de Sciences Po, 2009.

UNFPA. *Mashrū`da`m al-istrātijiya al-wataniyya li-l-shabāb fī sūriya.* Project of National strategic support of the youth in Syria, 2008.

Wedeen, Lisa. *Ambiguities of Domination, Politics, Rhetoric and Symbols in Contemporary Syria.* Chicago: Chicago University Press, 1999.

Winckler, Onn. *Demographic Developments and Population Policies in Ba'thist Syria.* Portland: Sussex Academic Press, 1999.

Yetiv, Steve. "The Iraq War of 2003: Why Did the United States Decide to Invade?" in *The Middle East and the United States: A Historical and Political Reassessment,* edited by David Lesch, 401–407. Boulder: Westview press, 2007.

Zisser, Eyal. *Asad's Legacy, Syria in Transition.* New York: New York University Press, 2000.

CHAPTER 5

Together, but Divided: Trajectories of a Generation[1] of Egyptian Political Activists (From 2005 to the Revolution)[2]

Chaymaa Hassabo

Introduction

Since demonstrations broke out all over Egypt on January 25th 2011, culminating in the toppling of Mubarak after 18 days of mass protests and inaugurating a "revolutionary situation" (Tilly, 1978), observers have focused on the role of *Shabâb al-thawra,* the 'youth of the revolution.' This designation has come to encompass not only the youth activists, groups and movements that called for the 'making of the revolution,' but more generally all young Egyptians who participated in the revolutionary events. In fact, both media and academic circles have presented this *shabâb al-thawra* as a 'concrete group' of individuals who, because they are young, share a generational belonging and therefore partake in the same attitudes, political orientations and methods of revolution.

This use of the term *youth of the revolution* as a category designating a concrete group has glossed over many questions and issues regarding how the participation of certain strata of society (or, for that matter, of age-based groups of populations) in historical events should be understood, as well as the more complex theme of generational phenomena and the identification of concrete generational groups. Moreover, this categorization denies the peculiarities of people's different individual or collective trajectories, as well as of the groups and networks these people create. A confusion of sorts is apparent here between *belonging* to an age-based group and having the *same orientation* towards historical events or sharing common political views. This

---

1 Some clarifications should be made regarding the use of the term generation: I use 'political generation' and 'generation(s) of activists' interchangeably to address those activists who joined a wave of mobilization at approximately the same moment and came into politics together. When generation is used in the singular, it is generally has this meaning. On the other hand, 'generational units' is used to identify the decomposition of political generations into groups and networks with ideological affiliations similar to those of the decomposed generation of activists. A 'youth movement' designates an organized age-based group, whose members share the same political opinions and attitudes.

2 I would like to deeply thank Nancy Ali and Victor Salama for their editing of this text.

© KONINKLIJKE BRILL NV, LEIDEN, 2017 | DOI 10.1163/9789004344518_007

interpretation may originate in generational gap theory, which posits the simplistic assumption that the "'young' generation is (always) 'liberal' and the 'old' generation is 'conservative'" (Rintala 1963, 512). Thus, a revolution must be a *youth* action that responds to a *youth* demand. Certainly, the major participants in the revolutionary events come from a *younger* age-based group, if we follow a demographic analysis, but this should not lead to the automatic assumption that only one unique group or generation was present.

Furthermore, this categorization has also been largely exploited and manipulated by the various Egyptian governments and regimes that have come to power since Mubarak, either to find the 'causes' of this youth participation (generally found in theories of *relative frustration*) or to yield some concessions to relieve the anger of youth (Allal and El Chazli 2012).[3] In other words, by associating the revolution with youth, its causes could be simplistically reduced to a reaction to unemployment and socio-economic deprivation (Jamal and Hoffman 2012), themselves consequences of the substantial youth bulge.

Moreover, substantial attention has been placed on the pivotal role of the Internet and the use young activists made of digital social networks. In a way, digital technology is a marker of these youth, their generational marker. It is therefore commonly proclaimed that this 'Revolution 2.0' was created by a Facebook and Twitter generation. All of these interpretations tend, as Jean-François Sirinelli noted of the '68 generation(s)' in France, to identify a "homogenous actor of the events, with an emblematic character, *the* young" (Sirinelli 2008, 116). In the Egyptian context both academic and media circles tried to answer the question of 'why' the youth participated or were naturally keen to participate in the Revolution by in general adopting a macro-scale approach, considering the presence of youth as reflecting a single reality and movement.

Still, a burning question remains, a question that is at the core of the discussion about generational phenomenon and that goes well beyond the Egyptian case: *what age bracket does this title of 'youth' encompass, and what is youth?* Does 'youth' automatically refer to the 15–25 age group? Could it be extended to 30 or even 45?

In Egypt, for instance, the dynamics of politics and of 'generational' phenomena are caught up in the opposition between young/reformist and old/conservative. The official representation of what *youth* is, of what a *new guard* is, and the automatic association of these criteria with being 'more modern, more open to the West' and with a more reformist vision of politics, was for a

---

3   In their article, Amin Allal and Youssef El Chazli criticize – through a comparison between Tunisian and Egyptian revolutionary situations – the interpretation of the motivation of youth participation in politics implied by such approaches.

long time encapsulated by the former president's son Gamal Mubarak and his clique. When they entered into politics they were between their late thirties and late forties (even extending to mid-fifties in some cases). When Mohamed Morsi, after he was elected president in 2012 after the revolution, decided to make room for some 'young' opposition representatives within the government or in the Constituent Assembly, nominees were in their early thirties or early forties. When a number of activists from many political groups created the 'Coalition of Revolutionary Youth' they were on average between twenty-five and thirty-nine, although the largest mass of young participants in revolutionary events were between fifteen and twenty-five years old. In this sense, this article departs from generalizing patterns and adopts a micro-level approach. Thus the main concern here is not to ask why youth are keen to participate in revolutionary events, but rather how historical and personal trajectories converge at a given moment, in order to observe "what is made by actors who are themselves being made by the events" (De Queiroz and Ziolkowski, cited in Fillieule 2001, 100).

This focus on trajectories has two main goals. Firstly, it helps to identify political generation(s), drawing on Mannheim's definition, as going beyond biological belonging to an age group. Mannheim's definition points to the impact of historical moments on the formation of concrete groups based on self-conscious belonging to a generational 'collective identity' (Mannheim 1952). Secondly, it leads to the question of the impact of historical moments on the individual trajectories of young activists, and how such moments actually determine the decomposition of political generations. Through a particular case study of one Egyptian group of activists, I will argue that they have formed a 'political generation' that acts as a self-conscious group, whose members share the same location from a socio-historical viewpoint (Mannheim 1952). I will show how the members of this generation of activists have changed following contact with a historical event, a 'turning point' (Abbott 2001), in this case the revolution. This will lead to a discussion of the notions of youth and of generation, as well as to an inquiry into how the evolution of events and of mobilization momentum can provide a significant and concrete example of the formation of political generations. At the same time, though, these influences might also enable decomposition into rival 'generational units' that, if we follow Karl Mannheim, relate to how individuals within the same generation can interpret and re-appropriate events and circumstances (Mannheim 1952). More precisely, the main intention here is to discuss the transformation of a political generation when it comes in contact with a revolutionary moment.

To demonstrate how this generation of activists has been formed, and why it can in fact be referred to as a generation following Mannheim's definition, it is necessary to first retrace the historical background in which this generation

TOGETHER, BUT DIVIDED

of activists was formed. A description of the political context of Mubarak's last few years in power is required to explain how the emergence of a political context marked by a number of events and 'protest moments' (Favre 1990) contributed to the formation of a political generation of activists. (1) A number of theoretical and methodological aspects will be discussed, related to debates on the formation of a generation, on youth, and on how generational phenomena matter for the continuity and the maintenance of mobilization and for the transmission of activist values; (2) Focusing on generational experience, tracing trajectories of individuals will be necessary in order to understand the interrelation between events and generational phenomena; and (3) The shift in focus from a macro-level analysis of youth participation in the revolution to a micro-level analysis of youth trajectories is necessary in order to better understand the particularities of each case. All this will point to the absence of a concrete age-based group of *'shabab al-thawra'* as a political generational grouping that shares the same political attitudes and the same ways of making revolution, and which is systematically opposed to other groups that are not identified or represented as young. The idea here is to *shed light on the trajectories of 'young' activists* who shared the same political generation (the *Kifâya* momentum), and who, even though all are of Leftist political leanings, disagree on every step taken *since the establishment of the revolutionary stance.*

Notes on Methodology

Some methodological aspects and choices made in this chapter should be addressed, particularly regarding the identities of interviewees and of some groups of youth activists. Even though the interviewees are 'public' figures, i.e. generally well-known activists from before January 25th 2011, who make their ideas and their stances on events and affairs public, and who are 'institutionalized' in that they participate in both conventional and unconventional politics, I will not mention their names. Biographical details will only be given to help contextualize their backgrounds, as well as their socialization process and gradual involvement in politics. The issue of citing the names of youth activists – especially those who are 'well known' – is problematic, since the choice not to cite names is usually either an ethically-driven decision (Onodera 2011, 70)[4] or one imposed from a security viewpoint. In a political situation where the

---

4 I share here Onodera's point of view with regards to the sensitive issue of whether or not to cite the activists' names, especially the ethical argument he makes in his article that many of the observations made by researchers are based on the experiences of those anonymous activists and should thus be accredited to them.

arbitrary use of violence and repression is exercised against many sectors of youth activism, whether to give names or not is a delicate and contentious issue, and it is important to remain mindful of the fact that omitting their names might lead to neglecting the decisive roles these individuals have played in politics.

The interviews presented are biographical, tracing the trajectories of each activist (his/her socialization process, his/her interests, his/her engagement in political activism, his/her periods of abeyance, etc.). Some of the interviews were carried out longitudinally, meeting up regularly with activists since 2006 (or later) during each new mid- to large-scale political event. This long-term broad perspective has also made it possible to reconstruct, through individual trajectories, the trajectories of groups, networks and movements created by these young activists. My observations are Cairo-based, and mainly take into consideration biographical information, political trajectories and actions in the capital. Other studies show the existence of similar groups in other cities.[5]

Since January 25th 2011, I have started to broaden the circles of interviewees to include newcomers on the political scene. The use of longitudinal perspective as well as the widening of the sample of interviewees to include newcomers belonging to other generations of activists have made it possible to observe intra- and inter-generational conflicts between the generations of youth that have interacted together within revolutionary events, while also showing how this has contributed to the larger process of societal and political change. What is interesting about the interviews is that they also function as an important collection of oral testimonies about the recent situation in Egypt. In addition, new factors appeared to be crucial in the process of socialization of these activists, for instance the eruption and intensification of the use of violence as a component of political interaction, and the establishment of elections as a process of institutionalizing popular expression.

Some of the interviews since January 25th 2011 were conducted immediately in the aftermath of events, whereas others were carried out later on, letting activists narrate the events with more distance and perspective. The many events that Egypt has witnessed since the inception of a 'revolutionary situation' also influenced the flow of the interviews and the questions addressed to those activists: important self-criticisms could be tested over time, and connected to attitudes towards both individual and collective trajectories. This relates to the importance of a longitudinal approach in interviewing activists, in order to understand the process of participation and commitment in politics

---

5   Here it is worth mentioning the ongoing doctoral research of Youssef El Chazli on activism in Alexandria between 2000–2011.

Mubarak's Last Years in Power and the Return of "street politics"

From the year 2000 onwards, Egypt witnessed a renewal of 'street politics' as a mode of *unconventional* political participation (Bayat 1997).[6] This was first directed toward external events and causes, for instance demonstrations in solidarity with the Second Palestinian Intifada in 2000 and against the War in Iraq in March 2003. These mobilizations served as a platform to indirectly confront the Mubarak regime, and furnished a platform for discussing the domestic situation. During these years a new actor entered into politics, prompting a debate over a 'Syrian scenario' where the transfer of power in Egypt would be hereditary. The introduction of Gamal Mubarak, via the National Democratic Party, as an ostensible representative of a new guard, a young generation of reformists who would lead the process of modernizing both the party and the country, and as a man opposed to an old generation of incumbents, led to number of political changes. First of all, it made the regime allow some room for newcomers, adopting new constitutional amendments to potentially 'legitimize' the election of Gamal Mubarak through 'pluralistic' elections. It also changed the equilibrium the incumbents had maintained until then between the government and the party. On the other hand, this newly created situation revived the debate over the transmission of power and opened the way for contestation.

A large front of opposition members was formed to oppose Mubarak's hold on power, directed against both father and son. A number of movements for change were created as early as 2004. One of the first concrete movements of this kind was the Egyptian Movement for Change, better known under the name of *Kifâya* ('enough' in Arabic). Its originality lay in the fact that it was composed of representatives from across the entire political spectrum who were bringing politics to the streets, and was thus without a clear ideological line. Yet its numbers remained limited to a few thousand even at its most heated level of momentum. Movements such as *Kifâya*, or its successors like

---

6 What I call here *unconventional* political participation is the taking of political debate to the streets without seeking institutionalization of any kind, as opposed to conventional political participation through political parties, parliaments, etc.

the Egyptian Association for Change created in 2010, which revolved around the personality of Muhammad al-Baradî,' were attempting to create an alternative opposition to the formally existing political parties, those legal political parties that were largely considered to be an opposition tolerated by or in support of the state (Zartman 1988, 61–87). Furthermore, these movements tried to find a third option between the legal and official parties and the Muslim Brotherhood, described often as the only and the most important – but hence controlled – opposition to the Mubarak's regime. These movements, and other forms of mobilization that touched all spectra of society, especially workers, served between 2004 and 2010 as a platform for the inauguration of newcomers, essentially young Egyptians, into activism. In fact, the years between 2005 and 2010 witnessed multiple youth-initiated movements and networks that led to the major protest moments that occurred during this time. Many of those movements and networks were the same ones that called for revolution on January 25th, 2011.

It must be noted that direct or indirect protests against the regime extended to nearly all sectors of society. This made it obvious that there was a development of a "culture of protest" (Beinin 2007, 234). In general, even though the regime and the political authorities would sometimes bend to the demands of some of the strikes and protests by socio-economic actors, most often they responded by intimidating political demonstrators or repressing them with riot police. It is worth mentioning that one of the main changes that occurred during this period was that Mubarak gave unprecedented power to the Ministry of the Interior and to the State Security Services (*Amn al-Dawla*, a political police of sorts), both of which had (and still have) unlimited and arbitrary powers.

The Formation of 'Political Generation(s)' of Young Activists

I argue that the period of 2005–2010 witnessed the formation of three main political generational units of activists – all located in Cairo – who made up the main spectrum of youth activism and politics in the Egyptian capital. A particular event or moment of mobilization marked each of these groups of activists. In that sense, they form *de facto* a 'political generation.' Actually, as Marvin Rintala points out in his essay on political generations, "the major emphasis of a generation's approach to politics…has been upon the reaction to very specific and concrete historical events of those in their formative years during these events" (Rintala 1963, 518). The common characteristics shared by these generations of activists were, mainly, that their action was directed toward the internal sphere, that their intention was to *'change something,'* that

TOGETHER, BUT DIVIDED

their uniting feature was their age and thus the feeling of being young, and the fact that they shared a common perception of their socio-political context.

In fact it appears here that "...the dynamics of the formation of political generations appears to be that historical circumstances...and mobilization forces...have combined during certain periods in history to form active political generations" (Braungart and Braungart 1986, 217–218). The first wave of these generational movements was formed in the momentum of the *Kifâya* movement. This first generation coalesced in various forms. The most 'structured' grouping came under the name of *Youth for Change* (Hassabo 2009), and the loose networks of bloggers-activists grouped in a network called the Movement of February 30th. This federation of youth activists, most of them newly committed to politics, transcended all political orientations and affiliations and went beyond ideological differences. This first generation of activists and early networks of activists and political bloggers operated as a sort of 'incubator movement' for other generations. The second generation of activists was created around the aftermath of the 6th of April, 2008, when a Facebook page created by two activists, one of them belonging to the first generation of activists, called for a day of general strike in solidarity with the workers of Ghazl al-Mahalla.[7] Later in June, the two co-founders of the Facebook page created the Sixth of April Youth Movement. This movement was interested in peaceful change, and has been generally compared to the Serbian Otpor youth movement. During the summer of 2010, a young man named Khaled Sa'îd from Alexandria was killed after being beaten up by two sub-officers. An anonymously administrated Facebook group under the name of *Kullina Khâlid Sa'îd* (We Are All Khaled Said) started to call for simultaneous silent demonstrations in several cities. It would later become news that the page administrator had known Islamist tendencies during the years of political protest in Egypt, and had somehow been linked to the blogosphere network and to the *Kifâya* generation. The murder of Khalîd Sa'id converged with the entry onto the political scene of Muhammad al-Barad'î, who was introduced as a potential president of Egypt and as a symbol for change. Newcomers to politics who began their commitment in this context have contributed to creating a new generation of activists. This third generation's experience, under the authoritarian rule of the Mubarak regime, differs from the previous ones in their commitment to silent,

---

7 The Workers of Misr Company for Spinning and Weaving, one of the biggest textile company in Egypt, went on one the biggest strikes of the last years of the Mubarak era. On April 6th, 2008, the workers were not successful in going on strike, but their city, Mahalla al-Kubra, saw a three-day riot.

apolitical, 'conservative' demonstrations, at least in the first actions led by the *Kullina Khaled Sa'id* facebook page.

It should be noted that at each of these moments, previous networks and generations of activists mobilized and created new movements. Between each wave of momentum of political mobilization, structures would not survive, and activists would go into *abeyance* (Taylor 1989). Therefore, in between surges of mobilization momentum there were small-scale events that united those activists again on more focused campaigns and activities, and helped maintain the relations between activists within each generation and between them. More obviously, these in-between moments would also make possible the small-scale entry into politics of new activists who joined any of the existing generations. Furthermore, those in-between moments have had major impacts on the socialization and politicization processes in activists' trajectories. They are 'abeyance' moments, or a suspended time of reflection about activism or course to be taken. They are also moments where activists would take care of personal lives that sometimes were put on hold or even damaged by the risks of activism (this is especially the case, for example, when activists received prison sentences).

The 'Kifâya Generation'

> We have realized that we have lived all of our lives under Mubarak's presidency and under the Emergency Law...This is the keyword of our generation. We are generations who in reality have lived under Emergency Law, we have not known Egypt in any other situation that one of Exception. For us, Egypt has always been a State of 'Emergency' / 'Exceptional' [laws]. We have not known Egypt in any other state.[8]

Margaret and Robert Braungart have noted that "a political generation is said to come into existence when an age group rejects the existing order, joins together, and attempts to direct the course of politics as its generational mission" (Braungart and Braungart 1986, 217). When asked why they became interested in and participated in politics, a number of activists responded with a very simple answer: they had the feeling that 'something must change.' This feeling was further fueled by the opportunity presented to them by the rise of the *Kifâya* movement, which offered them a chance to experience engagement with politics. When a number of relatively young individuals (generally those

---

8   Interview with female activist, January 14th, 2008.

TOGETHER, BUT DIVIDED 131

born between the mid-seventies and mid-eighties and still in higher education or just entering adulthood) began to interact with the older political activists of *Kifâya*, they realized that their age-group's condition was leading them to develop a generational "self-conscious identity" (Alwin and McCammon 2003, 25). They thus started to do politics in their own way. In other terms, this was clearly the development of a *"generational consciousness that makes possible the creation of a political generation"* (Boumaza 2009, 194). While addressing generational phenomena, it is useful to refer to Mannheim and his definition of generation not as determined by biological age, but as a social definition based on the location of an age-based group in time and its connections with the socio-historical context. By witnessing the same socio-historical context, and by realizing their shared 'collective problem' – having been born and raised under only one president (Mubarak, from 1981 to 2011), and having always lived under the state of emergency (lifted only in July 2011, with new forms established since then) – this *Kifâya Generation*[9] (if a political generation can be named after its adhesion date or its marking event) was an important player in the political dynamics under an authoritarian context.

Each trajectory of commitment in politics has its own paths and particularities, but these newcomers into politics shared certain patterns of socialization, and would sometimes take part in the same events. This could be related to *period effects* and more specifically to the authoritarian political context of Egypt under Mubarak, where critics of the regime were silenced. In general, activists would come into politics at major moments of mobilization or following the arrival of new political figures or ideas: for instance, the Second Palestinian Intifada in 2000 or the War on Iraq in 2003. Those two moments paved the way for the initial development of political consciousness that would lead to political participation in street demonstrations. For some other activists, the catalyst was the aura of certain opposition figures like Ayman Nûr, the ex-president of al-Ghad Party, subsequently imprisoned by Mubarak regime, whose party promoted a 'Third Way' and created a base for socializing newcomers into politics. Moreover, these youth witnessed an important technological development, the introduction of the Internet, which created a platform for the relatively free exchange of information as a tool to express visions of politics and civil rights. For some, the Internet provided a source of information on demonstrations, and created a location to learn about Egyptian and international politics, something not available through mainstream media. In addition, satellite television offered another venue, further opening viewers' perspectives. Talk

---

9   This generation could also be called the 'Emergency law generation,' as Egypt has been continuously under emergency law for the last thirty years. (El Chazli and Hassabo 2013).

shows broadcasted on the satellite private channels, which became popular in the mid 2000s, contributed to the process of providing political information by allowing a 'free' arena where the opposition could debate.[10] In addition, the rise and spread of independent newspapers has marked some of those activists in that they created an arena for opposition viewpoints to be expressed (though still within certain red lines), which was not feasible inside official information channels.

In the formation of some activists' political trajectories, their university years played the classic role of shaping initial political interests and establishing contact with political groupings of students that reflect the general political spectrum (Farag 2007). Some activists were already acquainted with the world of politics, having been raised by activist parents, but others hid their political commitment from their families. They also went through different paths of ideological engagement and indoctrination: some vacillated between several ideologies and political formations before settling on one; others converted to ideas that ranged from moderate Islamism to Anarchism; and still others declared an absence of ideological preferences. The momentum of the *Kifâya* movement, its ideal of heterogeneity and its mode of action attracted these young people interested in politics. In addition, it provided them with the opportunity and framework to create their own political rally. They found a *keyword* for their affiliation to a generation that eventually became a central actor of 'street politics' in Cairo (Bayat 1997). They set up daring actions, such as surprise demonstrations in popular quarters of the capital. They even organized a sit-in at Tahrir Square on the night of 16th to 17th March 2006, in solidarity with the movement of Judges for Independence. During 2005 and 2006, both the Youth for Change and the loose network of activist-bloggers launched a number of demonstrations and campaigns, and their actions were not always in line with their elders, the leaders of *Kifâya*. The latter belonged to the generation of the sixties and the seventies, which became politically engaged while they were students under Nasser and Sadat, and were the main players of student movements during that time (Abdallah 2008; El Khawaga 2003).

The *Kifâya*'s momentum faded after a while with the closure of a 'cycle of protest' (Tarrow 1995), and the unity of youth groups and networks began to split.

---

10   Many channels and talk shows, have benefited from a relatively 'free' tone compared to public media. The talk show *al-'ashira' massâ'n* (*10:00 PM*) on Dream TV, presented by Mona El Shazli, gave space for bloggers to talk about a famous sexual harassment case that happened in 2006. Also, days before the 25th of January 201, ONTV invited some activists to talk about their expectations for the day during its show '*Baladna bil masri*' (*Our nation in Egyptian*).

TOGETHER, BUT DIVIDED

However, it launched processes of reconversion, of transfer to a new group or new networks, or evolution into 'generational units.' This *Kifâya* generation of activists still shared the same 'collective problem' and, generally speaking, still had the same demands during these years.[11] They participated together in similar protest moments, for instance the April 6th 2008 demonstrations in Cairo, or the Khaled Sa'ïd demonstrations against torture in the summer of 2010. Still others became militants in favor of more social struggles like the battle for a minimum wage in the public sector launched in May 2010. In brief, they were united in the years preceding the Revolution by sharing the same general values of liberty, by experiencing the same 'collective problem' and by having the same objective for their commitment, namely that 'something must change.'

Mubarak Leaves, but What is Left of a Generation's Unity?

Revolutions are without a doubt among those historical moments that make an important impact on those who live them and participate in them. However, they are lived differently by each individual and thus are subjective events. Each individual experiences the same event differently and acts in her/his own way, therefore having his/her own narrative of it. If we consider the *Kifâya* generation of activists, we can observe a multiplicity of attitudes towards the Revolution, a moment which is perceived as 'traumatizing,' 'big,' 'unbelievable,' 'long awaited,' and so on. Because of the various perceptions of and attitudes toward this historical event, rivalries between *generational units* become obvious during a revolutionary situation. The 'collective problem' that made the members of this generation stand together no longer exists. Their goal has been achieved: 'things have changed' and Mubarak was removed. They no longer share the same enemy, and thus find themselves divided on every other matter. In order to illustrate this, three activists' trajectories will be described in detail to show how attitudes within the same political generation are influenced by the political situation and, as a result, become opposed to one another, thus denying the presence of a united youth movement on a large scale. For this, the political situation since the departure of Mubarak must be briefly described.

Since February 2011, Egypt has undergone a frequent reshuffle of power, with four regime changes. With each new reshuffle, there has been a convergence

---

11   Still, these demands remained vague. They dreamt of a revolution, but knew that demonstrations were not enough, and they agreed largely in their support of demands for general liberties (liberation of prisoners, end of torture and police brutality, freedom of expression, etc.).

between institutional dynamics (i.e., elaboration of new constitutions, the holding of parliamentary and presidential elections) and massive mobilization momentum. When Mubarak stepped down on February 11th, 2011, after eighteen days of widespread demonstrations with violence, culminating in the Day of Anger, January 28th, the Supreme Council for Military Affairs (SCAF) succeeded him. Since the Day of Anger, the Army has become an integral and pivotal actor in the political sphere. The SCAF's eighteenth months in office saw numerous violent clashes between revolutionaries and either army soldiers or riot police. In June 2012, political power was handed to the Muslim Brotherhood following Muhammad Morsi's election in the first presidential elections after the revolution. Soon, however, protests rose against the Muslim Brotherhood's hold on power, in a configuration in which both supporters of the revolution and of Mubarak's ex-regime joined the mobilization against the Muslim Brotherhood, and in which violence continued to mark protest dynamics. Clashes occurred either between civilians and anti-riot troops, or between civilians themselves (pro-Muslim Brotherhood sympathizers and anti-Muslim Brotherhood). A year later, on June 2013, a new wave of mobilization was organized against the Muslim Brotherhood in a day of rebellion that would again bring down the president and bring the army once again into the foreground. This created a new political configuration in which members of the oppositional elite were to gain positions in the new transitional regime. But soon after, the counter-revolutionary tendencies of the new transitional regime appeared, as violence and repression became widely used. The Muslim Brotherhood were the object of harsh repression when approximately 1000 persons were massacred in August 2013 during the dispersion of the sit-in at Rab'a al-'Adawiyya. Counter-revolutionary proclivities became even more visible after the Ministry of Defense's Abdal Fattâh al-Sissi was elected president in June 2014, when government restraints were imposed not only on the Islamists but also on protestors and activists who had themselves also opposed the rule of the Muslim Brotherhood.

The positions and attitudes of this generation of activists have been fundamentally transformed by their perceptions of the events involved in this important acceleration of history, and the multiple political changes that took place. They also had to come to deal with new phenomena such as elections or violence. But above all, the fundamental point of contestation was *how to make a revolution*, especially when events far exceeded their expectations: what was basically a Facebook-created event that would have otherwise gone unnoticed ended up amassing millions of protestors in the streets. In the authoritarian context, they once had been only a minority demonstrating against the regime. But in the revolutionary context, they were only a few among millions of protestors. For some, the revolution ultimately changed their

TOGETHER, BUT DIVIDED 135

status: some were activists transformed into revolutionaries, others became more institutionalized, others more radicalized, etc. To a certain extent, the context imposed the necessity of elaborating decision-making processes and organizing among themselves, as well as managing violence and dealing with a multiplicity of new actors. Divergences started to appear within this political generation. The unity that rallied its members before the revolution against *one enemy* dissipated once this enemy was defeated. Thus, friends of yesterday became enemies of today. 'Generational units' became more functional and more apparent, revealing opposing views. Each generational unit began to re-appropriate events differently and therefore to position their attitudes based on these perceptions.

A Generation across the Revolution: Trajectories of Activists

This generation was maintained above all by its sharing the same location, a socio-historical context that made "many of its members become aware that they are bound together by a shared age-group consciousness and mobilize as an active force for political change" (Braungart and Braungart 1986, 217). The coming together of this generation of activists had set aside its members' political differences and ideological beliefs: they were Trotskyists, Islamists, Communists, Liberals, Socialists, Nationalistic, Anarchists, etc.; in brief, they had conflicting ways of thinking politics, but shared the same 'collective problem' and the awareness that their action must be directed to resolve this collective problem. When the problem is not collective any more, divergences became visible.

Through three trajectories of activists from the *Kifâya* generation, a variety of attitudes and reflections about revolutionary events and how to deal with or achieve political change will be detailed here. Even though the selected activists all share leftist ideologies, their attitudes differ entirely from one another, specifically around topics such as elections, violence, demonstrations and negotiation with officials. In sum, they disagreed on the way to carry out the revolution, what paths it should take, and what kind of processes would best bring about change, and particularly on the question of whether it should follow an institutional path or a revolutionary one.

Activist 1: Hassanein

Born in the mid-seventies, Hassanein began his political initiation and process of socialization during the beginning of his university years, in the late nineties. Nasserism first attracted him, but he then joined a radical left-wing movement. By the time of the *Kifâya* moment, he was already an experienced activist, and was older than most newcomers to activism. He served for some of them as a 'mentor' (he is today in his forties). After the *Kifâya* momentum tailed off, he joined several initiatives and co-founded a group of youth activists in 2010. This latter group joined the calls for the Revolution of January 25th, and Hassanein would be a member of a coalition of youth movements, and among those who organized the call for demonstrations in January 2011.

Since that date, divergences of opinion with his comrades started to take a more prominent place. These revolved around how to continue the revolution, what steps should be taken to make a 'transition,' and what tools should be used.

Activist 2: Mohsen

Mohsen, the second activist, was born at the beginning of the eighties. His political career went through some fluctuations and different instances of socialization. The internet also created opportunities for such socialization, through forums and then via blogs. He was also interested in several different ideologies, and after an extensive period of study he converted from a certain strand of political Islam to an extreme leftist ideology.

His first participation in collective action was in *Kifâya*'s demonstrations. He was then arrested during the Mubarak years in 2006 while demonstrating in solidarity with reformist judges. He spent more than a month in prison. He participated in nearly all the demonstrations in the two main protest moments of 2008 and in 2010. Then, too, he was briefly arrested on several occasions. During the revolutionary events of 2011 he was seriously wounded by police rubber bullets.

We can find differences in attitude between Mohsen and Hassanein. Hassanein, for example, went through a 'partisan' experience by joining a political party that merged multiple leftist ideologies. He argues that building organization, mainly found in political parties, is the best way to produce change. It is an important tool for regulating political interactions and for doing politics. For instance, elections are important to channel popular demands and to allow political parties to build a popular base; and in revolutionary times negotiations with members from ex-regimes could be necessary.

Mohsen stands on the opposite side, as he refuses hierarchical forms of organization. For him, negotiating with members from the ex-regime is a form of treason. Elections – through the imposed system of representation – are not

TOGETHER, BUT DIVIDED

genuinely democratic. A few days after Mubarak stepped down from power, a second sit-in, a gathering of no more than one thousand people, was organized in Tahrir Square, with some activists and some of the 'people': the sit-in's main purpose was the removal of the Prime minister Ahmad Shafîq, who had been nominated by Hosni Mubarak. It also aimed to pursue the revolution's demands: a priority was to bring the officials from the Mubarak regime responsible for 'crimes' against Egyptians – mainly those committed during the early days of the revolution – before the courts. Even though Hassanein agrees with these same demands, he thinks that the tools to achieve them must be changed. He was completely opposed to the sit-in, even though he participated in the previous one in Tahrir Square, from January 28th to February 11th 2011. He felt that the sit-in went against the general ambiance (the main debates at this time focused on the return to normality and stability) and would make people hate the revolution. His attitude was mainly shaped by the new revolutionary conjuncture that associates a mobilization's success with the number of people who participate in it. He sees this period as more suited for negotiations and national dialogue. It should mark the start of the building process; in other words, an institutional process should be launched. On the contrary, for Mohsen, the revolution is still in the streets, and pressure from below should be maintained, even if only by a minority. No negotiations should be made until all of the demands are satisfied.

Activist 3: Mourad

Mourad, born in the early eighties, was politicized before university when he joined the Salafis. In his university years, he joined the Muslim Brotherhood but then decided to leave them. He made a career shift as part of his professional trajectory. He became close to the *Kifâya* groups and the associated youth. He became active on internet forums and blogs, and he even started a blog where he wrote about several subjects. He defines himself as a leftist, and more precisely as center-left. After the revolution, he was a co-founder of a league for progressive youth. He also joined a center-left political party but was not particularly active in it.

It can be said that Mourad occupies a conciliatory position between those of Mohsen and of Hassanein. For him, negotiating with former members of ex-regimes is not bad, if pressure is still maintained on the streets. Negotiations could be good, or at least helpful for understanding how the 'other' thinks. Participating in elections is important: the revolution must have its voice in parliament.

The period of the elections and constitutional referendums provided an ideal moment to observe, for instance, how these activists' attitudes differed with regards to the voting. Let's take into consideration a concrete case of divergence: the presidential elections of 2011. In the second round, the ballot boxes opposed Ahmad Shafiq, the Prime minister under Mubarak and during the first days of the SCAF in power, to Muhammad Morsi, a representative of the Muslim Brotherhood. Hassanein, even though he is a leftist, voted for Morsi, considering the latter to be the better choice because the Muslim Brotherhood were in some way '*our*' allies, at least during the early days of the revolution. Mohsen decided to completely boycott the elections from the very beginning, even though he had considered participating in March 2011, when a number of public figures and politicians declared their intentions to run, among them an eminent judge. Mohsen even criticized the idea of electing Muhammed Morsi. According to him, the Muslim Brotherhood were not to be considered comrades of the square (*rufaqâ' al-midân*), since they sat at the negotiation table with Omar Sulayman, the former chief of intelligence and Mubarak's vice-president in his last days, when "there [were] still people bleeding." Later on, both Mohsen and Hassanein would oppose Muhammed Morsi and support the demonstrations against his rule on the 30th of June, both standing firm in their position: *no to Muslim Brotherhood, no to a military regime*. Even though recent developments since June 30th would slightly change their positions, in the sense that they were firmly opposed to the 'massacre of Rabi'â,' when new elections arrived Mohsen insisted on boycotting them, this time again even more convinced that the 'results were known in advance.' These elections pitted the former minister of Defense Marshall 'Abdal Fattâh al-Sissi against the Nasserist Hamdin Sabahi, and everyone knew al-Sissi would be elected president. By contrast, Hassanein considered that, even though results were known beforehand, going to ballots boxes was a way to prove that *the voice of the revolution* still exists.

Conclusion

In one of his interviews, Pierre Bourdieu insisted that "youth is only a word" (Bourdieu 1992, 143–154), and that it is actually a 'category' that can be manipulated and instrumentalized by authorities. In the Egyptian context, the term *youth of the Revolution* (Shabâb al-Thawra) has been widely used by successive regimes: every regime attempts to talk to the youth, for instance Mubarak depicting the revolution's demands as those of the young (mainly unemployment), or the SCAF releasing communiqués on Facebook to be 'close to youth.'

Thus, when the regime associated the revolution with its youth, it thought it would be easier to canalize the massive mobilizations.

Therefore, the ways in which this category has been an 'object of manipulation' from the start of the revolutionary situation in Egypt are, I argue, of utmost importance and demand nuanced analysis. The category of the *Shabâb al-thawra* has been represented as the 'mainstream' figure of the young Egyptian *active* in the revolution. In fact, this figure represents educated, politicized, non-violent, urbanized, internet-savvy Egyptians who should and would vote in elections and participate in political debates and political parties. Youth who do not fit this description are not considered representative of the revolutionary youth. Furthermore, the expression *shabâb al-thawra* is also used to refer to a 'concrete group,' a single generation of *all* youth who are interested in the public domain, who share the same vision and political orientation, and who give voice to the demands of the youth since it is, after all, a youth revolution. In effect, this has led to delegitimizing every other youth expression that did not adhere to those dominant representations. In many cases, the young front-liners in conflict with anti-riot police or soldiers would be described as thugs (*baltaguiya*), people not at all representative of the image of the revolution.

The perception of the existence of a unified 'youth movement' and a united 'young generation' participating in the revolution, described and explained by academic and media circles on the one hand, and by every regime in power, whether Mubarak or any of the authorities who succeeded him (the SCAF, Mohamed Morsi, the interim regime of Adly Mansour, and most recently with Marshall al-Sissi) on the other, has not generally taken into consideration the micro-level of the individual. Nor has it answered what seem like simple questions: How has each of the trajectories of experienced activists belonging to the same political generation been affected by revolutionary events? How have attitudes been shaped and how have political commitments been restructured?

The focus here on a micro-level approach to these trajectories, addressing them through a generational lens, was meant to reflect the heterogeneity and the multiplicity of the generational belonging of the youth who participated in revolutionary events. From a macro-scale perspective, we observe that the formation of generational units takes place around the ways that individuals experience particular events and develop their political views in response to such events. This observation leads to several questions. For instance, does geographic location influence the way individuals react to particular events? More specifically, do the youth living in cities that witnessed little or no mobilization during the revolution share the same political views as those who participated in the violent events in the cities of Cairo, Alexandria and Suez in early 2011? Furthermore, what sort of effect does "occupational milieu" (Berger 1960, 10–23) have on the creation of generational units? For instance, can we talk about a generation of young journalists who covered the revolutionary events or a generation of young physicians who volunteered in the makeshift 'field hospitals' during the clashes, and so on?

In this chapter, I have attempted to analyze the problem posed by a categorization that homogenizes the youth movement by unifying all its units. Considering all the youth who participated, called for or initiated the successive events that shaped the reality in Egypt over the past four years as part of the same politically united 'group' does not take into account the variety of their profiles – their geographical location, their social class, their experiences in politics, etc. In addition, the notion of 'political generation' or the more complex concept of 'generation' (in the Egyptian context generally understood as biological generation) overlooks the diversity of the subjects. By analyzing young activists, along with their trajectories, the dates they joined a movement and entered politics, and the 'events' that motivated them to engage in politics, we have been able to uncover the existence of multiple (political) generations of activists in the revolutionary moment. Even though these generational units converged on general demands, they disagreed about every other step that was taken to pursue revolutionary goals and to actualize evolutionary changes. Such momentum can thus reinforce the rivalries between generational units, the groups and network of activists resulting from the decomposition of political generation(s).

References

Abbott, Andrew. *Times Matter: On Theory and Method.* Chicago: Chicago University Press, 2001.

Abdallah, Ahmad. *The Student Movement and National Politics in Egypt 1923–1973.* Cairo: American University in Cairo Press, 2008.

Allal, Amin and Youssef El Chazli. "Figures du Déclassement et Passage au Politique dans les Situations Révolutionnaires Egyptienne et Tunisienne," in *Sens Politique du Travail,* edited by Ivan Sainsaulieu and Muriel Surdiz, 321–336. Paris: Armand Colin, 2012.

Alwin, Duane F. and Ryan J. McCammon. "Generations, Cohorts and Social Change," in *Handbook of Life Course,* edited by Jeylan T. Mortimer and Michael J. Shanahan, 23–50. New York: Kluwer Academic/Plenum Publishers, 2003.

Bayat, Asef. *Street Politics: Poor People's Movements in Iran,* New York: Columbia University Press, 1997.

Beinin, Joel. "The Egyptian Workers Movement in 2007," in *Chroniques Egyptiennes 2007*, edited by Hadjar Aouardji and Hélène Legeay, 217–238. Cairo: CEDEJ, 2007.

Berger, Bennet M. "How Long is a Generation?" *The British Journal of Sociology* 11, 1 (1960): 10–23.

Boumaza, Magali. "Les Générations Politiques au Prisme de la Comparaison: Quelques Propositions Théoriques et Méthodologiques." *Revue internationale de politique comparée* 16, 2 (2009): 189–203.

Bourdieu, Pierre. "La 'Jeunesse' n'est qu'un Mot," interview with Anne-Marie Métaillée, in *Questions de Sociologie*, 143–154. Paris: Editions du Minuit, 1992.

Braungart, Richard G. and Margaret M. Braungart. "Life-Course and Generational Politics." *Annual Review of Sociology* 12 (1986): 205-231.

El Chazli, Youssef and Chaymaa Hassabo. "Socio-Histoire d'un Processus Révolutionnaire. Analyse de la 'Configuration Contestataire' Egyptienne (2003–2011)" in *Au Cœur des Révoltes Arabes. Devenir Révolutionnaires*, edited by Amin Allal and Thomas Pierret. Paris: Armand Colin, 2013.

El Khawaga, Dina. "La Génération *Seventies* en Égypte. La Société Civile Comme Répertoire d'Action Alternatif," in *Mobilisations et Protestations dans les Sociétés Musulmanes*, edited by Mounia Bennani-Chraïbi and Olivier Fillieule, 271–292. Paris: Presses de Sciences Po, 2003.

Farag, Iman. "Quand 'l'Education Forme la Jeunesse': la Construction d'une Catégorie en Égypte," in *Jeunesses des Sociétés Arabes. Par-delà les Promesses et les Menaces*, edited by Mounia Bennai-Chraïbi and Iman Farag, 49–78. Paris: Aux lieux d'être/CEDEJ, 2007.

Favre, Pierre (ed). *La Manifestation*, Paris: Presses de la FNSP, 1990.

Fillieule, Olivier. "Propositions pour une Analyse Processuelle de l'Engagement Militant. Post Scriptum." *Revue Française de Science Politique* 51, 1–2 (2001): 199–215.

Fillieule, Olivier. "Temps biographique, temps social et variabilité des retributions," in *Le disengagement militant*, edited by Olivier Fillieule, 17–48. Paris: Belin, 2005.

Hassabo, Chaymaa. "Du Rassemblement à l'Effritement des *Jeunes pour le Changement* Egyptiens: l'Expérience de Générations qui ont Vécu et Vivent Toujours Sous la Loi d'Urgence." *Revue Internationale de Politique Comparée* 16, 2 (2009): 241–261.

Jamal, Amaney and Michael Hoffman. "The Youth and the Arab Spring. Differences and Similarities." *Middle East Governance and Law* 4 (2012): 168–188.

Mannheim, Karl. "The Problem of Generations," in *Essays on the Sociology of Knowledge*, edited by Karl Paul Kecskemeti, 276–320. London: Routledge and Kegan Paul Ltd, 1952.

Muxel, Anne. "Les Choix Politiques des Jeunes à l'Epreuve du Temps. Une Etude Longitudinale." *Revue Française de Science Politique* 53, 3 (2001): 409–430.

Onodera, Henri. "A Few Reflections on Not Naming Egypt's Young Revolutionaries." *Journal of the Finnish Anthropological Society* 36, 4 (2011): 70–74.

Rintala, Marvin. "A Generation in Politics: A Definition." *The Review of Politics* 25, 4 (1963): 509–522.

Sirinelli, Jean-François. "Génération, Générations." *Vingtième Siècle, Revue d'Histoire* 98 (2008): 113–124.

Tarrow, Sydney. "Cycles of Collective Action: Between Moments of Madness and the Repertoire of Contention," in *Repertoires and Cycles of Collective Action*, edited by Mark Traugott, 281–307. Durham (N.C.): Duke University Press, 1995.

Taylor, Verta. "Social Movement Continuity: The Women's Movement in Abeyance." *American Sociological Review* 54, 5 (1989): 761–775.

Tilly, Charles. *From Mobilization to Revolutions.* Massachusetts: Addison-Wesley Publishers, 1978.

Zartman, William. "Opposition as Support of the State." In *Beyond Coercion: The Durability of the Arab State,* edited by Adeed Dawisha and William Zartman, 61–87. London: Croom Helm, 1988.

CHAPTER 6

The Gezi Protests: The Making of the Next Left Generation in Turkey[1]

Gökbörü Sarp Tanyildiz

> To live! Like a tree alone and free
> Like a forest in brotherhood,
> This yearning is ours.
>
> NAZIM HIKMET (2007)

∵

Introduction

In the late evening of May 27, 2013 the bulldozers of Istanbul Metropolitan Municipality turned their steering wheels towards Gezi Park, one of the few green spaces left in Istanbul's landmark Taksim Square. Tearing down the walls of one façade of the park, the bulldozers uprooted five trees. This was supposed to be the first step of the demolition of Gezi Park, a part of the neoliberal-Islamist AKP (Justice and Development Party) government's urban transformation plan. The plan foresaw the replacement of Gezi Park with a replica of 19th century Ottoman Artillery Barracks, containing yet another shopping mall and mosque. Upon hearing about the uprooting of trees, a group of environmentalist youth and some members of a neighbourhood civil society organization, the Taksim Platformu, arrived at the scene to protect Gezi Park. Performing a peaceful sit-in, they spent the night in the park with the trees, and were successful in stopping the demolition of the park.

The following day (May 28, 2013) the police violently attempted to evacuate the park so as to allow the demolition of Gezi Park. They failed because, in addition to the activists' efforts, a socialist member of the Parliament from the

---

1 I would like to thank to Ratiba Hadj-Moussa and Mark Ayyash for their generous editorial support throughout the various stages of the chapter, as well as to the anonymous reviewers who contributed to the development of the chapter.

© KONINKLIJKE BRILL NV, LEIDEN, 2017 | DOI 10.1163/9789004344518_008

BDP (Peace and Democracy Party) stood in front of bulldozers. On the third day (May 29, 2013), Prime Minister Recep Tayyip Erdogan, who in August 2014 became the President of Turkey, gave his first speech about the protest in an aggressive and dismissive tone making it clear that the urban reformation plan was unalterable (Kongar and Kucukkaya 2013, 101). Following Erdogan's speech, on the fourth and fifth days of protests, the police attacked the protesters with disproportionate use of tear gas, water cannons, and physical violence, including burning their tents to the ground (International Federation for Human Rights 2014, 7). The stark brutality of the police in contrast to the peaceful protesters and the ignominious absence of the mainstream media coverage sparked public outrage.

As a result, on the sixth day of the protests (June 1, 2013), Turkey awoke to the largest popular protests of its 90-year-history (Oncu 2014, 151). Spread through mainly social media, the protests that began in Istanbul to protect a park had snowballed into countrywide demonstrations protesting a wide range of problems and concerns. Challenging the authoritarian and anti-democratic atmosphere created by the AKP government, the protests in the streets and squares lasted powerfully until the end of June. Mainly due to the state violence enacted by the police, in the beginning of September the Gezi Protests became attenuated. According to the report of the International Federation for Human Rights, between May 28 and the first week of September, "5532 protests were organized across all (81) provinces of Turkey with the only exception of Bayburt. Approximately 3,600,000 people attended the protests, and 5513 were detained by the police, 189 were arrested. 4329 were wounded, and 5 demonstrators were killed" (International Federation for Human Rights 2014, 6).

The Gezi Protests have radically changed the socio-political landscape of Turkey. This is because of the composition of its participants; the diversity of the problems and concerns it has raised; the tactics and strategies it deployed; the unexpected solidarity it has created between unlikely groups; and the new political modalities it has introduced to the country. In short, the Gezi Protests have become a seminal reference point of socio-political life in contemporary Turkey.

The research and analysis of these protests is diverse and varied, but there are two points that are agreed upon: (1) the protests were utterly novel for Turkey, (2) they were driven by the new generation of the country. On the one hand, I agree with these observations. On the other hand, I am not convinced that they have much explanatory and analytical power. In these accounts, the novelty of the protests and the newness of this generation are often taken for granted. Even though it is invaluable to have comparative social knowledge, discussed synchronically in relation to other social movements, such as the Arab Spring, the European Summer and the Occupy Protests, the novelty of the Gezi Protests in such a trajectory becomes pre-empted because it appears as the latest manifestation of these trendy events. Such a claim contends that the protests are new to Turkey, but have already been developed in other places and were exported to Turkey – much like the latest smartphone arrived at the Turkish market after making its debut in the United States of America. In these accounts, the agents of the protests appear as 'the new generation' simply by virtue of their birthdays. Yet, their newness is also pre-empted: they are not new because of their agency, but merely because of the position they occupy in the calendars of linear-time.

As someone from this 'new' generation of Turkey who participated in the Gezi Protests, I argue that understanding these protests in their ecological, political and socio-cultural ways is crucial to an analysis of both the neoliberal-Islamist-authoritative transformation that Turkey has been experiencing since the early 2000s, and how the left in Turkey changes within this context. Such an understanding necessitates complicating the novelty of the protests through a diachronic investigation of the Turkish left that organizes itself around 'generations.' If you listen to two leftists in conversation, you will hear them asking one another: "What generation are you from?" Any answer to this question will bring forth an array of emotions, memories, and nostalgia. Each of the age groups of leftists constitute and define themselves, through struggle, as a generation with common values and a shared system of symbols (Mannheim 1952; Pilcher 1994). I suggest that, in the context of Turkey, generation as such might be defined as a common denominator that delineates the sociological specificities (i.e. the problems and imagined solutions) of each historical era. Therefore, it does not solely describe a rank in genealogy, or a stage in the succession of natural descent (Kertzer 1983; Eyerman and Turner 1998). The repository of the strategies and tactics of the former generations informs the newer generations' political struggles (Whittier 1997). Yet, at the same time, new modalities of politics produced by the newer generations encourage the former generations to reconsider their traditions.

My objective in this chapter is to develop an analysis of the internal relationship between the novelty of the Gezi Protests and its agents, the new generation of Turkey, through a specific focus on the classed subject formation of the Gezi Protests situated in the particular context of domination and dispossession that took place under the AKP rule. In the first section, I establish a theoretical framework that allows for a dialectical understanding of the two main conditions that underlie the Gezi Protests: (1) the protection of Gezi Park and its trees, and (2) the lack of democracy and increasingly authoritarian rule of the government in Turkey. By drawing on cultural productions about the neighborhood of the district of Beyoglu that encompasses Taksim Square and the Gezi Protests, I show that the significance of Gezi Park as the natal space of protests can be examined through an analysis of the socio-political history and the social texture. In the second section, I examine the discussions and debates on the class composition of the Gezi Protests, and suggest a shift from subject positions to subject formation on the basis of *a socialized conception of class*. Finally, I investigate the subject formation of the next left generation of Turkey through an emphasis on *the recognition amongst the protestors* and the *ethics of solidarity*. In order to better explicate the process of recognition and the realization of Gezi's ethics of solidarity, I focus on three crucial dimensions of the protests: (1) the actual experience of living together, (2) the deployment of socio-cultural performances as political strategies, (3) the Anti-Capitalist Muslim Youth's participation in and contribution to the Gezi Protests. In lieu of a conclusion, I discuss the current relevance of the protests in Turkey, through a story that has moved me deeply.

Understanding the Gezi Protests: A Historico-Spatial Analysis

'Are the Gezi Protests about uprooting a bunch of trees, or are they about the crippled democracy of Turkey under the AKP rule?' This was the question that occupied the minds of many politicians, commentators, analysts, and academics. From the very beginning, Erdogan dismissed the protesters' concerns about the environment. He arrogantly asserted that the AKP was an environmentalist party and that the protests were not about the trees, but merely an ideological conspiracy to overthrow the government (Samanyolu 2014). In order to refute Erdogan, some protestors argued that the demonstrations of course were not an ideological conspiracy, but were rather about the crippling of rights and freedoms under the authoritarian rule of the AKP. Ironically, this strategic emphasis on the lack of democracy and the increasingly authoritarian rule of the AKP government served as a 'counterproductive rhetorical opposition' (Tugal 2013a). It reduced the Gezi Protests' attempt of direct democracy to a civil-society action that strives to mend the faulty mechanism of representational democracy. Hence, it created a public expectation that the protesters ought to come up with a list of demands, and negotiate with the state authorities. The protests were straightjacketed into the conventional politics that organized around a 'rights' discourse that is in fact contrary to what is called the 'Gezi spirit' (Tugal 2013b).

To be sure, the uprooting of the trees cannot be reduced to a mere concern about nature, but has to be situated in its broader social context. However, I argue that a critical sociological analysis should not facilely take the trees of

THE GEZI PROTESTS   147

Gezi Park as a metaphor for socio-political problems of Turkey. If the protests erupted from the uprooting of trees and demolition of the park, sociological analysis has to begin right from that point.

Perhaps unintentionally, Cemal Ozay, who had been the head gardener of Gezi Park for 20years, draws attention to this methodological point when talking to *The Guardian*'s Turkey correspondent a year after the Gezi Protests. After recounting that when he started, Gezi Park "was a huge garden, green and full of flowers" that he had grown, Ozay poses a simple question: "What is it with this government's love for concrete?" (Letsch 2014). He answers his own question: "They don't like trees, because trees don't generate a profit. Even the smallest city gardens and parks are now seen as a possibility for investment" (ibid.).

Drawing on his real life experiences and observations, what Ozay describes is indeed the process of the accumulation of capital under the AKP rule. In a recent journal article, Ahmet Oncu, a sociologist from Turkey, explicates the AKP's story in relation to this process of accumulation in a historical context. It is worth rehearsing in full (Oncu 2014, 171):

> The Turkish neoliberal media created a climate of positive opinion for the AKP's 'conservative democracy' as the exclusive guarantor of individual freedoms and rights against the oppressive state and the legal system. The reformed Islamist party in its turn guaranteed an unconditional adherence to the ongoing IMF led stabilization policy and the structural reforms. In November 2002, just one year after its establishment, Erdogan's AKP won the national elections with a clear majority. Due mainly to favorable global economic conditions, the first AKP government did not face any serious bottleneck in the flow of capital from international markets. Economic growth rates increased, unemployment rates decreased. Thus, the 'moderate' Islamist Erdogan came to be the most successful prime minister of neoliberal Turkey. Securing the confidence and support of the U.S., the EU and global financial circles, he became victorious once again in the 2007 national elections – followed by a third victory in 2011. Although the capitalist class as a whole gained from the AKP's successful implementation of neoliberal policies, the government was certainly 'the executive branch' of the rising Islamic bourgeoisie, who succeeded in accumulating billions of dollars of extra capital in less than a decade by means of the advantages and favoritism provided in privatization initiatives and public tenders.

The ripest fruit of the sinful union of the AKP and the Islamist bourgeoisie is the construction sector (Sonmez 2013), which became "the backbone of AKP's political economy, the influence of which undermines agricultural and industrial sectors as foundations for genuine economic development" (Gurcan and Peker 2014, 74). I suggest that the AKP government's emphasis on urban policy should be considered through this connection. The Housing Development Administration of Turkey (TOKI) in this respect constitutes the most strategic link between the AKP and the Islamist bourgeoisie. TOKI is a crucial actor due to its unparalleled power to "create and implement urban plans, grant building permits, nationalize land and determine the price of building over slums, and all without being required to get permission from the local authorities or being subject to the control of any other specific legislations" (Moudouros 2014, 187). Endowing this power to TOKI required the AKP government to legislate 14 different bills, which it fulfilled with a great dedication (ibid.).

TOKI, directly under the command of Erdogan's office, functions as an ideological state apparatus because it appears to provide affordable housing to the urban poor, and therefore creates a strong link between the party and its electoral base (Chouraqui 2014, 183). In effect, TOKI displaces the urban poor, commodifies public spaces, and transfer capital to its Islamist bourgeois contractors (Sonmez 2013). For instance, "the largest 25 TOKI projects in Istanbul serve to distribute the rent of previously public lands to firms that build luxury housing and shopping malls" (Gurcan and Peker 2014, 77).

I argue that unless we situate the Gezi Protests in this context of the rise of the AKP, its umbilical relation to the Islamist bourgeoisie and the process of capital accumulation through the urban development plans, our understanding of the protests is bound to be reductionist and one-dimensional: either trees *or* rights. The Gezi spirit necessitates a dialectical articulation of both trees *and* rights. I suggest that Marx's theorization of "so-called primitive accumulation" (Marx 1976, 871) offers us an analytical framework that allows for such an articulation.

In his magnum opus, *Das Kapital,* Marx explains that the relations of the capitalist mode of production cleave workers from ownership of the conditions for the realization of their labour (ibid., 874). Furthermore, it has to reproduce this separation "on a constant extending scale" (ibid.). The so-called primitive accumulation, for Marx, is nothing else than the historical process in which producers are "forcibly torn from their means of subsistence, and hurled onto the labour-market as free, unprotected, and rightless proletarians" (ibid., 875–6).

Rosa Luxemburg reinterprets Marx's theory of the so-called primitive accumulation in a way that allows her to further theorize the territorial expansion and imperialist impulses of capitalist mode of production. Capitalist accumulation, according to Luxemburg, does not wait for the internal disintegration of socio-economic non-capitalist formations. It systematically destroys and annihilates these formations. Thus, Luxemburg argues "force is the only solution open to capital; the accumulation of capital, seen as an historical process, employs force as a permanent weapon, not only at its genesis, but further on down to the present day" (Luxemburg 1913).

Despite their different understandings of the crises tendencies of capitalism, David Harvey draws on Luxemburg's reinterpretation and coins the term "accumulation by dispossession" (Harvey 2003, 144) so as to emphasize the ongoing and persistent character of Marx's theory of the so-called primitive accumulation. In relation to the Gezi Protests, accumulation by dispossession can be defined as the following: Caused by urban redevelopment, a process of displacement that gives "rise to numerous conflicts over the capture of valuable land from low-income populations that may have lived there for many years" (Harvey 2008).

The Gezi Protests, thus, constitute an example of resisting accumulation by dispossession under the neoliberal-Islamist rule of the AKP government (Lowy 2013). I argue that the demolition of Gezi Park is an instance of accumulation by dispossession insofar as the park's qualities that satisfy its users' needs of whatever kind (its use value) are brutally torn from them and the enjoyment of this use value can be achieved only through the capitalist market relations (i.e. the shopping mall), while this forcible market-boundness intensifies and accelerates the accumulation of capital for a certain group (the Islamist bourgeoisie and its executive branch, the AKP government). Considered in this light, the people defending the park and trees are simultaneously resisting the marketization of the conditions for the realization of their use of the park. In other words, seen through lenses of accumulation by dispossession, protecting Gezi Park and its trees and defending democratic rights and freedom are not mutually exclusive categories, but the mediated realization of one another.

I will discuss the political implications of understanding the Gezi Protests through the analytic lenses of accumulation by dispossession in the following section. Here, let me give some examples to concretize my above-stated point. When a high school student is protesting the demolition of the park, she is at the same time defending her right to lay on the shade of a tree with or without her lover after a long day of school and unwind without worrying about engaging in capitalist market relations. When another woman joins the protests, she is at the same time defending her right to gossip about her husband with her friends in the park without worrying about the possible patriarchal rules of the household. When a gay protester occupies the park, he is at the same time defending his right to cruise at the park during the night without worrying too much about the stifling homophobia of society. The realization of the urban redevelopment plan means that the high school student will have to go to a café (only if she has some money); the older woman will have to self-censor herself at home; and the gay man will not be able to actualize his sexual potentialities, unless he can afford going to gay bars or bathhouses.

Perhaps I can better demonstrate this dialectical articulation of protecting Gezi Park and its trees and defending democratic rights and freedom with the help of a poem by Nazim Hikmet that presages the dialectical articulation of the freedom provided by an uncommodified park space and democratic rights, without the linear-logical constraints of prose (Hikmet 1957):

> my head foaming clouds, sea inside me and out
> I am a walnut tree in Gulhane Park
> an old walnut, knot by knot, shred by shred
> Neither you are aware of this, nor the police
>
> I am a walnut tree in Gulhane Park
> My leaves are nimble, nimble like fish in water
> My leaves are sheer, sheer like a silk handkerchief
> pick, wipe, my rose, the tear from your eyes
> My leaves are my hands, I have one hundred thousand
> I touch you with one hundred thousand hands, I touch Istanbul
> My leaves are my eyes, I look in amazement
> I watch you with one hundred thousand eyes, I watch Istanbul
> Like one hundred thousand hearts, beat, beat my leaves
>
> I am a walnut tree in Gulhane Park
> neither you are aware of this, nor the police.

Here, Hikmet is telling his story as a communist poet who is escaping from the police, in a socio-historical context where his political thought renders him a threat to the monolithic unity of the nation. Expressing his political commitment to freedom through evoking the images of foaming clouds and the ebbing and flowing sea, Hikmet identifies with a walnut tree that cares about its lover and the city. In Hikmet's poem, this caring relationship, which does not separate one's private commitments from their public commitments, takes place in a park that is not fully colonized by the state apparatuses. Thus, Hikmet in his poem offers an alternative political modality, which is based on the co-existence of all human concerns in a space where nature is not dominated by

THE GEZI PROTESTS   151

the state and the market. I argue that the Gezi generation takes up a similar politics and transforms its modality of recognition: In Hikmet's poem the lover and the city do not recognize his existence as a tree, whereas the Gezi Protests makes the existence of a variety of radical politics intelligible through recognizing one another intimately by sharing the same park space, a phenomenon that I discuss in the last section.

Here I focus on the space of the protests. Despite the fact that the Gezi Protests began at the Gezi Park of Taksim Square and snowballed all across Turkey, I suggest that a critical sociological analysis ought to avoid seeing Gezi Park as an immediately singular instance of the genus it represents. A critical sociological analysis should investigate its differential particularity within the general countrywide protests. Gezi Park was not the first urban space subjected to accumulation by dispossession, and unfortunately it is proved that it is not the last one either. Why then did the largest popular protests in the history of the Republic of Turkey erupt from this particular space?

The answer to this question resides in the socio-political history of the district of Beyoglu (also known as Pera), which encompasses Taksim Square and Gezi Park. Considered the heart of Istanbul, Beyoglu is "a settlement comprising 45 neighborhoods and approximately 225,000 resident population" (Beyoglu Municipality 2014), but usually implies "the avenue Istiklal Caddesi, stretching from Tunel, through Galatasarayi, to Taksim, as well as the many abutting side streets" (Schick 2009, 1).

Beyoglu established its fame in the Ottoman era through the Commercial Treaty of 1838 which "opened the floodgates to British commodities, most of which found their way to stores" (Schick 2009, 1) in the neighbourhood, which was largely populated by "the non-Muslims comprising the Greeks, Armenians and the Jews and the Levantines and people of foreign citizenship" (Beyoglu Municipality 2014). Schick argues that the Crimean War (1853–1856) secured Beyoglu's role "as the shopping and entertainment capital of the city" (Schick 2009, 1), due to the existence of large numbers of French and British military personnel in Istanbul.

Beyoglu was not celebrated and adored in all times. For instance, during the Balkan Wars (1912–13) and the First World War (1914–1918), the neighbourhood "became synonymous with...unpatriotism, since many of the businesses there were owned by non-Muslims, and much of the merchandise they sold was imported from the very countries that were now waging war against the Ottoman Empire" (Schick 2009, 2). The animosity against the inhabitants of the neighbourhood found, perhaps, its most cruel expression on September 6–7, 1955 under the rule of the right-wing DP (Democrat Party) government. The houses, shops and workplaces of the non-Muslim inhabitants of Beyoglu were plundered; some of their churches and even cemeteries were attacked (Erogul 2014, 164–8).

Unfortunately, this was not the only abominable event that happened in Beyoglu. The symbolic meaning of Taksim Square was inscribed into the collective memory of the Turkish left in the aftermath of May Day, 1977. At a memorial event, taking place in Taksim Square, a group of assailants began firing guns when the workers were engaged in a moment of silence for their departed comrades. Following gunshots, the police intervened events with "firing soundbombs with high-pitched sirens...[which] created a mass panic with the result of several people being trampled by the crowd and others falling under police vehicles" (Baykan and Hatuka 2010, 63). At the end of the day, 34 people died and hundreds were injured. Ever since, "the Turkish left claimed the hegemony of the square, turning it into a spot for collective action and political organization" (Moudouros 2014, 190).

In addition to its complex social and political history, Beyoglu also occupies a special place in the cultural imaginary of Turkey. Beyoglu's rich social texture represents both the conventional and unconventional sides of Turkey. Perhaps, for this reason, there are so many authors who chose Beyoglu as the site of their novels, stories, poems and plays. From Huseyin Rahmi Gurpinar to Halid Ziya Usakligil, from Halide Edip Adivar to Abdulhak Sinasi Hisar, from Ahmet Hamdi Tanpinar to Resat Ekrem Kocu, from Sait Faik to Sabahattin Ali, from Orhan Veli to Oktay Rifat, from Haldun Taner to Salah Birsel, from Edip Cansever to Ece Ayhan, from Bilge Karasu to Sevim Burak, from Leyla Erbil to Furuzan, from Murathan Mungan to Orhan Pamuk (Hizlan 2008)...In their stories the protagonists are mostly the underdog: the poor, the vagrant, the vagabond, the foundling, the beggar, the queer, the sex worker, the drug addict, the non-Muslim, the non-Turk. The visibility of these people is much higher in Beyoglu than everywhere else. In other words, they are those who negate the entire ideological credo on which the bourgeoisie, the conservative Islamists, and the Islamist bourgeoisie build their existence, such as cleanliness, respectability, diligence, intelligence and frugality. That is why since the multi-party period in the Republic of Turkey, the right has been obsessed with Beyoglu/Taksim.

Reflecting on this obsession, Murathan Mungan, an important literatus of contemporary Turkey, writes that Beyoglu is a part of Turkey that since the 1453 conquest of Istanbul could not be fully captured. Mungan (2009) argues that, in the eyes of the right, Beyoglu was not Turkified and Islamized enough. Thus, he concludes, the 'noble' Turkish right's obsession of erecting a mosque in Taksim is a political project (ibid., 36–7). Indeed, "various mosque proposals for Taksim have appeared in newspapers during almost all election campaigns

THE GEZI PROTESTS   153

since the 1960s" (Gul, Dee, and Cunuk 2014, 68). A late prime minister and
Erdogan's former political master, Necmettin Erbakan and his Islamist party
WP (Welfare Party) got closest to building a mosque in Gezi Park (ibid.).

Betraying Erbakan and establishing the AKP after separating from him,
Erdogan upgraded Erbakan's will: not *in*, but *instead of* Gezi Park, complete
with a plan for an Ottoman Artillery Barracks and a shopping mall. Erdogan's
perception of Beyoglu, too, was in line with the rightist tradition. Against the
demands to stop the police violence on protestors, he declared that "The police was there yesterday, they are there today, and they will be there tomorrow.
Why? Because Taksim Square cannot be a place where the extreme groups run
wild" (Samanyolu 2014). For him, Taksim is a place that needs to be chastened.

Thus, I argue that the urban redevelopment plan of Taksim was not arbitrary.
On the contrary, Gezi Park was the target of a neoliberal ideological project
aimed at Turkfying and Islamizing the area through the displacement of its
inhabitants who represented the negation of nationalist, Islamists and bourgeois ideals, while intensifying and accelerating the accumulation of capital of
the Islamist bourgeoisie through plunder. The protests erupting from this park
and snowballing all across Turkey were, therefore, against such a neoliberal,
Islamist, nationalist project at once.

From the Revolutionary Subject to Revolutionary Subjectivity in the Gezi Protests

In this section, I focus on the doers of the Gezi Protests, and their sensuous
human activity. 'Who is the subject of the Gezi Protests? Middle class, or working class?' During and after the protests, this question has been at the center
of many discussions and debates. I argue that this question itself and various
answers that have been offered do not adequately capture the Gezi Protests'
novelty in the left political tradition of Turkey.

In an interview, one of the best known and well-respected marxist econo-
mists in Turkey, Korkut Boratav cautions against the depiction of the protests
as middle class spectacles (Boratav 2013). According to Boratav, the term 'middle class' does not hold much explanatory power for the participation of high
school and university students in the protests, who constitute a crucial section
of the protestors. He continues, "the objective configuration of the students,
in the broadest of aspects, is a belonging to the working-class as a *potential*"
as they will become a part of workforce or the reserve army of labour (ibid.,
n.p.). After highlighting the proletarianization of the independent professional groups, such as participating doctors, lawyers, engineers, pharmacists,

and financiers, Boratav argues that the Gezi Protests constitute a mature class-based rebellion.

The protests are class-based, according to Boratav, because "highly qualified and educated workers, together with their future class comrades (students), [also] with the inclusion of professionals [are] confronting the attempt of [the appropriation of Gezi Park] by the pick-pocketing bourgeois and [its] political power" (ibid., n.p.). At the same time, the Gezi Protests are mature because the protesters are not defending their immediate interests, but the general interest of the society. He explains that the appropriation of the park (ibid., n.p.):

> does not have negative effects on the incomes, wages, working conditions of the people who are trying to resist; or it does not increase their rents, student loan paybacks, fuel prices or the inflation in general. There is no operation that seeks to increase the rate of exploitation or the extraction of surplus-value. What is being done is *the giving away of the common-wealth of the present society, which has bequeathed from past generations, by the political power to the pick-pocketing bourgeoisie.* People resisting today are resisting against the transformation of their collective property, which has been left by the past generations to present society, into bourgeois private property (italics in original).

Notwithstanding the fact that Boratav's discussion about the potentiality of the objective configuration of student protestors' class belonging to the working class seems dubious, his argument about the maturity of the Gezi Protests alludes to a more dynamic genesis of classes. Going beyond their immediate interests, in Boratav's representation of the protests, the working class is able to create a transcendental solidarity that can accommodate all existing concerns of the Gezi protestors.

In contrast to Boratav, Cihan Tugal acknowledges the occasional multi-class quality of the Gezi Protests, yet nonetheless highlights its predominantly middle-class character. Referring to Boratav's position on the matter, Tugal writes "labeling the Gezi revolt as the movement of the proletarianized middle-class or the white-collar working class stands on shakier ground than analyses that emphasize the middle class core" (Tugal 2013c, 166). Tugal finds the predominant participation of "well-paid and fashionably dressed professionals" (ibid., 167) puzzling. He is convinced that "exploitation, (socioeconomic) marginalization, impoverishment, and other categories that emphasize the process of production and/or the redistribution of resources cannot tell us much" (ibid.) about their participation in the protests. According to Tugal, the answer to their participation is the impoverishment of their social lives. He also asserts that "if we stick to the illusion that Gezi is a working class

THE GEZI PROTESTS   155

movement, we cannot theorize the reason why there is no organized class alliance in the body of the movement" (ibid., 170).

Tugal's approach to the concept of class swings like a pendulum, from economic pole to cultural pole. When he seeks an explanation for the participation of the professional middle class, Tugal culturalizes class by rejecting the relevance of economic exploitation, and by emphasizing the impoverishment of their social lives. Conversely, when he calls for a demystification of the Gezi Protests as a working class movement, Tugal economizes the concept by drawing attention to the negligible presence of working class organizations that are traditionally organized on the basis of economic concerns. Furthermore, Tugal's reading of the Gezi Protests does not allow any solidarity building between the professional middle class and working class because the immanent nature of his classes assumes a static genesis. Thus, he often positions the proletarian character (the concern of working class) and the low-quality common life (the concern of middle class) in antagonistic ways (ibid., 21–2). As a result, he encounters a "class-blindness among the participants" (ibid., 168).

What complicates the problem of the class composition of the Gezi Protests is that the immense participation from all segments of society does not allow us to identify class either as an economistic concept, nor as a cultural concept. I argue that the Gezi Protests could more productively be understood through a conception of class that bypasses economistic and culturally reductive formulations and, therefore, allows an analysis of such social diversity. Himani Bannerji's notion of the *socialization of class*, according to which class ought to be theorized as a social concept that "constitutively implicates both social relations and forms of consciousness" (Bannerji 2005, 147), is useful here. Such a theorization needs to "broaden 'class' into a sociological category, thus making it stand for an entire ensemble of social relations, signifying practices and organizations" (ibid., 150). Situating Bannerji's insight in the context of the Gezi Protests, I argue that in order to understand the togetherness of the protestors who are resisting accumulation by dispossession and its destructive effects, we have to shift the conversation from the revolutionary subjects (i.e. simply detecting protestors' class positions) to the classed subjectivities of revolution. I argue that this shift offers us the possibilities of comprehending the formation and deformation of the protestors' political subjectivities vis-à-vis their different identifications and backgrounds.

Recognition amongst the Gezi Protestors

On the eighth day of the protests (June 3, 2013), Ali Ismail Korkmaz, a 19 year-old protestor, was beaten by pro-government civilians and plain clothes police officers in Eskisehir. Due to severe injuries, Ali Ismail died on July 10, 2013 (International Federation for Human Rights 2014; Amnesty International 2014). In the evening of the following day, I decided to take a stroll with a friend in Ankara. Arriving at the intersection of John F. Kennedy Avenue and Bestekar Street, we stumbled upon a small group that gathered together for a vigil for Ali Ismail (Bianet 2013). About a block south of Bestekar Street on John F. Kennedy Avenue, the police were present with their arms and armoured water cannon trucks, outnumbering the small group. We decided to join the group to remember Ali Ismail and the others who were killed before him by the police during the protests. For almost two hours our only activity was to call out their names non-stop: ALI ISMAIL KORKMAZ. ABDULLAH COMERT. ETHEM SARISULUK. MEHMET AYVALITAS.

It is very difficult to describe how I felt that evening, though it must be familiar to those who have participated in a powerful political demonstration. I have been struck and overwhelmed by that evening, not only because of its moving and vivid emotional memory, but also because it was a moment marking the subject formation of Turkey's next left generation.

Before explaining and exemplifying what I mean by 'the subject formation of Turkey's next left generation,' let me emphasize that this subject formation is of a *classed* kind – otherwise, the idiom of our discussion would shift into purely psychoanalytical terms. I argue that resting on "intersubjective relations of bodies and minds marked with socially constructed difference on the terrain of private property and capital" (Bannerji 2005, 149), what I have experienced and witnessed was a working class event, so long as working class is not understood as the mere bearer of trade union banners. It was a working class event because the young people we were calling out were killed because they were rejecting the existing neoliberal-Islamist social, political and economic order of Turkey that denies livable lives for all (Tanyildiz 2013), never mind their working class backgrounds. However, calling this moment a working class event does not adequately exhaust its specificity if we want to be able to capture "an entire ensemble of social relations, signifying practices and organizations" (Bannerji 2005, 150).

Such an important undertaking requires a distinction between subject positions and subjectivity. Kelly Oliver explains, "subject positions, although mobile, are ... determined by history and circumstance. [They] are our relations to the finite world of human history and relations" (Oliver 2001, 17). On the other hand, subjectivity "is experienced as the sense of agency and response-ability that are constituted in the infinite encounter with otherness, which is fundamentally ethical" (ibid.). Thus, I argue that an investigation of the classed subject formation and deformation in the Gezi Protests offers an understanding of the tension between different classes' participation in the protests (the so-called 'subject position' which is indicative of Tugal's main emphasis) and the agentic movement and activities of the protestors (the process of making their classed subjectivities which rearticulates Boratav's emphasis on maturity).

As an example of such an investigation, I suggest that the moment of the Gezi Protests I experienced exemplifies how the political subjectivities of Turkey's next new left generation are constituted. Faced with the murderer of Ali Ismail and the others, we were not demanding recognition from the state. In this situation, they were the one who irretrievably erased the subjectivity of our comrades by a brutal rejection of any kind of recognition and reciprocity that exists between the state and the protestors. Against the will of the state and its police, those who gathered in vigil were recognizing subjectivity by calling out the names of those who had been erased but not forgotten with the despair of impotence. In summoning our deceased ones, we were, in effect, engaging in a moment of recognition and reciprocity *amongst ourselves*. I suggest that this moment and similar moments of recognition and reciprocity among protestors is the trademark of the protests constituting the Gezi spirit.

Despite the myriad of *differences* among the protestors (across class, gender, ethnicity, religion, sexual orientation, and so on), all the existing 'I's are transformed into a common 'we,' without losing their unique qualities in an internally differentiated unity of all. I suggest that this emerging *ethics of solidarity* marks the next generation of the left in Turkey, who do not form their subjectivities only in relation to the master (the state, capitalism, patriarchy, ethnic and religious domination, heteronormativity etc.), but rather these new subjectivities constitute themselves mostly in relation to one another.

Gezi's *ethics of solidarity*, which opens up the possibilities of classed subject formation in Turkey's next left generation, can be seen in different events throughout the protests. Yet, I argue that (1) the experience of living together at the Taksim Commune in Gezi Park, (2) the centrality of performance to the protests, and (3) the contribution of the Anti-Capitalist Muslim Youth are crucial components of the creation of Gezi's ethics of solidarity, and therefore of the recognition and reciprocity among the protestors.

An Ethics of Solidarity in the Gezi Protests

In a public meeting on the twentieth day of the Gezi Protests (June 15, 2013), Erdogan threateningly stipulated that if the protestors would not evacuate the park willingly, he would unleash the police on them. Two hours after this speech, the police, in an orgy of hostility, attacked the park with hundreds of gas canisters, tear bombs and water cannons (Kongar and Kucukkaya 2013,

165). As a result of the criminal and disproportionate use of force, they managed to evacuate the park and the bulldozers were allowed to entry into the park (as if demonstrating the organic relation between the bourgeoisie and the state) to 'clear' the park from the traces of the protestors, their tents, placards, books, kitchens.

Until that day, the protestors had lived in the park for 20days together. Some called this togetherness the Taksim Commune, others the Republic of Gezi. The protestors were of different political tendencies: feminists, LGBT block, anarchists, environmentalists, socialists, marxists, anti-capitalist Muslims. Living together, they organized the given space into commons, cafés, an infirmary, kitchens, library, daycare, warehouse, garden, orchard, *masjid*, radio, TV, stage, concert areas (Babac 2013). Their republic did not have borders and customs; no one was illegal there. In the Taksim Commune decision-making was absolutely transparent and organized in accordance with grassroots democracy. Gezi Park became a de-commodified space. The use value of goods and services was enjoyed without a monetary exchange relation. The Gezi people were taking as much as they needed from the stocks of goods without a care for accumulating or hoarding.

The Gezi people cared for each other. While anti-capitalist Muslims were engaged in their prayers, communists were watching over them in anticipation of a possible police attack. Considering Turkey's political history, this constituted an unimaginable alliance. The Gezi people recognized one another in answer-able and response-able ways. For instance, the protestors were initially calling the government 'faggots' and 'son of a bitch.' After feminist protestors explained that LGBT folks and sex-workers were also active participants of, and remarkable contributors to the protests, the slogans of the protests were divested from their sexist and heterosexist implications. Until the Taksim Commune, the representation of LGBT in Turkey was generally stereotypical and demeaning. Perhaps for the first time, LGBT groups were recognized as legitimate political actors through Gezi Park at the national scale.

In a similar fashion, due to their being at the forefront of the protests, feminists were recognized as key actors in the political landscape of Turkey. To put it differently, prior to the protests and as a matter of fact, both LGBT groups and feminists had been very active and important in political activism, yet they were, to an important extent, marginalized. Challenging the perception that feminists only fight for the end of sexism, and LGBT groups' goal is to end heteronormativity, the experience of living together with these groups helped the protestors to realize that these struggles were inseparable from geopolitics and political economy. As a result, they were recognized as central figures of politics.

What I am describing here might sound romantic or utopian. Nonetheless, this is how people lived their lives for 20 days (Iplikci 2013). I argue that this experience of living together in a de-commodified and radically democratic space allowed them to go beyond the banality of difference resulting from blood, birth and belonging. They stopped misrecognizing each other as limits to their freedom, and begin recognizing one another as their own mediated realizations. Within this context of an ethics of solidarity and political subject formation, difference was also radicalized, as it was no longer a mere marker of diversity, but a means to create different modalities of lives, an example of which was realized in the Taksim Commune.

I argue that the experience of living together is a decisive moment in the formation of the protestors in the new left generation of Turkey. According to Nancy Whittier, the process of producing a new generational self-identification is realized through the renegotiation of group boundaries, developing an oppositional political consciousness and politicization of everday/night life (Whittier 1997, 762). In living together, the Gezi protestors produced themselves as a new political generation. For the very first time in the history of Turkey, so many different political groups occupied the same space for an extended duration of time. As a result of co-existing in Gezi Park, they delineated their ideological boundaries anew with respect to their class, gender, sexual, ethnic, ecological, religious politics. Through this negotiation, the oppositional political consciousness that the former radical generations transmitted (Kertzer 1983, 137–138) was transformed in the context of highly politicized quotidian practices during dwelling in Gezi Park.

The experience of co-existing in the park also illustrates that the class character of a social movement cannot be inferred from the class origin of its proponents, rather it ought to be looked for in its historical significance. As the 20 days of living together in the park demonstrates, the Gezi protests are a mass movement pursuing a set of aims very clearly defined: equality, respect for particularities, solidarity, rejection of institutionalized authority, sharing, refusal of economic privileges, respect for the natural and cultural environment. These practical objectives express very concretely the programme of the next great social revolution: the establishment of a classless and stateless society, living in abundance and sorority. In the capitalist Turkey, there is only one major group of classes, which can accomplish such a thorough transformation, that is working classes. As a structural positioning, working classes do not appear as subjective agency, but realize themselves through diverse age, gender, ethnic, religious, sexual subjectivities. These various subjectivities are the most current means of expression of class situations. They are the modalities of being, the empirical manifestations of classes. Therefore, the working-class character of Gezi cannot exist independent of these different concrete subjectivities, but it can only exist in and through them.

Two days after the evacuation of the park (June 17, 2013), something strange happened in Taksim Square. A young man with his hands in his pockets and a knapsack at his feet, stood still and silent from 6 p.m. to 2 a.m. (Kongar and Kucukkaya 2013, 172). This man was a performance artist, whose name was Erdem Gunduz and epithetically became known as the 'standing man' (Sanul and Erali 2013). The political significance of this event was obvious for the protestors who had been terrorized by the police: the standing man was *witnessing* the brute force of the police, the state's violent silencing of its own citizens, and in so doing he was signifying the resilience of the Gezi Protests. Standing man's still, silent and singular performance went viral on Twitter, the main medium of the protestors.

As a result, standing man was multiplied everywhere in Turkey. Standing still and silent with a book, or a bottle of water, or a small pack of biscuits for hours, people became standing-persons, so as to show that the Gezi Protests did not terminate. The police detained some standing men, yet they could not legitimize their action against the inactive action of standing-men. The government officials tried to ridicule the standing man in a desperately cheap discourse, arguing that they wanted to stop Turkey's advancement, whereas the government was tirelessly working towards greater progression. This discourse did not have credibility in the eyes of the public, and the standing man became another symbol of the Gezi Protests.

I argue that the event of standing man is also a moment in the creation of Gezi's ethics of solidarity and the subject formation of the protestors. The phenomena of the standing man demonstrates that even when the possibilities of occupying a space and living together is obliterated by the state, the protestors can create a space of solidarity in which they turn their bodies into a monument of collective action. Each individual performing a standing man witnesses the unbearable violence inflicted on the protestors. However, the temporality offered by this performance exceeds being a signifier of a past event, since at the same time it alludes to a common future. In implying this future through what has been lost, it becomes the embodiment of the Gezi spirit. Thus, the protestor-performer realizes her particular political being in the unity (not *identity*) of this collective spirit.

Standing man was not the only example of such performances taking place during the Gezi Protests. For instance, until the end of August 2013, there had been 135 songs written, produced, arranged, and rearranged (Yildirim 2013, 265). In addition to pop, jazz, classical, folk music performances, there were modern, classical, and folk dance performances, theatre performances in pre-organized, spontaneous and *ad hoc* forms. Through intertextual citationality

THE GEZI PROTESTS　　161

and aesthetic displacement (Yildirim 2013; Snyder 2014), these performances draw on the collective social, political and cultural memory. By situating them in the present moment of the Gezi protests, they generate a "playful construction of a community that bound together disparate groups who want, among other things, a say in how their world [is] administered" (Snyder 2014, n.p.).

Ron Eyerman and Bryan Turner argue that "a generational cohort survives by maintaining a collective memory...[that] produce[s] an affective basis for generations, namely, an emotional substratum which is sustained by ritual practice" (1998, 97). Following Eyerman and Turner, I suggest that the re-production and vast distribution of images, songs and other Gezi-related cultural productions through social media, and constant repetition of performances, such as standing man, provide the affective and sensuous engagements for the sustenance of the new left generation after the possibility of living together was eradicated by the state. What made this generation new, and the protests novel, was also the way in which they produced cultural and aesthetic productions. To be sure, former left generations had great artists who produced cultural and aesthetic productions in order to support the radical movements of the day. Yet while those productions were usually perceived as providing moral support behind the front lines, the Gezi protestors deployed cultural and aesthetic productions *as the very form* of the protests – inseparable from its content.

Besides living together and the transformative power of performance, the Anti-Capitalist Muslim Youth group's participation in and contribution to the Gezi Protests constitutes a crucial juncture in the course of the protests. This group made their political debut in 2012 on May Day by marching from a mosque to Taksim Square to join the May Day celebrations/demonstrations (The New York Times, 2012). The intellectual leader of the group, Ihsan Eliacik, identifies as "a Muslim with an anti-capitalist and revolutionary understanding of Islam" (Hurriyet Daily News, 2013). Demonstrating their religious political stance, some of their famous slogans include 'inshallah socialism will prevail,' 'all property belongs to Allah,' 'down with capitalism with Islamic ablution,' 'all oppressed are equal,' 'freedom from slavery,' 'Allah, bread, freedom' (Antikapitalist Muslumanlar, 2012).

The existence and appearance of such a group in the Gezi Protests was an unusual phenomenon. From its entrance in politics, Islamism had generally merged with the bourgeois interests in Turkey. Political Islam found its zenith with Erdogan's AKP, from its inception to today, resulting in the implementation of an aggressive set of bourgeois politics. Yet, to be sure, like all religions, Islam has various interpretations. Therefore, some Islamist political currents, such as Erbakan's National View, had an anti-imperialist tinge to their overall political stance. However, this anti-imperialism has never been articulated in terms of class and social justice, but mostly in terms of religious xenophobia (Oncu 2014, 169).

The Anti-Capitalist Muslim Youth, on the other hand, appeared as an overtly working-class organization. They participated in the Gezi Protests starting from its very early stages. Their valuable role and visibility in the protests, to a large extent, prevented the marginalization of the protest and protestors through the ideological efforts of the government. One of the main ideological tactics deployed against any kind of political dissent by Erdogan and government officials had been to marginalize dissenters through a religious, moralist discourse. This time, too, Erdogan called the protestors 'drunkards,' 'looters,' 'alcoholics,' 'extremists' in order to degrade them before the public. The pro-government groups fabricated gossip that the protestors were drinking beer, even having group sex in mosques where they sought refuge from police violence. The Anti-Capitalist Muslim Youth testified against these allegations and their participation in the protests proved the legitimacy of the protestors for the broader public opinion.

More importantly, the existence of an Islamic political organization working in solidarity with leftists for socialism fractured the deep-seated secular/religious duality in Turkey, which has been one of the major political fault lines in the history of the Republic of Turkey (Arat-Koc 2013). Thus, the Gezi Protests, as Oncu argues, constitutes "a moment of overcoming the laïc/Islamic dual opposition of Turkish capitalist modernity" (Oncu 2014, 173). I argue that this fracturing and momentary overcoming contributes to the subject formation of the next left generation in Turkey by showing that the existing borders of the political landscape are well-worn and demand a radical transformation. In other words, the Gezi generation's relationship to religion mediated through the Anti-Capitalist Muslim Youth, constitutes a "novel approach in assimilating, using and developing" (Mannheim 1952, 293) the given social, political and cultural conditions (Pilcher 1994, 491). Unlike the former generations of the left, whose attitude towards religion was mostly monolithic and dismissive, the new generation has shifted the focus from the content of religion (inherently reactionary, or progressive) to its different interpretations and practitioners. In doing so, this new generation has opened up the possibilities of integrating a significant number of religiously identified people of Turkey into radical revolutionary politics.

In Lieu of a Conclusion: After the Gezi Protests?

The Gezi Park Protests ended around September 2013. In the meantime, Erdogan and the AKP have managed to fight off serious allegations of corruption, which erupted on December 17, 2013 with the arrest of three cabinet minister's sons. Also, they gained a victory in a country-wide local election on March 30, 2014. Finally, Erdogan was elected as the President of the Republic of Turkey on August 10, 2014. Drawing on these facts, some politicians, commentators, analysts, and academics have asserted that the Gezi Protests have lost any remaining power.

I believe that the specter of Gezi is haunting Turkey. Its memory is vivid and it is still the main reference point in the political arena. As I argue throughout the chapter, in the political history of Turkey, the Gezi protests constitute the moment in which the next left generation makes its debut on the historical stage. To be sure, the Gezi protests do not create this new generation single-handedly. Socio-political events prior to Gezi, such as the 2009–10 Tekel workers' strike, are the parts of the process of making of this generation. However, this new left generation that implies a common sensitivity and a sharing of feeling and worldview manifests itself through the striking social event of Gezi. There might not be concrete victories for the working-classes who have begun to recognize themselves in their gendered, ethnic, religious, sexual diversity. Nevertheless, the peoples of Turkey are experiencing the Gezi-spirit-related transformative moments everyday/night. I would like to end this article with one of them.

***

My friend was not in Turkey when the protests had started although he had many friends who participated in the protests. After the first brutal crackdown on the protestors, he learned through Facebook that his friends were injured and having difficulties getting help. He immediately contacted and told them to go to his mother's place, who was a retired nurse. He knew that his mother would not turn them away.

The friends he was sending home for help were all from the LGBT block. He was also gay. He had never discussed this with his mother, but he had suspected that she already knew. This was obviously going to be his coming out to her and hence he felt anxious. After taking care of the injured protestors, she called him and said that his friends were safe and sound, but she did not mention anything about sexuality. My friend learned from his friends that they quickly had become friends with his mom. She was serving as a nurse at the park during the day. Her home was also functioning as a LGBT infirmary.

My friend went to this year's Pride Parade in Istanbul with his mom. He was pleasantly surprised when he saw that his mother had become a local celebrity among the LGBT protestors, and admitted that he was a bit jealous because his mother was at the center of attention and love.

You cannot buy the revolution. You cannot make the revolution. You can only be the revolution. It is in your spirit, or it is nowhere.

URSULA K. LE GUIN (2001, 301)

References

Amnesty International. *Adding Injustice to Injury: One Year on From the Gezi Park Protests in Turkey,* 2014. Accessed September 20, 2014. http://www.amnesty.org/en/library/info/EUR44/010/2014/en.

Antikapitalist Muslumanlar. "Homepage". 2012. Accessed September 27, 2014. http://www.antikapitalistmuslumanlar.org.

Arat-Koc, Sedef. "Three Suprises of the Gezi Park Protests." *Peace Magazine.* July-September 2013: 6–7.

Babac, Alp Tekin. "Welcome to Chappulcity." Sendika.org, June 13, 2013. Accessed September 26, 2014. http://www.sendika.org/2013/06/welcome-to-chappulcity-alp-tekin-babac/.

Bannerji, Himani. "Building from Marx: Reflections on Class and Race." *Social Justice* 32, 4 (2005): 144–160.

Baykan, Aysegul and Tali Hatuka. "Politics and Culture in the Making of Public Space: Taksim Square, 1 May 1977, Istanbul." *Planning Perspectives* 25, 1 (2010): 49–68.

Beyoglu Municipality. "Short History." 2014. Accessed September 16, 2014. http://en.beyoglu.bel.tr/beyoglu/beyoglu_guide.aspx?SectionId=1674.

Bianet. "Ali Ismail Korkmaz Anmasina Polis ve Jandarma Saldirdi." [The police and gendarmerie attacked the vigil of Ali Ismail Korkmaz] 2013. Accessed September 20, 2014. http://bianet.org/bianet/insan-haklari/148425-ali-ismail-korkmaz-anmasina-polis-ve-jandarma-saldirdi.

Boratav, Korkut. "A Matured Class Based Contumacy." June 28, 2013. Accessed September 17, 2014. http://www.sendika.org/2013/06/korkut-boratav-1-evaluates-the-gezi-resistance-a-matured-class-based-contumacy/.

Chouraqui, Frank. "Turquie: Gezi Park et le Sauvetage de la Politique." *Les Temps Modernes* 677 (2014): 162–186.

Erogul, Cem. *Demokrat Parti: Tarihi ve Ideolojisi.* [The Democrat Party: Its History and Ideology]. Istanbul: Yordam Kitap, 2014.

Eyerman, Ron and Bryan Turner. "Outline of a Theory of Generations." *European Journal of Social Theory* 1, 1 (1998): 91–106.

Gul, Murat, John Dee and Cahide Nur Cunuk. "Istanbul's Taksim Square and Gezi Park: the Place of Protest and the Ideology of Place." *Journal of Architecture and Urbanism* 38, 1 (2014): 63–72.

Gurcan, Efe Can and Efe Peker. "Turkey's Gezi Park Demonstrations of 2013: A Marxian Analysis of the Political Moment." *Socialism and Democracy* 28, 1 (2014): 70–89.

Harvey, David. *The New Imperialism.* Oxford: Oxford University Press, 2003.

Harvey, David. "The Right to the City." *New Left Review* 53 (2008). Accessed September 14, 2014. http://newleftreview.org/II/53/david-harvey-the-right-to-the-city#_ednref12.

Hikmet, Nazim. "The Walnut Tree." 1957. Accessed September 14, 2014. https://www.marxists.org/subject/art/literature/nazim/walnuttree.html.

Hikmet, Nazim. "Plea." 2007. Accessed September 09, 2014. http://www.nazimhikmet.org.tr/kronolojik3-en.asp.

Hizlan, Dogan (ed). *Beyoglu'ndan Esintiler: Beyoglu'nun 150 Yillik Edebiyatindan Secmeler* [(Breezes from Beyoglu: Selections of Beyoglu's 150 Years of Literature)]. Istanbul: Istanbul Kultur Sanat Vakfi, 2008.

Hurriyet Daily News. "Anti-Capitalist Muslim leader says Gezi youth want a new approach to Islam." July 22, 2013. Accessed September 27, 2014. http://www.hurriyetdailynews.com/anti-capitalist-muslim-leader-says-gezi-youth-want-new-approach-to-islam.aspx?PageID=238&NID=51138&NewsCatID=338.

International Federation for Human Rights. *Turkey: Gezi, One Year On.* Accessed September 10, 2014. http://www.fidh.org/IMG/pdf/turkey_avril_2014_uk_web.pdf.

Iplikci, Muge. *Biz Orada Mutluyduk* [We Were Happy There]. Istanbul: Dogan Kitap, 2013.

Kertzer, David. "Generation as a Sociological Problem." *Annual Review of Sociology* 9 (1983): 125–149.

Kongar, Emre and Aykut Kucukkaya. *Turkiye'yi Sarsan Otuz Gun: Gezi Direnisi.* [The Thirty Days that Shook Turkey: The Gezi Resistance]. Istanbul: Cumhuriyet Kitaplari, 2013.

Le Guin, Ursula K. *The Dispossessed: An Ambiguous Utopia.* New York: HarperCollins, 2001.

Letsch, Constanze. "A Year after the Protests, Gezi Park Nurtures the Seeds of a New Turkey." *The Guardian,* May 29, 2014. Accessed September 10. http://www.theguardian.com/world/2014/may/29/gezi-park-year-after-protests-seeds-new-turkey.

Lowy, Michael. "Surekli Birikime Karsi Yanit; Surekli Devrimdir!" [The Answer to Permanent Accumulation is Permanent Revolution!] in *Gezi Direnisi Ustune Dusunceler* (Reflections on the Gezi Revolt), edited by Ozay Goztepe, 155–169. Ankara: Nota Bene, 2013.

Luxemburg, Rosa. *The Accumulation of Capital.* 1913. Accessed September 14, 2014. https://www.marxists.org/archive/luxemburg/1913/accumulation-capital/ch27.htm.

Mannheim, Karl. "The Problem of Generations," in *Essays on the Sociology of Knowledge,* edited by Karl Paul Kecskemeti, 276–322. London: Routledge and Kegan Paul, 1952.

Marx, Karl. *Capital: Volume 1.* London: Penguin Books, 1976.

Moudouros, Nikos. "Rethinking Islamic Hegemony in Turkey through Gezi Park." *Journal of Balkan and Near Eastern Studies* 16, 2 (2014): 181–195.

Mungan, Murathan. *Hayat Atolyesi.* [The Atelier of Life]. Istanbul: Metis Yayinlari, 2009.

New York Times. "Pious Turks Push for Labour Justice." May 9, 2012. Accessed September 27, 2014. http://www.nytimes.com/2012/05/10/world/middleeast/pious-turks-push-for-labor-justice.html?pagewanted=all&_r=2&.

Oliver, Kelly. *Witnessing: Beyond Recognition.* Minneapolis and London: University of Minnesota Press, 2001.

Oncu, Ahmet. "Turkish Capitalist Modernity and the Gezi Revolt." *Journal of Historical Sociology* 27, 2 (2014): 151–176.

Pilcher, Jane. "Mannheim's Sociology of Generations: An Undervalued Legacy." *British Journal of Sociology* 45, 3 (1994): 481–495.

Samanyolu, Haber. "Basbakan Erdogan'dan Taksim Icin Ilk Aciklama." [PM Erdogan's First Reaction to Taksim], 2014. Accessed September 10. http://www.samanyoluhaber.com/web-tv/basbakan-erdogandan-taksim-icin-ilk-aciklama- 1964-video-haberi/.

Sanul, Gokce and Ceylan Usaki Erali. "In Between Reality and Illusion: Occupy Gezi." *FWSAblog,* July 19, 2013. Accessed September 27, 2014. http://fwsablog.org.uk/2013/07/19/in-between-reality-and-illusion-occupy-gezi/.

Schick, Irvin Cemil. "Nationalism Meets the Sex Trade: Istanbul's District of Beyoglu/Pera During the Early Twentieth Century." Paper presented at the Amherst and Hampshire Colleges Workshop. Amherst College, February 16–18, 2009.

Snyder, Stephen. "Gezi Park and the Transformative Power of Art." *Roar Magazine* January 8, 2014. Accessed September 27, 2014. http://roarmag.org/2014/01/nietzsche-gezi-power-art/.

Sonmez, Mustafa. *Kent, Kapital ve Gezi Direnisi.* [City, Capital and the Gezi Resistance] Ankara: Nota Bene, 2013.

Tanyildiz, Gokboru Sarp. "Yasanilabilir Hayatlar Yaratma Mucadelesi." [A Struggle for Making Livable Lives] In *Direnisi Dusunmek: 2013 Taksim Gezi Olaylari.* [Thinking About the Resistance: 2013 Taksim Gezi Events], edited by Volkan Celebi and Ahmet Soysal, 75–79. Istanbul: MonoKL, 2013.

Tugal, Cihan. "Occupy Gezi: The Limits of Turkey's Neoliberal Success." *Jadaliyya,* June 4, 2013a. http://www.jadaliyya.com/pages/index/12009/occupy-gezi_the-limits-of-turkey's-neoliberal-succ.

Tugal, Cihan. *Gezi'nin Yukselisi, Liberalizmin Dususu.* [The Rise of Gezi, the Decline of Liberalism]. Istanbul: Agora Kitapligi, 2013b.

Tugal, Cihan. "'Resistance everywhere': The Gezi Revolt in Global Perspective." *New Perspectives on Turkey* 49 (2013c): 157–172.

Whittier, Nancy. "Political Generations, Micro-Cohorts, and the Transformation of Social Movements." *American Sociological Review* 62, 5 (1997): 760–778.

Yildirim, Baris. "Gezi'nerek Sanat: Bir Elim Sanatta Bir Elim Gazda." ["The Wandering of Art at Gezi."] In *Gezi Direnisi Ustune Dusunceler* [Reflections on the Gezi Revolt], edited by Ozay Goztepe, 265–277. Ankara: Nota Bene, 2013.

PART 3

Memory, History and the "New Generation"

∵

CHAPTER 7

'Freedom is a Daily Practice': The Palestinian Youth Movement and *Jil* Oslo

Sunaina Maira

In March 2011, a series of dramatic protests by young Palestinians erupted in the West Bank and Gaza and also inside Israel. The protesters set up camps in the center of Ramallah, Gaza City, and Haifa, engaging in a hunger strike and demanding an end to the division between Fatah and Hamas and later, in solidarity with Palestinian prisoners in Israeli jails. The stenciled slogan, 'Hungry 4 Freedom,' appeared on walls around Ramallah and Haifa as young activists from both sides of the Green Line were galvanized by the protests, which took place in conjunction with cultural events and music performances by young artists and rappers. This new youth movement, inspired partly by the Arab uprisings, called for a change in the political status quo and is a new phase of ongoing resistance against Israeli occupation, colonialism, and apartheid. But it largely remained in the shadow of the much more dramatic revolts in North Africa which generally eclipsed this difficult and complex struggle that a new generation of Palestinian activists were trying to wage for democracy *as well as* national liberation.

The label, the 'youth movement,' referred to a range of political actions and campaigns by a loose coalition of young activists, with diverse political orientations and organizing strategies, who generally shared the core political belief that it was time for an alternative politics and a refusal of party-based factionalism. What was striking and complex about these protests by what I call '*jil Oslo*,' or the 'Oslo generation,' is that they were opposed to Israeli occupation and colonization and also to the vision of nationhood and national politics of the Palestinian regime, in both the West Bank and Gaza. The independent youth movement (*al-Herak a-Shebabi al-Mustakil*), as it came to be called, emerged from the political malaise of the period following the Oslo Accords of 1993 and fundamentally represents a critique of the political paradigm and policies of normalization and repression, as well as neoliberalism and depoliticization, that Oslo consolidated in Palestine.

My ethnographic research in Palestine in 2011–2013 explored how Palestinian youth involved in this movement have been producing new strategies and languages of protest against colonial dispossession and displacement, as well

© KONINKLIJKE BRILL NV, LEIDEN, 2017 | DOI 10.1163/9789004344518_009

as recreating earlier political principles that they, and many others including in the diaspora, feel have been abandoned by the Palestinian national leadership since Oslo. This movement has built on and emerged from previous histories of national struggle in Palestine, while challenging or rethinking the contemporary political conjuncture and striking a path independent of the major political parties and factions. In this sense, the youth movement is very much crossing generational lines to align itself with an earlier notion of militant resistance and revolutionary struggle that they, and others, feel have been abandoned by the Palestinian Authority (PA). At the same time, young Palestinian artists have been using new, or recreated, cultural forms to resist Israeli occupation and apartheid policies and express a critique of the PA. From visual art and music to dance and theater, Palestinian youth in the West Bank, Gaza, and Israel have been continuing a tradition of using the arts to oppose the erasure of their collective identities and to (re)imagine what collective struggle might look, or sound, like. One of the significant expressions of this cultural politics is that produced by Palestinian rappers and graffiti artists who have been drawing on hip hop culture and combining it with Palestinian and Arab musical and visual idioms to express political critiques and solidarity with political struggles, within and beyond Palestine. These young artists are experimenting with aesthetic idioms and new cultural practices, and are also often deeply engaged with political movements as well as social critiques that involve a reshaping of the public sphere and national politics. The 'jil' in 'jil Oslo' is thus not meant to privilege the concept of generation as such but rather to point to a particular historical *moment* in which young Palestinians who came of age after Oslo, and were shaped by the second Intifada of 2000–2005, are confronting the retreat from mass mobilization since the Intifadas and the depoliticization of public space in the context of an emerging neoliberal order in Palestine. Thus, 'jil Oslo' indexes questions about temporality as well as space in thinking about youth protest which is engaged with political imaginaries as well as material forces.

The research in 2011–13 included field work and interviews in the West Bank (Ramallah, Dheisheh camp in Bethlehem, and Balata camp in Nablus), East Jerusalem, and Haifa. I did a total of 39 individual interviews in the West Bank, Jerusalem, and '48 Palestine, or inside the 1948 borders of Israel,[1] with young people who were between the ages of 18 and 25 years. These included nineteen rappers and artists; eleven young activists; two young artists who have worked with youth doing graffiti, break dancing, and hip hop; and four youth program workers. In addition, I did focus group discussions with college students in

---

1 Palestinians inside Israel are commonly referred to as "'48 Palestinians" thus including them in the national Palestinian body.

order to talk with young people who were not themselves hip hop artists or hip hop fans, which included 40 students at Bir Zeit University in the West Bank from different cities, towns, villages, and camps, followed up by individual interviews with some students.[2] I also did a focus group discussion with fifteen Palestinian youth from a variety of locations in Israel at a youth forum organized in Nazareth by Baladna, a Palestinian youth organization based in Haifa. In addition, I have had numerous informal conversations with many other young people – students, activists, and artists – and with older activists and artists, community members, and scholars about this topic, in the West Bank, Jerusalem, and in '48 Palestine.

In this research, I link the political and the cultural fronts of resistance and experimentation in order to offer a preliminary discussion of the ways in which new youth cultures and political movements in Palestine are challenging the dominant political paradigms of the post-Oslo era. My field work and interviews focused on the emergence of Palestinian hip hop artists and young activists on the public stage, the ways they transformed that arena, and the sentiments of inspiration, disapproval, and solidarity they have evoked. I explored the ways in which youth are grappling with the meaning of what 'politics' means, in a moment in Palestine in which it seems that political vocabularies and strategies have been exhausted or eviscerated, and when political skepticism and fatigue is pervasive.

In thinking youth culture and youth activism together, the larger project on which this essay is based explores how the politics of cultural production is related to the culture of protest politics for a particular segment of Palestinian youth in the West Bank, Jerusalem, and Israel in the post-Oslo moment (Maira 2013). I view hip hop as a form of cultural production that is inextricably intertwined with the political and the social. Hip hop is not just as a musical form but a youth subculture, that is, a group of young people defined by consumption or production of specific cultural forms, such as rap or graffiti art, in relation to the social contradictions faced by these youth in particular political and historical contexts (Hall et al. 1976). Furthermore, young Palestinian activists, or those engaged in various ways with 'politics' but who may not fit conventional definitions of what activism looks like, are also part of a youth

---

2 While the focus group discussions were roughly evenly divided between male and female youth, only eight of the individual interviews were with young women. This reflects the dominance of hip hop by male artists as well as the preponderance of male activists in the West Bank, an issue that I discuss in the larger work. In contrast, there are many more female hip hop artists among '48 Palestinians so while I interviewed a much smaller number of '48 Palestinian youth, three of the six artists I spoke to were young women and the two youth activists I interviewed were female.

subculture – or multiple subcultures – based on political protest and organizing; in some cases these subcultures overlap with and draw on subcultural expressions such as hip hop, but also on many other cultural forms proliferating in Palestine.[3]

Youth culture is a key site where young people express their social identities, political perspectives, and imaginings of the future. Palestinian youth culture, however, has generally been neglected in scholarly research in favor of psychological studies focused on issues of trauma, self-esteem, and coping skills for Palestinian youth, as well as quantitative studies and surveys assessing young people's political views within a largely pre-determined framework of existing political movements and what counts as 'politics' itself (Barber 2001, Elbedour 1998, Shadid and Seltzer 1989). More recent research on Palestinian youth has highlighted the agency of young people in conflict situations or refugee youth in the context of intergenerational shifts in national identity and there is a small body of qualitative research exploring how religion, gender, class, and generation shape the political perspectives of Palestinian youth (Collins 2004, Hart 2008, Nguyen-Gilham et al. 2008, Peteet 1994a). Some of this work is focused on Palestinian refugee youth in Lebanon or Jordan, and much of this literature is situated in the context of the first or second Intifadas, that is, spanning the late 1980s to the early 2000s. Other studies have highlighted education, social life, and the gendered dimensions of adolescent identity and political commitment for Palestinian youth (Hammer 2005, Kevorkian 1993, Kevorkian 2012). However, there is a need for more research that investigates how this generation of Palestinians that has come of age in a globalized youth culture is producing political and national identities through new cultural expressions. The under theorization of youth culture in this literature is related to the under theorizing of the concept of 'generation,' in that the construct of youth is itself often not interrogated enough, in my view, as a political and cultural – not just developmental – category. 'Generation,' is of course, not synonymous with 'youth,' but those who are defined as not-quite adults or not-yet citizens are more often that not viewed through the lens of generation and often, also, of intergenerational differences or conflicts. Thinking about the epistemology of youth as a generational category, fundamentally based on the notion of transition into the social order, allows us to understand how this category for identification and interpretation is generally burdened by the assumption

---

3   There are, of course, many youth subcultures in the West Bank, Gaza, Jerusalem, and among '48 Palestinians that may or may not be directly engaged with questions of national politics – from car racing (or drag racing) that involves young men and women and fandom among youth who support Real Madrid and Barcelona soccer teams, to parkour (an acrobatic sport popular among young men in Gaza) and Islamic fashion styles.

THE PALESTINIAN YOUTH MOVEMENT AND JIL OSLO   175

that certain forms of cultural expression or political activity are legitimate for a particular age group. This is why, I argue, the youth movement and Palestinian hip hop are often bedeviled by critiques of representing inauthentic national culture or improper national politics.

In this essay, I will focus in particular on the graffiti associated with Palestinian hip hop culture and the youth movement, given that a fair amount of attention has already been given to Palestinian and Arab rap in relation to the Arab uprisings. Palestinian graffiti art, I argue, is a poetics of displacement, protest, and decoloniality, which simultaneously unsettles and recreates national cultural imaginaries. Furthermore, graffiti art is an important tool for production of a counter-public in contexts of repression as well as demobilization. For example, Murid, a young artist from Ramallah, said that graffiti is "an effective way to tell a story, especially when people have things to say and they are not always heard." Graffiti art is a potent medium for political communication, particularly of subversive or dangerous messages, as it can be produced anonymously in public spaces, and so it is not surprising that it has historically been used as a tool of political communication in Palestine and is increasingly visible in places such as Ramallah, Bethlehem, Haifa, or Jaffa.[4]

It is interesting to consider Palestinian graffiti and the youth movement as expressions of what Walter Mignolo and Rolando Vasquez (2013) describe as 'underground conversations' promoting a decolonial aestheSis, which enunciate a critique of the violence of Euro-American modernity and coloniality. In their confrontation with coloniality, young artists and activists attempt to offer an alternative discourse of decoloniality to the national vision of the Palestinian leadership and the violent erasures of the settler colonial project.

Jil Oslo

The youth of *jil* Oslo, particularly those who are in their late teens to mid-twenties today and were born just before or after Oslo, have come of age in a very different political reality than the previous generation. The use of the word *jil* – as in *jil al-Nakba* (the generation that endured the Nakba of 1948), *jil a-Thawra* (the generation of the Palestinian revolution of the late 1950s and 1960s), or *jil al-Intifada* (the generation that experienced the first intifada that began in 1987) – underscores the national significance of the concept of

---

4 I focus here on graffiti produced by Palestinian youth, not the graffiti that has proliferated on the Wall which is largely by international solidarity activists and artists, such as Banksy, which has already received a great deal of attention and about which there is an active debate among Palestinians, including criticism (see Parry 2011).

generation in Palestine and also the historical experiences of different generations in resisting colonialism and warfare, including before 1948 (Collins 2004, 16–17). These generational markers do not necessarily signify historical or political discontinuity but rather speak to the process by which generational development is articulated with political resistance across time, and highlights the persistence of both colonial violence and Palestinian collective resistance. The label '*jil Oslo*' does not fit easily within this historical genealogy given that it refers not to a phase of resistance but to a new phase of colonial governmentality (indexed by the term 'Oslo'), in which colonial violence has taken a different, sometimes more ambiguous form – a moment when collective resistance has been undermined and is shrouded in ambivalence. It is possible that it is the ambiguity and ambivalence encoded by using 'jil' and 'Oslo' together that make this label rather uncommon. But this is also what makes it important in order to confront the current political conjuncture in Palestine and foreground the challenge faced by those whose political development has occurred in a time when the belief in, and perhaps romance of, revolutionary resistance has faded but when radical critique is as urgent as ever.

The public protests by the jil Oslo activists were in part a critical response to Mahmoud Abbas' bid for statehood in the United Nations in fall 2011, and the degraded vision of national sovereignty it enshrined, as well as in solidarity with the dramatic hunger strikes by hundreds of Palestinian prisoners that began in spring 2012, which was dubbed the 'prisoners' intifada.' Youth organized protest camps in cities and towns such as Ramallah, Haifa, and Nazareth in solidarity with Palestinian prisoners incarcerated by Israel, engaging in hunger strikes themselves and spearheading a protest movement that Palestinian political parties in the West Bank eventually supported or tried to hijack. While I was living in the West Bank in the fall of 2011 and in 2012–13, there continued to be waves of intense protests involving or initiated by youth, in solidarity with Palestinian prisoners and against the Oslo accords and the PA's economic policies, evolving from the protests in solidarity with the Arab revolutions in March 2011 and against the splitting of the West Bank and Gaza. Young activists also mobilized publicly during this period against rising prices and the PA's economic and security agreements with Israel, as well as meetings in Ramallah between Abbas, President Obama, and Israeli officials. The youth movement in the West Bank included groups such as Youth for Dignity, Free Palestinian Youth, Intifada, Youth against the Settlements, Youth who Love the Homeland, and others. Many young activists have also been involved in ongoing organizing against the Wall, the settlements, and the Freedom Riders campaign against the segregated Israeli transport system in the West Bank, as well as part of the Boycott, Divestment, and Sanctions movement.

Within Israel, there is also a growing Palestinian youth movement that has been mobilizing against police brutality and state violence, in opposition to conscription into the Israeli national civil service, discrimination and repression in Israeli universities, land confiscation, and housing restrictions, among other issues (Abed 2011). Activists and artists, from both sides of the Green Line have collaborated and coordinated with one another in a protest culture and movement that defies Israeli colonial borders. In fact, I argue that the youth movement has remapped the Palestinian nation, as one of its core principles is insisting that the Palestinian nation and the national movement has to include those from the West Bank, Gaza, East Jerusalem, '1948 Palestine' (Israel), and the diaspora.[5] This call for a unified Palestine and national movement is not a new political vision, and the youth movement and hip hop are not the only sites in which the call to resist the partitioning of Palestine is being revived or recreated. However, the recent youth movement as well as hip hop subculture have brought together youth from different locations in Palestine, who cannot always meet but who coordinate virtually and engage in a common challenge to 'proper' politics and acceptable national identity.

Furthermore, this political and cultural activism has emerged outside of the established parties and factions in the West Bank, Gaza, and in Israel, hence the label, the 'independent youth movement.' The surveys conducted by Sharek Youth Forum of youth in the West Bank and Gaza report an increasing distrust, if not outright rejection, of existing political factions. In 2013, 73% of youth surveyed said that they did not belong to any political faction, 39% saying this was due to their "lack of confidence" in these parties (Sharek Youth Forum 2013, 52). The disillusionment with established political factions, including left factions, which had historically provided established youth wings that were the basis for campus politics, increased in the wake of the second legislative elections in 2006 and the subsequent violent conflicts between Hamas and Fatah (see Sharek Youth Forum 2010). Many of the young activists who have been protesting in the streets share a refusal of party-based factionalism or are former members of factions, and they seek an alternative, more unified, national politics and, for some, a revival or reform of the Palestine Liberation

---

5 I want to note that I use the term '48 Palestine' because it is the category that Palestinians, including youth and hip hop artists, themselves use and generally prefer for referring to Palestinians in Israel. This appellation is not a denial of the existence of Israel, as some assume, but it is a complex geographic as well as temporal label that encodes a critical analysis of the colonial nature of the condition of Palestinians within Israel that is rarely acknowledged, generally unknown outside of Palestine, and often denied. I thank Mark Ayyash for some of these insights.

Organization as a national framework representing all the Palestinian people, as do some Palestinian youth in the diaspora (Nabusli 2014, 116).

This movement-like all political activism in Palestine-was met with skepticism and criticism by some Palestinians, including by other young activists and artists, who variously felt that the protests were not sufficiently connected to grassroots mobilization or were led mainly by middle-class or Western-educated youth and young people working for NGOs; these were critiques that some youth within the movement also shared, as I found, and tried to address as the movement evolved. I want to note that this movement does not represent *all* of youth politics or youth activism in the West Bank, Gaza, and '48 Palestine. There are clearly many young Palestinians who were not part of these protests and others who may not share these political views or may be nationalist but within a different political framework, such as Islamist politics. My interviews with college students who were neither activists nor hip hop artists helped me situate the movement within a broader spectrum of political views among youth. The youth movement that emerged in the West Bank, Jerusalem, and '48 Palestine in this period was not based on religious identity or Islamist politics and not affiliated with any Islamist parties; indeed, these young activists and artists rejected the political vision of both Hamas and Fatah. It was evident that the core political analysis of the youth movement regarding Oslo was shared by many progressive and left activists and artists, even if some disagreed with its tactics or rhetoric, particularly with the protesters' initial call for unity between political parties that many had no faith in any more. It was also apparent that the movement drew youth from across the class spectrum and helped break the 'fear barrier' about protesting in public spaces, for example, by rallying in front of the President's compound in Ramallah and confronting the PA security forces in the streets.

These public protests were significant for Palestinian national politics for by the time of Oslo, according to George Giacaman (1998, 4), "most parties, including those on the left, were quickly losing whatever mass base" they had during the first intifada and there was a decline in the grassroots involvement of student groups, women's organizations, and popular committees throughout the West Bank and Gaza.[6] Giacaman observes that the Oslo Accords precipitated a 'crisis' for the Palestinian national struggle, marked by "loss of a clear cause, lack of hope, and perception of the end of the national project." (ibid., 8) The supposed political withdrawal or apathy of Palestinian youth today has to be

---

6   The Oslo Accords weakened the revolutionary movement, as did the internal problems that plagued the different factions as a new political class and bureaucratic elite was established. See Sayigh 1999.

understood in the historical context of the crisis for the Palestinian national movement, one in which youth are currently not represented in the "leadership and decision-making," even though they have been key actors in the national struggle and especially the first Intifada (Seif 2000, 20). Ruanne Abourahme, a young artist from Ramallah who formed the multimedia performance collective, Tashweesh ('disruption'), with Basel Abbas and the rapper Boikutt (which evolved from Ramallah Underground, a pioneering hip hop collective), said incisively that for Palestinian youth in the 1990s, "It was a moment when the revolutionary movement was, in a sense, dissolving after Oslo. I think probably young Palestinians started looking for something else to articulate their experiences, for they were still experiencing the full force of the racist state."

The contradictory reality of this new phase of colonization is marked by the fact that the PA did not achieve full sovereignty after Oslo – in fact it has limited sovereignty only over a fraction of the Occupied Territories – and became the subcontractor for the occupation, in a sense, managing security and repressing dissent through its own internal police and intelligence apparatus. Ramzy Baroud (2013) observes of the crisis of faith in Palestinian political leadership since the concessions made in the Oslo agreements:

> These carefully molded leaders often cater to the interests of their Arab and Western benefactors, at the expense of their own people. Not one single popular faction has resolutely escaped this seeming generalization… This reality has permeated Palestinian politics for decades. However, in the last two decades the distance between the Palestinian leadership and the people has grown by a once unimaginable distance, where the Palestinian has become a jailor and a peddling politician or a security coordinator working hand in hand with Israel.
>
> BAROUD 2013, 1

Echoing this view, Hafez Omar, a well-known graffiti artist and activist based in Ramallah who is from a village near Nablus, was critical of the PA's willingness to comply with externally imposed frameworks and 'demands of self-governance' based on neoliberalism and pacification. According to him, and many other young (as well as older) activists with whom I spoke, the PA is a 'comprador regime serving Western interests' and the Israeli colonial regime that has undermined genuine grassroots or collective resistance. The politics of normalization, or what Lisa Taraki (2005, 68–69) calls the "new normal politics" of this period, has been marked by a "new individualistic ethos" that has distanced itself from collective struggle. In this context, then, the youth movement and Palestinian graffiti enact a politics of anti-normalization as well as decoloniality.

As the lines of national struggle became less clear after Oslo, Palestinians were also increasingly disconnected from one another in the West Bank bantustans created by Israel's Wall and Jewish settlements; in an encircled and increasingly peripheralized Jerusalem; and in a besieged and blockaded Gaza. In fact, the Oslo agreements gave "birth [to] what Jeff Halper has called Israel's 'matrix of control'" in Palestinian areas with the construction and expansion of the Wall, settlements, bypass roads, and checkpoints (Quoted in Seikaly and Erekat 2012, 275). The colonial state apparatus has also generated ambiguous legal categories and forms of identity documentation for the colonized population and territories – differentiating between peoples and geographic spaces, for example, in Israel, East/West Jerusalem, Gaza, and West Bank Areas A, B, C. One of the shifts generated by the colonial partitioning of national space and management of bodies and social lives is that "the withdrawal of the IDF [Israeli Defense Force] from the Gaza Strip and the removal of many of the internal checkpoints in the West Bank have created fewer arenas for direct confrontation with the Israeli enemy..." (Christopherson et al. 2012, 9). As Ruanne observed, the fragile semblance of 'peace' has created a schizophrenic reality for this generation: "There is a classic colonial context of double consciousness. The more people here do not interact with Israelis as a colonial force, the more removed they are from that reality." Fajr Harb, a young activist from Ramallah well known in the youth movement, observed of youth in the West Bank, "There has been a de-politicization of the population. My generation was not expected to understand anything about politics but just be interested in daily life." This generation, then, was meant to be the generation of neoliberal individualism and privatized consumption. In other words, the modicum of economic stability and increased opportunities for consumption available after Oslo, especially in the West Bank and within the 'Ramallah Bubble,' was expected to divert youth from political mobilization, if not to pacify them (what some call 'pacification by capuccino') (Shams 2014). The youth movement was an attempt to burst this bubble, as were other eruptions of protest in various sites across Palestine.

(Re)Thinking Youth and Generation

I found in my interviews with young Palestinians that there are deep tensions and complex debates about national identity and cultural authenticity that surface in discussions of Palestinian hip hop and the youth movement. Both are often viewed with some ambivalence as constituting inauthentic culture and improper politics by observers of all ages, so this is not a specifically intergenerational tension. The debate about what constitutes 'proper' national culture and 'proper' political identity is framed by the familiar dialectic of resistance and co-optation. But it is also apparent that to some degree it is the association with 'youthfulness,' both for graffiti as a cultural genre and for the youth movement that arouses suspicion for observers, as is the case for youth protests and cultures in other sites around the world. I argue that these tensions are indicative of deeper concerns about the social and political that Palestinian youth are grappling with in the context of the shifts in Palestinian politics and society since Oslo.

These tensions signal what I think is the always ambivalent response to the specter of youth as generational and political subjects. As Linda Herrera and Asef Bayat (2010, 355) suggest, "The 'question of youth' often gets articulated as a paradox, as a problem and an opportunity." Youth politics is often suspect for onlookers, because youth are seen as either too 'radical' – and thus naïve or utopian – or too conformist – and thus available for co-optation and manipulation. These binaries, as I have argued elsewhere, are what make it so difficult in many cases, including in the case of Palestinian youth culture and youth politics, to think the generational category of 'youth' outside of over-determined polarities of resistance/conformity (Maira and Soep 2005). What kinds of insights into young people's politics might be closed off if they are viewed only or primarily through the lens of generation? And how is this lens in certain instances shaped by a developmentalist approach to geography that views certain regions of the world as lagging behind, and having to 'catch up' with Western modernity and democracy?

The label jil Oslo captures the ambivalence about youth as a generational category associated with radicalism as well as conformism. The notion of youth as a site associated with instability often permeates discussions of Palestinian and Arab youth at large. Scholars suggest that youth in the Arab world and Middle East, as elsewhere, are generally viewed as a symbol of crisis due to their association with the project of 'national and social reproduction,' of saving and advancing the nation-state, and thus with the possibility of both a threat to or continuity of the status quo, for their own societies as well as for western states invested in the region (Lüküslü 2014; Swedenburg 2007, 6). Discussions of the 'youth bulge,' or youthfulness of the Arab population, as well as youth unemployment and underemployment in the region, position youth as a demographic problem and an always present threat to social and political stability – a threat that was realized in ways that many did not anticipate with the Arab uprisings and also the Palestinian youth movement. On the one hand, in dominant frameworks and policy-related research, "youth are treated as a group that needs to be understood and trained for purposes of political containment, ideological monitoring, and economic reform," that is, deprived of agency (Herrera and Bayat 2010, 356). On the other hand, Muslim youth, in particular, are increasingly framed through the discourse of securitization and the war on terror and are viewed as especially vulnerable to what counterterrorism experts call 'radicalization' or indoctrination into militant or Islamist movements. National as well as (mainstream) Western state and media discourses often frame Middle Eastern and Arab, including Palestinian, youth as a threat to the 'integrity of the nation' and to western strategic interests and neoliberal capitalism, that is, as having *too much* agency.

Youth are in general associated with modernity, progress, and the *telos* of the nation, but for some observers the fear is that some groups of young people may be excessively or inappropriately modern. John Collins (2004, 13) argues these tensions are acute in the case of Palestine – a nation without a sovereign state – because the notion of generation has always been used to inscribe the struggle for nationhood, and the "processes through which social identities and political projects are symbolically produced, reproduced, and transformed." Given that the question of resistance and rebellion, across different national contexts, is generally pinned onto youth, I am interested in how the notion of 'youth' itself is produced and negotiated in these sites of protest and youth culture that are defined in relation to generation, a category that refers to more than simply an age cohort. Furthermore, it is important to clarify that the Palestinian youth movement was not a protest movement focused solely or even largely on the concerns of young people per se. It was a movement *by* youth, not necessarily *about* youth, if expressing a particular critique emerging from a specific generational location and intertwined with youth culture idioms, including but not restricted to hip hop.

Palestinian Hip Hop and Graffiti

Palestinian hip hop artists in the West Bank, Gaza, Jerusalem, '48 Palestine, and in refugee and diasporic communities around the world have become part of a growing cultural movement since the early 2000s and a globalized Arab youth culture that is inflected by local cultural expressions and also by other subcultures. Palestinian hip hop first emerged among '48 Palestinian youth in the late 1990s, particularly with the group DAM from Lid in Israel; they found in progressive rap an idiom to challenge Israeli state violence, racism, and colonial practices and to connect with global publics as an often invisibilized Palestinian population that identified with the political critiques of urban youth of color in the U.S. (Eqeiq 2010; Maira and Shihade 2012; Stein and Swedenburg 2004). Palestinian hip hop artists have also been part of the soundtrack for the Arab uprisings and involved in many cross-border projects with young artists in the region that preceded the Arab revolts (El-Zein 2012).

Palestinian hip hop (which includes rap, graffiti, deejaying, and breakdancing) is part of a much longer genealogy of protest music and poetry within Palestine, not to mention a long and rich history of oppositional artistic practices more generally (Gana 2012; Massad 2005). Graffiti, in particular, has been a pervasive form of collective expression and public memory in Palestine since the first Intifada so while it has increasingly incorporated elements of urban graffiti, tagging, and stenciling, it is not at all a new form of public visual expression in Palestine. As Julie Peteet (1994b, 155) writes, Palestinian graffiti "affirms community and resistance, debates tradition, envisions competing futures...and registers memory." Graffiti or stenciling do not require expensive equipment or elaborate training, which partly explains their allure for youth who cannot afford to buy tools other than a paintbrush or spray can. Graffiti is a form that is often associated with youth culture, but it is not intrinsically restricted to a particular generational category, so it lends itself to an interrogation of the ways in which youthfulness is often associated with subversion, political and cultural. It is important not to romanticize the potential of resistance through youth culture or popular culture but it is clearly a site in which the contradictions and tensions in political and social struggle are expressed, negotiated, challenged, and rewritten.

The Search for an Alternative Politics

The youth movement drew together rather disparate groups of youth in protests that were independent of established parties and based on the search for a new political vocabulary or an alternative discourse, fundamentally emphasizing the unity of Palestinians partitioned between '1967' (referring to the West Bank and Gaza, or the territories occupied in 1967), '1948,' Jerusalem, and the diaspora. The narrative of unified nationhood is not new in Palestine, but it is significant because it challenges the Oslo paradigm (accepted by the PA) that fragmented the nation by situating what could be Palestine only in the West Bank and Gaza, and deferring the status of Jerusalem and the right of return of refugees, within the degraded terms of sovereignty supplied by Israel. Fajr Harb, observed thoughtfully:

> To understand Palestinian youth today, you have to understand the previous generation's politics and Oslo...After Oslo, things changed and the Palestinian cause changed. The purpose of Oslo was to divide the West Bank from Gaza from Jerusalem – the purpose was to divide Palestine.

The youth movement has, in fact, created a network connecting young people who are involved in ongoing activism and cultural projects across Palestine, including Bab al-Shams and the other 'resistance villages' erected across the West Bank in winter 2013, the 'return camps' and cultural activities on the sites of destroyed Palestinian villages (such as Ikrit) in Israel, the mock weddings staged at checkpoints by the campaign 'Love in the Time of Apartheid,' and the regular protests against Jewish settlements and the Wall. Protest activities thus constitute a site in which youth from different parts of Palestine who can travel meet and connect with one another to challenge the spatial and biopolitical confinement of life under apartheid and reclaim the national struggle (Nabulsi 2014, 116).

The call for a unified Palestinian nation is a consistent motif in graffiti art as well. For example, the young artist Hamza Abu Ayash has done graffiti art in many public places in Ramallah and al-Tireh featuring a signature white figure in various poses, with one image of the figure carrying the map of historic Palestine strapped to its back. The Atlas-like figure is faceless, if masculine, symbolizing the common Palestinian or the Palestinian nation, generally depicted in a state of confinement or stress, for example, in a shackled pose. His graffiti art suggests the ways in which Palestinians live in a daily state of enclosure and incarceration and Palestine itself is a prison.

The second major feature of this youth cultural production and protest movement is that it has offered a medium for reimagining the political itself, in dialogue with the Arab revolutions and drawing on new cultural idioms. As Ahmed, a young activist from Ramallah, astutely observed, "Popular culture plays a massive part in building the national narrative, especially when there's a problem with that narrative." The youth movement is a response to the retreat from mass mobilization in the wake of the first and second intifadas, the establishment of a virtual state or a state without real sovereignty, and the formation of separate political regimes governing the West Bank and Gaza after 2007. The issue of depoliticization is a theme persistently running through cultural production associated and protest activities that directly challenge the decline of mass politics. One young woman activist from Nablus, Feryal, who is also active with the BDS [Boycott, Divestment, and Sanctions] movement, said, "The fact that there is this sort of youth movement is inspiring in itself... to have that kind of commitment is very inspiring, given how depressing the situation is…there's so much that's disappointing so it gives us hope that we are doing something and not accepting the status quo."

The young people I spoke to, students as well as artists and activists, in the West Bank and also Israel persistently observed that the pursuit of new cultural forms overlapped with their search for a new politics in the post-Oslo era. Basel said, "We were trying to give voice to an alternative art scene in Palestine, an alternative voice in Palestine that was trying to say something different and to find a different language." Duaa, a young activist and artist from Haifa, said thoughtfully that youth needed to rethink political resistance 'in a deeper way,' to produce a truly 'alternative music' and politics that was not simply based on filling old 'frames' of protest with new content or slogans. The point, thus, is not simply about finding a new generational discourse or idealizing the old. For Duaa, 'revolutionary art' had to be based in a democratic as well as anti-capitalist politics, and have a 'connection to the local community.' It was this 'dialectical analysis' of the relationship between individual artists or groups and a larger collective, as well as between struggles – based on gender, sexuality, class, or nationalism – that she thought needed to be deepened in the youth movement.

Ruanne observed that the search for an alternative politics in her generation had begun before Oslo but it took a while for the implications and 'disasters' of the Second Intifada to crystallize into a new political moment. Palestinians now had to grapple not just with the Israeli regime but also with the Palestinian "security apparatus and their training with the Israelis and the CIA." (Abbas and AbouRahme, "The Zone") Tashweesh's project, 'The Zone,' directly addresses "the way in which this new regime displaced the old collective 'dreams' and gave birth to new political discourses and desires largely centered on consumption." (ibid) Ruanne and Basel describe this eloquently in the project:

> In what would appear to us as one of the darkest moments in Palestinian lived history, a 'dream-world' has somehow emerged in the West Bank: a host of commodified desires, semblance of normality, have been constructed atop the debris of political failure and collapse. Here, new lifestyles, desires, senses of self mingle and collide with a persistent denial of the disasters of Palestine's current situation…in order for us to invest in this new dream we must somehow ignore the increasingly visible violence of the colonial situation. (ibid)

The Zone captures the ways in which the dreams and disasters of jil Oslo are enmeshed with fantasies of consumerist freedom and individualized 'normality' – what some call the Ramallah Syndrome – that mask neoliberal economic restrictions and repressive securitization, not to mention dispossession and annihilation. It may appear that this critique encodes a nostalgia for an old era of collective resistance but the language of dreams and nightmares emphasizes the element of political imagination, and its failures, and also the materiality of the current moment of disaster. Salim, a young theater artist from Balata refugee camp in Nablus, commented, "It's hard to understand why so much money is put into security, not education" and why the Palestinian security forces have attacked young protesters in Nablus or Ramallah. The surveillance, policing, and repression – both by the PA and Israel – experienced by young activists has created a climate of fear and insecurity that underlies some of what is glossed as youth 'apathy' in the West Bank.

It is strikingly apparent that after the Oslo Accords and the establishment of the PA, and with the profusion of local and international NGOs in the West Bank, Gaza, and (less so) Jerusalem, the class schism has widened even as new consumer lifestyles have emerged under occupation. In Ramallah, the de facto capital city, upscale restaurants, cafes, and bars have mushroomed, and real estate prices have sky-rocketed while the general population, including youth, suffers from unemployment and also, increasingly, from debt (Harker 2014). This 'five star occupation' has led to a sense of disconnection in the city from the realities in the rest of Palestine – or even the daily reality at the Qalandia checkpoint just outside Ramallah.

Artist Yazid Anani (2010) points out that the 'thriving neoliberalism' under the PA has led "to [the] economization and depoliticization of public spaces... prohibiting their use for collective assembly, collective political exchange, accessibility and self-criticism." So while privatized public spaces, such as malls and art galleries, have sprung up, many lament the shrinking of spaces for collective political resistance and also for collective cultural practices. In the context of the PA's state-building project, the struggle over public space is part of the larger contest over a public political culture, and the boundaries of permissible public and social behavior. This is what is at stake in the emergence of new forms of popular culture and protest, including graffiti art and hip hop, that attempt to politicize public culture visually and through public protest. However, while graffiti is a form of public art available to youth, it is *still* produced and consumed within a neoliberal cultural sphere shaped by the contradictory forces of globalization and commodification, as well as institutionalization by NGOs, which have transformed both artistic production and political culture (Hanafi and Tabar 2003). Murid pointed out that many of the youth who are producing graffiti are visual artists who want to display their work for the public – and are using walls and public spaces that are free and accessible. There have also been graffiti workshops and collaborative projects between Palestinian youth and foreign artists, in a landscape in which collaborations with 'internationals' and the politics of solidarity are often contentious and, understandably, fraught.

Graffiti: Re/Creating Public Culture

Young artists and as well as activists of jil Oslo are engaged in this quest that has drawn on or revived, in many cases, earlier frameworks of Palestinian resistance or discourses of national identity while (re)creating new cultural idioms or political vocabularies. Yasmine, a young activist from al-Bireh in the West Bank, said that the independent youth movement's "aims were to go back to resistance and resuscitate the Palestinian struggle as a national movement." I want to note here that this is not conceived as a simple 'return' to an idealized politics, but a struggle to challenge the post-Oslo national paradigm that has suppressed collective resistance by drawing on historical memories of radical resistance and contemporary political languages and strategies from within, and beyond, Palestine.

For example, the question of political memory is addressed by an artist from the West Bank, Majd Abdel Habib, who plastered large black and white posters with photography and text on the walls of Ramallah. One of them featured an enlarged photograph of a *Time* magazine cover with an iconic image of Yasser Arafat as a 'fedayeen leader' from 1968 [December 13] in kaffiyeh and sunglasses with the title, "Arab Commandos: Defiant New Force in the Middle East." The other was of an older woman in a thobe (traditional Palestinian dress) with the pointed question: "What's happening to us?" The letters resembled the shape of a key, symbolizing the right of return which was abandoned in the concessions made in Oslo, and the portrayal of the female figure in traditional dress plays on gendered imagery in nationalist art. These images wryly mimic the form of a political poster and signal what Peteet (1994b, 156, 161) describes as the "civil disobedience and self-reflection" conveyed by the Palestinian graffiti of an earlier era targeted to a "discontented Palestinian readership" (if discontented now for somewhat different reasons). The posters, like much of the graffiti I saw on the walls of Ramallah, questions the disappearance of militant resistance, generational discontinuities, and the meaning of Palestinian national identity today. This new flowering of street art is variously critical, cynical, and exhorting of collective solidarity and public political action.

For example, there has been a flourishing of graffiti by youth in solidarity with the prisoners' mass hunger strike, including ubiquitous stenciled images of Palestinian prisoner Khader Adnan with a lock on his mouth, produced by Hafez. This image, which spread widely through social media, and the stencils of Adnan in general speak to the centrality of the issue of Palestinian prisoners and prison in general as a symbol and sphere of national resistance. Derek Gregory (2004, 125) describes occupied Palestine as a "carceral archipelago" across which Palestinian bodies are moved around, directly or indirectly, by the settler colonial state and its policies regulating residence, marriage, work, travel, and property ownership. Another stencil in solidarity with prisoners that was common on Palestinian walls inscribed the words 'Hungry 4 Freedom,' which was reportedly first produced by '48 Palestinian youth in Haifa, as part of this transborder youth culture and movement. (I should note that since this is in English, it was clearly intended for Israeli and foreign audiences and international media as part of an outreach tactic).

Graffiti art also proliferated in conjunction with what became known as the 'March 15 movement' in the West Bank and Gaza, sparked most immediately by the Tunisian and Egyptian revolutions in 2011. '48 Palestinian youth also organized demonstrations at the time in solidarity and in support of a revived pan-Arab identity. 'Revolution' (*thawra*) was another popular stenciled slogan that also popped up next to stenciled images of the faces of young men killed by Israel, for example, along the road between Ramallah and Birzeit University. The conjoining of these two images underscores a situation in which many youth are deeply aware that the Arab revolts had very different implications for Palestine, and that a popular uprising would have different consequences for Palestinians still living under occupation and colonization. As Boikutt observed, "No one relates to Fatah and Hamas anymore, their time is up. It's like with Hosni Mubarak. But it's a different situation because we're not in a postcolonial situation, we're still colonized." One large painting by Abu Ayash on a wall along the main street in Ramallah depicts the white figure carrying the map of historic Palestine strapped to his back, with the words 'The Land is Hungry.' The metaphor of hunger suggests a larger critique of the deprivation of sovereignty and freedom that Palestinians crave and that is key to the youth movement. Street art provides a canvas for political debate, as in the sardonic question ('Where?') scrawled on a wall in al-Tireh in response to the statement, 'The Intifada is continuous,' stenciled under a map of historic Palestine. A generational romance of resistance is constantly challenged in the streets even as it is being invoked or recreated.

Repression is also the focus of many stenciled images, for example, featuring a policeman with a baton crossed out by a red slash. Protesters in the youth movement have been attacked or arrested by PA and Hamas security on multiple occasions since they started taking to the street. Yasmine, a young activist from al-Bireh, talked about the rallies by youth in late June 2012 protesting the meeting of Abbas with Shaul Mofaz, who was the Israeli defense minister during the war on Gaza, and which led to a violent crackdown by PA security in the streets. Yasmine said the last day of protests was 'like Tahrir Square,' with throngs of people coming out after they heard the news of the crackdown on the protesters: "That was a shocking thing to everyone – how did we reach the point of Palestinians beating up other Palestinians, including raising the baton against women?" Significantly, the meeting with Mofaz was cancelled after the protests. But some youth pointed out that the fear of reprisals was what in part led to the hesitation of many to join the public protests and their eventual dwindling (though the militant protests by young Palestinians in Jerusalem and the West Bank during Israel's invasion of the West Bank and war on Gaza in summer 2014, which some labeled the 'third intifada,' underscores the persistent commitment to protest in the face of violence). The repression, co-optation, and in some cases brutal assaults on protesters reveal the multiple fronts of authoritarian rule they confront. In fact, one of the popular graffiti motifs that sprouted on the walls of Ramallah was a simple stencil of the word *fakkir* (think) – with the shape of the calligraphy echoing the silhouette of a policeman with a baton. Other stencils that were ubiquitous during the spring of 2011 were the slogans in English, '#Un-Occupy' or 'Occupy Wall Street, Not Palestine,' making links between global movements against capitalism, militarism, and repression.

Surveillance, Repression, and Transgressions

Scholars have discussed how graffiti during the first and second Intifadas provided a (communicative) medium of defiance that evaded Israeli censorship and helped produce and address an audience, locally as well as globally, for the Palestinian struggle, assembling Palestinians into a sovereign entity (Bishara 2010; Peteet 1994b, 155). Hafez recalled that as a young boy, he secretly did graffiti during the night so that he would not be caught by Israeli soldiers. He also noted, however, that these announcements in the street were not signed by individuals at the time, but by parties or groups, and that 'signature graffiti' has taken an individualized turn as it has become an 'artistic practice in the street.' Murid similarly observed that there has been a shift from graffiti as a display of political slogans or announcement of strikes during the intifadas to a more visually interesting form of public art, that is also part of hip hop's visual idiom of DIY art.

Yet there seems to be some continuity between these different phases of street art as well, for while contemporary graffiti by youth is generally not associated with political parties, it is often produced to galvanize support for political campaigns or public awareness about specific issues. In fact, much as political communiqués were criminalized by Israel and had to be anonymously broadcast on walls before the advent of Palestinian mass media, issues that are not discussed on the official and new Palestinian TV channels are now surfacing on the walls of Palestinian towns and Israeli cities. Many graffiti artists still work anonymously and apparently there are young women as well as men who do graffiti, such as an underground group of women I heard about who do political stencils around Jerusalem where they are under direct Israeli surveillance.

In some cases, youth in the West Bank as well as Israel have tried to assert their right to freedom of political expression and to a democratization of Palestinian politics by visually challenging repression and surveillance. For example, Abu Ayash has done a series of graffiti paintings in Ramallah and al-Tireh challenging police brutality and repression by the PA. Marwan, a young activist from al-Bireh who was involved in an experimental film that featured graffiti art projects in villages in which he had himself participated, said that he used Facebook to counter surveillance by documenting attacks on protesters, as do other youth who use new media to challenge the electronic surveillance by both the PA and Israel (Shalhoub-Kevorkian 2012). Palestinian youth live in a state of permanent surveillance, whether in the West Bank, Jerusalem, or Israel, as they navigate checkpoints and borders or simply go to college. Ilan Pappe (2011) describes Israel as a '*mukhabarat* (secret service) state' for the logics of surveillance and securitization are key to militarized states. As Collins (2011) argues, the Israeli settler colonial regime views the indigenous population as a constant security threat to be surveilled and contained, if not eliminated.

Surveillance and counter-surveillance are key issues for '48 Palestinian youth, and for Palestinian students in Israeli universities, given the militarization of Israeli educational institutions and the deep links between "Israeli academia and the state's security and occupation systems" (Academic Watch 2012). Surveillance and censorship on Israeli campuses is used by both Zionist student groups and university security to target Palestinian students and activists, sometimes in conjunction with racist assaults and physical threats. Israeli universities have banned Palestinian cultural festivals, documentary film screenings, and talks by Palestinian political leaders. This repression has made the campus an important battleground for young '48 Palestinian activists and is linked to the larger project of erasure of Palestinian national identity and histories as well as to the garrison state's logic which views '48 Palestinians as internal security threats and suspect citizens (Sa'adi 1996; Shihade 2011). For Duaa, given this context, there is a need for a clearer 'Palestinian discourse' that gets to the 'root of the issue' of the experiences of '48 Palestinians and challenges the Israeli university itself as a 'colonial institution,' rather than focusing solely on discrimination and equality within the liberal democratic framework of the Israeli state.

It is also interesting to note that feminist graffiti and stencils have also cropped up around Ramallah. There are stencils of Handala, the iconic Palestinian figure created by cartoonist Naji al-Ali, holding the female symbol with a clenched fist inside, in the center of Ramallah with the credo, 'Freedom is a daily practice.' Another stencil I saw in various places had an image of what could be the face of a woman in hijab but was ambiguously gendered. A young activist from Nablus revealed to me during our interview that it was she who did this work and that the stenciled slogan was inspired by a stencil from Beirut; I was later told this originated in Tunisia. This transnational circulation of protest imagery and language is thus able to cross generational boundaries to re-imagine iconic symbols of Palestinian national identity and resistance and to challenge the Olso framework of what freedom means. This happens in ways that are viewed by some as transgressive and by others as improperly national. For example, there is a queer political current in graffiti in conjunction with queer youth activism. In May 2013, the Palestinian queer group Al Qaws launched a youth music project, '*Ghanni A`an Taa`rif*' (Singing Sexuality), which included a website and concert in Haifa, as well as graffiti in Jaffa, Haifa, and other cities.[7] Graffiti that introduces questions of feminism and sexuality into the public sphere is part of a larger debate among youth about issues of feminist and queer politics in relation to the national question and protest culture in various sites in Palestine that I dwell on in the larger project. It is a complex discussion that speaks to what it might mean to have feminist and queer perspectives on Palestinian national identity and Israeli colonization.

In this sense, graffiti associated with the youth movement is visually forcing attention on "vital internal dialogs" that Bishara (2010, 78) argued were not adequately addressed in graffiti produced during the second intifada. Yet like the youth movement itself, which is viewed by critics as not politically authentic and radical or not effective enough, hip hop is often viewed as culturally

---

7 www.ghanni.net.

inauthentic and not properly 'Palestinian.' In the larger project, I explore the ways in which this suspicion of new forms of cultural and political expression, as "troubled or treasonous" in relation to the national liberation struggle (Stein and Swedenburg 2004, 8), emerges through a discourse that is both gendered and generational.

Graffiti art is heterogeneous in form and motivation and persists as a successful technology of resistance and of politicization of the public sphere, especially by those who are marginalized or repressed by institutionalized politics or critical of an increasingly neoliberal public and political culture. But this visual resistance also elicits its own repression. While there has not been much crackdown on graffiti art in Ramallah, where Murid said "there's more freedom, as there are more foreigners and more eyes watching," this was not always the case in other locations in the West Bank beyond the Ramallah Bubble. Palestinian graffiti is not illegal in the West Bank unless it is on private property, but apparently in most cases there has been little conflict with property owners. However, in some locations outside of Ramallah political graffiti has been erased by Palestinian authorities (as often happens in U.S. cities where graffiti is considered vandalism). Furthermore, the PA restricts, censors, and sometimes arrests activists as well as hip hop artists, even as Israeli repression and violence continues. Thus graffiti and street art is an important site where questions of repression and democracy, colonialism and resistance, and national identity and public culture are being visualized and contested.

Conclusion

The public cultural production and political culture that has emerged in the context of the youth movement reflects a deeper attempt to politicize public space, in the context of the post-Oslo malaise, and to articulate a decolonial political subjecthood that exceeds the discourse of statehood and rights. The challenge to the Oslo paradigm is threatening to those who defend and benefit from the status quo, and the challenge to the boundaries of what constitutes authentic Palestinian national resistance – and also Palestinian culture – creates some unease and suspicion. The association with commercialization, globalization, and Westernization haunts youth culture in sites where political struggle is intense and ongoing – in particular, in zones of colonialism and occupation where the production of national imaginaries is crucial, a matter of survival. In the context of the management of life and death in sites such as Palestine, that is, the biopolitics of colonial rule, youth culture and popular protest perhaps cannot *not* be contested expressions of what is truly 'popular' and what is authentically 'national.' Furthermore, it is also generally apparent that 'the popular' is a notion deeply invested with imaginaries of what 'the people' think – or what they *should* think or *can* think – in relation to hierarchies of 'high' and 'low,' elite and mass, authentic and inauthentic, resistant or accomodationist.

The youth I spoke to seemed to be aware of these tensions and grappling with how to rethink political resistance 'in a deeper way,' including in cultural production. Duaa was concerned that 'alternative music' and arts was becoming the basis of a new Palestinian youth subculture in Haifa, and offered a thoughtful critique of 'alternative evenings' or 'alternative parties' that in her view were ultimately based on the "idea of having a 'cool' nationalism or a 'cool' struggle." This touches on an interesting tension, and one which exists in many locations around the world: at what point does popular protest become too 'popular,' or even trendy, and not sufficiently subversive? How can youth walk this line between the popular and the radical when 'youthfulness' itself is often seen as inherently embodying both the 'popular' and 'radical'?

These questions are ongoing and constantly occupy the uneasy location encoded in the concept of 'jil Oslo,' that undoes the association of generation with a *telos* of political progress toward national liberation. The youth movement and the graffiti associated with it use a decolonial paradigm focused on the concepts of dignity, freedom, and collectivity, expressing a hunger for a less compromised notion of national sovereignty and rejecting a vision of a state based on neoliberal democracy and securitization. I conclude with a manifesto distributed at a rally in Ramallah organized by the youth coalition, Palestinians for Dignity, that I attended on September 11, 2012. The protest was held during a period of mounting frustration with rising prices and increased taxation in the West Bank, due to economic policies put in place with Oslo. The flier (in Arabic) stated boldly:

> We stand today for dignity, not just against hunger, but also against repression. You president, your politics is standing in the way of ending the occupation. It has become clear to everyone that these political, economic, and security agreements…are a burden on our people and are hindering our national liberation from Zionist occupation…How could our land be liberated if you make the people slaves?
>
> In plain Arabic, what connects us as a people is not the crumbs of your aid, but hope, dignity, and freedom.
> Down with the Paris economic protocols!
> Down with the Oslo strategy!

References

Abbas, Basel and Ruanne Abourahme, "The Zone," Artterritories. http://www.artter ritories.net/designingcivicencounter/?page_id=633.

Abed, Rabi'. "Youth and Students: The Youth Movement 'Inside' and the Horizon Envisioned." (Translated from Arabic). 15 November 2011. Accessed 25 April 2012. www .arabs48.com.

Academic Watch. *Annual Summary Report 2011–2012*. Nüüazareth: Arab Culture Association: Ar-Rased Project and the Youth Empowerment Project, 2012.

Anani, Yazid. "Interview with Shuruq Harb." *Artterritories*. September 7, 2010. http:// www.artterritories.net/?page_id=889.

Barber, Brian. "Political Violence, Social Integration, and Youth Functioning: Palestinian Youth from the Intifada." *Journal of Community Psychology* 29, 3 (2001): 259–280.

Baroud, Ramzy. "The Unity Charade and Prisoners' Intifada." *Ma'an News*, January 17, 2013. http://maannews.net/eng/ViewDetails.aspx?ID=557063.

Bishara, Amahl. 2010. "New Media and Political Change in the Occupied Palestinian Territories: Assembling Media Worlds and Cultivating Networks of Care." Middle East Journal of Culture and Communication 3: 63–81.

Chirstopherson, Mona, Jacob Hoigilt, and Age A. Tiltnes. *"Palestinian Youth and the Arab Spring."* NOREF (Norwegian Peacebuilding Resource Centre), February 5, 2012. http://www.peacebuilding.no/Regions/Middle-East-and-North-Africa/Israel-Palestine/Publications/Palestinian-youth-and-the-Arab-Spring/%28language%29/ eng-US.

Collins, John. *Occupied by Memory: The Intifada Generation and the Palestinian State of Emergency*. New York: New York University Press, 2004.

Collins, John. *Global Palestine*. London: Hurst and Company, 2011.

El Zein, Rayya (ed.). *Shahadat: Exploring Popular Literature Series – Hip Hop*. New York: ArteEast, 2012.

Elbedour, Salman. "Youth in Crisis: The Well-Being of Middle Eastern Youth and Adolescents During War and Peace." *Journal of Youth and Adolescence* 27, 5 (1998): 539–557.

Eqeiq, Amal. "Louder than the Blue ID: Palestinian Hip-Hop in Israel." In *Displaced at Home: Ethnicity and Gender among Palestinians in Israel*, edited by Rhoda A. Kanaaneh and Isis Nusair, 53–71. Albany, NY: State University of New York Press, 2010.

Gana, Nouri. "Rap and Revolt in the Arab World." *Social Text* 30, 4 (2012): 25–53.

Giacaman, George. "In the Throes of Oslo: Palestinian Society, Civil Society and the Future," in *After Oslo: New Realities, Old Problems*, edited by George Giacaman and Dag J. Lonning, 1–15. London: Pluto Press, 1998.

Gregory, Derek. *The Colonial Present*. Malden, MA and Oxford, UK: Blackwell, 2004.

Hall, Stuart and Tony Jefferson (eds.). *Resistance through Rituals: Youth Subcultures in Post-war Britain*. London: Hutchinson/Centre for Contemporary Cultural Studies, University of Birmingham, 1976.

Hammer, Juliane. *Palestinians Born in Exile: Diaspora and the Search for Homeland*. Austin: University of Texas Press, 2005.

Hanafi, Sari, and Linda Tabar. 2003 "The Intifada and the Aid Industry: The Impact of the New Liberal Agenda on the Palestinian NGOs." *Comparative Studies of South Asia, Africa, and the Middle East* 23, 1–2: 205–214.

Harker, Christopher. "Debt and Obligation in Contemporary Ramallah." *Jadaliyya*, October 19, 2014. http://www.jadaliyya.com/pages/index/19665/debt-and -obligation-in-contemporary-ramallahn.

Hart, Jason. "Dislocated Masculinity: Adolescence and the Palestinian Nation-in-Exile." *Journal of Refugee Studies* 21, 1 (2008): 64–81.

Herrera, Linda, and Asef Bayat. "Conclusion: Knowing Muslim Youth." In *Being Young and Muslim: New Cultural Politics in the Global South and North*, edited by Linda Herrera and Asef Bayat, 355–364. New York: Oxford University Press, 2010.

Kevorkian, Nadera S. "Trapped: The Violence of Exclusion in Jerusalem." *Jerusalem Quarterly* 49 (2012): 6–25.

Kevorkian, Nadera S. "Fear of Sexual Harassment: Palestinian Adolescent Girls in the Intifada," in *Palestinian Women: Identity and Experience,* edited by Ebba Augustin, 171–180. London: Zed Books, 1993.

Lüküslü, Demet. "Cyberspace in Turkey: A 'Youthful Space' for Expressing Powerful Discontent and Suffering," in *Wired Citizenship: Youth Learning and Activism in the Middle East*, edited by Linda Herrera with Rehab Sakr, 76–88. New York and London: Routledge, 2014.

Maira, Sunaina. *Jil Oslo: Palestinian Hip Hop, Youth Culture, and the Youth Movement*. Washington, D.C.: Tadween, 2013.

Maira, Sunaina and Elisabeth Soep. "Introduction," in *Youthscapes: The Popular, the National, the Global,* edited by Sunaina Maira and Elisabeth Soep, xv–xxxv. Philadelphia: University of Pennsylvania Press, 2005.

Maira, Sunaina, and Magid Shihade. "Hip Hop from '48 Palestine: Youth, Music, and the Present/Absent." *Social Text* 112, 30/3 (2012): 1–25.

Massad, Joseph. "Liberating Songs: Palestine Put to Music," in *Palestine, Israel, and the Politics of Popular Culture*, edited by Rebecca Stein and Ted Swedenburg, 175–201. Durham, NC: Duke University Press, 2005.

Mignolo, Walter, and Rolando Vasquez. "Decolonial AestheSis: Colonial Wounds/ Decolonial Healings." *Periscope, Social Text*, July 15, 2013. Accessed September 28, 2013. http://socialtextjournal.org/periscope_article/decolonial-aesthesis-colonial -woundsdecolonial-healings/.

Nabulsi, Mira. "'Hungry for Freedom': Palestine Youth Activism in the Era of Social Media," in *Wired Citizenship: Youth Learning and Activism in the Middle East*, edited by Linda Herrera with Rehab Sakr, 105–120. New York and London: Routledge, 2014.

Nguyen-Gillham, Viet, et al. "Normalizing the Abnormal: Palestinian Youth and the Contradictions of Resilience in Protracted Conflict." *Health and Social Care in the Community* 16, 3 (2008): 291–298.

Pappe, Ilan. *The Forgotten Palestinians: A History of the Palestinians in Israel.* New Haven: Yale University Press, 2011.

Parry, William. *Against the Wall: The Art of Resistance in Palestine.* Chicago: Lawrence Hall, 2011.

Peteet, Julie. "Male Gender and Rituals of Resistance in the Palestinian 'Intifada': A Cultural Politics of Violence." *American Ethnologist* 21, 1 (1994a): 31–49.

Peteet, Julie. "The Graffiti of the Intifada." *The Muslim World* LXXXIV 1–2 (1994b): 155–167.

Sa'adi, Ahmad H. "Minority Resistance to State Control: Toward a Re-Analysis of Palestinian Political Activity in Israel." *Social Identities* 2, 3 (1996): 395–413.

Sayigh, Yezid. *Armed Struggle and the Search for a State: The Palestinian National Movement, 1949–1993.* Oxford: Oxford University Press, 1999.

Seif, Samir. "Youth in the Palestinian National Movement: Painful Truths." *Palestine-Israel Journal of Politics, Economics, and Culture* 4 (2000): 20.

Seikaly, Sherene and Noura Erekat. "Tahrir's Other Sky," in *The Dawn of the Arab Uprisings: End of An Old Order?* edited by Bassam Haddad, Rosie Bsheer, and Ziad Abu-Rish. London: Pluto, 2012.

Shadid, Mohammed and Seltzer, Rick. "Student-Youth Differences among Palestinians in the West Bank." *Youth and Society* 20, 4 (1989): 445–460.

Shalhoub-Kevorkian, Nadera. "E-Resistance and Technological In/Security in Everyday Life: The Palestinian Case." *British Journal of Criminology* 52 (2012): 55–72.

Shams, Alex. "Nablus Conference Imagines Life in 'Glocal' Palestine." *Ma'an News*, October 27, 2014. http://www.maannews.net/eng/ViewDetails.aspx?ID=731722.

Sharek Youth Forum. *Palestinian Youth and Political Parties: From a Pioneering Engagement with Political Parties to Fear and Disappointment.* Al-Tireh, Palestine: Sharek, 2010.

Sharek Youth Forum. *The Status of Youth – 2013: The Future is Knocking.* Al-Tireh, 2013. Palestine: Sharek.

Shihade, Magid. *Not Just a Soccer Game: Colonialism and Conflict Among Palestinians in Israel.* Syracuse, NY: Syracuse University Press, 2011.

Stein, Rebecca L., and Ted Swedenburg. "Popular Culture, Relational History, and the Question of Power In Palestine and Israel." *Journal of Palestine Studies* 33, 4 (2004): 5–20.

Swedenburg, Ted. "Imagined Youths." *Middle East Research and Information Project* 245, Winter (2007): 4–11.

CHAPTER 8

The Double Presence of Southern Algerians: Space, Generation and Unemployment[*]

Ratiba Hadj-Moussa[1]

Introduction: On Monumentality and the Revolutionary Generation

The 'November Generation' has been a recurrent theme in the official discourse that justifies Algerian national unity, as well as the nation's political and economical orientation. The term 'November generation' refers to the beginnings of the War of Independence on the 1st of Novermber 1954, and includes more or less all those who participated in it.[2] It has allowed the 'revolutionary family' to continue its work of 'national edification'[3] for almost three decades (1962–1988). Although it underwent a gradual disappearance during the 1990s, this genealogical and teleological construction of the nation continues to shape the modes of discourse of monumental history, which has been the dominant form of thinking and acting in Algeria, in spite of opposition from different quarters, and despite the great suffering and conflicts caused by the country's Civil War (1991–2002).

Our analysis begins from the notions of monumentality and monumental history – used interchangeably here – because they are determinant in all post-independence discourses on social and political struggles. Drawing from

---

[*] I would like to thank Karine Côté-Boucher and Johan Giry for their in-depth comments on the first drafts of this article. Thanks to Mark Ayyash for his acute reading and comments on the first and last drafts, to Rana Sukarieh for her help with creating Map 8.1, and to Jonathan Adjemian for his editorial work and remarks. This article has benefited from the Support of the Social Sciences Research Council of Canada (435-2013-1104).

[1] With assistance from Samir Larabi.

[2] Up until 1988, this discourse came from one sole source, the single-party regime. The institution of multipartyism and the right of association liberated other voices (1989). But this new liberty paradoxically allowed a further spread of the idea of the 'November generation,' and enhanced its sacred status. For example, the plethora of publications on the War of Liberation reinforced the idea of the 'November generation.'

[3] All expressions were heavily used during the 1970s and the 1980s.

© KONINKLIJKE BRILL NV, LEIDEN, 2017 | DOI 10.1163/9789004344518_010

THE DOUBLE PRESENCE OF SOUTHERN ALGERIANS   199

Nietzsche's conception of monumental history as developed in his *Untimely Meditations* (1993 [1874]),[4] we understand monumental history as the process through which the past is petrified into past moments, which resist the forces of 'life' and render the present inadequate. Indeed, if in the Algerian context the "unity of the nation is the red line," as the Algerian Prime minister recently put it (APS, 2016), "its revolution" and those who carried it out are its horizon line, its present and its past. Monumentality colonizes the newness of actions and freezes them.

In this chapter we use the example of the movement of the unemployed, one of the new social and political struggles, to analyze how monumentality functions in the relation of one generation to another, and how these become actualized in the context of their production, that is to say of the socio-historical phases that have followed the period of independence, focusing particularly on the last two decades in the 2000s. First, we explore how the revolution and the so-called November generation have occupied the social fabric and made expression of free thought highly difficult. Second, we analyze how the Saharan segment of the movement of the unemployed has taken a corporatist demand (the demand for employment), and transformed it into a political demand that laterally dismantles the architecture of the November generation and its monumental construction. This 'in fact' should not, however, be interpreted as a conscious practice, or at any rate not as a thought-through and developed strategy, but rather as a series of acts that sometimes respond to contingencies, and sometimes are supported by a renewed reading of the history of the struggle for independence.

The 'November generation' owes its perennial existence to the National Liberation Front (*Front de libération nationale* –FLN), the party that dominated the political scene for three decades (1962–1988). The FLN was the connecting thread, if not the organic element, in the elaboration of genealogic continuity. Its mass organizations, such as the *Union nationale de la jeunesse algérienne* (National Union of Algerian Youth) and the *Organisation nationale des moudjahidines* (National Organization of the Mujaheddin) amplified its rhetoric by continuously reviving the spirit of the 'revolutionary family.' The November generation's specificity lies in its seemingly homogeneous and almost untouchable character, with a symbolism firmly established to counter any criticism

---

4   For Nietzsche, monumental history also has a positive version. This is exemplified by the actions of creative men who know to take up the past and make renewed use it. Instead of imitating the past, they make of it something other, something alive. Nietzsche posits this creative aspect of 'life' in opposition to the crushing version of monumental history or the nostalgic version of 'antiquary history' (1993 [1874], 217).

that might tarnish the image of the Revolution. It has indeed been slow to put the history of the War of Liberation and its actors into perspective and has done so with difficulty, along with the conscious and sustained repression of the memory of certain important figures of Algerian nationalism.

The November generation is inescapable, not only because of the monumentality that is its foundation, but also because of how permeable Algerian social fabric is to its imaginary universe. The fight for freedom was a slow and extremely violent process which had profound consequences for society. The construction of monumentality is thus also anchored in deeply rooted local memories, and has by no means been an evil process consciously concocted by an elite. To understand the ways in which the rise of Algerian monumental history and its paradoxical manifestations have been possible, we can usefully draw on Jean-Nöel Ferrié's theorization (2004) of what he called 'solidarity without consensus,' which is based on agreement by individuals on the form but not on the content of the subject under debate, and which limits deliberation within the constraints of the shared reference (in his case, Islam). Following Ferrié's approach, an Algerian may oppose the content (how such or such an event took place), but not the form – that is, the framework of the revolution and the generation that carried it out. In the case of the 'November generation,' the one that started the war and led to victory, connections remain very significant and 'real.' To give only one example of the weight of this generation, in the April 2014 presidential elections three out of the six candidates were children of *chouhada* (martyrs), and one was a former *mujahed*.[5] This generation continues to mark the present by putting it in a specular relation with the past, one which takes two forms. On the one hand, in its official version it justifies political actors' actions and reinstates the past as *the* framework for political decisions, while mobilizing the past positively as a mirror that reflects a present apprenhended as its logical continuation. On the other hand, in its popular 'lay' version, which at present is often critical, the past represents tangible proof that can lay bare the political perversions of the present, in which the past and the purity of the revolutionary epic are subjected to hidden manipulation. In both cases, the past – i.e. the November generation – remains the reference point.

---

5   Four out of the six candidates directly belonged to the 'revolutionary family,' either as participants in the war or those 'having rights' (*ayants droit*) according to the formula applied to the children of the *chouhada*. The November generation refers exclusively to those who participated in the war or sacrificed their life. The powerful organizations of those 'having rights' include, among others, the National Organization of the Children of the *Chouhada* (ONEC) and the National Organization of the Children of the Mujaheddin.

THE DOUBLE PRESENCE OF SOUTHERN ALGERIANS   201

In a sort of temporal inversion, but while still keeping the reference to the past, the November generation is invested with the capacity to judge present-day actions, favouring retention over emancipation or projection into a 'time still to come,' hence its teleological and monumental function. This apprehension of the past has profound implications for territorial space, which was at the centre of the ferocious fight against the colonizer and which, after liberation, became 'shrunken,' as it was centralized, homogeneous and hierarchized – in a word, a Jacobin space.

Turning Point: The Emergence of the 'Unemployed Generation'

This model of historical reference continued to play out until the end of the 1980s, when it was fractured during the massive riots in October 1988, where for the first time the horrified Algerian people saw 'their army' kill 'their children.'[6] Until the early 1980s, divisions within the political elites had not gone beyond their own circle. The slogan 'by and for the people' began to lose its hold as identity claims (e.g. Amazighity or Berberity) and large social in-equalities came to light in a country that still defined itself as socialist, egalitarian, and the standard bearer of the 'November Revolution.' The Civil War (1991–2002) widened the fracture, as these two events and the bloodshed in-volved confirmed a subjective rupture which became increasingly apparent when contrasted to the reverse linear construction involved in reference to the November generation.

What effects did this ordering of generations and their temporality have on the emergence of protest movements? We subscribe to the argument that monumentality is not merely a process of 'simple domination,' to use Luc Boltanski's expression (2009) – a raw and direct imposition – but is rather something that actors integrate and incorporate into their discourse. It estab-lishes filiation while at the same time integrating contradictory statements and, like most ideologies, it imposes totality. However, believing in the Novem-ber generation or being unable to deny it entirely does not imply the absence of parallel or even contradictory discourses. Acknowledging these discourses opens the possibility of breaking with old ways of thinking and being, and

---

6   In fact, there was a precedent to October 1988 – on June 19, 1965, the day of the *redressement révolutionnaire,'* the coup d'état where President Ahmed Ben Bella was deposed by the army, the tanks of the 'Popular National Army' were deployed in the streets to disperse opponents of the coup.

creating new ones which will constitute the present generation. But in this case, what characteristics do these latter have, and how are they shaped?

In what follows, we will address these questions by considering the recent movement of the unemployed in Algeria, aiming to understand how an emerging generation constructs its relation to the past and to monumentality, and the expressive modes that position it in relation to the November generation. Through the number and energy of its members, and the activities that it has chosen to emphasize, this movement establishes temporal and spatial parameters that let it claim to be the 'spokesperson of a generation in formation.' Its interest to us, but also the difficulty it poses, is that it is a forming and emerging force. It has the characteristics of a 'split habitus' (*'habitus clivé'* Mauger 2009): that is to say, it evolves both from within a structure, which Mauger calls 'genetic,' and outside of it, in a 'plural action' (Lahire 2001) which supersedes the former. How will this movement, which started 'just like that' (an activist[7]) and reacted 'tit for tat with the police' (idem), be able to construct its own temporality by opposing or imitating temporalities constructed by other generations, in this case by and in the projection of the 'November generation'? It seems that the movement of the unemployed, despite its recent creation, is an example of an attempt to cut loose and to open the way for new things, but it also exemplifies the difficulty of disaffiliating from the past.

Born in the wake of the revolutionary circumstances of the 2011 Arab Spring but preceding it in its initial form, this movement is not linked to any political party,[8] and defines itself as a movement fighting for fundamental rights, especially the right to work. As if to echo the uprising that took place in the *peripheral* South Central regions of neighbouring Tunisia at the outset of the revolution there, this movement started in the South, from where it spread to the rest of Algerian territory. Our decision to explore the movement through its southern 'section' is justified, on the one hand, because it involved new protests with specific modalities, particularly non-affiliation with political parties. On the other hand, the movement is fairly recent and remains largely undocumented in comparison to other protest groups in Algeria, for instance the Amazigh (Berber) movement, which has received substantial attention. And

---

7   R. Hadj-Moussa met activists from this movement in the spring and summer of 2014. For anonymity reasons, few names will be used with the exception of those that are already public.

8   The movement was supported by the National Autonomous Union of Public Administration Personnel (*Syndicat national autonome des personnels de l'administration publique* – SNAPAP) but it distanced itself from it later. The Algerian League of Human Rights, in particular its section in the city of Toughourt and its first leader, Yacine Zaid, were the main support and backing of this movement.

although initially guided by regional leaders, the movement nonetheless has involved many *wilayat* (administrative region; sing. *wilaya*) in the country.

Since the movement's main preoccupation has been employment, we will first of all focus on the latter contextualization on a national scale in relation to public policies, particularly those specifically related to jobs and unemployment. Then, secondly, we will identify how the movement itself is a site of the emergence and creation of a generation, and how local space – here the Sahara – becomes an inescapable element in the mobilisation of actors and a site of the redefinition of monumentality. This emphasis on space helps to identify the unique articulation between generations, and contributes to revisiting the way that a generation is conceptualized by including space.

Public Policy and Unemployment

Algeria's socialist path and its economic policy choices, based on heavy industry with gas and oil as its main products, have long coloured its public policies. The State was a large employer, leaving little legroom for private industry. After 1994, when Algeria was required to follow the neo-liberal guidelines of the Structural Adjustment Plan (SAP) imposed by the major international monetary organizations, the State did not withdraw from the social sector, and has continued to address the imbalances that resulted from these policies. Even though the largest and most viable public corporations were sold to foreign corporations, and that layoffs affected "320,000 workers in three years"– that is, 8% of the active population (Safar Zitoun 2010, 54 and 64)[9] – the State's presence remained 'palpable' in vital social sectors such as healthcare, education and housing. However, as Madani Safar Zitoun shows, it is difficult to reconstruct the implementation of social protections, not only due to the "tendency towards an opaque system,"[10] but also due to the syncretism that gives the State the ability to undo harm done elsewhere by imposing levies and using part of

---

9   These numbers can be revised upwards, as the General Labour Inspectorate (*Inspection générale du travail*) recorded 514,000 job losses between 1994 and 1998. (In Mohammed Saib Musette, "Jeunesse et politiques publiques en Algérie*..." (nd)).

10   External studies on the impact of the PAS after 1994 are not available, due either to their being confidential or extremely technical and thus difficult to use (Safar Zitoun 2010, 55). The level of State disengagement is still a subject of debate. While most authors agree that there has been disengagement, some analyze its devastating effects on 'households' and buying power, whereas others approach it from different angles by examining State actions towards target groups such as "the poor," "youth," etc. Musette notes a profound mutation in the "structure of the employed" (*ibid.*).

its oil revenues to cover the gaps or insufficiencies of social programmes. In a flurry of State interventions, numerous programs targeted general employment (e.g. labour-intensive public utility work (TUP-HIMO)) or specifically youth employment, with the creation of the National Agency for Support to Youth Employment (ANSEJ) in 1996[11] and the National Micro-Credit Agency (ANGEM) in 2004, both directly reporting to the President's Office. But these efforts to put safeguards into place to avoid large social disparities clashed with the informalization of economic activities, paradoxically encouraged by the social policies that were implemented (Safar Zitoun 2010, 65).

The level of informal economic activity grew exponentially, whereas job programs bore fruit for only a small number of young programme recipients. Badly structured, these programs, which had no upstream or downstream follow-up, gave precedence to the financial dimension – i.e. relation with a bank – as the sole link between recipients and the whole system, and failed in encouraging innovative initiatives or at least in having a more humane dimension. As described by Nacer Abbaci (2010) in his article on the implementation of employment policies and its workings in a small Algerian town, successful individuals were those who were persistent and systematically used family resources, felt to be "inexhaustible capital" (118), to counter the precariousness of their employment and the uncertainty in which they found themselves for an indeterminate time. Furthermore, permanent job security was scarce when compared to demand and to the goals of the employment programmes themselves. Between 1990 and 1994, 3.3% of young people were hired at the end of their pre-employment contracts, and only 2% between 1994 and 1999, with most permanent jobs being in administration rather than in the economic sector (Abbaci 2010, 97). These observations are corroborated by Safar Zitoun's conclusions, which took into account the support mechanisms in the fight against poverty and unemployment. According to him, between 2000 and 2006 "the 'social safety net' had a real effect on reducing poverty" (Safar Zitoun 2010, 84), but this reduction did not result in the creation of "true jobs by the economy" but rather an intensive development of unemployment reduction programmes (ibid, 85), which itself became a major social and political issue.

The statistics we present in this chapter are approximate due to technical and methodological weaknesses in data gathering,[12] but they nonetheless

---

11   The Youth Employment Plan (*Plan emploi jeune* – PEJ) was the first employment assistance plan, created in 1988.

12   Figures from the Statistics National Office (*Office national des statistiques* – ONS) are incomplete and problematic. As well, the survey techniques used do not accurately show the disparities between *wilayas* in terms of unemployment.

indicate the seriousness of the problem. Employment is at present dominated by the private sector, which in 2011 provided 60% of jobs as against 40% in the public sector, a reversal of the situation in 1989 when 54% were in the public sector (Musette 2013, 4). This reversal was accompanied by an informalization of the economy and of employment, estimated at 40% in 2011. Temporary work was estimated at 79.5% (ibid, 4; Musette 2014) in the private sector, and accompanied by a rather high rate of precarious employment, all the more so as union affiliation is almost non-existent and social assistance benefits are absent, which lifts the curtain on another aspect of the reality of employment in Algeria. In fact, having a job is no longer a source of socio-political stability and integration, as had been the case in the past. The segment of the population that was and is most affected by precarious employment are recent entrants to the job market. Unemployment in the officially defined 'youth' bracket, i.e. those between 16 and 24 years old, was 24% in total, 19.1% for young men and 38% for young women (ibid, 4). According to an IMF report, unemployment among young people will probably increase more than among the general labour force due to the lack of employment 'flexibility' (FMI 2012).

The Rise of a Movement

During the decade of terrorism (1991–2002), these extremely high numbers led to few reactions among the unemployed and the general population, who were paralyzed by terrorism and forced into silence by a State that viewed their demands as a threat to national sovereignty. However, many voices rose up after the end of terrorism (e.g., Amazigh demands,[13] the formation and consolidation of independent unions, Human Rights associations, etc.), and among these were the unemployed, who formed a committee on February 6, 2011. Although initiated by 'youth' in the South, shortly thereafter it was named the "National Committee for the Defense of the Rights of the Unemployed" (*Comité national pour la défense des droits des chômeurs* – CNDDC) to avoid any hints of regionalism, and included representatives from thirteen *wilayat*. In addition to its primary focus on work, the CNDDC proposed the introduction of an employment policy based on the renewed engagement of public authorities, restoring measures that had allowed municipalities to create their own companies. Its platform of demands, although very category-specific – i.e. 'corporatist' – remained strongly open to other political and social struggles. Furthermore, in contrast to Tunisia and Morocco's committees of the unemployed, which

---

13   In fact, Amazigh demands have been continuously voiced.

were comprised solely of diploma-holders, the CNDDC included those with and without degrees. Since its inception it has operated illegally, sometimes 'tolerated,' sometimes controlled, and often suppressed.

From the outset, the committee wanted to differentiate itself from State structures and chose to not seek accreditation because "for them [the committee's founders], if you are accredited you are integrated into the system," as we were told by an unemployed activist. However, after many debates and several years of seeing its actions and activities getting lost in the here and now, the CNDDC is torn today between becoming accredited or being independent because, as one the Southern activists stated, "the country is governed by individuals [individual interests,] and not incarnated in the State." This rejection of authority is quite significant for our argument about monumentality, because it relates to what Algerians call 'system,' i.e. those who govern and constantly instrumentalize the 'November generation.' The 'system' refers to a government structure, but also to a group of people who share the same 'generational habitus' (Mauger 2009), who benefit from the same material conditions and share the same imaginary, which feeds off of the liberation war and the 'November generation.'

While the principal demand of the unemployed is for work, other types of demands are more central because they better account for the formation of the 'unemployed generation' of unemployed and offer opportunities of developing new forms of protest. On a strictly practical plan, however, the Committee of the Unemployed should not be ignored because it has allowed a new voice to have greater freedom and to be heard. Hence, the demands of the unemployed for a 'decent' job are absolutely crucial, as they are supported by an indescribable precariousness and high unemployment among working-age people marginalized by the Algerian economy.

That said, it seems less valuable to treat the issue of generations head-on through the generational specificity represented by the Committee of the Unemployed and its anchoring in the history of struggle in contemporary Algeria, than to approach it laterally by examining a group of unemployed activists from southern Algeria. This means that the analysis of generational emergence requires that we are attentive to the geography and space of its inception. To take the Committee of the Unemployed by one of its sections helps identify its complex composition while offering a better understsnding of the stakes that characterize it.

This generational category has had to deal not only with the general demands of the movement of the unemployed but also with unequal relations between peripheral regions and the centre, and the differing relations of regions to the revolution (seen as an exemplary struggle), its history, and the history of post-independence protest movements. Hence, the 'question of generations' can be treated more deeply by means of a cross-sectional approach, which relies on the various angles, particualry on space. Our own perspective was shifted in this direction in light of the historical specificities of the South and by our 'witnessing' an ongoing groundswell in Algerian society, which social scientists have treated with some difficulty under the heading of 'youth,' largely failing to consider the dynamic relationships that these people have built with their ecological milieu, which makes them a generation rather than merely a group sharing the same age bracket.

To shed light on this generation in formation (we will discuss its status as emergent later on), we must bring together the often heterogeneous elements that define a scale of generations in time or over a short time span, and in relation to space. To our knowledge, research on generations, which is dominated by references to time and temporality, has not developed the notion of space. The case under study here forces us to reflect on the relation between space and the formation of generations. Here space, around which diverse affiliations are expressed, does not designate 'location' as defined by Karl Mannheim (1964), which refers to a specific positioning of individuals vis-à-vis certain past or contemporary phenomena and events. An emphasis on space seems somewhat unorthodox in light of the predominance that Mannheim and many others after him (e.g., Mauger 2009) give to temporality – as if the relation between spatiality, or the lived environment, and the acquisition of a positionality and subjectivity could remain separate from the identification of an individual or a group, and their qualification. The experience of space and the subjective attachements it encourages can indeed be regarded as equally formative as the experience of time.

An exception to this tendancy is Abdelmalek Sayad (1994), who deconstructs the concept of generation as it has been applied to Maghrebin émigrés in France, and who sees it as already visible in the country of origin. He does not think through this reference to space directly in relation to generations themselves, however, but rather through a critique of the notion of integration, which refers to degrees of inclusion (or its lack) among immigrants in the host society, and categorizes generations according to sequence (first, second, etc.). For Sayad, the integration that the immigrant, an outsider in French society, undertakes is already present in the space and time in which the idea of immigrating appears in his mind. To properly understand the relation to space that Sayad proposes, as someone critical of the idea of integration as intrinsic to and underlying the notion of generation, it is important to note that for him the category of generation is "performative" (1994, 167) and involves power. In other words, when he explores the sociological criteria that define the generation, the author shows how this category becomes an imposition whose justification is based (or comes back to) the space of origin. From this approach we retain the idea that generation has a performative function in Austin's sense – i.e. as a language act that has a relation to authority – and, especially, the idea that place of origin is a significant marker in the process of 'generating a generation' (Sayad), even though it is temporality that dominates most analyses of generations of immigrants.

Moreover, space and the projection that it allows inform individuals' experiences. The line of analysis followed by Henri Lefebvre in his book "The Production of Space" (1974), and the complexity he sees there, can illuminate the relation between space and generation. The triptych he proposes, distinguishes between 'spatial practice,' 'the representation of space' and 'space of representation.' The first pertains to the competence and performance of the actors, the second is related to relations of dominance in producing space, and finally, the third is linked to resistance, that is, "to the clandestine and underground side of social life, but also to art..." (Lefebvre 1974, 42–43, trans.). It is this third element that, we argue, permits deconstructing the monumentality of history, in particular through the strong presentation of present necessity by evoking of a space called in our case either the 'South' or the 'Sahara,' which unfolds into the notion of region (*mentiqat es'hara*).

Within the movement of the unemployed, the group comprised of the southern unemployed is clearly attached to two elements: the movement of the unemployed properly speaking, its activist projects; and the space it belongs to, the South or the Sahara. Both are structuring, but the first is also contingent. We will see later how contingency can assist the emergence of demands specific to a generation and, in the same movement, the construction of a generation.

Generations and Conjunctures

In Algeria, the category of 'youth' officially corresponds to a specific age bracket (19 to 24 years old), but it is generally accepted that a person who has not started a family is 'young,' even if that person is almost forty. Due to the seriousness of the issue of unemployment, and also to housing policies that make it difficult to fill the high demand for housing among people of marriagable age, Algeria is increasingly populated by 'young' people; and the growing figures available on this do not take women into account. The unemployed in the South share this situation, but it is aggravated by the vast inequality that

MAP 8.1   Map of Algeria
© RATIBA HADJ-MOUSSA, 2015.

affects the region, which largely explains why the movement 'caught on' there rather than in other regions that also suffer inequalities. Our hypothesis is that inequality and the sense of injustice are at the heart of the movement's viability and of the generational formation that brought it to life. But there is more to these specificities, as the sentiment of injustice is related to space and to territory, as mentioned earlier. The wide disparities between the North and the South in Algeria have begun to come to light and to be denounced by people from the southern regions, whose voices, since February 2011, have begun to resonate and even to drive demands at the national level. They have pushed the political regime to use all sorts of strategies against them, from corruption, to beatings, to intimidation and even prison sentences.[14] This is 'an anomaly,' since until 2011 the South had not been heard.

On Saturday, November 1st, 2014, the 60th anniversary of the Algerian liberation war, the coordinator of the unemployed movement at that time, Madani Madani, a journalist and activist born in Ouargla, one of the large cities in the Algerian South where the unemployed movement started and around which movements across the region gathered, reported that the city did not have a sewage system in the 1990s (Abane, 2014a). In fact, because of oil revenues, there had been important and substantial infrastructure investments in the southern regions, but these mostly responded to the needs of gas and oil exploration.[15] Employment was offered, but by oil companies who hired their own workers, often foreigners, and by sub-contracting companies who hired people from other regions of Algeria even for positions without special qualifications, leaving the local workforce without many jobs. For the majority of Algerian workers who worked in the sub-contracting sector, working conditions resembled "modern slavery" (Benfodil 2012) and certain cities, such as Hassi R'mel (see Map 8.1), were no-go areas. "Algeria is a rich country with poor people," said Tahar Bellabes, one of the pioneers of the unemployed movement. Thus, beyond the demands for jobs there is the shadow of a dispute and a disagreement that runs from one end to the other of Algerian history, in particular the history of the people of the South and their relation with the North, the centre of decision-making.

How can we understand the emergence of this generational spirit, and what are the central moments that made it possible? We propose to answer this question by recourse to the notions of event and domination as they have been developed by historical sociology and the sociology of critique.

To do so, we will need to look back over the short term, as the movement took on its meaning within the temporal folds of recent history. Various economic and structural elements must be considered if one wants to avoid falling in the trap of seeing generations as homogeneous groups chronologically following one after another, or of thinking that the post-independence generation "has

---

14   We have witnessed this police and judiciary harrassement. To give just one example, in December 2014 thirty-two unemployed people were being tried in Aflou, with six among them receiving a one-year prison sentence. During a second revision of this article in February 2015, "nine unemployed rights activists were sentenced, in Laghouat, to sentences of six to eighteen months in jail without parole, and eight others to six-month suspended sentences" [Our translation] (Allilat 2015).

15   The city of In Salah has only recently (2015) had some roads asphalted, despite being close to important gas plants in which the Algerian government and its partners invested 1,185 billion USD (Algérie-Focus 2011).

THE DOUBLE PRESENCE OF SOUTHERN ALGERIANS   211

run its course," as President Bouteflika famously stated in a speech given in 2012, where he acknowledged that "his generation had run its course" [*"jili dab edjanou"*] and that the *'shabab'* (the young) must take their place in a linear succession dictated by the sacrifices of the sacralised Algerian people.[16] Such a discourse smoothes, flattens, and makes continuous the uneven road that is the life of subjects, of events, of men and women and their histories.

In contrast to this continuist vision of history and generations, it is possible to see the formation of generations in the way that Williams Sewell Jr. (1990) does, by beginning from events. For Sewell Jr., who views events as the product of bifurcations provoked by the conjunction of a series of actions or character-istics proper to situations, recourse to broad frames of analysis that ignore the role of events and situations is ineffective.[17] He suggests going beyond these by better integrating the notion of event, in order to treat changes through the characteristics of the phenomenon being studied, rather than through an already established framework, and to explain events through attentiveness to conjunctures. Following Sewell Jr., we can argue that the movement of the un-employed, its anchoring in the South, and the ways it has been brought to life by the 'young' have to do with "multiple registers of causation" (1990, 21). These registers can be essentially summarized as the impacts, starting in the 1990s, of the Structural Adjustment Plan (SAP) on the parents of today's unemployed, these parents often being unemployed or precarious workers themselves. To this economic situation can be added two major political conjunctures, the riots of October 1988[18] and the Civil War.

---

16   *'jili tab ajnanou'* (literally: 'the garden of my generation is ripe' meaning that his genera-
      tion must give its place to the next).
         "You, youth of Algeria, who have lived with the generation that freed Algeria, who have
      told you, 'Oh, brothers! We cannot take it anymore.' You must get ready for your future re-
      sponsibilities. [...] Time is over for my generation." Commentators, the people, and those
      opposing Bouteflika's fourth presidential term, kept repeating this broken promise during
      the election in April 2014 (Bouteflika, 2012).
17   Sewell Jr. analyses Charles Tilly's and Emmanuel Wallerstein's work, whose methodologies
      he describes as 'teleological.' For example, Sewell shows that the counter-revolutionary re-
      volt in Vendée is attributed by Tilly to the delay in urbanizing the communities involved,
      whereas according to Sewell, its reasons can be found in the local social structures which
      permitted the passing from the *ancient regime* to the revolutionary government. Altough
      Tilly describes these structures, he nonetheless ignores them because they remain hidden
      by the main factors he had previously identified (Sewell Jr. 1990, 7–8).
18   On the importance of the 1988–1992 period, see a rare book by Myriam Ait-Aoudia (2015),
      which focuses on the emergence of political parties as new political players.

The riots, which are more important for our purposes, shattered the image of the regime's durability and emphasized the voice of the people (the voice of the street, not the 'sacred people' of the dominant discourse), along with a certain idea of rule of law that Algerians had lost in the 1970s, during the glorious years of the Houari Boumediene[19] presidency, which offered them comforts but forced them to remain quiet and silent. The riots in October 1988 were the start of an era of freedom, not only because they forced the regime to authorize the right of citizens to form political and labour associations and to allow the initiation of a multiparty system, which offered the hope of the democratization of Algeria, but also because it facilitated the *rise of a political subject* that aimed to rethink its relation to the public sphere. The fact that this experience veered off into the Civil War (1991–2002) after the cancellation of legislative elections which the Islamist party was winning should not lead us to think that October 1988 left no traces. For example, music on the Internet, of all types, shows how pivotal this moment was (Hadj-Moussa 2013). An important breach was opened, and with this came new ways of doing and thinking that remained dormant, like sleeping cells, throughout the Civil War, but were reactivated as soon as the war was brought under control.[20]

The second political conjuncture – the Civil War – was paradoxically a period of security in the South, especially in certain locations where gas and oil plants existed and the interests of multinational corporations were at stake. Indeed, while there were many collective massacres of civilians perpetrated in the North, no terrorist attacks were reported against the gas and oil fields, which spread across a large territory.

In this decade, during which everything seemed to be drenched in blood, the arrival of satellite television, also an important event in the overall political conjuncture, occurred at the same time as the Civil War. This new form of television was a major issue in the dramatic struggle between Islamists and the regime over the public sphere. But beyond its intrumentalization by both sides, and the undeniable opening up to the world it provided after decades of state-controlled television, this new television brought media coverage of

---

19   Houari Boumediene was the second President of Algeria, who came to power in June 1965 after a coup d'état. During his presidency, Algeria adopted a policy of '*socialisme spécifique*,' and became a champion of the Third World and hosted revolutionaries from around the world. The rate of growth during his term was 7.5% and the employment rate doubled between 1965 and 1975. Large infrastructure projects were started, particularly in heavy industry and the oil sector (Hassan 1996, 27).

20   We do not refer here to structured activities or those deployed within an activist framework.

world events, different modes of governance, and the divergent views of opposition figures. It made visible what before had been only rumour and innuendo, and permitted a dismantling of the official discourse that surreptitiously continued the acts of rebellion and defiance triggered by the riots of October 1988. We describe this as surreptitious because this dismantling following the viewing of satellite television not because of a growing awareness re/activated by organized political mobilization, but rather through the uncertain and diffuse circulation of ideas as to the meaning of justice, the rule of law, democracy, corruption, and inequality alongside the focus on entertainment that predominates in this media.[21]

Generations: Algeria Contested by Its South

'The generational spirit' of the movement of the unemployed in the South was thus constructed around and at the crossroads of three conjunctures, which themselves were articulated around a structural inequality with deep and powerful roots. The movement of the unemployed, as it was expressed in the South, led to explosive 'political' demands.

We can initially read the point of connection between these situations and the double demands of Southern actors in terms of brute, or in Luc Boltanski's terms (2009) 'simple,' domination.[22] Indeed, responses to demands by the populations of the South usually came from the security forces, not the administration. "At the slightest protest, we suffer police repression. The police are our sole interlocutor. In the North of the country, you can go see a local official, but in the South it's only the security forces," said Tahar Bellabes.[23] The security situation became more delicate after an attack by a major terrorist group on a gas site in Tinguentourine (Ain Amenas; see Map 8.1) on January 16, 2013. Still, it was in the South that the most important Algerian social movement of the last decade began, and this requires us to nuance both the idea of simple or brute domination – which according to Boltanski blocks the manifestation of

---

21 For more details see Hadj-Moussa (2015).

22 Boltanski, in his work *De la critique* (2009), distinguishes simple or first-degree domination, which brutally impose its justifications, from more sophisticated forms of domination that are supported by a discourse of managers and experts which use 'change' as their ultimate justification. Simple domination is the main mode used by totalitarian (and authoritarian) regimes.

23 R. Hadj-Moussa did three sets of interviews with activists or members of the movement of the unemployed in the spring and the summer of 2014 and in the summer of 2015. She met with activists from both the North and the South.

criticism by weakening its intensity or forcing it to become dormant – and the reframing of activity that it involves.

There is still much left to clarify about this movement, but we can already posit that a certain anthro-political imaginary universe has begun to implode, under which the South and its population were ruled through a mode of quasi-colonial domination, albeit under the cover of an ideological discourse that claimed peaceful national unity. Undoubtedly, this explains the great tension in the movement's discourse – which we should note is supported by the local population – between on the one hand the justification of belonging to the nation, out of deep conviction and in fear of being accused of secessionism, and on the other hand a self-definition supported by a strong demand for equality, made even stronger by the idea that "Algeria's wealth comes from its South," as an activist said.

The demand by people in the South for access to employment (a 'right,' according to the Algerian labour code) is thus framed by a larger geo-anthropological and ecological entity: the Sahara. Although we believe these cannot be dissociated from each other, analysis should proceed on to two different registers. The first (employment) concerns criticism related to reality, or more precisely to the confrontation between what are valued and established principles of justice (e.g. the right to work), and what exists "in the actual texture of reality" (Boltanski *op. cit.*, 160, our trans.).[24] In other words, these operations allow criticism to use evidence in order to show its compliance to and application of the 'roadmap,' which is to provide employment for the largest number. The unemployed used their present 'situation,' i.e. 'what exists,' to show how distant this was from 'what ought to be.' Like vigilantes, they caught the State in the act, and deconstructed the scaffolding of its claims of equality, often paying a high price (all types of humiliations and punishments, jailings, etc.).

The second register relates to a 'deeper malaise,' as the whole Algerian Sahara has become concerned, not merely affected. This 'concernement' has happened through justifications that are not institutionalized, but belong rather to the life and lived experience, and which pertain to what 'touches' or 'renders' affective sentiments in individuals and collectivities. They are based on humiliating experiences that are difficult to thematize or to generalize, as they lack a frame of expression, or simply because they are seen by the political regime

---

24 This section of the article is inspired by Boltanski's *On Domination* (2009), where he distinguishes between the 'reality tests,' and 'existential tests.' The first type of tests determines the difference between 'what it is' and 'what ought to be.' The second type of tests refers to realities that lack institutional forms but that allow for more radical changes.

as outside of the order of things. Due to the fact they do not correspond neatly to reality or go beyond it, these justifications have a radical critical capacity.

Thus, an activist met in the summer of 2014 stated:

> The regime makes reference [to the term] the 'South' (*el djanoub*) to better split up and divide our forces. In fact, it was the regime that created regionalism and terrorism. Just look at what is happening in Ghardaïa [a city in the South that experienced serious inter-community clashes that set the M'Zab region abalze for at least 6 months in 2013–14]. [Its rhetoric is] 'It's me or terrorism.' 'It's me or bombs.' Why does the regime want to free the Sahrawis [in Western Sahara], but does nothing for the Algerian Sahara?
> Why don't they say that we are Sahrawis?

Here we find a new scene, which brings us back to our discussion on monumental history, the 'November generation' and the 'unemployed generation.' This scene is built, on the one hand, from the historical background that led people from the South (e.g., the representative of the movement of the unemployed centred on the city of Ouargla) to remind others that the Southern population voted for a united Algeria in the referendum forced on them by France on February 27, 1962. The unemployed, and by extension the population of the South or at least the population of Ouargla, declared this date the 'Day of National Unity' (*Youm el wahda el watanya*), which has been celebrated ever since. Using a double strategy, they thus remind others of the debt that Algeria has towards the South while ostensibly celebrating a united Algeria according to official tradition. This has further significance given that the city of Ouargla, where Algerians protesting in favour of Algerian unity were killed by French bullets, is now the point around which discontent and opposition gather. In terms of strategy, there is no doubt that the invocation of the war of national liberation, and by association the 'November generation,' situates the movement in the same wake as the elites in power who use this reference; but the movement has also built, in a new manner, the foundations of a generation, a population, and a region.

At this point it will be useful to return to the idea of solidarity without consensus as presented by Ferrié, mentioned above, which rests on the constraint exercised by reference (to revolution, the November generation, etc.), but which attributes a great flexibility to social actors. From the angle of the emergence of a generation, represented by the unemployed from the South, the retrospective appropriation of the date of February 27, 1962 institutes a new group while ensuring continuity and recalling the South's earlier sacrifices for the unification of Algeria. November 1st, 1954, the day when the Algerian revolution started, now has as its counterpart February 27, 1962, the day when the nation was united, a date that is certainly anchored in continuity but at the same time transforms and shifts the terms of reference by conferring new positions to emerging actors.[25]

This new scene is thus constructed, on the one hand, on an argument about participation in the liberation war (the inter-community clashes in winter and spring 2014 in M'Zab showed the centrality of this argument), and on the other on an anthropological reality that often goes unnoticed and draws inspiration from the model of a civilized person face-to-face with a boorish and almost barbarian ignoramus, which embodies the administrative practices and the ordinary beliefs of people from the North that make Southerners feel humiliated and ignored. Rejection of this dominant model is expressed on various registers, both by activists and by citizens. Thus, in a letter sent to the 'High Authorities'[26] on November 26, 2014, asking them to censor some research by an Algerian anthropologist they felt had betrayed them, the "sheikhs, women and the young people of Djanet" (a city deep in the Algerian South, see Map 8.1) were aiming at more than the disapproval they perceived coming from the researcher. We take the liberty of quoting the letter as it was published, since it gives a remarkable example of the sentiments and perceptions of people who feel marginalized in their own country, and also echoes the demands of the movements in the South.

> In this country, it is reasonable to send the condemned and the sanctioned among us to the Sahara; to give the opportunity to a person beginning their professional career to use us as subjects to acquire skills; to send those that are near retirement here so that they will have a better pension. Even police officers and doctors ask that their period of service in the South be reduced; and there are pilots who refuse to come South.
>
> Furthermore, those who obtain high positions in the State say [of us]: 'they can even taste yogurt!'...and others accused the Touareg of being accomplices in the Tiguentourine operation even before the investigation had been started. An official at the University of Constantine [East North] stated it will not let people from the South enrol until they show negative test results for Ebola and AIDS, since it is us and the Africans [Sub-saharan migrants] who carry such diseases! All this is followed by a long list of offences...

---

25   Our reading of the consequences of the appropriateion of the events is inspired by Sewell and his suggestion for developing sociology of events (Sewell Jr. 1990, 23–24).

26   With "a carbon copy to national and international media."

THE DOUBLE PRESENCE OF SOUTHERN ALGERIANS

To these sentiments of rejection and humiliation, a relatively recent but *significant* event can be added, which informs the discourse and strategies of the unemployed in the South even though in the actors' discourse itself it often remains a presupposition. It is understandable that actors are careful in what they say, since when seen from the point of view of the Algerian State something unprecedented has taken place, namely the creation a local citizen and civic movement initiated by a group of young men called "the Movement of Southern Children for Justice" (*Mouvement des enfants du Sud pour la justice* – MESJ). This movement began in Ouargla in 2004, following the merger of the platforms of the movement based in Ouargla and the citizens' movement in Labiodh Sidi Cheikh, another city in the central South and the administrative centre for the *wilaya* of El Bayadh (see Map 8.1), which was created in 2001 following riots in the region barely one year after the official end of the Civil War. In September 2003, a visit by President Bouteflika to the *wilaya* of El Bayadh led to further riots and to anger among residents and associations, who tried to prevent him from meeting the local dignitaries who they did not consider their representatives. They asked, in vain, to be allowed to speak to the President in order to present their platform of demands, which "contain[ed] a series of cultural, political and economic demands. Substantially, the drafters of the platform demand[ed] a better distribution of national wealth and a real administrative division to allow *for the founding of a federation in the South*" (Benseba 2003, our italics). In this platform, the federalist option, which they expressed here for the first time, had as its corollary a demand for justice clearly enunciated as a political demand.

After its creation, the Movement of Southern Children for Justice was quickly and violently repressed. Already geographically isolated, its members were accused of being separatists and terrorists. They were harassed, jailed, tortured and summarily tried. Some members were pushed to armed violence following the sanctions, humiliation and torture that were applied on them and their families. The local population felt that the State was unduly criminalizing the movement's actions by calling its members terrorists.[27]

---

27   In February 2014, citizens protested even in Djanet [see Map 8.1] demanding that the State stops its attacks on the movement led by Abdessalam Tarmoune, the brother of Taïb Tarmoune, one of the leaders of the "Movement of Southern Children for Justice." "We want the ANP [Armée nationale populaire] to stop bombing Tassili and to enter in talks with Abdessalam Tarmoune and his men in the Movement of Southern Children for justice," states its communiqué. The protestors justified their demands with the following arguments: "We fear that the youth will take to the *maquis* [remote regions, historically the base for armed opposition]," they claim. "We advocate a federal option for the State, and we demand social justice and the fair distribution of wealth in Algeria," assures Ahmed Arbi, spokesperson for the citizen movement in Labiodh Sidi Cheik (El Bayedh).

If it seems then that the activist and civic version of the Movement of Southern Children for Justice was decapitated, its armed version was both combatted and maintained by the State (see note 29), in what appears to be one of its strategies to curb actions by the unemployed. But this neutralization of the leadership was not totally successful, as the unemployed movement, while making 'social' demands, in the words of one of its leaders, shows some affinities with the MESJ's political demands. Between 2004 and 2011, MESJ supporters and the 'youth,' as an activist told us, "led a continuous struggle (*moustamira*). We were like a school out on the street. We taught people what peaceful struggle is, the principles of pacifism. The street was instructive (*mounaoura* – which also means enlightening). And then there were issues on which everyone agreed." The Saharan actors of the movement of the unemployed and those who shared the same conditions supported this dual demand. However, this demand differentiated them from other members of their generation in other regions of Algeria, and gave them a unique perspective, where their learning on the street – "We started with the street, we had the street" – which all members shared, was strongly associated with their '*assassiyat el djanoub*,' their 'southern sensibility.' To avoid their actions being systematically transformed into political demands, they limited their claims to their 'social' dimension, hoping in this way to avoid the accusations of 'terrorism' and 'violation of State security' that brought some members of the movement under martial law (Section 40 of the military penal code). They knew that "the one who will say that [his actions are] for the South, that one will be burnt," "he will be assassinated" (activists).

In its present state, the movement of the unemployed gathers together the suffering and the inequality endured by the Southern population, and demonstrates its organizational capacity by drawing on two orientations that come into tension – on one side non-violence, an opposition to armed violence which has proven to be fruitless, and on the other the street violence and riots that were its mode of operation in the past. The choice of the 'pacifist way' results from their experiences in action and their confrontations with the police: "we fought on the street...but we learned that our protests, our actions had to be peaceful. When the police beat us up, we did not respond. That is how we could defeat them," as an activist said. This path is fed by social demands

---

"The [MESJ's] members received an amnesty in 2008 according to the National Reconciliation Charter [implemented in 2005]. The members of the MSJ (sic) laid down their weapons, on the sole condition that the State take up their platform of demands, for the most part social and political. But the State did not keep its promises. The MSJ members were stabbed on the back" – these views are heard from Ouargla to El Bayedh. (Abane, 2014b [Our translation]).

THE DOUBLE PRESENCE OF SOUTHERN ALGERIANS 219

for a 'decent job,' which must be accompanied by 'human development' and policies of 'professional training,' which have been crossed out with a "red line as far as the children of the South are concerned." On the other side, 'the movement's illegality' prevents it from positioning itself as a sustainable interlocutor with the authorities, and has recently pushed it to consider civil disobedience strategies. If this choice is confirmed in the future, the movement will find itself caught up in 'politics,' which will push it back into its initial insurgent radicalization.[28] With its dual nature, social and political, the movement is trying to redefine the contours of a reality that has long been taken for granted and accepted as such, with no possibility for change. The shift these demands initiated represents an extraordinary opening, whose effects are double-edged: it can open towards the further deployment of domination, or towards the possibility of an acknowledgment of harm suffered in the past. The movement and the generation that sustains it are currently at this juncture.

Work for Dignity: Generations in Equality

Another tension is superimposed onto this, as demands for decent work lead to a search for dignity and justice: this is why the MESJ rose up in 2004, allowing, by default, an echo of the uprising and the referendum on February 27, 1962 to resonate through the movement of the unemployed. Indeed, as Rainer Forst (2013) shows while defending a political approach to justice, a call for justice never stops with the distribution of goods but first and foremost has to do with power (34). In the Algerian authoritarian context, the call for justice exemplifies the pertinence of this 'political shift.' It allows both an insistence on relational and contextual dimensions while producing a discourse

---

28 A comparison with the movement of the unemployed in Tunisia and Morocco would be useful on this point. The fact that the Algerian movement is not only comprised of degree-holders gives it a more 'radical' character, as non-degree-holders, "who are more numerous in the structure, have nothing to lose. They are more radical. They are more determined in their action. They are not afraid of physical confrontations. They suffer greater hardship than degree-holders, who say 'I have a degree' and thus are covered by pre-employment policies," in the words of an activist. This concurs with observations by Asef Bayat (2008, 100) who notes that the unemployed movement was the most radical of the protest movements at the start of the Iranian Revolution. Furthermore, in the present case, members of the Committee who get a job do not cut ties with the movement and continue to provide financial support. This continuity makes it possible to limit state manipulation and to reduce co-opting of the newly employed, as has been the case in Morocco (see Emperador Badimon 2013).

of justification, and a call for the necessity of an ethical dimension. In fact, its discursive, i.e. normative dimension (e.g. the right to work) is not sufficient. It is intertwined with an ethical dimension that finds its meaning within anthropological discourse, among others, on the humanity of human beings – here all Algerians – and their unconditional *equality* with their fellow humans. This can be a way to read the use of the word 'dignity' (*el karama*) chanted by protesters throughout the Arab world, and is strongly suggested in demands for a 'decent job.' As Forst states, "to *possess* human dignity means being an equal member in the realm of subjects and authorities of justification, an attribute, I would add, that does not depend on the active exercise of capacity of justification, which would exclude infants or disabled persons" (2013, 101).

Two types of protests have cut across the South of Algeria, led by two generations that overlapped in a condensed temporality during a very short period – between 2004 and 2011 – and whose issues were the fair distribution of wealth and the ability to decide. The forms of protest used by the Southern segment of the movement of the unemployed, on which we have more information (the history of the MESJ still remains to be written), cover a wide range of practices that all seem to differentiate them from the generation that took the reins of power after independence, and involve a different perception of 'the November generation.' In fact, although the recent movement is still in the shadow of that generation, it has shifted its centre by renaming the main square of Ouargla 'sahat el Ouhda el wataniya' (the Square of the Nation Unity), and by adding an event, February 27, 1962, taken from the fringes of monumental history. In doing so, it has revealed one of the pieces missing from the truth. This event reminds everyone that Algeria owes much to the South, although History is still silent on it. The Algerian political regime was not fooled. Its attempts to weaken the impact of the movement of the unemployed by all means possible shows the importance of the issues at play, which go beyond economic demands: the Saharan element in the movement of the unemployed breaks the continuity of generations posed by monumental history, problematizing it and tending to rearrange the historical and geographical pieces essential to its creation.

Conclusion

The movement of the unemployed as it has formed in the South of Algeria presents a generation whose 'unity' (Mannheim) is built on overt class differences and on an outsider relationship to political decision-making. Although employment is its main leitmotif, the movement frames itself within demands for justice that surpass it. The movement formed and constituted itself in relation to history by picking certain historical events. Thus February 27, 1962 constitutes the founding and federating event of union with the rest of Algeria, and in two respects: in a regional crystallization that gathers '*hassassiyat el djanoub*' (Southern sensibilities), and in the celebration of the unified nation, which was for long the missing event in the writing of Algerian history. Furthermore, while being formed the movement declared its attachment to the Sahara, which complicated its emergence within the Algerian authoritarian context, where unity is the dominant form of national acknowledgement. This is a political complexity, as identity demands have always been the cause of bitter battles and are considered unacceptable in a centralized political system, as demonstrated by the Amazigh (Berber) struggle. It is also an economic complexity, as the Sahara is Algeria's 'wealth,'[29] in particular for the elites who, according to popular criticism, became its exclusive owners.

In terms of protest, the movement's actors, as members of one sole generation, the adopted a sort of "split habitus" (Mauger 2009, 117), which draws inspiration from the liberation struggle, while at the same time displacing it and adding innovation, since the history of contemporary protests continues to be very patchy, or even absent – "we must know the history of the region, its labour history and the history of rights," says an activist. This is a needed innovation but also a default choice. In fact, the lack of transmission of the movement as it has been expressed in the South continues to be its major stumbling block. Lastly, this political transmission is not the only element that should be put into question, as a better understanding of the ins and outs of the movement will also require studying issues of family lineage, and other forms of expression such as literature, poetry and music.

References

Abane, Meziane, "L'Histoire Secrète du Mouvement des Enfants du Sud," *El Watan*, 28 March 2014a. Accessed March 28, 2014. http://www.elwatan.com/actualite/l-histoire -secrete-du-mouvement-des-enfants-du-sud-28-03-2014-250892_109.php.

Abane, Meziane. "60 ans après la Révolution. L'Algérie est Libre, les Algériens pas Encore," *El Watan,* 31 October 2014b. Accessed October 31, 2014. http://www.elwatan .com/actualite/l-algerie-est-libre-les-algeriens-pas-encore-31-10-2014-276118_109 .php.

---

29   One of the Southern activists summarizes the reality of the relation between South and North this way: "People in the North say: 'the cow is home with you but the milk is with us.'"

Abbaci, Nacer. "Traitement du Chômage en Algérie. Des Politiques Publiques d'Aide à l'Emploi aux Solidarities Familiales," in *L'État Face aux Débordement du Social au Maghreb. Formation, Travail et Protection Sociale*, edited by Myriam Catusse, Blandine Desmetrau and Éric Verdier, 95–127. Aix-en-Provence & Paris: IREMAM & Karthala, 2010.

Aït-Aoudia, Myriam. L'experience démocratique en Algérie (1988–1992). Apprentissage politique et changement de régime. Paris: les Presses de Sciences Po. 2015.

Algérie-Focus. "Développement des champs gaziers du sud d'In Salah en Algérie." *Algérie-Focus*, April 12, 2011. Accessed May 4, 2016. http://www.algerie-focus.com/2011/04/developpement-des-champs-gaziers-du-sud-d%E2%80%99in-salah-en-algerie/.

Alilat, Yazid. "Laghouat: Neuf Militants des Droits des Chômeurs Condamnés," *Le Quotidien D'Oran,* 13 February 2015. Accessed February 15, 2015. http://www.lequotidien-oran.com/index.php?news=5209662.

APS (Algerie Presse Service), Wikalet el Anba' el Djazaïria. "L'Unité nationale est une 'ligne rouge'." April 16, 2016. http://www.aps.dz/algerie/40514-l-unit%C3%A9-nationale-est-une-ligne-rouge.

Bayat, Asef. "Workless Revolutionaries. The Unemployed Movement in Revolutionary Iran," in *Subalterns and Social Protest. History from Below in the Middle East and North Africa*, edited by Stephanie Cronin, 91–115. London& New York: Routledge, 2008.

Benfodil, Mustapha. "Les Chômeurs 'Professionnels' au Pays du Gaz." *Algeria Watch*. September 22, 2012. Accessed October 29, 2014. http://www.algeriawatch.org/fr/article/eco/soc/scorpions_bidonville_hassi_rmel.htm.

Benseba, Nadir. "En visite à Labiodh Sidi Cheikh, Bouteflika provoque l'émeute," Algeria Watch, September 10, 2003. Accessed December 11, 2014. http://www.algeria-watch.org/fr/article/pol/revolte/bouteflika_emeute.htm.

Boltanski, Luc. *De la critique. Précis de Sociologie de l'Emancipation*. Paris: Gallimard, 2009.

Bouteflika, Abdelaziz. Public speech broadcast on Algérie Direct. May 9, 2012. Accessed July 16, 2014. http://www.youtube.com/watch?v=dbWkQHi1XuE.

Emperador Badimon, Montserrat. "Does Unemployment Spark Collective Contentious Action? Evidence from a Moroccan Social Movement." *Journal of Contemporary African Studies* 31, 2 (2013): 194–212.

Ferrié, Jean-Noël. *Le Régime de la Civilité en Égypte. Public et Réislamisation*. Paris: CNRS Éditions, 2004.

FMI (Fonds monétaire international). *Questions Choisies. Algérie*. Rapport 12/22, 2012. Accessed February 7, 2015. http://www.imf.org/external/french/pubs/ft/scr/2012/cr1222f.pdf.

Forst, Rainer. *Justification and Critique: Towards a Critical Theory of Politics*. Cambridge, UK & Malden, MA: Polity Press, 2013.

Hadj-Moussa, Ratiba. 2013. "L'Émeute dans le Maghreb. La Révolte sans Qualité," *L'Homme et la Société*, 187–188 (2013): 39–62.

Hadj-Moussa, Ratiba. *La Télévision par Satellite au Maghreb et ses Publics. Espaces de Résistance, Espaces Critiques*. Grenoble: Presses Universitaires de Grenoble, 2015.

Hassan. *Algérie. Histoire d'un Naufrage*. Paris: Seuil, 1996.

Huyssen, Andreas. "Monumental Seduction." *New German Critique*, 69 (1996): 181–200.

Lahire, Bernard. *L'Homme Pluriel. Le Ressort de l'Action.* Paris: Hachette Littérature, 2001.

Lefebvre, Henri. *La Production de l'Espace.* Paris: Anthropos, 1974.

Mannheim, Karl. *Essays on the Sociology of Knowledge.* London: Routledge & Kegan and Paul, 1964.

Mauger, Gérard. "Générations et Rapports de Générations." *Δα΄ιμων. Revista Internacional de Filosofía,* 46 (2009): 109–126.

Musette, Mohammed Saib. "Jeunesse et Politiques Publiques en Algérie*: D'une Préoccupation Socio-Educative à une Prise en Charge en Termes d'Emploi," in *Contribution à la Construction des Savoirs dans les Politiques d'Inclusion Sociale et de la Jeunesse* (13). Consultation pour le Conseil intergouvernemental du Programme MOST, Nd. Accessed June 2, 2014. https://www.google.com/search?q=Contributio n+%C3%A0+la+construction+des+savoirs+dans+les+politiques+d%E2%80%99in clusion+sociale+et+de+la+jeunesse&ie=utf-8&oe=utf-8.

Musette, Mohammed Saib. "Le Marché du Travail en Algérie: une Vision Nouvelle?" FCE – *Journées de l'Entreprise Algérienne: Emploi, Formation et Employabilité,* October 29, 2013, Algiers: 1–11.

Nietzsche, Friedrich. *De l'Utilité de l'Inconvénient de l'Histoire pour la Vie: Deuxième Considération Inactuelle*, edited by Jean Lacoste et Jacques Le Rider. Paris: Robert Laffont, 1993 [1874].

Safar Zitoun, Madani. "La Protection Sociale en Algérie. Évolution, Fonctionnement et Tendances Actuelles," in *L'État Face aux Débordements du Social au Maghreb. Formation, Travail et Protection Sociale*, edited by Myriam Catusse, Blandine Desmetrau and Éric Verdier, 53–93. Aix-en-Provence & Paris: IREMAM & Karthala, 2010.

Sayad, Abdelmalek. "Le Mode de Génération des Générations 'Immigrées'." *L'Homme et la Société* 11–12 (1994): 155–174.

Sewell Jr., William. "Three Temporalities: Toward an Eventful Sociology." Presented at a conference on "The Historic Turn in the Human Sciences," University of Michigan, October 1990. Accessed February 3, 2011. http://deepblue.lib.umich.edu/bitstream/ handle/2027.42/51215/448.pdf?sequence=1.

CHAPTER 9

"We are not heiresses": Generational Memory, Heritage and Inheritance in Contemporary Italian Feminism[1]

Andrea Hajek

Introduction

> We are nine/new feminists. We are not heiresses, we are precarious workers.

This declaration encapsulates the message of the Femministe Nove – or 'nine feminists,' a group of young Italian women who participated in workshop number nine of the Paestum conference in 2012 (Terragni 2013). This national gathering held in the South-Italian city of Paestum was organised by a number of so-called 'second-wave' feminists, in remembrance of the last national feminist conference that was held in the same city 36 years earlier, but also in response to the current financial crisis and its impact on women's conditions in Italy today. A follow-up event was organized in 2013, this time with the more active involvement of younger generations of women. On the second day of the follow-up conference, the Femministe Nove – all from Rome and mostly in their 20s and 30s – interrupted a debate as they stepped on stage and unfolded a provocative banner while they read their polemical manifesto.[2] In Italian, natural numbers are normally placed *before* nouns, but by positioning the natural number nine ('nove') *after* the noun 'feminists,' the women created a wordplay where 'nove' comes to resemble the adjective 'nuove,' which in Italian means 'new,' and which would normally be placed *after* the noun, as indeed happens here. In other words, the Femministe N(u)ove identify themselves not only as the feminists from group number nine in the 2012 conference,

---

1 This work was supported by the British Academy [grant number pf130101]. The author would like to thank Deborah Withers, all interviewees who have contributed to this research, and the editors of the volume for their useful feedback and assistance.
2 The manifesto – from which the declaration above was taken – was subsequently published on a blog and in the feminist magazine DWF. All translations from Italian are mine.

© KONINKLIJKE BRILL NV, LEIDEN, 2017 | DOI 10.1163/9789004344518_011

but also as 'new' feminists. This explicit self-identification reflects not only the generational tensions that typically determine any relationship between different age cohorts, as we will see throughout this chapter, but it also shows how these younger groups acknowledge and build on memories and legacies of previous generations as they construct their own feminist identity, in the present and looking towards the future.

In my exploration of the relationship between feminist generations, I will focus on the question of how memories of feminism are produced and subsequently transmitted, and thus 'travel' to future generations. First, however, I will briefly analyze the transmission – more generally – of memories of protest since the 1970s, through a process that has been defined as 'remediation.' This occurs both via the re-enactment of past methods of activism and modes of communication as through the more 'material' or 'textual' remediation of images, texts and narratives, which allows present-day activists to connect with the past and strengthen their protest identity in the here and now. Next, I will move to an exploration of the legacy of feminist activism in Italy by studying the way memories of second-wave feminism are constructed, transmitted and perceived in the present, while questioning the very concepts of generation and generational waves. Other than the Femministe Nove, I will also briefly discuss two other contemporary groups composed of feminists, the cultural association Femminile Plurale and the student collective Fuxia Block.

Memory and Protest

In recent years, protests in various parts of the world have seen the widespread application of digital media technologies and social media. Consequently, patterns of protest have changed (Eaton 2013, 5), and the production of short-term, immediate memories that are circulated among global networks and communities in a limited amount of time have downplayed the existence of long-term processes of remembering. Yet, we must remain critical of the fact that these technologies are often no more than a tool to get messages across or to organize mobilization. Nor should we underestimate the importance of collective memories in the construction of political identities among contemporary activists. Indeed, very often these identities draw on the appropriation of 'counter-memories,' that is, alternative memories that oppose themselves to hegemonic views of the past, and as such challenge dominant versions of the past (Hajek 2013, 7). Counter-memories are transmitted to future generations in a process Ann Rigney has defined 'memory transfer,' and this increasingly happens via the media:

> With the help of various media and memorial forms later generations recall things other people experienced, and do so from the conviction that those past experiences have something to do with the sense of 'our history'.
>
> RIGNEY 2005, 25

The concept of mediated memory has been further developed by Rigney and Astrid Erll, who argue that collective and cultural memories are shaped not only by social factors, but that they also draw on "available media technologies, on existent media products, on patterns of representation and medial aesthetics" (Erll and Rigney 2009, 4). Indeed, media are becoming ever more important in the recording, producing and mediating of memories in the present as they allow collective remembrance to take root in a community, via the intermedial reiteration of a particular narrative across different platforms in the public sphere (ibid., 2–3). This is particularly relevant when studying contemporary protest movements: in a previous study, where I analyzed the transmission of memories of the 1977 student movement in the Italian city of Bologna, I found that a process of 'memory transfer' took shape precisely through the remediation of texts, images and mnemonic practices. For example, during the 30th anniversary of the student movement in 2007, its memory was remediated very explicitly through the publication of a new edition of a key text which was published by the student movement back in 1977, as a means of denouncing the violent death of a left-wing student during clashes with police. The new version of the text was published on initiative of a local, antagonist youth collective, which also wrote an afterword to the new edition. Here it drew a line of comparison between the incidents of 1977 and the contemporary situation, which saw the youth collective involved in a dispute with local authorities over high rents and a new public order policy directed mostly against local youth groups, and which called back memories of the suppression the student movement had suffered at the hands of local authorities in 1977. Thus, the local mayor of the Democratic Left party is described as continuing the 'tradition' of the Italian Communist Party – which governed Bologna throughout the 1960s and 1970s, and which in the 1990s transformed itself into the Democratic Left – in 1977:

> Once again mayor Cofferati has mobilized the police in order to deal with the student protests against high rents...Now as then, for the heirs of the [Italian Communist Party] nothing on its left-hand side is acceptable.... .
>
> quoted in HAJEK 2013, 141

Another example of remediation, this time of a visual memory, is a mural painted on a wall in Bologna's university zone during a protest march to

"WE ARE NOT HEIRESSES"

commemorate the 1977 incident in 2014, depicting the student who was killed by the police 30 years earlier. The portrait was copied directly from the photograph published on the front cover of a radical left-wing newspaper the day after the student's death in 1977. It was also one of the few images of the student to have circulated in the local memory community since his death.

Memory transfer not only occurs though via the transmission of similar 'impact events' (Erll 2011, 11), even if the 1970s in Italy do have a reputation for having witnessed many violent incidents, consequently producing images and narratives that have 'travelled' through time and space. Yet, other factors play a role in this memory travel as well. In her description of the concept of 'travelling' memory, Erll (2011) proposes five dimensions of movement to explain this travel: carriers, media, contents, practices and forms. If we return to the example of the memory of 1977 in Bologna, the carriers are primarily the victim's family as well as the former members of the student movement of 1977, who have endeavoured to keep the memory of 1977 alive throughout the following decades. Media, secondly, include oral testimonies, gathered in texts such as the above mentioned book published by the 1977 movement itself, as well as many other, often nostalgic texts that have appeared since then and that give evidence of what was otherwise a very colourful and playful student movement, as it manifested itself in Bologna.[3] Indeed, in Bologna the student movement had a particularly artistic character which has been documented extensively by local photographer Enrico Scuro. Recently, Scuro has published a series of online photo albums on Facebook, where the visual – and again, quite nostalgic – memory of 1977 was reinforced (Hajek 2012), as also happened in a series of documentaries, films and retrospective photographic exhibitions about both the 1977 incidents and the 1977 student movement at large. It should be noted, though, that local and national media have contributed instead to a highly negative, condemning representation of the incidents, which has produced a very different memory of 1977. Contents, thirdly, privilege memories of what Erll (2011) calls political 'impact events,' of which the death of the student is of course a good example. Protest practices that travel through time are various: university occupations, public demonstrations and the self-reduction of prices are all typical forms of protest during the late 1960s

---

3 Experiences in larger cities such as Rome or Milan have been tainted more by violent incidents, contributing to an otherwise predominantly negative, collective memory of the 1970s. In particular, the second half of the decade was characterized by an explosion of terrorist violence, perpetrated mostly by left-wing terrorists. This has resulted in the assimilation of the 1977 student protests with political violence, in media and historical reconstructions of this period. For more information see Hajek 2010; Hajek 2013.

and 1970s. Practices also include commemorative rituals, which – considering the large number of fatal incidents that occurred in the 1970s – have also contributed to memory travel. Finally, mnemonic forms – or 'floating signifiers' – are another important dimension of movement, due to their 'powerful transgenerational tenacity.' They refer to those symbols and icons that are "handed down unwittingly, via not-conscious ways of speaking and acting" (Erll 2011, 14), for example rhetoric, bodily aspects and symbols.

What happens, though, when we apply these five dimensions of movement to the memory of second-wave feminism? As we shall see in this chapter, memory transfer or 'travel' is a more complex operation in the context of feminism, and this is in large part due to the more complicated generational paradigm of feminism.

The Generational Paradigm

Returning to the example of the Femministe Nove, who so explicitly rejected the idea of being heirs to the legacy of a previous generation of feminists ("We are not heiresses"), it is indeed difficult to trace any clear-cut continuation or travelling of the memory of second-wave feminism. On the contrary, the Femministe Nove seem not even to consider their relation to previous generations in any linear, historical sense when they make the following claim: "We are historical feminists." Through this provocation they clearly place themselves on the same level as the feminists of the 1970s generation, who in Italian are usually referred to as 'historical feminists.' What do they mean by this and how must we understand the concept of generations and generational 'waves' in this context?

The concept of generation as we know it today originated after the First World War, which saw the emergence of a 'war generation' (Erll 2014, 387). It is precisely this definition of generation that inspired photographer Enrico Scuro when he created the abovementioned Facebook photo albums of the 1977 generation, entitled "I ragazzi del '77" ("The '77 kids"): it was an explicit reference to the definition with which the soldiers who came of age during the First World War – 'I ragazzi del '99,' i.e. born in 1899 – are generally known in Italy.[4] In both cases we are witnessing "the conscious identification of a group of people, either by itself or by others, *as* a generation" (Erll 2014, 387). With

---

4 Enrico Scuro explained the origins of the title during the launch of a book drafted from the online photo albums, on 17 January 2012. See Hajek 2012.

regard to the 1968 and 1970s generation, this identification has taken shape mostly in the writings of the former participants – or "witness-historians" – themselves (Bracke 2012, 639).

The explicit reference to the war generation in the name of Scuro's online photo albums reflects a certain dependence on the very existence of such a generation. From this it follows that generation units, in Karl Mannheim's words, do not exist in or by themselves but must be constituted and produced – as the editors of this volume also sustain – against other generations. Thus, if the Femministe Nove reject the idea of being heirs to the 1970s generation, the very use of the adjective 'new' in their name nevertheless reflects a certain genealogy, as the young women themselves also acknowledge in their manifesto: "We were born after." In Erll's words, "no generationality [is] without its genealogical other" (2014, 396). However, unlike Mannheim's contention that personal memories and collective – or 'appropriated' – memories cannot overlap, we must acknowledge the fact that memories are never limited to first-hand experiences (Erll 2011, 10). As we have seen, collective and cultural memories are shaped not only by social frameworks but also, and increasingly, by media frameworks: "What [Mannheim's] conception of generational memory appears to rule out is the possibility of secondhand, mediated experience in the formation of identities" (Erll 2014, 389). Since we have become increasingly reliant on media technologies in the formation of our memories, the media must be considered "as catalysts and 'travel agents' of generational identity" (ibid.), an identity which is increasingly transnational and global. Hence, if generationality depends on the specific construction of a generational identity by members of that generation, experiences of the past and transmissions of memory that increasingly take place via the media allow for generationality to be transmitted. In other words, generationality not only presents itself in the form of a horizontal relation of synchronicity or contemporaneity – what Erll refers to as 'familial inheritance' (ibid., 396) – but also as a diachronic and vertical genealogy, a sort of 'social heritage' where by heritage I imply something that is handed down by tradition and, increasingly also media, as opposed to inheritance which is closer to the idea of a shared genetic characteristic or trait. A transition from familial *inheritance* to societal *heritage* takes place where the memories existing *within* the same generation (the intra-generational aspects of memory) and those memories transmitted *between* generations (the inter-generational aspects of memory) are increasingly connected (ibid., 396). Put simply, memories existing among members of one generation, who feel part of that generation as if members of a large family (hence Scuro's references to his online photo albums of the 1977 generation as a 'family album'), cross over with memories transmitted to and from other generations, and which are appropriated by those other generations. The very concept of generation is therefore no longer constructed solely on the basis of some form of synchronicity or contemporaneity, but also – and increasingly – becomes a product of the transmission of memory.

The idea of a generational memory of feminism that is transmitted to other generational cohorts is supported by the wave metaphor that is so often applied to feminism, though less so in the Italian case. Indeed, much has been written about the generational paradigm of feminism and the logic of succession and differentiation that lies behind the application of the wave metaphor (see for example Gillis and Munford 2004; Dean 2009; Withers 2015). Although the division into three waves – i.e. first-wave for the suffragette movement at the beginning of the 20th century, second-wave for the 1960s–1970s women's movement, and third-wave for the cohort that manifested itself in the 1980s and beyond – is commonly accepted today,[5] several scholars have criticized this temporal (but also spatial, considering its focus on developments in Western civilisations) delineation of generational cohorts of feminists. Jonathan Dean summarizes the criticism as follows:

> Such an approach is, I argue, problematic in that it domesticates feminism's capacity to be a dynamic and disturbing political force, it risks reinscribing a specifically Euro-American feminist historiography as hegemonic, risks imposing artificial and divisive cleavages between feminists, and may also lead to a complicity with certain hegemonic post/ anti-feminist discourses.
>
> DEAN 2009, 335

Indeed, the wave metaphor imposes a highly linear, teleological perspective on feminist history as,

> a progressive series of successive 'phases' or 'waves.' This hegemonic model severely curtails the ways in which diverse feminist histories can be mapped and understood, as it functions by blocking out or distorting trajectories which do not fit into the dominant frame.
>
> BROWNE quoted in WITHERS 2015, 29

---

5 Note that third-wave feminism is not the same as 'post-feminism,' which actually 'undoes' feminism as Angela McRobbie explains when she defines post-feminism as an "active process by which feminist gains of the 1970s and 80s come to be undermined" (2004, 255). In addition, more recently a fourth-wave has also been identified.

Similarly, Stacy Gillis and Rebecca Munford observe that "[t]he wave paradigm also means that figures who write 'outside' of it…are regarded as anomalies at best or ignored at worst" (Gillis and Munford 2004, 176). It is precisely this linear perspective that the Femministe Nove rejected when they stated that they too are 'historical feminists.' In doing so they criticize the wave metaphor which – as I mentioned above – is rarely applied in Italy anyway; this might be because the first-wave feminists are far less known than and celebrated as their English or American counterparts (they did not, for example, obtain women's vote, which wasn't granted in Italy until after the end of the Second World War). Rather, members of the second-wave feminist generation are commonly referred to as 'historical feminists,' giving them a sort of landmark position in women's history. Yet, in her recent book on the transmission of feminist knowledge, Deborah Withers warns not to reject the generational paradigm altogether, arguing that "waves are a symptom of the centrality of generational processes through which feminist knowledge is transmitted" (Withers 2015, 31). The problem, rather, lies in the fact that feminist generations or indeed waves are taken for granted 'as an established fact,' whereas feminist thought is something that must always be elaborated: feminist generations "are a site of fragile contestation, tireless struggle and political transformation…" (ibid., 32). The polemical statements of the Femministe Nove reflect this perfectly, so let us now take a closer look at the question of transmission with regard to the memory of second-wave feminism in Italy.

"We are not heiresses"

It should be clear by now that such a transmission has been problematic, to say the least, and that any cultural memory of 1970s feminism has been far less in-fluential as opposed to that of the 1968 protests, for example. A predominantly celebratory and often nostalgic memory of 1960s and 1970s protest movements began circulating in the 1990s. Alongside the production of this cultural mem-ory, or what we could call 'heritage,' a communicative and living memory of the 1970s had been developing steadily since the end of the 1970s: the latter comes closer to the notion of 'inheritance,' as it is less interested in celebrat-ing a heritage than it is in keeping alive contentious memories of violence and social injustice. As such this living or 'militant memory' is firmly rooted in the present and concerned with present issues that could be linked to the recent past (Hajek 2013).

A similar influence of a cultural memory of 1970s feminism on younger gen-erations has, on the other hand, not taken place. Nor does there seem to be a comparable co-existence of heritage and inheritance, let alone any particular connection between the two, and I would like to argue that this is largely because of the presence of a generational conflict. As Gillis and Munford state, we are dealing with a "competitive generational model [that] does not allow for a collective memory of female-based thought, empowerment and activism" (Gillis and Munford 2004, 176). The difficult transmission of cultural memory in this case is mostly a result of the relatively few violent incidents – or any other types of 'political impact' events – involving feminist activists and, accordingly, the absence of any commemorations or monuments. Indeed, with the exception of the influential public manifestations of the women's movement (most notably during the pro-abortion law protests in the second half of the decade, see Bracke 2014), feminist activism was less 'spectacular,' less visible and therefore less memorable as opposed to the radical demonstrations of other social movements and the various (usually male) victims of violence that mark the collective memory of the 1970s. Similarly, highly private or intimate feminist practices such as consciousness raising and self-help visits were more difficult to 'remember' publicly. Finally, feminism was marginalized within the social movements themselves, which failed to give priority to women's issues and gender discrimination. Consequently, feminism features less in any publications by those 'witness-historians' mentioned earlier on: these were mostly educated, white and male who have turned generation into a 'hegemonizing narrative,' and in doing so marginalized other forms of conflict, including gender (Bracke 2012, 639). This is particularly evident in the Italian case, as for example in the title of Scuro's online photo albums, "I ragazzi del '77" ("The '77 kids"): the word 'ragazzi' is the plural of 'ragazzo' or 'boy,' though in the plural form it may refer to both genders ('kids'). Yet, in doing so it renders the female gender (linguistically) invisible.

This lead feminist historian Elda Guerra (2005) to declare, in the early 2000s, that a history of Italian feminism had yet to be written. This is due in part to the fact that there is a predominance of memory over history, "a tendency to favour specific and separate, historical narratives focused on identity," and consequently, a persistent lack of historical studies which contributes to an "historical void," as another leading feminist historian, Anna Rossi-Doria, stated during a recent conference which addressed precisely the problematic transmission of a history of feminism in Italy. She attributes this to the difficult definition of the term 'feminism' and to the melancholy which involves various generations of women in the face of the loss of the utopian, feminist dimension, the fears of a too painful and conflicting, personal involvement when coming close again to the ideological and political contrasts of the past

(Mazzanti 2014). It has been mostly the task of second-wave feminists – who continued their activism in the 1980s and beyond, creating a vast network of cultural women's associations and women's aid organizations, or engaging in the promotion of equal opportunity politics – to produce a history and memory of feminism. For a long time these remained localized experiences which failed to contribute to any encompassing cultural memory of feminism on a wider, regional and national level. Similarly, not many films, novels or theatrical plays that might transmit feminist ideas and practices to a wider audience, and which do exist for 1968 and the 1970s, have been created. In recent years this lack does seem to have been countered by an increased production of history and memory, which includes the experimental documentary films by feminist director Alina Marazzi, a photographical book (published in 2014) about 1970s feminism, various literary and autobiographic texts and essays written by different generations of women, and a number of historical documentaries that have very recently been aired on the national news channel RAI ("History of the feminist movement in Italy"), and the educational RAI Storia channel ("The Feminist Movement"). In terms of feminist readings, finally, a number of young feminists whom I interviewed for my research project declared having become interested in feminism through what we could define key feminist texts, such as Simone De Beauvoir's *Second Sex*, but there is no regular pattern that I could trace in these reading habits, and for many of the women born in the 1990s this 'intellectual' coming of age often occurred via the internet.

If the feminist heritage struggles to move beyond the local dimension, beyond the personal testimonies and beyond the specific locations of feminist culture and politics as these have been upheld by second-wave feminists since the early 1980s, how then have memories of second-wave feminism been transmitted to the present, and how exactly does this memory travel? Let us go back to Erll's five dimensions of movement: carriers, media, contents, practices and forms. The carriers are obviously those feminists who have pursued their activism beyond the 1970s: many of these have founded women's associations, archives or libraries, and therefore have a certain presence or authority in local communities. This, however, frequently results in conflictual relations with younger generations, as several of my younger interviewees confessed. This seems to be related to a certain "obsessive need of recognition from younger people," as well as the presence of an element of ownership. In those cases where members of the older generation have carried forward a particular, material legacy in the form of a women's association, library, documentary centre or bookshop, for example, there is a fear that this legacy is somehow 'contaminated' or transformed in a way they aren't always happy or comfortable with.[6] Speaking from my personal experience, I encountered some reticence myself when I approached one of these associations with a proposal for a public event, which would involve participation from younger feminists. Doubts were raised about the necessity of the event: thus, the topic was said to have been discussed on various occasions among members of the older generation, in the past. Similarly, the launch of a recent publication about second-wave feminism, written largely by younger historians and feminist activists, saw the very active – and according to one of my younger interviewees, rather dominant – involvement again of some of the second-wave feminists in the local community. We may therefore speak of a 'possessive' memory that marks the attitude of former members of 1960s–1970s protest movements in general, as I encountered in my previous study on the 1977 student movement in Bologna, and which explains the problem Rossi-Doria raised when she observed that the history of feminism was dominated by memories, that is, by "those who experienced the events at first hand and who tend to see their personal involvement as a privilege" (Mazzanti 2014; see also Hajek 2013, 50). In sum, the 1970s feminist generation seems to keep a tight rein both on feminist inheritance and heritage.

The role of media in the movement of memories of feminism is again strongly dependent on the carriers and their personal input in the writing of feminist history: as mentioned above, any memories of feminism have – at least until very recently – been transmitted mostly through personal testimonies and local researches, and are therefore often based on oral testimonies. As for contents, we have already seen that there are not many of what Erll calls 'political impact' events that characterize the women's movement of the 1970s, if we exclude the passing of important legislation such as the abortion law in 1978. It is more at the level of reflections and elaborations of specific themes related to sexuality, sexual violence and work, that we might identify relevant contents for the women's movement and its collective memory, and these, again, have been transmitted mostly by the protagonists of the women's movement themselves. Finally, protest practices such as university occupations, sit-ins and demonstrations, which were performed by social movements generally and by feminist groups, as well as the more specific feminist practices such as consciousness raising, and mnemonic forms (the typical feminist hand gesture or the feminist symbol, for example) perhaps best contribute to the idea of an 'inheritance' brought forward by second-wave feminists, as opposed to a more material or tangible 'heritage.'

---

6 EB, interview with author, 19 December 2014.

Nevertheless, younger generations of feminists continuously claim their place on the feminist stage. I would argue that this is because "[g]enerational claims are integral to the formation of feminist identities and modes of belonging," as Deborah Withers (2015, 4) observes. We could argue, for example, that the age-span for feminist activism ranges from the late teens to the late 30s, and that some of the main issues of second-wave (but not only) feminism is concerned with – sexuality and sexual self-determination (e.g. abortion rights and birth control) – are issues relevant to this specific age cohort (after all, women in their 40s or 50s are less likely to be concerned with issues of pregnancy or abortion than those women pertaining to a still fertile age cohort). Withers continues:

> Generational claims, fashioned most clearly through the metaphor of the wave, operate within feminism as meta-narratives which structure and account for the back-and-forth quality that underpins feminism's long and continuous struggle for social revolution.
>
> WITHERS 2015, 4

In other words, the return to feminist activism among younger generations is not to be seen in causal terms, that is, as a linear, teleological process of continuation of an interrupted or failed struggle, stimulated by the transmission of knowledge and the presence of a specific heritage. As Victoria Browne explains, rather than to consider repetition as a sign of failure and to think about the history of feminism

> in terms of an endless spiralling between the forward movement of linear progress and the backsliding movement of repetition forced by backlash politics: a two-steps-forward, one-step-back model that results in an overwhelming sense of despair and frustration.
>
> BROWNE 2013, 918

We must, instead, "rethink the nonlinear and 'untimely' progressions of feminist politics as a site of generation and change":

> [T]he idea that feminist histories are 'untimely' may help to bring energy and hope to the process of repeating: 'recollecting forwards' and reactivating the radicality of challenges that have long been forgotten, misunderstood, taken for granted, or simply not seen or heard (ibid., 918).

This might explain the generational conflicts that frequently resurface, as demonstrated by the irruption of the Femministe Nove at the Paestum conference in 2013. Although the very use of the adjective 'new' in their name reflects an acknowledgement of genealogy ("We were born after"), as we have seen, the young feminists nevertheless reject the idea of repetition and thus seem to respond to Browne's idea of 'recollecting forwards' as they counter the acknowledgement that they were born after by a subsequent statement which argues that, in spite of this, "we don't feel at all 'post'." In other words, while respecting the older generation and recognizing their belonging to a different generation, they wish to overcome this divide and, with it, the almost inevitable generational confrontation with that other generation, making a call for equality:

> We acknowledge the fundamental value of our genealogies in feminist thought and practice. And we wish to live the confrontation between feminist generations neither in the asymmetry of power and authority nor with envy of the epic dawning of a new decade.

What the Femministe Nove are advocating is not so much a sort of belated claim of post- or neo-feminist identity and agency, but a rejection of the mother-daughter conflict and of any competition between different age cohorts. Ultimately it is a rejection of the wave metaphor, in which – Gillis and Munford remind us – "generations are set up in competition with one another and definitions of feminism are positioned around the 'leaders' of these generations..." (Gillis and Munford 2004, 176).

Generation – a False Dichotomy?

The position of the Femministe Nove was criticized by three young women who in 2009 founded a cultural association called Femminile Plurale ('Plural Feminine'), and who also participated in the Paestum conference of 2013. Femminile Plurale was initially present mostly through a blog, but a strong interest in feminist theory, literature and art led to the opening of a women's bookshop in the women's native city Padua, in 2014. In a commentary piece that was published on their old blog, written shortly after the Paestum conference, they criticize the generational wave metaphor in their own terms, speaking of a 'false dichotomy of generation':

> Feminist generations. Different women apart have already noted that the dichotomy young/old is unsatisfactory and, on various levels, even false. It's false, for example, on the level of economy and class: granted that a generation – incidentally also the generation who is writing this – has

been struck in a more systematic way by the erosion of rights and the structural absence of employment, we can't ignore the fact that there are young, well-off women who enjoy the privileges of solid economic situations, and at the same time women with quite advanced ages who find themselves in precarious economic conditions. Young/old an inter-class trap?

Next, the young/old dichotomy is false on the relational level, given that there is no reason to believe that age in itself should create favourable conditions for an authentic relationship among women. Sisterhood is not only a logical but an emotional consequence of the gaining awareness of the personal/political.

Last but not least, the dichotomy is false on the concrete level of the women present in the here and now, up to the point that it becomes an introjection of conceptualities derived from an elsewhere which is by no means feminist in nature: can the Nine (new) feminists truly define themselves as 'young,' when it's obvious for years now that one of the symptoms of social inferiorisation of our generation occurs through the expansion of 'youth' to age cohorts that were unimaginable until a few years ago? Are we certain that young women in their 30s, nearly 40s, are still 'girls'?

FEMMINILE PLURALE 2013

Indeed, what is to be considered a generation? Femminile Plurale's reply echoes Gillis' and Munford's warnings that "[t]he wave paradigm not only ensures that each generation must 'reinvent the wheel' but also lends power to backlash politics and rhetoric" (Gillis and Munford 2004, 177): "Perhaps the 'generational clash,' which we are told is taking place in the political class, is a media message which has influenced us more than we would like to admit?" It may be wiser to speak in terms of age cohorts rather than 'generations,' which is after all a construct, as Astrid Henry confirms: "A generation is an imaginary collective that both reveals truths about people of a particular age and tries to mold those people into a unified group" (Henry 2004, 6), and as such is a generalizing force. Similarly, the concept of 'waves' should be reviewed as they too reflect a generational category, which necessarily leaves out those generations who came of age in the in-between periods.[7] They fall in the middle of the 30-year period Mannheim identified as separating different generations:

---

7   The title of a recent book about the first female parliamentarians in post-war Italy, *The Lost Wave* by Molly Tambor, is a perfect illustration of this exclusion of feminist generations.

They are subsumed under the category 'second wave,' and their inability to be read as a distinct generation is compounded by the dyadic mother-daughter relationship used to represent feminist generations. As they can be understood as neither 'mothers' nor 'daughters' within feminism's imagined family structure, such feminists are frequently absent from recent discourse on feminism's (seemingly two) generations (ibid., 4).

Femminile Plurale also criticizes, however, the reaction of the 'old cohort' at the Paestum conference. The latter, in part, applauded the spontaneous action of the Femministe Nove:

> [I]f 'they' are the 'young ones,' then who makes up 'all the others' in the assembly? That would be the 'old ones': that other 'generation,' of which so many suddenly reveal to be offhandedly willing to justify a practice and also tones of voice – which, it must be noted, they would never have accepted from a group of peers – simply to appreciate the 'young ones,' an a priori approval which seems almost a value in itself. An a priori approval from which I personally, for as far as I myself am considered 'young,' and harshly safeguard myself, at least with whom I would like to have an authentic relation with.
>
> The mechanism of infantilisation on the one hand (the group, the playful blitz, the joyful homologation) and the maternage, on the other (assumption of the maternal role, with the aim of caring for the growing up of the 'small ones') creates between women an unhealthy mechanism.
>
> FEMMINILE PLURALE 2013

In spite of their different, more 'appreciative' approach to the older generation, clearly this second group also resents a certain maternal positioning of the latter, which again reflects the mother-daughter trope that is so central in the relationship between different generations, or age cohorts, of feminists. From this we may conclude that, other than the absence of any tangible, feminist heritage, in the sense of a remediation of memory and transmission of feminist knowledge as discussed earlier on, and no transition from familial *inheritance* to societal *heritage* – which Erll (2014) identified as being inherent to the construction of generational identity – taking place, there is also a rejection – in particular among the Femministe Nove but also Femminile Plurale – of the familial generational model which so often characterizes the relationship between different feminist age cohorts, and where this relationship is described in terms of a mother-daughter relationship. Rebecca Dakin Quinn has coined this phenomenon the 'matrophor,' that is, "the persistent nature of maternal metaphors in feminism" (quoted in Henry 2004, 2), where second-wave feminists become mothers to the third-wave feminists, and as such the potential relationships between women are reduced to a single relationship: that of mother and daughter (3). Femminile Plurale is uncomfortable with this interpretation, but also the Femministe Nove try to back out of this relationship as they claim to be a political generation, going against the assumption "that feminists of a certain age will, *naturally*, share a generational identity" (ibid., 4; 6–7). They very explicitly identify with current times, in particular with regard to the financial crisis and its devastating impact on female employment opportunities, as the second part of the sentence with which I opened this chapter demonstrates: "We are not heiresses, we are precarious workers." By no means do they take their generational identity for granted. As such they illustrate the "simultaneous identification with and rejection of second-wave feminism" that Henry attributes to younger feminists, speaking in terms of cross-generational identifications and disidentifications, i.e. an identification against something:

> for many younger feminists, it is only by refusing to identify themselves
> with earlier versions of feminism – and frequently with older feminists –
> that they are able to create a feminism of their own.
>   HENRY 2004, 7

In the last section of this chapter I will discuss a third example of contemporary feminist activism and its relation to feminist inheritance and heritage, by exploring the way the Padua-based *Fuxia Block* collective relates to the memory and legacy of second-wave feminism.

Fuxia Block

The Italian women's movement was an extremely heterogeneous and fragmented movement, consisting of a myriad of small collectives and groups, which varied in their practices and ideologies (see for example Hellman 1987 and Bracke 2014). The Northern city of Padua characterized itself by the strong presence of the feminist group Feminist Battle, closely linked to the extra-parliamentarian Marxist party Worker's Power, and mostly engaged in the issue of domestic labour and the waging of housework. It was one of the leading groups in the Italian branch of the International Wages for Housework campaign, set up in 1972, and as such strongly contributed to transnational connections and collaborations with feminists in the USA and in the UK (Bracke 2013).

In 1974, Feminist Battle also founded the very first, self-managed women's health clinic in Italy. Women's health clinics aimed at providing specialized care and support for women's health issues, in particular with regard to the issue of illegal abortion: until a law was passed in 1978, several thousands of women per year lost their lives due to dangerous, illegal abortions (Caldwell 1981). More generally, though, the self-managed health clinics were constituted in a climate of increased attention to the woman's body and health, due also to an overall negligence – on the part of the state – towards such issues. Political parties and lawmakers did eventually acknowledge the necessity of legislation,

> which would deal with the problem of modernizing rights with regards to the protection of women's health through the presence of dedicated services and a wider attention to their needs…
>
> MURA, n.d.

And in 1975 a law was passed which institutionalized women's health clinics.

Although Feminist Battle remained active throughout the 1970s, the nationwide protests for the abortion law that was eventually passed pushed the domestic labour issues to the margins, and the legacy of the wages for housework struggle remained limited mostly to feminist sociological research (Bracke 2013, 636–37). In the second half of the 1970s, second-wave feminism became monopolized by the abortion debate, among other things, and by the pro-abortion law protests that gained considerable media attention and public visibility (see Hajek 2014). Nevertheless, the abortion law has frequently been under attack, and continues to be so in the present. This in part explains why feminist activism keeps coming back, confirming Browne's notion of 'recollecting forwards' and the idea of feminist politics as a site of generation and change, not as repetition because of failure. In other words, the abortion law was a successful outcome of the protests of the women's movement in the late 1970s, but continues to be under attack, which means that every generation needs to reactivate this struggle in order to defend itself.

Abortion is in fact one of the main themes of Fuxia Block, a mixed collective active in Padua since 2006. It consists of some two dozens of women and men, mostly university students or researchers, with an average age of 25 years. Fuxia Block is not an explicitly feminist collective: it self-defines itself as a 'biopolitical' collective. This is due to its origins in a mixed, university collective with a wider range of political interests, called Bios Lab. In terms of its objectives, Fuxia Block sets itself political and social objectives, as we can read on the 'about' page of the collective's blog: it proposes "to open a place of critical discussion and analysis on the politics of life, of the control over bodies, on the government of society." The issues it engages with most include job insecurity and sexual self-determination and control, i.e. the right to abortion, for example by organizing demonstrations and public events around these issues. More importantly, in May 2014 it opened a self-managed women's health clinic, the Queersultoria (a wordplay drawn from the words 'queer' and 'consultorio,' the Italian word for women's health clinic which is declined to the feminine here, see Figures 1–2). The autonomous women's health clinics that arose around 1974 and 1975 closed soon after the law was passed, in 1975, and the clinics were institutionalized, and no actual, feminist heritage in any physical or material form persisted in Padua, due also to the fierce repression of political activism towards the end of the 1970s in general. Where then did the idea to open the Queersultoria come from? Does it build on any direct contacts or collaboration with second-wave feminism? One member of Fuxia Block, although acknowledging the significant input of three local second-wave feminists during a public event Fuxia Block organized shortly before the launch of the clinic, stressed the fact that the collective did not explicitly look for inspiration in past experiences.[8]

And yet, the following text published on internet explains the reasons behind the creation of the Queersultoria in terms of a continuation of the experience of the 1970s feminists:

> Much like the self-managed women's health centres were, in the 1970s, places of liberation, we believe it is necessary today to rethink the practices and the discourses of contemporary feminism…[N.a., 2014]

Similarly, a document published online by the Bios Lab collective again draws a line of continuation:

> The refusal to adhere to predetermined roles, to the naturalization of bodies and the normalization of lives produced an epochal short circuit, operated by the feminists through the re-appropriation of knowledge and experiences of women and transferred in real laboratories of political subjectivity which multiplied in neighbourhoods, universities, spaces of movement: thus the self-managed women's health centres were born, the centres for health and self-help which became the point of reference for all the women that felt the need to free themselves from the medicalization of the body and the biopolitical control of their lives.
> Bios Lab N.D.

---

8   BM, interview with author, 22 December 2014.

242   HAJEK

Any remediation of second-wave feminism as we have seen in the case of the 1977 protests in Bologna, however, is rare: it is reflected, at the most, in the collective's occasional use of photographs of 1970s feminists in some publicity posters, or in commentaries published on the collective's blog. These are often long and rhetorical, and therefore read very much like the political manifestos of Feminist Battle, for example. Generally, though, remediation of key texts and images is limited and rather takes places at the level of contents (mostly sexual self-determination and right to abortion), practices (the very presence of the Queersultoria), and forms of protest. Hence we are confronted with a paradox: in spite of the refusal to define itself as 'feminist,' Fuxia Block reflects the presence of a feminist legacy, most explicitly in the creation of the Queersultoria. It does not, however, limit itself to an appropriation of memory and reflects a 'living,' future-oriented and progressive memory with a clear political function in the present and looking towards the future. It is precisely that 'recollecting forwards' that Victoria Browne (2013) refers to in her study on backlash politics.

Concluding Remarks

This chapter evolved around the idea that generationality exists both in relation to its genealogical other and as a result of mediated experiences of the past, whereby intra- and intergenerational aspects of memory are increasingly connected. I applied this idea to the memory of 1960s and 1970s protest movements in Italy at large: the latter was shown to be subject to an explicit remediation of texts, images and commemorative practices that allow current generations of activists to forge relationships with past incidents of social injustice and political violence. Next I demonstrated that the situation is more complex in the case of the memory of second-wave feminism, and the transmission of feminist knowledge to the present. As we have seen throughout the chapter, both a memory and history of feminism have failed to deposit themselves in the present, due in large part to a competitive generational model where definitions of feminism and feminist identities are 'guarded' by the 'leaders' of these generations. In other words, the transmission of a (cultural and collective) memory and history of feminism, marked by the dominant presence of the protagonists of 1970s feminism, is complex and delayed, resulting in the relative absence of a feminist *heritage*. Instead, younger generations of self-proclaimed feminists seem to call for a shared *inheritance* of feminism by rejecting the linear, teleological perspective on feminist history as a progressive series of successive waves, which (re)produces a mother-daughter relationship. To quote Browne again, there is a "simultaneous identification with and rejection of second-wave feminism" which reflects itself in the very name of the Femministe N(u)ove, as it necessarily constitutes its generational identity against the backdrop of the previous generation and in relation to that generation. However, the 'new' feminists seek to evade the diachronic terms of that relationship altogether, placing themselves on the same level as their chronological predecessors and calling for a more horizontal, synchronic level of mutual understanding not just within the same generation, but across generations: "We are historical feminists." Whether the *actual* 'historical' feminists are ready to share this inheritance in the full is yet to be seen.

References

Bios Lab. "Editoriale – La Crisi Logora Anche i Nostri Corpi e le Nostre Menti," *Bios Lab*. ND. http://www.bioslab.org/editoriale-la-crisi-logora-anche-i-nostri-corpi-e-le -nostre-menti/.

Bracke, Maud Anne. *Women and the Reinvention of the Political. Feminism in Italy, 1968–1983*. New York: Routledge, 2014.

Bracke, Maud Anne. "Between the Transnational and the Local: Mapping the Trajectories and Contexts of the Wages for Housework Campaign in 1970s Italian Feminism." *Women's History Review* 22, 4 (2013): 625–42.

Bracke, Maud Anne. "One-dimensional Conflict? Recent Scholarship on 1968 and the Limitations of the Generation Concept." *Journal of Contemporary History* 47, 3 (2012): 638–46.

Browne, Victoria. "Backlash, Repetition, Untimeliness: The Temporal Dynamics of Feminist Politics." *Hypatia* 28, 4 (2013): 905–20.

Caldwell, Lesley. "Abortion in Italy." *Feminist Review* 7 (1981)· 49–63.

Dean, Jonathan. "Who's Afraid of Third Wave Feminism?" *International Feminist Journal of Politics* 11, 3 (2009): 334–52.

Eaton, Tim. "Internet Activism and the Egyptian Uprisings: Transforming Online Dissent into the Offline World." *Westminster Papers in Communication and Culture* 9, 2 (2013): 5–24.

Erll, Astrid. "Generation in Literary History: Three Constellations of Generationality, Genealogy, and Memory." *New Literary History* 45, 3 (2014): 385–409.

Erll, Astrid. "Travelling Memory." *Parallax* 17, 4 (2011): 4–18.

Erll, Astrid, and Ann Rigney. "Introduction," in *Mediation, Remediation, and the Dynamics of Cultural Memory*, edited by Astrid Erll and Ann Rigney, 1–11. Berlin: Walter de Gruyter, 2009.

Femminile Plurale. "Sulle Femministe Nove a Paestum." *Femminile Plurale*. October 12, 2013. https://femminileplurale.wordpress.com/2013/10/12/paestum-2013-femministe -nove/.

Femministe Nove. "Manifest@F9," *Femministe Nove*, 2013.

Fuxia Block. Nasce la Queersultoria Facebook event page for Fuxia Block, https://www
.facebook.com/events/491954717600453/?pnref=story. (Page expired).

Gillis, Stacy, and Rebecca Munford. "Genealogies and Generations: The Politics and
Praxis of Third Wave Feminism." *Women's History Review* 13, 2 (2004): 165–82.

Guerra, Elda. "Una Nuova Soggettività: Femminismo e Femminismi nel Passaggio Degli
Anni Settanta," in *Il Femminismo Degli Anni Settanta*, edited by Teresa Bertilotti and
Anna Scattigno, 25–67. Rome: Viella, 2005.

Hajek, Andrea. "Teaching the History of Terrorism: The Political Strategies of Memory
Obstruction." *Behavioral Sciences of Terrorism and Political Aggression* 2, 3 (2010):
198–216.

Hajek, Andrea. *"Mmmmm Quanti, ma Quanti Ricordi mi Evocano Queste Foto...* Facebook and the 1977 Family Album: The Digital (R)evolution of a Protest Generation."
Italian Studies: Cultural Studies 67, 3 (2012): 375–96.

Hajek, Andrea. *Negotiating Memories of Protest in Western Europe. The Case of Italy*.
Basingstoke: Palgrave Macmillan, 2013.

Hajek, Andrea. "Defining Female Subjectivities in Italy: Motherhood and Abortion in
the Individual and Collective Memories of the 1970s Women's Movement in Bologna." *Women's History Review* 24, 4 (2014): 543–59.

Hellman, Judith Adler. *Journeys among Women: Feminism in Five Italian Cities*. Oxford:
Oxford University Press, 1987.

Henry, Astrid. *Not my Mother's Sister. Generational Conflict and Third-Wave Feminism*.
Indiana: Indiana University Press, 2004.

Mazzanti, Roberta. "La Storia Che Verrà." *Società Italiana Delle Letterate*, 2014. http://
www.societadelleletterate.it/2014/11/convegno-bologna/.

McRobbie, Angela. "Postfeminism and Popular Culture." *Feminist Media Studies* 4, 3
(2004): 255–264.

Mura, Bruna. "I consultori familiari." Unpublished Thesis, n.d.

N.A. "Nasce la Queersultoria – Spazio di autodeterminazione e desiderio," *Fuxia Block*,
May 2, 2014. Available at: http://www.fuxiablock.org/nasce-la-queersultoria-spazio
-di-autodeterminazione-e-desiderio/.

Rigney, Ann. "Plenitude, Scarcity, and the Production of Cultural Memory." *Journal of
European Studies* 35 1, 2 (2005): 11–28.

Terragni, Marina. "Femministe 'Nove' a Paestum: il corpo torna al centro," *Femministe
Nove*, October 13, 2013. https://femministenove.wordpress.com/2013/10/12/femmini
ste-nove-a-paestum-il-corpo-torna-al-centro-di-marina-terragni.

Withers, Deborah. *Feminism, Digital Culture and the Politics of Transmission: Theory,
Practice and Cultural Heritage*. London: Rowman & Littlefield International, 2015.

CHAPTER 10

Echoes of Ricardo Mella: Reading Twenty-First Century Youth Protest Movements through the Lens of an Early Twentieth-Century Anarchist

Stephen Luis Vilaseca

An emergent territory is only as good as the codes that sustain it. Every social movement, every shift in the geography of the heart and revolution in the balance of the senses needs its aesthetics, its grammar, its science and its legalisms

BRIAN HOLMES, *Escape the Overcode* (2009, 14)

The great and noble cause of the worker has the need to create something that is essential, indispensable for any idea; it has to create its own literature and art that will serve as an active means of expression and propaganda; that will vouch for the importance of the pillars on which its principles are founded – Opening Remarks of the *First Socialist Literary Competition* (1885) in Spain

MORALES 1991, 47[1]

A key debate raging among radical activists and militant researchers in Spain is how to best extend the social, cultural and political dynamism of the 15-M movement, which began on 15 May 2011 (hence the name 15-M) when thousands of young Spaniards decided to occupy public squares in various major cities across Spain to protest the ineffectiveness of the two-party political system. The intense emotions triggered by the three-week-long collaborative association of protesters in the Puerta del Sol in Madrid and the Plaza Catalunya in Barcelona inspired many passers-by to engage in political action for the first time in their lives. If past events are indicative of future ones, the 15-M movement and related activist platforms will have difficulty sustaining social support. According to historian José Alvarez-Junco, collective protest in Spain since the late nineteenth-century has exhibited a "combination of chronic weakness with a surprising representative capacity at certain junctures" (Alvarez-Junco 1994, 323). Some of the tactics currently being discussed

---

1 All translations are those of the author unless otherwise noted.

© KONINKLIJKE BRILL NV, LEIDEN, 2017 | DOI 10.1163/9789004344518_012

to escape this historically uneven effectiveness of Spanish social movements are very similar to those put forth by the radical turn-of-the-twentieth-century thought of anarchist Ricardo Mella (1861–1925). The connection between nineteenth-century/early twentieth-century classical anarchism and the 15-M movement (and linked creative activism in general) is the shared perception that somehow these were new forms of protest that, in the first case, exploded Europe-wide and, in the second, worldwide. The encampments in the squares of Spain in 2011 did not occur in isolation, but formed part of a wave of social mobilization constantly in a process of being created again and again as witnessed in the Arab Spring of 2011 with the fall of Ben Ali in Tunisia, Mubarak in Egypt, and Gaddafi in Libya as well as in the Occupy Wall Street movement in the U.S. The two quotes in the above epilogue, separated by 124 years, reveal that just as the novelty of anarchism required the birth of an anarchist literary tradition to convey the anarchist message, the newness bound up with the early stages of the present global anti-capitalist struggle begs for its own cultural codes. Mella's theoretical and creative response to the internal conflicts raging within classic anarchist theory and practice over the use of violence, the process of experimentation in decision-making techniques, the value of collectivism and cooperatives, the practice of democracy, and the creation of values other than purely economic ones are relevant because of the clear intersections between his moment of protest and the current generation of youth protests in Spain. This chapter imagines Mella's past and the future of youth activism, and stitches them together into a new whole in order to stimulate innovation in current Spanish protest practices. Because Barcelona has a long history of anarchist activity, the majority of the examples referenced in this chapter are Barcelonan. Nevertheless, the anarchistic sensibilities historically present in Barcelona have extended to other major cities in Spain including Madrid, Valencia, Seville, and Málaga. Hence, the conclusions posed in this chapter, although based on Barcelona, are not limited to Barcelona, but are also applicable to the rest of the major cities in Spain.

Mella and the Generational Consciousness of Anarchistic Practices

Along with Mikhail Bakunin and Peter Kropotkin, Mella was at the forefront of the development of anarchist thought, not only in Spain, but internationally. According to respected Spanish anarchist Federica Montseny in her introduction to the 1975 edition of *Ideario* A Collection of Ideas, a compilation of Mella's best newspaper and journal articles:

ECHOES OF RICARDO MELLA

> He is considered, quite rightly, the most profound, most penetrating, most lucid of the Spanish anarchist thinkers. His writings, all concise, short in length, equipped the best theorists of international anarchism.
>
> MONTSENY 1975, 5

Mella's friend and fellow anarchist José Prat also notes Mella's status as a superstar of anarchist theory during his lifetime. In his prologue to the original 1925 edition of *Ideario*, he writes that Mella's articles, "The Problem with Emigration in Galicia" and "Differences between Communism and Collectivism," won prizes in *The First Socialist Literary Competition* (1885), a platform to promote debate among anarchists and to showcase the latest in anarchist thought (Prat 1975 [1925], 9). All of his texts were also awarded in *The Second Socialist Literary Competition* (1889) (Prat 1975, 10). Multiple editions of *Ideario* were published over the years (1925, 1955, 1975, and 1978) as a way to keep Mella's opinions circulating, even though his name would eventually be disassociated from those very notions.

For Mella, freedom and social justice, the two pillars of his thought, result from the entanglement of anarchy and socialism. He argued in the introduction to the section about anarchist socialism in *Ideario*:

> It is necessary to reach socialism in order to realize that freedom is a myth without the voluntary cooperation among men; that equality is a contradiction without the destruction of private property; that solidarity is impossible without the prior disappearance of how much in the everyday fight some men are placed opposite others. It is necessary to reach anarchism in order to warn that any system of government, no matter how radical, of some men over others makes impossible any solution of equality and freedom, and blocks the way to the future.
>
> MELLA 1975, 26–27

Social justice and equality under capitalism is impossible because, as Mella pointed out, "the person without property in our individualistic societies lives obligated to submit his or her freedom and labor force to whomever pays the best" (Mella 1975, 26). Any restriction of freedom is condemned in Mella's thought. As an enemy of authority, he did not believe revolutionary changes could be reached through political parties. Capitalism, a system of production that puts money above human beings, and government, a system of laws that impose limitations, are methods of forced cooperation that need to be countered with voluntary collaboration. Therefore, Mella advocated anarchist collectivism, the organization of production through autonomous, federated collectivities in which the means of production are shared, but the fruits of labor are distributed according to the effort and quality of work of each individual.

Mella is, on the one hand, a significant forefather of Spanish anarchism, but, on the other, a highly underappreciated voice. Nevertheless, despite being underrepresented, the spirit of his ideas has been transmitted over time, and has contributed to a generational consciousness of anarchistic practices both in Spain (Juris 2010) and worldwide beginning with the Seattle anti-World Trade Organization protests in late 1999 (Day 2005).[2] The question that must be asked is: Why have Mella's ideas been more successfully communicated from generation to generation than his name? A logical point of entry is the notion of generational consciousness and its actual workings within Spanish youth protest movements and activist groups. The concept of generational consciousness used in this chapter is not reduced solely to basic biological factors like birth, life span, and death. People born during the same time period do belong to the same generation in terms of historical moment. However, people who are not part of the same age group, but who do share core characteristics and beliefs, can also be said to belong to the same generation, according to Karl Mannheim's framing of the nature of the generation as a dynamic social category. Instead of being determined exclusively by a static constant like age, generation can be thought of as, in the words of social scientists Michael Pickering and Emily Keightley, "a subject position, a consciousness and a domain of social action" (Pickering and Keightley 2012, 117). The generational consciousness relevant to this study is that of anarchistic practices. Anarchists, both past and present, are critical of capitalism and the state, and share, according to Randall Amster, "some basic points of agreement: (1) opposition to hierarchy, (2) decentralization, (3) a commitment to freedom and autonomy, and (4) an opposition to vanguardism as it was expressed in authoritarian socialist traditions" (Amster et al. 2009, 3). Present-day anarchists, in addition, see a need for revolutionary struggle, because the divide between the rich and the poor is growing, political corruption is rampant, the criminalization of everyday life is on the rise, restrictions of access to public space in the city and culture on the Internet are deepening, and the invasions of privacy through constant surveillance are escalating.

A general contention of this chapter is that the generational consciousness of anarchistic practices in present activism would benefit from "a fresh contact" with the actual raw materials of Mella's thought (Mannheim 1993, 368).

---

2 Mella's defense of anarchist collectivism was shared by fellow theorists Anselmo Lorenzo, Farga Pellicer, Serrano Oteiza, Josep Llunas, and Fernando Tarrida del Mármol.

ECHOES OF RICARDO MELLA

According to Mannheim, the reintroduction to forgotten cultural heritage sparks social change:

> In the nature of our psychical makeup, a fresh contact (meeting something anew) always means a changed relationship of distance from the object and a novel approach in assimilating, using, and developing the proffered material.
>
> MANNHEIM 1993, 368

By combining the narrative of protesters with that of Mella's writings, a heightened potential for creative and radical change could be possible. Despite this chapter's attempt to create and facilitate a dialectical relationship between past and contemporary activism, there are precious few examples from within Spanish protest movements and activist groups that try to actively and consciously accomplish and facilitate this dialectical relationship with the past. As a result, there are several questions that must be addressed: Why do they not do this? What is it about a generational consciousness that makes it difficult to facilitate, or to even observe this dialectical relationship? Why do Spanish protest movements and activist groups not read Mella in the way that this chapter tries to read his texts into their protests? What might it be about a generational consciousness that may itself block such a reading? Posing Antonio Gramsci's "active man-in-the-mass" (Gramsci et al. 1971, 333) and his "modern prince" (ibid., 129) against Michael Hardt's and Antonio Negri's "multitude" (Hardt and Negri 2000, 61), and then considering all from within Mella's critique of political idolatry, will begin to answer said questions.

A constituent part of the generational consciousness of anarchistic practices is the valuing of the collective over the individual. When a project, intervention or discourse produced in common is made visible, it is dislocated so that it cannot be attributable to only one cultural producer. If a name must be provided, it is a collective name and not an individual one. This is a reaction against bourgeoisie and neoliberal notions of individualism that foment a world of egotistical competitors. Gramsci famously wrote in his *Prison Notebooks* that "the active man-in-the-mass has a practical activity, but has no clear theoretical consciousness of his practical activity" (Gramsci et al. 1971, 333). Political activists who participate in anarchistic practices like direct actions and express anarchistic values like self-management and the rejection of illegitimate authority do not necessarily know the theory behind their actions or the names of the theorists who first conceived the radical positions that they take. This is because oftentimes anarchistic practices are handed down orally from "active man-in-the-mass" to "active man-in-the-mass" through social spaces like neighborhood clubs, bars, and other social centers (Esenwein 1989, 8–9). In other words, workers and activists do not tend to study theory. Although Gramsci gives a nod to the implicit knowledge behind much activism (whether that knowledge is actively dislocated to be anonymous or not), he views it as a weakness and not as a strength. It is incomplete without the guidance of and the theory produced by a group of named and recognized intellectuals who form part of a political party that he refers to as the "modern prince" (Gramsci et al. 1971, 129). Gramsci believes that workers and activists should regain a theoretical consciousness of their practical actions with the help of these intellectuals (ibid., 198). Whether the actions should be anonymous or represented by a collective name when confronting power is unclear. Hardt's and Negri's multitude is a collective subjectivity made up of multiple singularities (unique and different subjects instead of indistinguishable, identical ones). Unlike Gramsci, Hardt and Negri clearly argue that these singularities should come together visibly to challenge constituted power. Some intellectuals like Santiago López Petit, Professor of Philosophy at the University of Barcelona, and Marina Garcés, Professor of Philosophy at the University of Zaragoza, pose the need to rethink the category of visibility. Instead of constantly making social problems visible through traditional forms of public protest, they argue that activists should make themselves invisible and/or anonymous to be more effective. One example is the use of Guy Fawkes masks during protests to deemphasize identity and promote collectivity. The valuing of the collective over the individual that forms part of the generational consciousness of anarchistic practices strips the authorship and ownership of practical activity. Paradoxically, it is the very nature of the generational consciousness of anarchistic practices in particular that blocks a reification of its theory. Mella began to set the stage for his own eventual theoretical disappearance by criticizing the fanaticism of some of the followers of Alejandro Lerroux, leader of the Radical Republican Party during the Spanish Second Republic (1931–1939), and Francisco Ferrer, anarchist educator who founded the Modern School. For Mella, such fanatics who idealized these men and made them into political idols could not be anarchists or socialists or radicals. They were simply pseudo-revolutionaries who failed to understand that it is not the man who is important, but his ideas (Mella 1975, 169–171).

Antipoliticism: Violent Confrontations with the Spanish State

Antipoliticism is a legacy of Spain's classic stage of anarchism, of which Mella was a part (Alvarez-Junco 1994, 307). Both non-violent and violent

ECHOES OF RICARDO MELLA

confrontations with the Spanish State continue to populate the contemporary political landscape. The European Parliamentary Elections in Spain on 25 May 2014, the reactions to them, and the political decisions reached after them made visible the new spectrum of Spanish protest movements, activism and political action ranging from non-violent and violent antiauthoritarian groups and actions to reformist strategies, consisting of policy changes from outside institutions, negotiations with and legalization by institutions, and entering into institutions like political parties. The practice of squatting abandoned buildings to condemn property speculation and to underscore the lack of autonomous cultural spaces in the city is a clear affront to governmental authority. This challenge, on the whole, is non-violent, but it does have its moments of violence. A recent example is the case of the squatted social center Can Vies in Barcelona. In 1997, members of the Joventuts Comunistes [Communist Youth] and the Joves Independentistes Revolucionaris/es [Revolutionary Youth for Independence] squatted a building in the Sants neighborhood that had been abandoned and unused for seven years (Miró 2008, 19). The owners of the building, Transports Metropolitans de Barcelona (TMB) and the Barcelona City Council, accused the squatters of the crime of usurpation and attempted to evict them from Can Vies in 1998, but they failed. Eight years later, they filed a civil lawsuit to reinitiate the eviction process, but this bid was also unsuccessful. For 17 years, Can Vies has functioned as a peaceful squatted social center for the neighborhood. As I outline elsewhere, there are four types of squatters: 1) youth in search of independence; 2) the poor; 3) drug dealers and users; and 4) activists (Vilaseca 2013, 2). The squatters that interest this chapter are the activists, like those of Can Vies, who convert abandoned buildings into squatted social centers. Although the majority of these squatters known as *okupas* are under 30 years old, they are not a homogeneous group. The movements with which they are involved range from the anti-globalization movement to organic culture to housing, among others. What links them together is their anarchistic sensibilities.

The upper floors of Can Vies are designated for housing and the lower ones for spaces of encounter in which many different organizations and collectives meet to share informal knowledge, creativity and culture. It is in this vein that the squatters of Can Vies agree with Mella that the true field of struggle is the emergent territory of the libertarian spirit of free exchange and openness. The anarchist seeds of freedom and voluntary cooperation cannot flourish if they are not buried in a social ground conducive to its growth. Establishing social forms through which anarchist values and beliefs can be nurtured is essential for anarchism's survival. Mella encouraged anarchists in 1909 in the newspaper *Solidaridad Obrera* to "go and in every neighborhood open a secular school, found a newspaper, a library; organize a cultural center, a union, a worker circle, a cooperative" because politicians, sensing a change in values, would eventually "govern, in short, according to the environment created by you directly" in order not to lose votes (Mella 1975, 97). This dynamic occurred in Barcelona during Mayor Hereu's mayoral campaign for re-election in 2007. Hereu recognized that Barcelonans were growing weary of urban renewal plans that were more concerned with attracting investors and tourists than with improving the quality of life of citizens. Appropriating the squatters' discourse, he championed the value of collaborating and cooperating, and the importance of establishing networks of social solidarity and social cohesion through the creation of more cultural spaces, social centers, and sports complexes (Ayuntament de Barcelona 2008, 11). Hereu's campaign promises, however, never came to fruition because he lost the election.

To rely exclusively on the ideal that the squatters' daily acting out of sharing will consciously and unconsciously influence not only people, but more importantly, politicians to share more and be more critical of capitalism is not enough to instigate a social revolution, let alone a political one. When politicians feel threatened by the growing spirit of rebellion and social unrest sewn by squatters in response to political dissatisfaction, they try to find ways to take back both the ideological and physical ground gained by the squatters. It is at these times when the issue of violence and how to respond to forceful eviction arises. Mella was not an advocate of violence, and abhorred killing (Mella 1975, 125). However, he understood that the demands of reality could make the putting into practice of certain ideals complicated and messy. He explained in 1913 in the newspaper *Acción Libertaria*:

> If I condemn on the whole the idea of violence, I cannot but condemn conditionally bottom-up violence while top-down violence subsists. Reality is stronger than philosophy, but I cannot nor want to heed the reality that disgusts me, that repulses me and overwhelms me as a thinking being and as a free citizen. The need for revolution imposes itself on me. I am therefore revolutionary because freedom and justice can only be reached by jumping over the abyss in a revolutionary way. Give me the possibility of social transformation without appeals to force and I will stop being revolutionary (ibid., 132).

Intellectually, Mella is against violence, but, realistically, such a rigid stance is untenable in the world in which he lived and in which we live. The desire to stay true to his ideals is overcome by his yearning for equality and free exchange. Therefore, the violent response – not so much by the squatters themselves

ECHOES OF RICARDO MELLA

(although there was some conflict), but by neighbors, supporters, and fellow activists – to the eviction of the squatters from Can Vies on 26 May 2014 and the subsequent bulldozing of the building would have been seen by Mella as an unsavory but necessary part of the leap toward revolutionary change. Garbage containers were burned, the windows of small businesses and banks were smashed, a television news crew's van was torched as was the bulldozer that had been used to demolish Can Vies, and barricades were strategically placed in the streets in order to contain, surround and eventually ambush the police. The images of destruction and fire depicted a state of emergency.

Tiqqun, also known as Comité Invisible, a collective of radical contemporary French theorists whose texts have been widely distributed among Barcelonan activists, argues that in a world where alternatives to capitalism are constantly being criminalized and are becoming fewer and fewer, the dwindling non-capitalist spaces that remain – like squatted social centers – must be defended and maintained, violently if required, because "we cannot continually reconstruct our bases" (Comité Invisible 2009, 147). At the end of *Llamamiento y otros fogonazos* [*The Call and Other Flashes*], the recent translation in Spanish of various texts by Tiqqun, the comments collectively written by several Barcelonan activists provide a glimpse into the probable mindset of the squatters of Can Vies and their supporters, and a likely explanation for their actions. *Something 99* writes:

> In a closed world, every expression of life is criminal and, as a result, if you want to defend yourself there will be violence. Because there are no spaces left, every affirmation is criminal. I read their reflection [Tiqqun's] on violence from that point of view. As self-defense, so that life can live
> TIQQUN – COMITÉ INVISIBLE 2009, 197.

Soul Rebel in dialogue with *Something 99* responds:

> Indeed, I am totally against violence for violence's sake as a method. But I am not against directing violence against the everyday violence that uses violence against me. Reality imposes limits that constrain us daily and that use force upon us; or we push back or they leave us less and less space. As was stated before it is pure self-defense (ibid., 198).

Norms like the Bylaws for the Means to Foment and Guarantee Communal Living in Public Space passed in 2005 in Barcelona make it illegal to put posters in public spaces without the authorization of the Barcelona City Council. The pending 2014 reform of the national Law of Citizen Safety will give police greater power to restrict free movement in public space during protest events, and to fine not only those who commit antiauthoritarian acts of disobedience, but also those who are simply present. These new laws are clear moves to impede social protest (Comisión Legal Sol, 2013). The words of Judge Josep María Miquel, although originally a reaction to the 2002 attempted eviction of the squatters from Can Masdeu, apply to the current political trend to criminalize dissent: "To locate the action of the accused in the Penal Code would suppose criminalizing the ideological opposition to the economic system that is behind the occupation, hitting squarely against political pluralism" ("Diez de los okupas" 2002, 6). The right to be able to ideologically oppose capitalism is at the heart of a democratic society, and that right is slowly being whittled away. The everyday violence of which *Soul Rebel* speaks, therefore, is twofold: the impact of predatory capitalism on citizens, one example of which are the recent suicides related to foreclosures (Fontevecchia, 2012), and the brutality of the Spanish State against those who protest capitalism, such as Ester Quintana, a woman who lost an eye after being hit by a rubber bullet used to disperse a crowd of protesters during the General Strike of 14 November 2012 (Europa Press 2013). Pushing back against this double violence with Molotov cocktails and rocks sabotages the flows of capital and interrupts the fixed relations of power, but, more importantly, amidst the burning destruction, it creates a situation of emergency in which the normal relations of capitalism are suspended, and forces people to relate to one another in a different way. On a very simple level, if the ATM machine is smashed, and you do not have any money in your wallet or purse to buy your next meal, you will have to seek the help of your friends. You will begin to realize that if you have friends, money becomes less and less necessary. By creating a life in common with others, you are able to weather the precariousness of urban living. After the period of violence, five days in the case of Can Vies, the violent protesters' hope is that neighbors will have changed and will have become less dependent on capitalism than before.

In addition to the expectant transformations at the scale of intimacy, the urban violence surrounding the Can Vies case has had repercussions at the territorial scale. For the past seven years the Federación de Entidades Ateneu Harmonia [Ateneu Harmonia Federation of Entities], consisting of twelve collectives of the Sant Andreu neighborhood, has been requesting that the Sant Andreu Casal de Barri [Neighborhood House] form part of the Barcelona City Council's Gestión cívica [Civic Management] initiative. This program separates institutional financial management from organizational management. It grants neighbors the freedom to define a certain building's programmatic direction despite receiving city funding. After seven years of negotiation, the Federación de Entidades Ateneu Harmonia's request was finally denied on

ECHOES OF RICARDO MELLA

23 April 2014 (Pauné, 2014). After the eviction of the squatters from Can Vies and the first couple of nights of violence, the Barcelona City Council began making pleas for dialogue. The squatters cited Sant Andreu's fate as proof of the uselessness of negotiating with the City Council, and refused. The neighbors of Sant Andreu started threatening to extend the violence of Sants to their streets. To avoid greater chaos, Mayor Xavier Trias reversed the original decision, and designated the Sant Andreu Casal de Barri [Neighborhood House] a Gestión cívica [Civic Management] project. In an unprecedented move, he also returned Can Vies to the squatters, and will allow them to rebuild the social center and use it for the next two years until the finalizing of new urban plans if they agree to proceed through legal channels (Escofet and Vallespin, 2014). In this case, the Can Vies violence did create policy change in Sant Andreu. It remains to be seen, however, whether Can Vies will accept the Barcelona City Council's terms, and legally reconstruct by obtaining all the necessary building permits.

Antipoliticism: Non-violent Confrontations with the Spanish State

In the meantime, Can Vies is moving forward on its own, and is getting back to the work of bringing people together to share knowledge, language, technology, science and culture as common goods for self-enrichment. In order to remove the fallen debris from the site of the partially demolished Can Vies, hundreds of activists and neighbors voluntarily came together to form a human chain and passed rubble from person to person. Creating commons in the city and spreading the value of voluntary cooperation are hallmarks of Mella's thought. He believed that collectivism was the form of social coexistence that best allowed people to fully and freely cooperate with one another (Mella 1975, 35). David Harvey asks in *Seventeen Contradictions and the End of Capitalism* (2014) if there is an alternative to capitalism being offered now. He says no. I disagree. The alternative is collectivism and cooperatives, first championed in Spain by Mella in the nineteenth and early twentieth centuries, and now finding a resurgence, not only in Spain, but worldwide. The United Nations designated the year 2012 as the International Year of Cooperatives (IYC). Its slogan was 'Cooperative Enterprises Build a Better World.' That same year, Cooperatives de Treball de Catalunya organized a free tour of late nineteenth- and early twentieth-century historical buildings that once housed important cooperatives in various neighborhoods of Barcelona ('9 de juny' 2012), and the Associació de veïns i veïnes de l'Òstia [Association of the Neighbors of l' Òstia] coordinated and planned a talk about the history of workers' cooperatives in la Barceloneta neighborhood ('Memòria Cooperativa' 2012). Remembering the past cooperative movement is not meant to be an exercise in historical memory. Rather, the memory of cooperatives and collectivism in the form of photos, videos, and newspaper and journal articles by anarchists like Mella serve as raw materials to be constantly reinterpreted and recombined to imagine new relational possibilities. Imagination and memory work together to effect change. Pickering and Keightley (2012) explain that the incessant replaying of memory in creative, new narratives offers valuable insight into and a better understanding of one's original relationship to the secondhand experience (in this case, the memory of cooperatives and collectivism):

> In engaging with pasts that we did not experience and bringing them to bear in our own self-narratives and understanding of others, memory and imagination act in productive tension with each other, and in so doing, open up opportunities for the generation of new temporal meanings.
> PICKERING and KEIGHTLEY 2012, 122

One of the emergent opportunities in the growing cooperative movement became reality on 25 January 2014 when l'Ateneu Cooperatiu LA BASE opened its doors in the working class neighborhood Poble Sec in Barcelona. Before the inaugural presentation and grand opening, in order to introduce LA BASE to neighbors (and to anyone else interested) and to explain what it is and what it will offer, founding members of the athenaeum collaborated with Metromuster, an independent Barcelonan production company specializing in documentaries and non-fiction film. Together they made a visual manifesto declaring the objectives and principles of LA BASE in which images and videos depicting the manual labor and daily life of Barcelonan workers affiliated with anarcho-syndicalist labor unions in 1936 were repeated by videos showing similar types of manual labor and communal life of the members of LA BASE.[3] A sense of commonality over time is established in which LA BASE's values of self-management, community, equality, and solidarity are shared with those of the anarcho-syndicalists of the 1930s (who looked to Mella before them). The members of LA BASE form more of a community with anarchists of the first third of the twentieth century than with capitalists of the twenty-first century. The identification with the benefits of forging a cooperative instead of a business creates a common set of beliefs and values that can be understood as a generational consciousness. The visual manifesto is a creative replaying

---

3   The visual manifesto can be seen by watching the video posted online at http://metromuster .cat/project/la-base/.

ECHOES OF RICARDO MELLA

of anarchistic practices that is not a simple repetition of past experience, but a repetition with transformative possibilities. Pickering and Keightley (2012) clarify how the productive tension between memory, in this case the raw footage of the workers, and imagination, Metromuster's and LA BASE's creative retelling, results in the construction of generational consciousness:

> This repetition goes beyond a retelling: it requires an open interaction with secondhand experience which can be performed only in the liminal space of transmission between generations. In this sense, generational consciousness as a sense of difference over time is creatively produced not by making a complete break with inherited pasts, but through the dialectical relationships between continuity and rupture, intimate knowing and irreducible difference that occur vertically through time in genealogical relationships.
>
> PICKERING and KEIGHTLEY 2012, 126

The film and eventually the operating cooperative attempt to make the social and economic forms of self-management that were once prevalent in the early twentieth century an understandable part of the neighborhood's present story. Some of the projects being developed are a community kitchen, a food cooperative, a shared library, a communal computer lab, child care, and skill-sharing.

Reformism

In addition to the strategy of non-violent and violent confrontation with the Spanish State (as has been discussed in the cases of politically motivated squatters and collectivism and cooperatives), there is a more reformist approach within youth protest movements in contemporary Spain. Working with the system takes on three iterations: pushing for policy changes from outside institutions; negotiating with institutions; and, finally, entering into institutions like political parties.

Mella was against participation in political parties, but, at the same time, argued in favor of working through a legal structure, the trade union, in order to quicken the revolution. Historian and militant anarchist Miguel Amorós criticizes Mella's 'legalism' as reformist and a betrayal of Bakunin's critique of bourgeois culture ('Los dos anarquismos' 2003[4]). George Richard Esenwein,

---

4 See, http://www.nodo50.org/ekintza/spip.php?article104.

associate professor of Modern European/Iberian History at the University of Florida, suggests that the matter is far more complicated. He writes:

> The notion of 'legalism' itself, at least as it was understood by the syndicalists, bore no relation to the literal meaning of the term. That is to say, they did not interpret the policy as one which in any way bound the FTRE to the juridical system that granted these rights...On the contrary, as anarchists, they were implacably hostile toward politics and unwaveringly committed to the idea of completely overturning the ruling system. For the syndicalists, a policy of 'legalism' was nothing more than the most efficacious means of achieving this end.[5]
>
> ESENWEIN 1989, 82

Mella seizes control of the terms 'reformist' and 'legal,' and reverses their meanings. Legalization is a conduit through which to radicalize the public. Anarchist values and beliefs are able to circulate more freely and widely, and have a greater potential to undermine capitalism and instigate social and political transformation via a legal front rather than through illegal, clandestine and violent means. Contrary to Amorós' critique that Mella's ideas are a bourgeois, watered-down version of anarchism, the possible end result of Mella's thought is actually more revolutionary.

His brand of reformism is never one that tries to change policy directly, but, rather, one that attempts to saturate daily life with a spirit of rebellion. The reformist strategy furthest from Mella's thought in contemporary Spain is that of neighborhood associations that have blocked urban renewal plans, and platforms of the 15-M movement like the Plataforma de Afectados por la Hipoteca (PAH) [Platform of Those Affected by Mortgages] that have prevented evictions. That is not to say that the leveraging of real changes is less important than transformations in thought. Both are needed for true social revolution.

For Mella, the legal front through which to ignite a spirit of rebellion among the workers is the trade union. Connected to the question of trade unions is the debate over whether strike activity or violent deeds against authority is the most effective way to overthrow capitalism. Mella, again, sides with the syndicalists. Esenwein explains:

---

5   FTRE stands for Federación de Trabajadores de la Región Española (1881–1888) [Federation of Workers from the Spanish Region], the anarchist organization that succeeded the Federación Regional Española, the Spanish branch of First International established in 1870.

In one camp were the 'syndicalists,' comprising both anarchists and pure syndicalists, who followed the founders of the IWMA [International Working Men's Association, First International] in believing that the key to the emancipation of the proletariat lay in the development of trade unions. Furthermore, strikes were viewed as an important indicator of working-class strength and solidarity. For them, the growth of labor federations went hand in hand with the general strike tactic. Once the unions were strong enough to wield their own economic power, the belief was that a general strike could be called to bring about the collapse of the capitalist system.

ESENWEIN 1989, 56

Over a century later, that belief continues to be in force. To protest against the government's labor reforms and austerity plans, Spanish trade unions called for a general strike on 29 March 2012. Student unions also responded to governmental budget cuts to public education by staging three student strikes (17 November 2011, 29 February 2012, and 3 May 2012). Although a reformist strategy, strikes, also, can turn violent. Some businesses like the Barcelona Stock Exchange and Starbucks that remained open during the general strike were targeted and vandalized. Police reacted with baton charges, the firing of rubber bullets into crowds of protesters, and the use of tear gas.

Mella's legacy of working outside of political parties but within legal institutions to disseminate anarchist values and beliefs reverberates most strongly in the pacts made between city councils and radical spaces like self-organized art studios, squatted social centers, and autonomous athenaeums. L'Ateneu Popular 9 Barris is a non-profit, partially subsidized cultural center with autonomous management and a focus on social transformation in the Barcelonan neighborhood Nou Barris. Public subventions represent half of the budget. The other half is generated by the center itself so that it does not have to depend totally on the public administration (Junta de Bidó de Nou Barris 2008). Although publicly funded, the Association Bidó de Nou Barris has complete autonomy to manage and determine L'Ateneu Popular 9 Barris' cultural program. In Madrid, the Department of Fine Arts and Cultural Heritage and Archives and Libraries, the branch of the Ministry of Culture that oversees the management of all of the *Bienes de Interés Cultural* [Properties of Cultural Interest], and the Tabacalera, an autonomous social center housed in the old eighteenth century Embajadores Tobacco Factory, have reached an agreement in which said governmental institution temporarily transfers the right to use the national historic landmark to the social center. This new institutional arrangement is one that reimagines the relations between public institutions and social collectives from the standpoint of collaboration and cooperation, and not from that of antagonism. The Tabacalera, despite its legalization, is free to pursue its own programming based on autonomy, direct participation, free culture, and the sharing of informal knowledge and creativity as common goods.

Even Mella did not appreciate the full promise of his practice of producing new meanings from already existing symbols. He remained fervently against political parties, and never considered what would happen if an anarchist cloaked him or herself in the sign of the politician, entered the political system, and turned the sign on its head by infusing the figure of the politician as well as the state with a set of anarchistic practices. Revisiting Mella from the perspective of contemporary activism not only helps us understand the limitations of his thought, but also sheds light on political action in Spain and its future. In the introduction to this chapter, the related questions of how to best extend the social, cultural and political dynamism of the 15-M movement, and how to escape the historically uneven effectiveness of Spanish social movements were posed. Facilitating collective experiences of self-organization in reformist trade unions in order to spread anarchist values and beliefs among workers as well as inspiring a will to political action among the general population through art and emotions are two possible answers. One can see both practices occurring in Spain today, and the result is that the Spanish masses are being politicized more and more. However, because many collective experiences of self-organization eventually lose steam, the problem is how to take advantage of the heightened politicization, and channel it to make change. The key lies in maximizing both Mella's version of entrism, the entering in to a larger organization by a small revolutionary group, with that of Vladimir Lenin. In addition to being active in reformist trade unions while staying true to one's radical political beliefs, Lenin adds the need to participate in parliamentary elections. In order to reach the end goal of a new era of communism, he stresses the importance of tactical compromises and temporary political alliances. Lenin is critical of fellow revolutionaries who believe that working through state power is not necessary for social change. He views such a stance, one that is obviously anarchistic, as naïve and childish as the title of his famous pamphlet *"Left-Wing" Communism: An Infantile Disorder* suggests. In this leaflet published in April 1920, Lenin clarifies his position by referring to the workers' movement in Britain. He calls for British communists to form a temporary electoral bloc with reformist Labour leaders Henderson and Snowden in order to defeat the more conservative Liberal-Tory alliance. He explains the revolutionary logic behind this type of cooperation in the following way: "I wanted with my vote to support Henderson in the same way as the rope supports a hanged man"

ECHOES OF RICARDO MELLA

(Lenin 1940 [1920], 70). The collaboration is a means to eventually strangle to death bourgeois dominance from the inside.

Present-day Catalan activist Enric Duran embodies a hybrid approach to activism, one that combines Mella's practice of producing new meanings from already existing symbols with Lenin's expanded strategy of entrism and tactical compromises. Duran constantly asks the following questions: Can we live without capitalism? Can we live without banks? What role do banks, credit, and indebtedness play in our lives? In 2008, he opened 68 lines of credit from 39 banks equaling 492,000 euros. He did so to demonstrate the ease with which one could become indebted. There is no crime in that. However, he also decided that he would never repay the loans. Instead, Duran used the money to fund social movements and to publish 200,000 copies of *Crisis? Podemos!*, a newspaper of articles in Spanish that explains how to create alternatives to capitalism. Duran was charged with swindling money from the banks and with falsifying documents. He spent two months in prison (March 20, 2009–May 22, 2009) until he was released on a 50,000 euro bail.

Duran's creative activism was not recognized as activism. His act of asking for loans looked like any other person's act of asking for money. His performance was read as a normal action. What protesters can learn from Duran is not to mark activism as activism, but to hide activism within the everyday. In so doing, the protesters can make holes in capitalist reality. Once those holes are made, they can then go public to expose them. Like Mella who takes over already existing symbols and points them in new directions, Duran used the symbol of the borrower to enter into the lending system, and then from within, he changed the lender/borrower relationship in order to elicit a transformation in cultural attitudes toward the banking institution.

Simona Levi, founder and candidate of the Citizens' Network x Party, a newly formed political party that gained enough signatures to be able to participate in the 2014 European Parliamentary Elections, cites Duran as an inspiration for her approach to activism:

> This [Enric Duran's robbing of banks] for me is art because he is talking about the banks, not by going to a theater saying that speculation is bad… but he is making an artistic gesture because I define an artistic gesture as one that communicates content and emotion at the same time, and takes place in reality.
>
> LEVI 2009

Levi made an artistic gesture of her own when she founded the Citizens' Network x Party. Her idea for a form of political organization that will create social, economic, and political change is a blend of state-interventionism because it works through a political party, and anarchism because it stresses autonomy and a critique of illegitimate authority. In a move Mella never would have considered, Levi breaks into the two-party political system, and articulates a position from within that system in order to produce new information. She disposes of the dichotomies revolution/reform and non-statist/statist, and works from multiple centers. She eschews the limitations of a rigid ideology and describes the Citizens' Network x Party's approach as a practical methodology. Mella also defined anarchism as a method and not an ideology. He argued that "anarchist socialism follows...its own method, opposed to all dogmatism" (Mella 1975, 20). A precursor to present-day activists' aversion to the use of political labels is Mella's anarchist theoretical perspective known as *anarquismo sin adjetivos* [anarchism without adjectives.] He theorized "a doctrine without any qualifying labels such as communist, collectivist, mutualist, or individualist" and sought to foment "an attitude that tolerated the coexistence of different anarchist schools" (Esenwein 1989, 135). While Mella argued against exclusionary, totalizing thought, his defense of *anarquismo sin adjetivos* may have been prompted by an ulterior motive: the preservation of "the collectivist heritage to which he belonged" (Esenwein 1989, 140) which was being threatened by anarchist communism. Nevertheless, Mella's rejection of doctrinal systematization resonates with Levi, and she applies that logic to the organization of her political party. The Citizens' Network x Party's method consists of the voluntary cooperation of federated abilities across a network in order to develop real, practical solutions for the problems facing democracy in Spain today. The four planks of its platform are transparency in public administration, right to real and permanent vote, government under citizen control (wikigovernment) and citizen legislative power (wikilegislation), and the use of referendums to make decisions.

Another recently founded political party that is less a traditional party and more a network of grassroots activists is Podemos. Despite being formed only three months before the May 2014 European Parliamentary Elections, it earned 1.2 million votes and 5 seats in the European Parliament. Like the Citizens' Network x Party, it is driven by the desire to foment direct participation and return the democratic process back to the citizens. Its program is a collaborative work-in-progress whose method consists of online debates and contributions by individuals, collective amendments from its extensive network of small groups throughout Spain known as Podemos Circles, and online referendums on the amendments. Some of the policies for which Podemos argues are a wider use of Popular Legislative Initiatives and referendums, an unconditional basic income, and complete fiscal transparency.

ECHOES OF RICARDO MELLA

Lenin's electoral united front infused with Mella's spirit of rebellion reworked for the twenty-first century in Spain is a flexible network of politicized citizens whose various nodes range from political parties like the Citizens' Network x Party and Podemos to radical think tanks to collectives and cooperatives to squatted social centers to neighborhood associations to alternative media among others. The transversal relays between the nodes are both digital and corporeal. In many cases, people are members of various groups at once, facilitating a constant cross-pollination of ideas. In terms of strategy, the described nodes of the flexible network work with each other towards a common goal of real, direct participatory democracy from many centers and not just one.

Mella was a proponent of new social movement theory before that term ever existed. Although Mella was connected to the old social movement, namely the labor movement, and believed that the economic struggle and the strike tactic, along with propaganda, were important pieces in the revolutionary puzzle, he later developed his theory of *anarquismo sin adjetivos* that focused more on the social aspect. Like new social movement theory, instead of lobbying for changes in public policy, he stressed social transformations in thought, daily life and culture. More than interactions fueled by class relationships, he held that social action characterized by free, voluntary cooperation and association shaped social identity. For Mella, the most significant social actors were not necessarily workers, but those who lived their lives according to anarchistic practices. Therefore, the type of social actors mobilized in Mella's time was not so different from the kind rallied today. John Moore, echoing Hakim Bey's take on anarchist subjectivity, argues that anarchists live life poetically: "Anarchist subjectivity emerges in his work as a synonym for poetic subjectivity, and anarchist revolt as a synonym for the immediate realization of the creative or poetic imagination in everyday life" (Moore 2004, 57). Similarly, Félix Guattari contends that change occurs when life is lived at the same time that it is creatively represented (Guattari 1985). Enric Duran is a perfect example. His asking for a bank loan in everyday life was indistinguishable from his creative performance of soliciting credit. His artistic activism short-circuited the lender/borrower relationship. Protesters, also, understand the power of creatively framing resistance through art, be it a performance or a dance party to name just two, because, as Paul Routledge points out, "emotions...are a means of initiating action" (Routledge 2009, 86–87). Mella, too, realized the potential of art as experimentation to create values other than those focused solely on money-making. Hence, the argument that new social movements tend to overstate their novelty rings true in Spain (Brand 1990; Larana, Johnston and Gusfield 1994; Melucci 1994; Plotke 1990).

Despite the fact that Mella and present-day Spanish protesters do not share the same historical moment, they, nevertheless, do form part of the same generation. That is, they embody common characteristics and beliefs that connect them over time. This generational consciousness of anarchistic practices will be heightened and reenergized when activists come into contact once again with Mella's writings. This chapter facilitates such a re-encounter. The flows of new meaning developed after such a reunion are the application of Mella's practice of hijacking symbols to any institution including political parties, and the move away from ideology to methodology. Much like the figure of Mella himself, activism in Spain is a mixture of antipoliticism (politically motivated squatters, collectivism and cooperatives like l'Ateneu Cooperatiu LA BASE) and reformist strategy (*los indignados*, PAH, neighborhood associations, 9Barris, Tabacalera, political parties like the Citizens' Network X Party and Podemos), and calls for the continued experimentation with hybrid forms of organization to elicit social, political, and economic transformation.

References

"9 de Juny: Ruta per la Barcelona Cooperative (Final a la Barceloneta)." *La Barceloneta Rebel*, June 8, 2012. http://www.labarcelonetarebel.org/2012/06/08/9-de-juny-ruta -per-la-barcelona-cooperativa-final-a-la-barceloneta/.

Alvarez-Junco, José. "Social Movements in Modern Spain: From the Pre-Civil War Model to Contemporary NSMs," in *New Social Movements: From Ideology to Identity*, edited by Enrique Laraña, Hank Johnston, and Joseph R. Gusfield, 304–329. Philadelphia: Temple University Press, 1994.

Amorós, Miguel. "Los dos Anarquismos: Legalismo e Ilegalismo Libertarios a Finales del Siglo XIX." Lecture presented at Arus library, October 7, 2003. http://www.porta loaca.com/historia/historia-libertaria/2525-los-dos-anarquismos-legalismo-e -ilegalismo-libertarios-a-finales-del-siglo-xix.html.

Amster, Randall, Abraham DeLeon, Luis A. Fernandez, Anthony J. Nocella II, and Deric Shannon, (eds.). *Contemporary Anarchist Studies: An Introductory Anthology of Anarchy in the Academy*. London: Routledge, 2009.

"Ayuntamiento Cifra Daños en 200.00? Y da por Acabado Diálogo con Violentos." *La Vanguardia*, June 1, 2014. Accessed June 2, 2014. http://www.lavanguardia.com/poli tica/20140601/54409518079/ayuntamiento-cifra-danos-en-200-00-y-da-por-acaba do-dialogo-con-violentos.html.

Ayuntament de Barcelona. *Barcelona: La Ciutat de Tots: Programa d'Actuació Municipal (2008–2011)*. Barcelona: El Periódico, 2008.

Brand, Karl-Werner. "Cyclical Aspects of New Social Movements: Waves of Cultural Criticism and Mobilization Cycles of New Middle-Class Radicalism," in *Challenging* the *Political Order: New Social and Political Movements in Western Democracies*, edited by Russel J. Dalton and Manfred Kuechler, 24–42. Oxford: Oxford University Press, 1990.

Comisión Legal Sol. "Porque Sólo la Lucha Hace Justicia (II)." *Diagonal* December 20, 2013. Accessed June 2, 2014. https://www.diagonalperiodico.net/libertades/21167 -porque-solo-la-lucha-hace-justicia-ii.html.

Comité Invisible. *La Insurrección que Viene*. Barcelona: Melusina [sic], 2009.

"Diez de los Okupas de Can Masdeu Irán a Juicio por Vivir en la Masía." *El Mundo*, June 21, 2002. Catalunya sec.: 6.

Day, Richard J.F. *Gramsci is Dead: Anarchist Currents in the Newest Social Movements*. London: Pluto Press, 2005.

Escofet, Jordi Mumbrú and Ivanna Vallespín. "El Alcalde de Barcelona Devuelve el Centro de Can Vies a los 'Okupas.'" *El País* June 4, 2014. Accessed June 5, 2014. http:// ccaa.elpais.com/ccaa/2014/06/04/catalunya/1401881628_079231.html.

Esenwein, George Richard. *Anarchist Ideology and the Working-Class Movement in Spain, 1868–1898*. Berkeley: University of California Press, 1989.

Europa Press. "Ester Quintana: 'No soy la Primera Víctima de las Balas de Goma Pero Quiero ser la Ultima." *Público.es*, July 11, 2013. Accessed June 3, 2014. http://www .publico.es/actualidad/458769/ester-quintana-no-soy-la-primera-victima-de-las -balas-de-goma-pero-quiero-ser-la-ultima.

Fontevecchia, Augustino. "Spanish Woman Commits Suicide as Foreclosure Agents Walk Into Her Apartment." *Forbes*, November 9, 2012. Accessed February 20, 2014. http://www.forbes.com/sites/afontevecchia/2012/11/09/spanish-woman-commits -suicide-as-foreclosure-agents-walk-into-her-apartment/.

Gramsci, Antonio, Quintin Hoare and Geoffrey Nowell-Smith. *Selections from the Prison Notebooks of Antonio Gramsci*. London: Lawrence & Wishart, 1971.

Guattari, Félix. *Pragmatic/Machinic: A Discussion with Félix Guattari*, Interviewed by Charles J. Stivale, March 19, 1985. Accessed December 18, 2012. http://topologicalme dialab.net/xinwei/classes/readings/Guattari/Pragmatic-Machinic_chat.html.

Hardt, Michael and Antonio Negri. *Empire*. Cambridge Mass: Harvard University Press, 2000.

Harvey, David. *Seventeen Contradictions and the End of Capitalism*. Oxford: Oxford University Press, 2014.

Holmes, Brian. *Escape the Overcode: Activist Art in the Control Society*. Eindhoven: Van Abbemuseum, 2009.

Junta de Bidó de Nou Barris. "Les Obres i l'Economia." *L'Ateneu Popular 9Barris* 104 (2008): 2.

Juris, Jeffrey. "Reinventing the Rose of Fire: Anarchism and the Movements Against Corporate Globalization in Barcelona." *Historia Actual Online* 21 (2010): 143–155.

Larana, Enrique, Hank Johnston and Joseph Gusfield, (eds.). *New Social Movements: from Ideology to Identity*. Philadelphia, PA: Temple University Press, 1994.

Lenin, Vladimir. *'Left-Wing' Communism: An Infantile Disorder*. New York: International Publishers, 1940 [1920].

Levi, Simona. Personal Interview, Barcelona, May 20, 2009.

Mannheim, Karl. "The Sociological Problem of Generations," in *From Karl Mannheim*, edited by Kurt H. Wolff, 361–395. New Brunswick and London: Transaction Publishers, 1993.

Mella, Ricardo. *Ideario*. Toulouse: Ediciones C.N.T, 1975.

Melucci, Alberto. "A Strange Kind of Newness: What's 'New' in New Social Movements," in *New Social Movements: From Ideology to Identity*, edited by Enrique Larana, Hank Johnston, and Joseph Gusfield, 101–130. Philadelphia: Temple University Press, 1994.

"Memòria Cooperativa de la Barceloneta: Arrenquem de l'Oblit el Cooperativisme Obrer del Barri." *La Barceloneta Rebel*, September 21, 2012. Accessed November 9, 2013. http://www.labarcelonetarebel.org/2012/09/21/memoria-cooperativa-de-la-barce loneta-arrenquem-de-loblit-el-cooperativisme-obrer-del-barri/.

Miró, Ivan. "Assemblea de Barri de Sants, més d'una Dècada Revolucionant el Barri," in *més d'una Dècada Revolucionant el Barri*, 7–51. Barcelona: Assemblea de Barri de Sants, 2008.

Montseny, Federica. Introduction to *Ideario*, by Ricardo Mella, 5–7. Toulouse: Ediciones C.N.T., 1975.

Moore, John. "Lived Poetry: Stirner, Anarchy, Subjectivity and the Art of Living," in *Changing Anarchism: Anarchist Theory and Practice in a Global Age*, edited by Jonathan Purkis and James Bowen, 55–72. Manchester and New York: Manchester University Press, 2004.

Morales, Manuel. "La Subcultura Anarquista en España: el Primer Certamen Socialista (1885)." *Mélanges de la Casa de Velázquez* 27, 3 (1991): 47–60.

Pauné, Meritxell M. "Trias Cede Ante el Ateneu Harmonia de Sant Andreu en Plena Crisis por Can Vies." *La Vanguardia*, May 30, 2014. Accessed June 5, 2014. http://www .lavanguardia.com/local/barcelona/20140530/54408522547/trias-cede-ateneu-har monia-crisis-can-vies.html.

Pickering, Michael and Emily Keightley. "Communities of Memory and the Problem of Transmission." *European Journal of Cultural Studies* 16, 1 (2012): 115–131.

Plotke, David. "What's So New about New Social Movements?" *Socialist Review* 20 (1990): 81–102.

Prat, José. Prologue to *Ideario*, by Ricardo Mella, 9–15. Toulouse: Ediciones C.N.T., 1975 [1925].

Routledge, Paul. "Toward a Relational Ethics of Struggle: Embodiment, Affinity, and Affect," in *Contemporary Anarchist Studies: An Introductory Anthology of Anarchy in the Academy*, edited by Randal Amster, Abraham DeLeon, Luis A. Fernandez,

Anthony J. Nocella ii, and Deric Shannon, 82–92. London and New York: Routledge, 2009.

Tiqqun-Comite Invisible. *Llamamiento y Otros Fogonazos.* 2009. Madrid: Acuarela, 2009.

Vilaseca, Stephen Luis. *Barcelonan Okupas: Squatter Power!* Madison, N.J.: Fairleigh Dickinson University Press, 2013.

Index

abeyance 130
accumulation by dispossession 149
active man-in-the-mass 249
activism 27, 29, 35, 126, 178, 187
  consciousness of 20, 248
  creative 177, 246, 261, 263
  digital 38
  disappointment with 34
  feminist 225, 231–235, 235, 239–41
  grassroots 31, 36
  knowledge in 250
  lawyers 82–84, 92–93
  LGBT and feminist 158, 191
  new types of 28, 41–49, 251
  recruitment 33, 128
  risks of 130
  student 32
  youth *see* youth activists
activists, unemployed 206, 208, 210, 218–19
Algeria 1, 18, 198–221
Algerian economy 203–5, 206, 211, 221
Algerian North 209, 210, 212, 213, 216, 221fn
Algerian South 202, 205, 207, 208–9, 213, 214,
  215, 216, 217, 220, 221
Algerian workers 203, 210, 211
anarchism 132, 245–64
anarchistic practices 248, 249, 250, 257, 260,
  263, 264
anarchist theory, classic 246
anarcho-syndicalist labor unions 256
Anti-Capitalist Muslim Youth 146, 161–62
Arab nationalism 82, 83, 86, 88, 107, 116
Arab-Palestinian society *see* Palestinian
  society
Arab-Palestinian youth *see* Palestinian youth
Arab spring 10, 31, 40, 49, 144, 202, 246
Arab uprisings 8, 9, 11, 103, 171, 175, 181, 183
al-Asad, Hafez 102n, 105, 106, 113
al-Asad, Bashar 102, 107, 112, 114
Association of Young Lawyers (Tunisia) 83
authoritarian regimes 9, 31
  Algerian 219, 221
  Egyptian 40, 129, 131, 134
  fall of 73, 92
  harassment by 75

neoliberal 40
political dynamics 131
repression by 93
socialist tradition 248
Syrian 106
Tunisian 40, 73, 87n, 92
Turkish 144–6

Baladna (Palestinian activists) 29, 34–35, 36
Beyoglu 151–53
Bologna 226, 227, 242
Bylaws for the Means to Foment and
  Guarantee Communal Living in Public
  Space 253

Can Vies (Barcelona squat) 251, 253, 254–55
civic professionalism 74, 83
civil war
  Algeria 198, 201, 211, 212, 217
  Libya 40
  Syria 13, 40, 105n
classed subjectivity 145, 155–57
CNDCC (Comité national pour la défense des
  droits des chômeurs) 205–6
collective action
  Egyptian 136
  by lawyers 73, 76, 80, 84, 93
  Palestinian 29
  in Gezi park 152, 160
collectivism 246, 247–48, 255–56, 257,
  262, 264
collective identity 55–58, 64, 69, 124
collective memory *see* memory: collective
collective problem 131, 133, 135
Comité Invisible *see* Tiqqun
communicative memory 231
conjuncture 137, 172, 176, 208, 211–13
cooperatives 246, 252, 255, 256–57, 264
counter-memory 225
creative activism 246, 261
cultural memory *see* memory: cultural

Damascus spring 112–113, 115
Day of Rage 43–44, 47
decoloniality 17, 175, 180, 192, 193

dignity   193, 219–20
Duran, Enric   261, 263

education   28, 104, 105, 118, 174, 186, 203, 259
   education system, Syria   106–7
   in Iraq   115
   militarization of   190
   see also post-secondary education
Egypt   14, 40, 47, 122–140 *see also* revolution,
      Egyptian
Egyptian Movement for Change see *Kifaya*
   movement
Emergency Economic Stabilization Plan   39
emergency law   112fn, 130
employment   39, 199, 203–5, 210, 212n, 214,
      220, 237 *see also* unemployment
entrism   260–61
Ettajdid movement   80
European Parliamentary Elections   251
extra-parliamentary movements   27

family   7, 13, 36, 75, 101, 112, 227
   émigre   6
   feminism as   238 *see also* mother-
   daughter relationship
   generation as   22
   law   77
   lineage   18, 221
   and memory   14, 19
   presidents'   81, 88
   resources   204
   revolutionary   198–200
   and socialization   108–10
   vs. youth   208
Femminile Plurale   225, 236–39
feminism   19–20, 57, 158, 191, 224–243
   second-wave   224, 230–31, 233, 234, 235,
      240, 242
      legacy of   239
      memory of   225, 228, 233, 242
      as obscuring term   238
feminist activism *see* activism: feminist
Feminist Battle   239, 240, 242
Femministe Nove   19, 224, 228–229, 231,
      235–36, 238–39
February 27 1962   215, 216, 219, 220, 221
15-M movement   245–56, 258, 260
freedom   40, 85, 110, 115, 192, 251, 252

and art   109
collective   59
concept of   193, 247
consumerist   185
crippling of   146
defending   85, 149, 150, 248
of expression   133, 190
fight for   200
fundamental   74, 83
individual   147
in slogans   161, 171, 188, 191
seeds of   251
time of   107, 212
Fuxia Block   225, 239–42
frame   56, 59, 60–61, 62–63

Gaza   35, 43, 48, 49, 171, 177, 180,
      183, 186
genealogy   108, 145, 176, 183, 229, 236
general struggle   63–67
generation
   across historical periods   264
   concept of   2, 4–7, 75, 122, 140, 145, 174,
      210–11, 228–29
   as false dichotomy   236–37
   and memory   15–16, 19
   and nationhood   182
   new generations   3, 13
   political *see* political generation
   and protest   3, 7–8
   revolutionary (Algeria)   198
   and space   207–208
   and temporality   4, 6–7, 12–13
   and youth   3, 30–31, 100
   see also November generation
generational cohort   28–30, 161, 230
generational conflict   57–58, 233, 235–36,
      237
generational consciousness   3, 16fn, 20, 29,
      246, 248–50, 264
   production of   15, 19, 131, 256–57
   solidification of   34
generational formation   5, 12
generational habitus   206
generationality   229, 242
generational location   29–30, 49, 182
generational memory *see* memory: collective
generational model   232, 238, 242

INDEX

generational unit   28, 30–31, 49, 58–59, 122fn, 124, 128, 133, 135
generation Oslo   171, 175–176, 181, 185, 193
Gezi Park protests   9, 15, 143–44, 146, 149, 153–63
graffiti   13, 17, 172, 173, 175, 181, 183, 186–90
    feminist and queer   191
Gramsci, Antonio   249–50

Haifa   34, 36–38, 48, 171, 172, 175, 176, 185, 191, 193
Hama   101, 102, 106
Harakat A-Shabiba al-Yaffaweeya   29, 37, 43, 48
Hassi R'mel   210
heritage   31, 101, 228, 231–32, 233–34
    collectivist   262
    cultural   30, 249, 259
    feminist   233–34, 235, 238, 239, 241, 242
    societal   229, 238
higher education *see* postsecondary education
Hikmet, Nazim   150
Hiraq al-Shababi   29, 35, 37, 40, 41, 43–44, 47
hip-hop   17, 172, 173, 177, 180–81, 182–83, 186
Housing Development Administration of Turkey *see* TOKI
human rights defenders   82, 83, 85, 86
Hussein, Saddam   14, 99, 114–115, 116

inheritance   19, 228, 229, 231–34, 238, 242–43
Intifada   39, 174, 184
    second   27, 127, 131, 172, 174
    first   174
    generation   175
    prisoners'   176
    rekindling of   39
    in Syria   115
Iraq   99, 115, 116–17
    Iraq war (2003)   1, 14, 99, 101, 114, 115, 118, 127, 131
    Iraqi refugees   14, 99, 116
    role of neighborhood   112
Ikhwan al-Muslimin see Muslim Brotherhood
Italian women's movement   232, 239–40
Italy   2, 11, 13, 19, 55–69, 224–243

Jerusalem   35, 37, 172, 173, 178, 180, 183–184, 189, 190
jil Oslo *see* generation Oslo
justice   49, 85, 213, 214, 217–9, 221 *see also* social justice
justice system   75, 80, 92

Kasserine, Tunisia   84n, 87, 90–91
Khutwe (Palestinian activists)   29, 35, 38, 43, 48
Kifaya movement   127, 129, 130–33, 136, 137

LA BASE   256–57, 264
L'Ateneu Popular 9 Barris   259, 264
Law of Citizen Safety   253
lawyers   73–93
    cause lawyering   86
    lower-level   75–77, 80, 81, 83, 84, 92
    overcrowding of profession   76–77
    political activist   82–84, 93
legacy   1, 225, 233–34, 239–40, 242, 250, 259
Levi, Simona   261–62

Mannheim, Karl
    on acquired memories   17
    on contemporaneity   2, 6
    on generations   4–5, 7, 15, 18, 29–31, 56, 58–9, 100, 123–4, 131, 145, 162, 220, 229, 237, 248, 249
    on location   207
Maoists   82
Marxist-Leninists   67, 82, 87n
mass organizations   199
matrophor   238fn, 242
May 15 2011 protests (Spain)   245
Mbembe, Achille   8, 9, 12, 13
media   147, 182, 227, 233, 237, 240
    alternative   263
    event   47
    interpretation of youth revolt   122–23
    mainstream   131, 144
    mass   190
    and memory   20, 225–26, 229, 234
    television   212–3
    see also social media
mediated memory   226
Mediterranean   1, 9

MENA 1, 2, 9
Menzel Bouzaïane 87
Médenine, Tunisia 87, 91
memory
  collective 19, 28, 161, 225, 226, 227fn, 229, 232, 234, 242
  communicative 231
  counter 225
  cultural 161, 229, 231, 232, 233, 242
  generational 16, 18, 229–30, 233
  and media 20, 225–26, 229, 234
  mediated 226
  political 187
  possessive 234
  travelling 227–8
Mella, Ricardo 20, 245–64
memory transfer 225–27
Metromuster 256–57
micro-level analysis 124–25, 139
Middle East 1, 32, 99, 114, 117, 181, 187
modern prince 249, 250
monumental history 1, 18, 198–200, 220
monumentality 198–200, 201–3, 206, 208
mother-daughter relationship 236, 238–39, 242
multitude 249, 250
Muslim Brotherhood 14, 104, 113, 128, 134, 137–38
Mutahammisin 81

Nakba 28, 117, 175
Nakba Day 37, 44, 45
Naqeb (Palestianian activists) 41–42, 44, 46–47
National Committee for the Defense of the Rights of the Unemployed 205–6
Nietzsche, Friedrich 199
neoliberalism 10, 31, 38–39, 50, 69, 182, 186, 193
  culture 192
  democracy 193
  economic policy 11, 182
  and education 59–60
  era 45, 49
  impact on individualism 29, 249
  in Italy 55–56, 59–61, 63–64, 67, 69
  Islamist 143, 145, 149, 153, 156
  in Israel 38–40

media 147
neoliberal reform 55, 59–60, 63, 67, 145
  in Palestine 171, 172, 179, 182
  policies 56, 61, 64, 67
  in Turkey 143, 145, 147, 149, 153, 156
network society 36, 37
new social media *see* social media
New Social Movements 41, 57
  theory of 263
NGOS 28, 34–35, 48, 186
Non-Governmental Organizations, *see* NGOS
North *see* Algerian North
North Africa 1, 171 *see also* Algeria, Tunisia
nostalgia 19, 45, 186, 227, 231
November generation 198, 199, 200, 201, 202, 206, 215, 220

October Events (Israel/Palestine) 27–28
October 1988 riots (Algeria) 201, 211, 212, 213
oil 203, 204, 210, 212
Onda Anomala 63
Oslo Accords 13, 17, 27, 178, 184, 186
Oslo generation *see* generation Oslo
Ouargla 210, 215, 217, 218n, 220

Padua 236, 239, 240, 241
Paestum 224, 235, 236, 238
Palestine 10, 37, 39, 45, 111, 117fn 171–193
Palestinian Authority 172, 178–79, 183, 186, 189, 192
Palestinian society 27–29, 32, 35, 39–40, 50
Palestinian youth 17, 27, 29, 31, 44–45, 49
performance 48, 146, 157, 263
political generation 83, 123–25, 127, 128–129, 130–131, 139, 239
  concept of 58, 122n, 140
  divergence within 135
  formation of 101, 159
political lawyering 74
political impact events 232, 234
political idolatry 249
political memory 187
political parties 262
  AKP (Turkey) 145, 146, 147–48, 161, 162
  Balad (Israel) 32, 33–34
  BDP (Turkey) 144
  Citizens' Network X (Spain) 261–62, 263, 264

CPR (Tunisia) 83n, 88
FLN (Algeria) 199
Hadash (Israel) 32, 33
Hamas (Palestine) 177, 178, 188, 189
Islamic Movement (Israel) 32, 33
Muslim Brotherhood *see* Muslim
Brotherhood
PDP (Tunisia) 87
PCOT (Tunisia) 80, 85n, 87
Podemos (Spain) 262–63, 264
RCD (Tunisia) 80, 81, 86, 88, 90
Watad (Tunisia) 87
political socialization 32
political struggles 39, 46, 145, 198–99
popular culture 183, 184, 186
possessive memory 234
postsecondary education 28, 55, 59–60, 63,
65–66, 69, 107, 131–32
Prawer Plan 35, 42, 44, 46
production of space 208
protest
in Algeria 205–8
collective 245–46
concept of 7
cycle 55, 58
in Egypt 122–140
framing of *see* frame
forms of 3, 8–10, 19, 38, 43, 220, 227, 242
historical shifts 41
in Italy 55–69
in Israel/Palestine 42–43, 47–49
and memory 225–28
new forms of 1, 41, 45, 186, 206, 220, 246
non-violent 45, 49, 250–51, 255–57
peaceful 45, 112n, 143, 144, 218, 251
in Turkey 143–64
protest movements 75, 81, 84–86, 176, 184,
201, 202, 207, 221, 226
of the 60s / 70s 231, 234, 242
and social movements 9

Queersultoria 241–42

Ramallah 171, 172, 175, 176, 178, 179, 186,
187, 192
recollecting forwards 235–36, 242
reformism 251, 257–59, 260
refugees 117

Iraqi 14, 99, 116
Palestinian 115, 174, 182, 183, 186
remediation 225, 226–27, 238, 242
revolution
Algerian 199–200, 201, 206, 215, 216
Arab 184
digital 35
Egyptian 14, 43, 122, 124, 125, 133–5,
137–40, 188
French 16–17
idea of 164, 252, 262
Iranian 219n
Palestinian 175
social 159, 235, 252, 258
as slogan 188
Syrian 115
Tunisian 111, 188, 202
as youth action 123
revolutionary generation 198
revolutionary situation 122, 123n, 126, 133
revolutionary subjectivity 15, 153, 155
riots 9, 10, 90, 91, 201, 211–12, 217, 218
rule of law 85, 212, 213

Sahara 199, 202, 208, 214–18, 221
SAP *see* Structural Adjustment Plan
Sayad, Abdelmalek 6, 13, 207
Saddam Hussein *see* Hussein, Saddam
Scuro, Enrico 228–29, 232
secondary socialization 109, 110
second-wave feminism *see* feminism:
second-wave
Sewell , William Jr 211
Shabâb al-thawra 122, 125, 138–39
Sidi Bouzid, Tunisia 82, 84n, 87, 88, 89, 90
simple domination 201, 213
situation/state of emergency 131, 253, 254
socialization process 125–26, 130, 135–36
socialism 161, 162, 212, 247, 262
socialized conception of class 155
social justice 8, 16, 40, 162, 217fn, 247
social media 1, 8, 41, 114, 123, 161, 188, 190, 225
dissemination of protests 144
effect on organization 29, 35–38, 49
social uprising 56, 87
solidarity, ethics of 15, 146, 157, 159, 160
South *see* Algerian South
space, production of 208

state of emergency *see* situation/state of
emergency
strategic dilemma 64, 66, 69
student mobilization 56–58, 63, 66
student movement of 1977 (Italy) 226–28,
234, 242
student protest 56–68
surveillance 189–90, 248
Suweida, Syria 111
Structural Adjustment Plan 203, 211
Syria 1, 13–14, 40, 45, 99–118

Tabacalera 259–60, 264
Tahrir Square 40, 132, 137, 189
Taksim Square 143, 145, 151–53, 157–9,
160, 161
temporality 3, 6, 7, 12, 13, 160, 172, 201–2,
207–8, 220
Tilly, Charles 1, 8, 122, 211fn
Tiqqun 253
TOKI 148
trade unions 39, 65, 91, 93, 156, 205, 256–59,
260
trajectories 100, 126, 132, 133, 230
individual 11, 15, 109, 123–25, 126, 133,
135–9, 140
travelling memory 227–8
Tunis, Tunisia 31, 75, 82, 84n, 86n, 88, 89, 91
Tunisia 11, 40, 73–93, 103–4, 191, 202, 205,
219fn, 246
Tunisian National Bar Association 76, 77,
79–81, 83, 85, 87, 89, 91
Turkey 9, 15, 143–64
2011 social protests (Israel) 40

UGTT (Tunisian General Labor Union) 87,
90, 91
unemployed activists *see* activists:
unemployed
unemployed movement 199, 202, 208–210,
211, 221
unemployment 65, 110n, 123, 147, 186, 205–6,
214

graduate unemployment 76n
unemployment policies 203–4, 214
youth unemployment 63, 181

violence 90, 99, 113, 135, 231, 232, 252–53
debate over 246, 252–53
in protests 259, 218
against protests 134, 144, 153, 160, 189
everyday violence 254
sectarian violence 116
state violence 177, 182
political violence 242
as political tool 126, 134
of modernity and coloniality 175–76
sexual violence 234
urban violence 254–55
voluntary cooperation 247, 251, 255, 263

wave metaphor (feminism) 230–31, 235,
236, 237–39
West Bank 43, 46, 48–49, 176, 177, 178, 180,
183, 186, 192
women's health clinic 240, 241
work *see* employment

youth
activism 28–29, 126, 128, 173, 178, 191, 246
concept of 3, 13, 101, 104, 110, 174, 182,
208–9
culture 173, 174, 181, 182–183, 188, 192
and generation 16–17, 100–101, 175, 181
and resistance 182
subjectivity 15, 40
succession of 211
unemployment 63, 76n, 204–5
young/old dichotomy 237
youth activists 27, 29, 31, 34, 36–37, 48, 122,
125–33, 157, 161–62, 173, 246
youth movement 14, 122n, 129, 133, 139, 140,
171–93
Youth for Change Movement 129, 132
youth of the revolution see *Shabab al-Thawra*

Printed in the United States
By Bookmasters